History of Childbirth

History of Childbirth

Fertility, Pregnancy and Birth in Early Modern Europe

Jacques Gélis

Translated by Rosemary Morris

Polity Press

Editorial office:
Polity Press, 65 Bridge Street,
Cambridge CB2 1UR, UK

Marketing and production:
Blackwell Publishers Ltd
108 Cowley Road, Oxford OX4 1JF, UK

ISBN 0–7456–0677–6
ISBN 0–7456–1840–5 (pbk)

A CIP catalogue record for this book is available from the
British Library.

Typeset in 10 on 11 pt Ehrhardt
by Acorn Bookwork, Salisbury, Wiltshire
Printed in Great Britain by T.J. Press, Padstow, Cornwall

To Antoine, awaiting rebirth in a grandchild

Contents

x *Contents*

Introduction

This book is the fruit of some ten years of research into the anthropology of childbirth. It does not aim to trace the course of medical progress, but to examine the motivations and behaviour of the men and women – especially the women – who perpetuated the human race in time past, within the domain of Western culture.

The book covers four centuries which were crucial in the development of mental attitudes in Western Europe. Much regional variation exists, but I have sought to trace overall trends rather than local differences. The bulk of my documentation is from France, but for some subjects – for example, midwives, the placenta, sanctuaries and the 'wild hunt' – I have included material from neighbouring countries. Continual reference to peasant notions of cosmology reveals a substantial common stock of beliefs and customs vis-à-vis the most fundamental questions: the cycle of life and death, the imagery of childbirth, the awareness of time, the fear of stillbirth.

The way in which a society receives a newborn child into its bosom tells us a great deal about the fundamental attitudes of that society towards the experience of living. The last two hundred years have seen great changes in this reception of the newly born in Western societies. The main features are well known: a spectacular drop in deaths of women in childbirth and of newborn infants; a decline in the birth-rate which is now tending to cause anxiety among doctors and even politicians. The present rapid rate of progress in the life sciences and in obstetric techniques tends to obscure the fact that for very many years the process of childbirth remained remarkably unchanged.

In earlier times, a couple had in duty bound to accept all the children God might send them. The success of a marriage was gauged by the number of offspring it produced. After the Council of Trent the Church never ceased reminding men and women conjoined in holy wedlock of their duty of procreation, which was the sole justification for the sexual act. People lent a ready ear to this teaching, the more so because they dreaded sterility or the death of their children: a large family was a guarantee of continuity. However, an abundance of children was also to be feared, because the parents feared lest they be unable to feed them all. The Church, resolutely opposed to all forms of contraception, did its best to calm such fears, exhorting parents to trust in divine Providence. In a society redolent of social inequality, over which the spectre of Malthus began to hover from the eighteenth century onwards, it became fashionable to extol the merits of large families; needless to say these were mostly poor families. In fact, children were the poor man's riches.

What riches were these? In the great cities spawned by the rampant industrialization of the early nineteenth century, when children became an essential part of the workforce, it might have been possible to consider them as an investment. And in the country? Certainly country children began to help their parents at a very early age: they might gather firewood, search the hedgerows for berries or glean corn; they could herd the cow, goat or sheep, if the family was fortunate enough to possess any such animals. Where possible the child would go to work for a farmer, usually without wages; he would have a roof over his head – that of the stable or cowshed, maybe – and he would be fed. That was all; but at least he had the bare necessities of life. Sending him away to work meant one less mouth to feed and less strain on the family commissariat. 'The poor man's riches'? Hardly. The child brought nothing in; he was an expense, and all the parents wanted was for him to earn his own living. For poor homes were always at the mercy of any interruption in the food supply due to inclement weather.

In all Western European countries people have become 'sparing' in their production of children. In former years they were prodigal, abundant. But this should not be exaggerated. Until the 1950s a good many false notions existed among students of demography as to the attitudes of people in modern Europe. In the absence of census returns or any reliable statistics recourse was had to individual biographies and to incomplete testimonies which gave a false picture of reality. Thus it was believed that women married very young, an idea which may have gained credence from certain literary texts: in Shakespeare, for example, we see girls in highborn families marrying at fifteen or even twelve. It was also believed that large families were the norm, whether in a castle or a cottage. Now that parish registers have been made to yield their secrets, the truth must be accepted: in times gone by, people married late. Girls would wed at twenty-five, but boys had to wait a couple of years longer than that. Marriages were mostly local affairs, between people from the same village; indeed, the local young people would band together to ensure that no 'foreign' suitor was ever admitted. At the most a man might go some nine or ten miles in search of a wife from a nearby village. However, we should not exaggerate this tendency to endogamy. It was very pronounced in remote mountain communities, much less so in more favoured regions, especially in the eighteenth century.

Once married, these couples were indeed relatively fertile, producing an average of four to five children. There were very large families to be found everywhere, but nowhere did they constitute the norm. The first child would be born shortly after the wedding, within thirteen months in half the cases examined. But it was quite common for long periods, of up to four years or more, to occur between births, for reasons which remain unexplained. It can be observed that the interval depended on the mother's age: it was greater for those who married late (at age 35 it was some 14 months), and especially for the very young (17 months for women marrying before 20), who were often afflicted with a temporary sterility.

As one child followed another, the gaps became ever wider: two years, two and a half years . . .. It is quite untrue that couples tended to have a child every year. The practice of suckling a child for long periods, which was normal in the countryside, helped delay future births by prolonging the post-parturition amenorrhoea (cessation of menstruation) and thus preventing ovulation and so conception.

The rate of conceptions fluctuated notably through the year. This phenomenon did not escape contemporary observers. In 1778 the statistician Moheau noted that 'the month of June is that in which the largest number of women begin to earn the title of mother; and it is in the month of September that the smallest number do so'. The joys of springtime brought about a marked rise in conceptions in May and, especially, June, while in the autumn (September and October) and in March and December the tide of new life was on the ebb. The decrease in March and December is attributable to the 'closed seasons' of Lent and Advent, during which the Church demanded sexual abstinence. Bishops' pronouncements and recommendations in the confessional did bear fruit, it seems. It is in fact quite difficult to be sure if this drop in fertility was the result of sexual abstinence or of fasting, which might have induced temporary sterility in some women.

While new life was abundant everywhere, death was omnipresent too. If couples had an average of only four or five children, this was because many marriages ended with the death of one partner before the woman had ceased to be fertile. If both partners survived until her menopause, they would be able to bring some seven or eight children into the world.

The family in times past was often a residue of survivors. The population suffered severely from the epidemics which swept through it at fairly regular intervals. Often, food shortages and high prices added to the gravity of a crisis provoked by an epidemic. In good times or bad, it was the children who died most readily: only one in every two reached the age of twenty. It took two newborn children to make one adult. Thus, four or five children per family were barely enough to maintain the level of the population. Nor were the survivors assured of a particularly easy existence, especially if they had lost a parent.

Epidemics also affected the pattern of marriages. Many unions came to a premature end and were sometimes replaced by a second marriage. One man in four and one woman in five remarried, usually very quickly, especially in the case of men: two out of three remarried less than a year after the death of their first wife. The stepmother – often enough a 'wicked stepmother' to the children of the first marriage – is a familiar figure in documents of the time. The introduction of a stranger into the household often put an end to harmony between a father and his children, especially if the father was weak enough to fall under the influence of the young person whom he had married.

Nothing is more complex than the creation of new life, and any historian embarking on a study of childbirth quickly realizes the immensity of the task. Children are so central to the whole of human existence that it is hard to see how the historian can reject, *a priori*, any piece of evidence concerning marriage, the family, death . . . .. Historians are faced with a constantly widening horizon, a multiplicity of approaches, a need to juggle with a plethora of different sources, medical, ethnographic, religious, legal. They are in danger of losing themselves in a labyrinthine superabundance of documentation.

Almost all the sources give us a distorted image of childbirth, as it was among the urban elite or in institutions. Village women and the midwives who attended them in childbed have left little or no trace. The rural past is full of black holes which it is difficult to fill in: for the history of childbirth in rural communities we have to listen to the silence as often as to the solid evidence.

Manuscripts and printed texts give us a model for childbirth: chldbirth as the practitioners thought it ought to be, not as it really was. From the end of the sixteenth century, doctors and surgeons acquired the habit of giving a written account of the births they attended. Partly this was the desire to bring the cases and methods they had seen to the attention of colleagues; partly it was the desire to make a collection of facts which could be compared, classified, and form the basis of deductions which would lead to the founding of obstetrics as a science.

Birth as depicted by these experts is vivid and real, always compelling, often dramatic. After all, the doctor was only called in as a rule if the situation was desperate. There is a danger of letting our image of childbirth be coloured by these sad, but on the whole exceptional cases, while there is a vast area of ignorance about uneventful labour, when the child made its appearance without causing undue trouble. The same applies to manuscript accounts from the eighteenth century submitted to the French Royal Academy of Surgeons or the Royal Society of Medicine, and to articles published in the *Medical Gazette* or *Journal of Medicine*.

However, these texts from the pens of inquisitive and prolix medical men indirectly furnish much useful information about the practices of midwives and the drugs they used; on the attitudes of pregnant women; and on the behaviour of those attending the woman in labour. If we can disentangle the facts from the subjective observations of the doctor himself, such accounts give us some idea of the real world of childbirth: not a complete idea, for indirect evidence is always partial, but an idea.

Language itself is a special kind of source. Up to the seventeenth century, doctors were still profoundly influenced by rural culture; they were tending more and more to set themselves apart from it, but it permeates their writings in the form of richly significant metaphors. Among the sources I have consulted, some texts stand out for their exceptionally interesting content and for their pivotal position between two stages in the development of medical science. Such are the works of the Montpellier practitioner Laurent Joubert and of Jacques Duval of Rouen, and above all those of the midwife Louise Bourgeois and the obstetricians Jacques Guillemeau and Guillaume Mauquest de La

Motte: these records have contributed enormously to my understanding of the mental attitudes and the behaviour of people in times past.

Materials gleaned by nineteenth-century antiquaries and folklorists allow us to rediscover and compare fertility rites and practices associated with pregnancy and birth, though such sources must be handled with care, taking due account of the time and place at which they were collected. Certainly it is better to rely on Van Gennep than on Sébillot, but there is one exceptionally trustworthy and shrewd folklorist to whom I am indebted more than to any other, and that is Pierre Saintyves.

The chief regret of historians of the 1980s must be that they came on the scene some thirty or forty years too late. Field studies on beliefs relating to stones and springs, fertility beliefs and 'respite' chapels, have become extremely difficult, and require endless patience and caution. Cult sites have often been destroyed, and practices associated with churches have often suffered from the deplorable iconoclastic zeal triggered off by Vatican II. But there are still some places which bear witness to traditional practices and can help in understanding them.

Some information may also be harvested from ecclesiastical sources: synodal proclamations, rituals, accounts by parish priests of the methods of midwives, death in childbirth, symbolic practices, baptism and the burial of children who died before receiving that sacrament. Such documents throw light on the changing attitude of the Church towards children and women in labour from the seventeenth to the eighteenth century: the desire to save the soul was accompanied more and more often by the need to safeguard the body.

This slow assembling of the jigsaw of past time never really gives a complete picture. The significance of some gesture or expression escapes us; we long to know what is meant by the 'secret' which an author refuses to reveal for fear of it being abused by hostile elements. Labouring like ants, we bring in the gleanings seed by painful seed; in the end, the motley assembly will always have a few patches missing.

Any study of the anthropology of birth must necessarily take account of the main trends in contemporary historiography: for not only is childbirth the reflection of a whole society, the study of it places us at a methodological crossroads. As a historian of childbirth I am in debt to those who have trodden my paths before me: writers on the history of women, of mothers, of labour; those who have investigated the history of childhood and family life, or contemplated 'the story of mankind in the mirror of Death', or worked in the domain of the anthropology of religion to explain the nature of the sacred, or the meaning of a pilgrim's quest; or again those, ethnographers in particular, who have paid close attention to 'man and the human body in traditional societies'; and finally to those mythographers and philosophers who have attempted to 'define differences' and 'detect analogies at a distance'.

The present study aims to avoid two kinds of oversimplification. The first is to talk about 'traditional' pregnancy and childbirth as being easier and more reassuring for women: an ideal which, unfortunately for them, was eliminated by the all-conquering obstetrician. The second is to give undue credit to medical advance as having got rid of the obscurantist stupidities of the traditional midwife: this approach relies on statistics which show a sharp diminution of the risks attaching to childbirth through the last two hundred years and seem to show that the control of birth by medical science was a triumph of humanity. These antagonistic and frequently radical attitudes both contain a measure of truth. But in both cases the argument is complicated by moral considerations; and in both cases the viewpoint is too narrow. For in order to understand what changes have taken place in the process of childbirth over the last two centuries, we must first try to grasp its place in the mental outlook of the time: the image of child in the rural society of early modern Europe.

What, in brief, does this book seek to achieve? To describe and account for beliefs and customs; to observe and interpret ritual; to delve down to the ancient roots of beliefs which are no longer part of our mental outlook.

In the earlier modern period, birth was still seen from the mental viewpoint of a rural society whose world view was based on the rhythm of the seasons, a close relationship with the earth and a reverence for ancient custom. Even in the eighteenth century the lifestyle of the countryman remained close to that of the villager, the town-dweller and, thanks to the steady stream of immigrants from the countryside, to that of many city dwellers as well. It was not easy for new urban settlers to shake off their former habits; their everyday speech retained the words and metaphors of country life; bodily habits and eating patterns remained the same. The next generation, passing through the crucible of town life, no longer had the same frame of reference or pattern of thought, and had no memory of their ancestral village: they had new horizons, new beliefs, other ways of living.

For us today, the country ways which so permeated society just over a hundred years ago have become largely unfamiliar. For our present purpose it is necessary to reconstitute them, piece by piece, if we are to understand the experience of birth in a time now lost. A way of life, a way of living in a human body, an image of childbirth: they are all inseparable.

It is because they reflected a certain world view, a certain way of living, that the beliefs and practices which we are studying persisted for so long. Through-out the modern period they have been under constant threat from the growing power of the State and the medical establishment: they could survive only insofar as they could adapt. The Church, for its part, was well aware that it was not always wise to try to go too fast: it was willing to compromise and adapt its teachings to the analogical forms of thought of its peasant faithful. Even the medical profession was, up to the eighteenth century, so close to rural popular medicine – in its pharmacopoeia if not in its methodology – that there was no perceptible gulf between the two.

The contest between popular and professional medicine was an unequal one. It turned into a struggle between the go-ahead urban outlook and the back-wardness of the countryside with its superstitions. 'Superstition': a pernicious word which, by reason of its convenience as a substitute for original thinking, became an indispensable item in the pejorative armoury of churchmen, doctors, ethnographers and historians. Any belief or practice which the zealots of the Council of Trent were resolved to suppress, any 'cure' which the medical profession had suddenly decided to reject after centuries of acceptance, any behaviour which nineteenth-century researchers failed to understand, was dismissed as 'superstition'. Such a dismissal meant a refusal to contemplate a different way of thinking, to recognize the logic of behaviour motivated by concepts other than one's own, to seek out the network of common understandings which is the foundation of an individual culture.

In my quest for a proper understanding, the bitter and persistent condemnation to which the traditional care of mothers and babies was subjected proved a serious stumbling block. Obviously practices which were so widespread must correspond to something deeply rooted in human experience. I could rediscover their inner logic only by approaching them from the inside, combing the available evidence for the guiding thread which would take me further; I had to share the experiences of the childless woman, the woman in labour, the midwife; to enter the shadowy world of fertility rites; to seek out the hidden links between different beliefs and rituals. My ear was on the alert for the slightest nuance.

This difficult but fascinating quest often revealed the importance of apparently minor details: a single word, a folklorist's jotting, might supply the key to a ritual whose meaning had hitherto escaped me. To understand what was being said as it were 'in profile' I often had to turn to the 'oblique science' so energetically advocated by Roger Caillois. The interplay of shape and colour, the importance of certain gestures or certain parts of the body, the belief in 'sacred stones' or wonder-working springs, took me into a world of feelings and imaginings, a fresh cultural dimension, a new mythology.

My research soon began to form into three parallel movements. The study of life led back again and again to God, the source of all life, and above all to the Earth, to the slow rhythm of her breath. When a woman conceived, carried the child to fruition and was delivered, she helped carry on the race and took part in the great cycle of all life. Children, like the fruits of the earth, were *par excellence* the symbol of continuity.

But at times nature seemed to hesitate, to disobey her own laws. A child was born twisted or sickly, dead, deformed. At times even men contributed to these irregularities by killing or exposing the child. The first two movements of my research, however, intentionally stressed what was permanent, looking for structures rather than for change.

The final break with the old ways was long in coming. It took several centuries for a new relationship between man and the universe, a new outlook on life, a new relationship between parents and children, to be made manifest. The changes in the reception of the newborn child and the medical monopolization of birth, along with the material, psychological and mental alterations which ensued, will form the third movement of the present study.

PART I

The Rhythms of the Earth

Silencieusement va la sève . . .

Silently goes the sap . . .
Saint John Perse

The Mother of All Things

For they all came forth from the bosom of Mother Earth
Theodore Vulpinus, poet of Alsace

The myth of the all-nurturing Earth Mother, source of all fertility, was deeply rooted in the minds of people of earlier generations. All curiosity about the origins of life, about the growth and flourishing of plants, animals and all living beings, led back ultimately to her. From her sprang living souls; in her grew the creatures each after its own kind; to her returned the bodies from which the life had fled. She preserved and altered, modelled and perfected her creatures, labouring in her teeming womb to ensure the continuance of life.

The simplicity of this image hides a profoundly complex relationship between man and the first mother, between the body of man and that of Earth, and through her, the entire universe. From season to season of the year or of the human lifespan, the relationship was governed by notions of the sacred.

It is hard for us nowadays to comprehend the essence of this way of 'living in the world', to grasp the intricacies of a way of thinking which scarcely makes a distinction between the sacred and the profane, to 'rediscover the existential dimension of religion and ancient societies'. The modern desacralization of the universe has brought about a rapid collapse of former mental structures. We have another notion of rationality which has swept away the old world of wizardry and analogical thinking, the world in which the Earth Mother was the beginning and end of all things.

1

Man, the Earth and the Cosmos

If we are to perceive correspondences we must be prepared to suffer astonishment and abolish prejudice.

Roger Caillois

Awareness of the Environment

Rural man was very sensitively aware of the environment in which he lived: earth, heathland, woodland or forest, everything which sprang from the living soil. It was a sensitivity learned from childhood. 'The world we have lost' in the course of the last two centuries is first and foremost precisely this: the world of essential impulses, a particular way of feeling, listening, decoding the messages which come from plants, animals and stones.

Those country people saw things now hidden from our eyes. Not that the images they perceived were all that different from ours, but their way of interpreting them has become, at least in part, foreign to us. Their way of thinking was basically analogical: a sound, a word, a smell or a shape which had attracted their attention would act as a signal, taking its place in the richness of their symbolic universe. Even now, a countryman's speech will often lack conciseness, tending to frequent reiteration; both speech and thought progress a step at a time. He will seek a resemblance to someone known to him in an unfamiliar face, see the form of an animal or man in some aspect of a tree, a rock, or a landscape, showing his desire to keep in contact with nature, to get a grip on the world, to make it fit into his own notions of logic. He needs to know his world and his place in creation, and feels the need to answer the fundamental questions: who are we? Where do we come from, and where are we going to?

Creation means, first and foremost, what is immediately around us, the things we see every day: the world of the soil with its yearly cycle, its seasonal rhythms, its apparent death and rebirth, the ebb and flow of its life. Every springtime the 'all-nourishing earth' showed its power, pouring forth life from every part in endless variety. This teeming of life, this passion to reproduce, was seen as the only possible response of all mortal creatures to the inevitability of death. Mortal man endured through his children. Man's instincts echoed those of the universe: nature was a vast reservoir of life.

4

The Reservoir of Nature

Mortal man knew that since the Fall his destiny had been one with the rest of Creation. Birth and death were the only certainties. But in making man, his masterpiece, God, the 'great Prometheus', did not desire him to vanish without leaving a trace. He gave him a helpmeet so that 'that which was mortal in the individual should become immortal in the species, by and through its continual propagation'.[1] Man did not die if he could perpetuate himself in his children, 'For it cannot be said that that man has died who leaves his image alive and exactly represented in his successor.'[2]

In the womb of the first woman all succeeding generations were embedded, one within the other, ready to unfold through the years as man's reply to the great challenge of death, in an unbroken chain which transcended time. 'Thus the world remains always entire and perfect, though it suffer a perpetual vicissitude and alteration in all its parts.'[3] The idea of a world which never empties, which gains here what it loses elsewhere, of a world in continual mutation, striving unceasingly to keep in balance, runs through the medical and philosophical texts of the seventeenth and eighteenth centuries and crops up again in popular beliefs.

The wonderful and inexorable cycle of life and death continues without interruption, for one creature must die that another may come into the world; the seed in the furrow ferments and perishes in the earth to bring a new blade of corn to birth; a drop of semen, a fragment of life, rots in the womb, the 'fertile field of womanhood', so that a new person can be born and take the place vacated by another. 'Nothing is destroyed in the changeability of natural things.'[4]

The close association of beginnings and endings, birth and death, corruption and new life, renewal and decay, appeared day by day before the eyes of the countryman. The earth would not bear a fair harvest unless it was well fertilized with manure. The account in the myth of Aristaeus of the origin of bees is another good example of this recurring association between decay and new life: the swarm of 'honey'd flies' was born from the rotting corpse of an ox.[5] Even human offspring must dwell for nine months in close proximity with the maternal excrement; and yet from between the 'filth of the bowel' and the bladder – 'between the shit and the piss', as a popular expression has it – comes the beauty of the newborn child.

All animals, including human animals, are urged by instinct to pair and to procreate, making ready the future by the gift of life. In so worthy an enterprise, nature willingly comes to their aid by providing sexual attraction, that 'inborn gaiety', 'sweet titillation', 'bait of delight' which so advantageously conjoins 'pleasure and utility'. Numerous doctors took up their pens to express in metaphor the hidden role of nature in the continuation of the race. She 'urges mankind to cultivate the field of humanity'; the penis is the 'ploughman casting his seed'.[6] But to 'plant' a child or establish it securely in the 'kiln' or 'forge', the 'good seed' was in itself insufficient: the 'vessel' must also be a good one, the soil must accept the seed.

Country people acquired from simple observation some understanding of the reproduction of plants and animals, most notably of the aquatic plant vallisneria, whose reproductive cycle had been known since antiquity. *Vallisneria spiralis* is found in Greece and Mesopotamia, in India and southern France. It is common in watercourses, and has long ribbon-like leaves. The male plants have flowers gathered together on a single spike; the female flowers grow individually on a spiral shaft.

At the moment of fertilization, the male spathe releases its stamens into the water. The gas they contain brings them to the surface, where they scatter. The female flower is also brought to the surface by the action of the pedicle; after fertilization by the male flowers, the fruit is brought back under water by the retraction of the spiral shaft.[7]

The peoples of antiquity were struck by this extraordinary sexual behaviour; it features on Mycenaean vases alongside the favourite themes of angry bulls, goddesses and chariots drawn by sea-horses.[8] Sexuality takes on religious connotations – with a plant as the hero. Such images should be seen in relation to ancient notions about the origin of living things, especially to Empedocles' idea that the first plants and animals did not spring forth complete, but formed piece by piece, 'like a game of cut-outs', by means of borrowings from assorted other species. Beyond all myths, monsters and metamorphoses, we may keep it in mind that life came first from the water.

Mythology also bears witness to a belief that women could conceive from plants. In the cyclic worship of Attis as described by Pausanias, Sangarios gathered an almond flower and from this the god Attis was conceived. There are folktales in which a girl becomes pregnant by eating a rose-leaf. Plant life is the universal source of fertility: 'It transcends species in the propagation of life.'[9]

'Signatures': A Network of Correspondences

In our restless world, with all its diverse manifestations of life, species coexist but remain separate. There can be no real meeting or combination of the human species and that of any plant or animal; but there are strange correspondences, or 'signatures', which link them together.

The 'doctrine of signatures' is a theory of knowledge based on analogy. 'Symbolism was universal, and thinking was a perpetual process of discovery of hidden meanings, an endless "hierophany". For this hidden world was sacred, and symbolic thinking, with its refinement and subtlety, was no more than the learned man's equivalent of the "magical thinking" which characterized popular attitudes.'[10]

This doctrine, familiar in antiquity, was elevated into a fully-fledged theory by Renaissance scholars such as Jerome Cardano, Paracelsus, Campanella and Giambattista della Porta.[11] Cardano, for example, has a theory of nature based entirely on 'analogical word play' – though 'play' is not really the right word, since the intention is to gain 'an immediate, intuitive grasping of the complex of nature'.[12] All things in nature answer each other, correspond and communicate through a subtle network of connections. Everything comes together under the

surface. Even minerals under the earth are like 'underground plants' slowly
maturing: 'Metals are living things, as we can also conclude from this argument
that in the mountains they are born exactly like plants, with spreading branches,
roots, trunks, and after a fashion, flowers and fruit.'[13]

Everything is like something else, is the mirror of something else. Such a
vision of Creation is essentially magical: in fact, magic is the source and
fountain-head of all natural science, for it establishes relationships and seeks
the governing principles of the universe. 'Just as the peasant weds the vine to
the elm, so the magician weds heaven and earth and brings the lower world into
contact with the forces of the higher world.'[14]

Animals know by instinct which plants are useful to them; country folk,
similarly, have always known and benefited from the medical value of 'simples'.
Could not sympathetic magic therefore serve as a basis for the art of healing?
Any blemish or malady has some remedy on earth: one must seek the cure
simply by looking around one. The shape, colour or scent of a plant shows some
correspondence with such and such a part of the body or bodily function, and
therefore constitutes the antidote to the particular malady. Some plants are
harmful, others useful: the former are ugly, ill-formed and stinking; the latter
are 'fair to see and sweet to smell'. Plants which look alike have the same
virtues; those have no outward resemblance must have different properties.

This 'medicine by signatures' is directly concerned with human reproduction. Plants without stems, flowers or fruits advertise the fact that they are of no
use in inducing conception; those with an abundance of seeds are helpful to
those who wish for a similar abundance in their own progeny. The sex of the
plant to be used is of great importance: only 'female' plants can be given to a
woman, plants such as the strong-smelling *chenopodium vulvaria*, said to be
beneficial in controlling hysteria. For an impotent man there is nothing better
than a good dose of boiled orchid roots, which look exactly like testicles: they
render him instantly capable of paying his debt to Venus ....[15]

Man the Microcosm

The theory of signatures implies belief in the great harmony of nature: man's
destiny is ruled by the ticking of the cosmic clock. 'Man, finding his essence
extending out into the world, also found the world within himself: one was
mirrored in the other': the microcosm was mirrored in the macrocosm, and
these are two essential notions in modern and medieval culture.[16]

The distinction goes back to antiquity: it was known to the ancient Greeks
and to the Romans. Pythagoras stated that the same law, the Law of Number,
ruled both macrocosm and microcosm; and for Hippocrates 'nature in man is
constituted in the image of nature in the world'. Theophrastus called man the
'exemplar of the universe', and for Pliny he was 'the abridgement of the world'.
This image of man and his place in the world appears again and again in the
writings of Neoplatonists and neo-Pythagoreans.[17]

Medieval encyclopaedias and summas were equally affected by this way of thinking. But the thirteenth to fourteenth centuries saw a weakening, or rather transformation, of this system of representation.[18] The medical authority Arnauld of Villanova used it in an attempt to effect the increasingly difficult reconciliation of religion and the natural sciences. His ideas on physiology were largely the result of his vision of man as microcosm: the state of health of that microcosm depended on the balance of elementary humours which were subject to the influence of the stars, that is of the macrocosm.

The theory of the microcosm gained a new lease of life with the coming of the Renaissance. The human body was seen as the perfect mirror of the great universal body, and the two worlds were very closely connected, each and every element in the one finding its echo or symbolic double in the other. Everything went to show that the world we live in was no chaos, but the perfected product of the Creator's thought and organizing power. The universe is a mighty body to which the human body corresponds. The waters of the earth are to it as sap is to a tree and blood to a human body:

The springs which flow in the depths of the earth are the bearers of its life, like the veins in a well-constituted body; the rocks are its bones . . ... Man has been called a little world or microcosm because he seems to be a compendium of all the perfections of nature; and indeed our soul is to our body as God is to the universe.[19]

Thus man is the fulcrum or lynch-pin of the whole extraordinary edifice of Creation. But his position, privileged as it is, is also reciprocal: the stars, the constellations and the planets rule human life and influence its rhythms;[20] 'zodiac man', unendingly subject to the ebb and flow of cosmic forces, must endure what they send him for good or ill.

Not everything in this universe is harmonious. According to the early sixteenth-century theoretician Agrippa of Nettesheim, one of the leading proponents of the doctrine of signatures, things contrary to one another create discords which it is the doctor's task to discover: medical knowledge is based on the study of obvious or concealed sympathies and antipathies. Paracelsus also contributed to this theory in his *Book of Matrices*, in which he claims that there are not two 'worlds', but three: 'The first, the great universal world', in which we human beings are but as atoms; 'the two others are small', that of man, 'the superior of the little worlds', and that of woman, 'the inferior of the little worlds'.[21] Thus, at an important stage in the history of relations between the sexes in the Western world, woman finds herself relegated to an inferior status.

Since the human body was part of the great rhythm of the universe, it was dangerous to interfere with it: 'Operating on and, above all, penetrating the body – the microcosm – meant interfering in a transcendant interplay of forces.'[22] Only a madman would cut into a body to operate on it or to perform an autopsy after death, because he would, by 'sympathy', be attacking the constitution of the universe and the powers of the Creator. It was virtually sacrilegious to try to penetrate the secrets of the body, or of the universe. And yet the resurgence of interest in the microcosmic theory during the Renaissance must bear witness to a new eagerness for investigation, a fresh appetite for knowledge which threatened the whole edifice of science as then constituted. As the boundaries of the known world extended, a better approach to the human body developed. Microcosm and macrocosm together were caught up in the dynamics of an ascending spiral. New ways of perceiving the body were to have a profound effect on Western man's notions of cosmology. No longer, as hitherto, was the human body to be seen as the hinge between two worlds – the realm above, and the realm under the earth.

The Body as Hinge

For hundreds, perhaps thousands of years, man remained in close association with the world around him; he was just one element within the ever-changing but ever-consistent nature in which he had his being. He perceived his body as part of a natural topography: up above, the head rose towards heaven; down below, the genital organs and the entrails were drawn towards the Earth Mother – towards Hades.

It was, indeed, through his 'earthy body', through his 'corporeal grotesque-ness', that man set up a 'constant interrelationship with the Earth, which swallowed him up and from which he was again and again reborn'.[23] For Earth was womb and tomb to him; her perpetual cycle brought him to naught and saw him born again.

Man saw nature as an extension of himself; between himself and her there was no impenetrable frontier, for the passage was easy. Through myriad openings, cracks and appendages his body was open to the outside: mouth, genitals, breasts, phallus, protruding stomach, nose. His body was part of the world, of animals, of inanimate things: it was cosmic.[24]

Now, this body-as-hinge was ambivalent, rather like the 'Lespugue Venus', a huge, fat, grossly deformed female body which yet was the carrier of new life, symbol of the immanence of both life and death, two bodies in one: 'the one giving birth and dying, the other conceived, generated and born'.[25]

The grotesque image of the body which was at the heart of medieval theatre and of the works of Rabelais was thus very different from the image of a body 'made ready, fully formed, fully mature, purged as it were of all the refuse of birth and growth' which became the Renaissance ideal. It was a moving, changeable body, through which coursed the vital flux, 'the ever-unfinished, ever-creating body'.[26]

2

Daughter, Wife and Mother

> Wer ke Kinder het weiss net vorum'r lebt
> (He who has no children knows no reason for living)
> *Alsatian proverb*

Of all the demands made by nature on men and women, none was more urgent than the perpetuation of life. The species must servive. A young girl's first period was thus a happy omen, for those 'monthly red flowers' were her hope of bearing children. Their non-arrival was cause for anxiety: 'No seed without flower', as a proverb has it.

The Periods

A woman's body is most notably subject to cosmic influences: the regular upheaval of her periods shows her sensitivity to the rhythms of the macrocosm. The disturbance it causes her is in fact necessary to her overall internal harmony: by it her body is purged of its 'superfluities'.

The monthly red flowers

The 'overflow' of the periods constitutes a fundamental difference between women and men. Maiden or wife, the woman pours forth her monthly offering: her period, her 'ordinaries'; 'she is said to flower, as she sheds blood every month'.[1] These flowers are the principal sign of her capacity to procreate; they are the harbingers of the change from girl to potential woman, and of her eventual bearing of fruit.

When a woman says that she is 'bleeding', she is thinking of the colour of the lost fluid, the 'redness of difference'.[2] Nothing is more striking to the eye than the redness of blood on white cloth; a menstruating woman was said to be 'leaving her mark', or in nineteenth-century Picardy, her 'trail'. By contemplating the stained linen the woman 'learns the law of her body'; to have one's period is to 'see'. In any agrarian society learning is done mainly by looking. In former times the periods were a great secret, a taboo, which was almost never mentioned even between mother and daughter: thus the daughter had to discover her body the first time she *saw* . . ..[3]

The colour of menstrual blood was symbolically connected with everything to do with women. Red related to red, in particular to red earth. In south-western France, the body of the menstruating woman was connected with the blood-red soils of the Rouergue district; she did not 'have her monthlies', she 'went to Rodez'. The purple-red of blackberries also recalled the menstrual blood leaving the oven heat of the woman's belly: in the hamlet of Minot-en-Châtillonnais, the 'cooked' blood which thus came forth was crudely evoked by saying that the woman 'had a blackberry bum'.

The usual French word for the periods, *règles*, became general only at the end of the seventeenth century. It was probably learned and medical in origin, but swiftly passed into the everyday language. Like the English 'period', the word implies regularity and balance: the balance of the periods ensures that the body itself remains in balance. One could not be a real woman – that is, in the society we are talking about, a real mother – unless one had one's periods.[4] They must be sufficient but not too copious; if they got out of order the woman had recourse to 'analogical medicine' to restore the normal course of her 'monthlies': in particular, the 'simples'. In such treatments the colour of the plant involved was a vital element: thus mugwort, which has a red stem, was supposed to be particularly good against haemorrhage after childbirth, but could also produce the opposite effect and ensure the arrival of the period. Marigold had a similar reputation, which it owed to the monthly rhythm of its flowering and to its smell: some said that 'the smell of the flower is similar to that of the menstrual blood of a healthy woman'.[5] Women also made use of a 'month-stone', which had the virtue of restoring menstruation, or of a bead from a magic necklace.[6]

Sixteenth- and seventeenth-century doctors offered concoctions based on analogical principles, the rationale of which sometimes escapes us now. An old parchment manuscript from the Nantes region, dating from the reign of Louis XIV (1643–1715), has the following two recipes:

To start a woman's period: take a handful of hempseed which has been thoroughly crushed, infuse it for twenty-four hours with an ounce of fine white sugar in a pint of white wine. Drink a large glass of it first thing in the morning; if nothing happens, continue for three days in succession.

To stop the flux in women: take the powdered rind of a pomegranate, one dram, with two fingers of plantain water; have ready a skein of new thread, dip it in strong vinegar and place it on the part.[7]

The notion of the relatedness of milk and blood, and of the womb and the breasts, recurs constantly in medical texts from Antiquity and the Middle Ages. One saying has it that 'to stop the menstruation of a woman, one should apply a large cupping-glass to her breasts'; another insists that 'if a woman who is neither pregnant nor suckling a baby has milk in her breasts, it is a sign that her periods have ceased'.[8] Milk is in fact menstrual blood which has turned white and been diverted into the breasts: it circulates through several of the veins, 'which by their digestive virtue make the red colour turn to white, so that it becomes the same colour as the breasts, just as the chyle, which gets from the stomach to the liver, turns to red'.[9]

While women drew heavily on the 'medicine of signatures' for such purposes, it was often accompanied by religious devotions. Saints – female ones in particular – could correct the deviations of nature. In the Perche region, around 1820, 'women suffering from irregularity in their monthly purgation would attach to a statue of Saint Venetia, in the church of Nogent-le-Rotrou, a white or red ribbon: the white one was intended to slow the flux, the red one to stimulate it'.[10] This was not an isolated case: just such an 'image' was to be found at Ceton, in the Orne region (southern Normandy), and 'it was said that if its face blushed red in a kindly fashion, the prayer would be granted'.[11] Saint Venetia was one of those saints not officially recognized by the Church; she was believed to be the woman with a flux who had been healed by Christ, and this qualified her, in the eyes of many women, to deal with menstrual irregularities.

Even more rich in significance was the pilgrimage to Saint Ylie (Eulalia) at Flacé-en-Mâconnais. The folklorist G. Jeanton reports that newly wedded wives and adolescent girls often went there, the former to lay down their bridal wreaths and the latter 'the garlands they had worn at their first communion, that their periods might begin'; women also offered red or white ribbons which were supposed to 'bring back or put a stop to the periods'.[12] The first communion was a rite of passage into adolescence which was especially important to girls; the retreat which traditionally precedes it is seen by the ethnologist Yvonne Verdier as being analogous to the 'period of seclusion which in numerous societies is characteristic of the rites surrounding puberty in girls'.[13] But the symbolic threshold of communion did not really correspond to puberty: not all girls had their first period at the same age; moreover, the age of puberty has altered considerably in the last two centuries.

The age for menstruation

Detailed observations by doctors from the mid-eighteenth century onwards, coupled with statistical data from the nineteenth century which have recently been studied by Edward Shorter, show that in France the average age for the first period has gone from about sixteen (between 1750 and 1799) to less than fourteen (between 1900 and 1950).[14] The beginning of this change is hard to date; it may be earlier than 1750. The downward tendency certainly became more marked after the end of the nineteenth century, thanks to the improvement in both the quantity and the quality of nutrition.

It was long believed that puberty began earlier in a warm climate: that girls in the Mediterranean region and in Africa, with their 'warmer blood', started their periods much earlier than girls from the chill, damp countries of northern Europe. The idea accorded well both with the humoral theory of medicine and with current theory on climates. It has also been said that in the city, with its looser morals, the girls' hormonal system was stimulated into activity earlier than in the countryside, but this has yet to be proved. If such differences did exist, they must really have been social and thus connected with diet. The utter poverty of the lowest classes in both town and country and the considerable yearly variations in global food production – and thus in individual diet – did once influence not only the onset of the periods but also their temporary cessation: in times of famine amenorrhoea, with cessation of ovulation, certainly affected the birth-rate, though it is difficult to tell exactly to what extent.[15]

It is hard to tell whether temporary food shortages had any effect on women at the end of their fertile lives. The menopause occurred at around forty-five, sometimes a little later, but it was popularly believed that a well-fed woman bade an earlier farewell to menstruation. 'In very fat women, the monthly flow ceases earlier: they have their periods only up to the age of thirty-five, as Forestus remarks; at least, the flow does finish earlier than in other women.'[16]

Excess weight was certainly often believed to be an obstacle to conception: a well-grown girl or woman was seen negatively and often held to be barren; a fat body could not swell further with a pregnancy.

At that time, more than today, menstruation was the greatest measure of a woman's life: its onset marked the first ripening of her body, its cessation brought her abruptly into old age, to the threshold of death. The 'flowers' once lost, the body began to wither. 'The womb, and with it the breasts, contract little by little and become as small as they were before puberty', claimed a sixteenth-century doctor.[17] The body's cycle was complete.

A menstruating body was an active body: the periods were evidence of an intense inner life. When they stopped, the body became 'neutral', stable from then on, no longer capable of curdling the milk . . . .

Beware the menstruating woman . . .

Menstrual blood, in fact, was credited with 'diverse harmful properties, as causing meat to rot, curdling milk and sauces, stopping melons from fruiting and bread from rising, turning wine cloudy'.[18] Anything touched by a menstruating woman was soiled and wasted. Her very presence could make it impossible to preserve one's larder, at least those items in it which were uncooked. That was why on the critical days she was forbidden to enter the salting-room or the cellar. This was the case throughout Europe. In western France, about 1920, menstruating women were absolutely forbidden to engage in the salting of butter or pork; at the same period, in Brunswick, the killing of a meat animal was put off if the wife was 'indisposed'; in northern France, she was told not to enter a sugar refinery while the sugar was being boiled or cooled, because she would turn it black.[19]

Menstrual blood spoils things and fragments them; its power to cause rot 'hastens the natural processes and upsets the even tenor of the household'. It can scorch vegetation: 'It makes the grass to die, as is well known', said the fourteenth-century poet Eustache Deschamps.[20] It can even cause the death of an animal which has consumed any of it, or at least bring on rabies: 'Dogs go mad merely by touching such matter.'[21] When honey was being gathered in Limousin, no menstruating woman was allowed to approach the hives: the honey would be lost and the 'flies' would all perish.[22]

The woman's whole body was contaminated by this waste product, this 'sweat of blood', this effluvium; her breath was particularly pernicious, but so were her gaze, her touch. Pliny reports in his *Natural History* that just a glance from a menstruating woman could fog a mirror or take the edge off a knife; copper would take on a fetid odour and tarnish if she touched it.[23]

The 'great biological storm' of the periods made women both dangerous and vulnerable. The body, subject at that time to internal upheaval, recoiled from water, especially cold water which halted the flow by congealing the blood. So during her 'monthlies' the woman did not wash or change the linen which caught the flow, it being believed that white linen attracted more blood.

The monthly stepmother

The moon has always been believed to have a big place in the periodic purgation of women and in the continuance of the human race. The doctor Jacques Duval, who at the dawn of the seventeenth century was still profoundly influenced by the old naturalist doctrine, held that the best moment for the blood of a 'gay, healthy, vigorous, well-constituted woman . . . to flow from the orchard of mankind' was at the full moon, when that luminary had the greatest power over a woman's body. Girls and young wives, who had a more 'tender and delicate' disposition, had more fluid blood, so that their periods begin earlier in the lunar cycle, 'at about the first quarter'. Older women's bodies are 'hardened, and in consequence they do not so easily allow the passage of the rays of energy from the celestial body': thus the moon must be full, at least, 'or even, very often, in its last quarter' before this thicker blood can gain passage. Hence the French proverb which says that the old moon purges old women, and the new moon young ones.[24]

In the course of a year there were some moons which occurred at the wrong time; the most dangerous of these was the 'ruddy moon' which started at the end of April. It initiated a time of ice and snow, a sudden return of winter in the midst of spring. Like menstrual blood, it scorched buds and tender plants, but encouraged hens to lay and cows to produce milk. The moon, in fact, 'has its periods', and the May dew which scorched plants 'is as it were the menstrual blood of the moon'. Hence, if one firmly believed in the close correspondence between the phases of the moon and the rhythm of a woman's body, it would be madness to hold a wedding at the time of the ruddy moon; the fruit of such a union would infallibly be spoiled. 'Unwillingness to get married in May is in fact caused by the fear of conceiving' under this aberrant moon.[25]

Poor 'Carrots!'

For several hundred years it was widely believed in Western Europe that conception could take place during the time of menstruation. Laurent Joubert, a learned doctor of Montpellier, reports that some people took birthmarks and freckles in children to mean that they had been conceived at that time of the month.[26] Others made out that a husband who 'knew' his wife at the time when she was 'polluted and unclean' would be responsible for the birth of an infant leper![27] These 'popular errors', denounced as such by Joubert in the sixteenth century, can serve as a reminder of the repugnance which, since Antiquity, had attached to the performance of the sexual act during the 'monthlies'.

But it was the red-headed child, more even than the freckled or unhealthy one, which was a sure sign of its parents' lack of self-control. Red-headded children had a universally bad image: 'red-nob' in Champagne became *Griserli blunt* (horridly blond) in Alsace and 'Carrots' elsewhere.[28] As the living proof of a contravention of sexual taboos, they were the butt of jokes by other children and by adults in the village. As the product of menstrual blood they were universally believed to have bad qualities and evil inclinations. They were frightening, ill-disposed, untrustworthy. 'Never trust a red-head', as they used to say in Alsace.[29] Not forgetting that Judas was always portrayed as having red hair and a red beard . . ..

The 'dog of a red-head', doomed to vice and ill-health, was despised; children's rhymes even went as far as to wish death upon them:

Roti Figür	You red one
Spring iwwer d'Mür	Jump over the wall
Brich Hals und Bein	Break your neck and legs
Kumm nimmi heim!	Never come home (alive)![30]

It is easy to deduce that a red-haired woman at the time of menstruation was regarded with particular suspicion. She was a compendium of threats: a woman, in a state of impurity, and to compound matters, a 'child of the monthlies'. Red, the colour of fire and corrupted (period) blood, savoured of the demonic. She had the rank smell of earth after rain. Her effect on the outside world was always to be feared: she was supposed to be sensual and sexually eager; her 'bad breath' prevented the scabbing of wounds and infected newly delivered women with puerperal fever.[31] She was certainly something out of the ordinary!

Barren Earth

The profound need to have children is universal, as old as time. Rachel weeping at her husband's feet: 'Give me children, or else I die' (Genesis 30 : 1). The woman, sole bearer of the hopes of the married pair and of the family unit, since it is she who receives the seed, makes it fruitful and finally brings the child to earth, was for that very reason generally held responsible if no children appeared. After a few years of marriage the family began to worry, asked awkward questions, pressed the wife, even if she was still young, to go on a pilgrimage, to do 'what is necessary'. But their attitude could be much harsher at times; for while sterility was seen as a physiological defect, unnatural or magical practices were also sometimes suspected.

A woman barren as a mule

A childless woman was often subject to humiliation: 'There goes the mule', jeered people she met, recalling the cross-bred animal which can have no offspring.[32] To escape from this misfortune the infertile woman was supposed to drink the urine of a mule![33] Hagiographic tradition often draws on a similar line of symbolism. That churchmen, sterile by vocation because of their vow of chastity, should have made frequent use of the image of the genetically sterile mule was certainly no coincidence. A saints' relics were always transported on mule-back. According to the legend of Saint Bertrand of Comminges, that holy man once put some of his parishioners, the inhabitants of the Azun valley in the Pyrenees, under an interdict for their outrageous disrespect in cutting off the tail of his mule. The saint's punishment exactly fitted the crime: for five years, the trees dropped their flowers and gave no fruit, the seed sown in the earth rotted and failed to grow, female animals and women became barren.[34]

From the fifteenth century to the eighteenth, childless women were called *brehaigne* ('barren'), the term commonly used since the twelfth century for a field which never bore a crop; in the nineteenth century the same word was applied to female animals who produced no young. In the last century, therefore, the same word was used to describe sterility in the animal, vegetable and mineral kingdoms. In any rural society, the rhythms of farm life have a strong influence on attitudes of mind. These rhythms are often disturbed, to the point where lives are put at risk. Any break in the chain of family descent was felt by the family unit as an attack endangering its very existence. This put childless couples in a well-nigh intolerable position, making them feel useless and therefore guilty. Death could be accepted if one could hope to live on in one's descendants; a barren couple was an aberration, they might as well be dead already, since they had no future.

Sterility was a shameful thing, a curse; not surprisingly, attempts were made to detect and cure it. History does not tell us whether girls whose 'test' was positive were invariably doomed to spinsterhood; but it can be shown that the means of detection was usually inspection of the urine. Here is an example of the method used in the eighteenth century: 'To know if a woman is capable of conceiving, make her piss on a mallow-plant for three days; if it dies, she is barren; if it is reborn green and vigorous, she is capable of conceiving.'[35] The idea that the urine of a barren women will burn and wither – sterilize, in fact – everything it touches must be connected with notions of the woman's inner nature: like a scorching wind or a burning sun, she burns up the seed and destroys what she should make to bear fruit.

So ancient and so powerful was the association of women with fertility that barrenness was seen not so much as a disturbance of the spirit of life, more as an incongruity, a nonsense. It is worth noting that in Latin, and also in German, the names of trees – symbols of fertility – are almost always feminine in grammatical gender, as are the names of rivers and the words for all 'active forces' like night, snow, light . . ..[36] A barren woman turns her back on nature. By failing in her duty and breaking the continuity of the family she is damaging the very work of Creation.

Even the Queen . . .

In their longing for children, a royal couple were not greatly different from their married subjects; but they made more frequent and sustained efforts to remedy the situation, which involved the kingdom as a whole: witness the case of Louis XIII and Anne of Austria, whose long childlessness certainly left a profound mark on the first part of their reign. They did not disdain the 'resources of nature': in 1633, following the advice of their doctor, Bonsart,[37] they went to Forges-les-Eaux, whose iron-bearing 'sanguine' springs were supposed to cure anaemia and infertility. In the same year, the Queen went, alone this time, to sit ritually on the stone of Saint-Fiacre at Breuil (now Saint-Fiacre-en-Brie). But if they made trial of water and stone, they also engaged in devotions more suited to orthodox Christian conduct. Through those long years of anguished waiting Louis and Anne never ceased praying to the Virgin, and to any saint with any reputation for curing infertility. Every great place of pilgrimage in the kingdom, north, south, east and west, was visited by them or their representatives. Every journey they made was a further occasion to seek help, for, while the royal couple were faithful visitors to famous shrines, they also showed reverence to lesser-known images. While travelling in the East, Anne went to pray at Gironet-Sampigny in Burgundy, then to the hermitage of Dun-sur-Meuse in Lorraine, where the hermits of Saint Augustine were accustomed to pray to Saint Lucy of Scotland on behalf of childless women.[38] She also stopped at Saint-Nicholas-de-Port to ask for the intercession of its holy bishop. Saint Norbert, the founder of the Premonstratensian order, having had a green and mis-spent youth during which he sired innumerable bastards, was much solicited by childless women; naturally Queen Anne was careful to send a prayer in his direction.

Distance to a shrine was no object, as it was always possible to delegate the pilgrimage to a reliable subordinate. The clergy were willing supporters of the royal couple's quest, realizing that the very existence of the realm, locked in its long indecisive struggle with the Habsburgs, would be at risk if the Queen unhappily produced no heir. In 1637 Brother Fiacre de Sainte Marguerite, a member of the barefoot Augustinians of Paris, went on the orders of his superiors, and with the consent of the King and Queen, on pilgrimage to the Virgin of Grace at Cotignac (Provence). It was because a few days earlier, while at prayer, he had heard a baby cry and, turning, had seen the Virgin; falling at her feet to adore the Child she held out to him, he heard her say: 'This is not my son, but the dauphin which heaven is preparing to send to France.' While Brother Fiacre was on his way to Cotignac, a nun from Clermont, Sister Germaine, was *en route* to Our Lady of Grace at Gignac (Languedoc). From 1635 onwards the venerable Marguerite of the Holy Sacrament, foundress of the Carmelites of Beaune, had also been praying for the birth of a dauphin.[39] That is worth stressing, for at the time a new image of childhood was beginning to take shape; devotion to the childhood of Christ was a notable trait of the Carmelite order, and every new recruit to it was given a little statue of Jesus the Founder,[40] a sign of the fascination of these nuns with the babyhood of Christ. The venerable Marguerite seems to have been the first to associate intercession for a dauphin with devotion to the Christ-child. In 1638, when the future of the dynasty at last seemed assured, 'she had a crown placed on the head of the statue of the child Jesus to thank him for fulfilling his promise'.

The royal couple expressed their own gratitude in various ways. Anne of

Austria sent to the mother of the Carmelites of Beaune a little statue of the child Louis XIV;[41] the Carmel of Orleans, where another nun had been praying at the Queen's request, received ten thousand *livres*, together with other favours and donations. In 1639 Louis XIII entrusted a relic of Saint Anne to the Carmelites of Sainte-Anne d'Auray, where two years earlier Anne of Austria had founded a brotherhood of Saint Anne;[42] in various places the Queen arranged for the saying of masses *in perpetuum*, and at Saint-Nicholas-de-Port she even left her diadem as an *ex voto*.[43]

After the death of Louis XIII Anne and her son, the young king, went on pilgrimages whose symbolic significance should not be ignored. Thus in 1658 they went to pray at the Carmel of Beaune, and before the tomb of the blessed Marguerite of the Holy Sacrament, the Queen asked the nuns to pray 'for the safe preservation of the king and for his marriage'.[44] And, after the signing of the Peace of the Pyrenees, which was sealed by Louis XIV's marriage to the Infanta of Spain, mother and son decided to go together to give thanks to the Virgin of Cotignac. In 1667, a year after Anne's death, Louis XIV had a marble tablet affixed to the walls of the sanctuary there, bearing the arms of France and intended to draw the attention of future generations to his obligations to the Virgin:

> Louis XIV, King of France and Navarre,
> Given to his people through the vow
> Which Anne of Austria, Queen of France, his mother,
> Made in this church,
> Had this stone placed here
> As a monument for posterity
> And to show his gratitude
> And record the masses which he generously founded there
> For the soul of his said mother.

The conception of the future Louis XIV in the Louvre in 1637 had been attributed to a storm which providentially compelled the King to remain in the palace and to sleep with the Queen; thus the engendering was seen as a direct result of God's will. By making solemn pilgrimage to the sanctuaries where prayers for the dynasty had been offered up and granted, the young king was giving credence to the wondrous character of his birth and destiny. The 'vow of Louis XIII' had put the kingdom under the direct protection of the Virgin just at the time when the future of the dynasty was being assured. The near-miraculous conception of Louis Dieudonné – Louis the God-given – contributed without a doubt to the reinforcement in seventeenth-century France of the Divine Right of Kings.[45]

Before it is too Late

Our sources are generally reluctant to reveal much about the fertility rites enacted by all countrywomen in former times. The Church is partly responsible for this discretion in that it did its utmost to plunge such rites into oblivion. It fought against such practices, mentioning them only indirectly, for fear that others would learn from the examples given. A bishop on a pastoral visitation, or a priest reporting on the state of his parish, might allude to certain 'superstitious', 'unbecoming', or 'shameless' customs among the faithful, but no more. Even the most communicative of churchmen, such as the Abbé Thiers towards the end of the seventeenth century, show extreme caution in this domain. Not until the accounts of antiquaries from the turn of the nineteenth century, and the researches of folklorists, is there anything to throw some light on these rituals: they speak of partial or total nudity, imitation of the sexual act, ceremonial slides and throwing of pins.

However, the Church is not solely responsible for the lack of evidence. For the villagers themselves, fertility rites were one of those things that just were not talked about: gestures and words passed on in some mysterious way, but of which the initiated were reluctant to speak at any length. They were too intimately enmeshed in the rituals to be able to treat them lightly. Late nineteenth-century accounts, by contrast, are swarming with double meanings and improper allusions, but this merely goes to show that by that time the age-old practices and beliefs had begun to lose their power.

Barren women were not alone in making use of fertility rites. The need to reproduce is so deep-rooted, the fear of sterility so great, that it seemed natural to perform one's devotions in advance, even before the discovery that 'nature has been unkind to our blood'. While the proportion of men and of women who remained unmarried was almost exactly the same (around ten per cent), it was the unmarried woman, rather than the bachelor, who was cut off from the social fabric: husbandless and childless, she was effectively marginalized. In Brittany it was derisively said that she had 'run to seed', while in the Bordeaux region she was 'in hock'.[46]

The woman desirous of having offspring had to pay attention to three decisive moments in her years of fertility. In adolescence she must seek a husband: fear of loneliness was not the only reason for rejecting celibacy, it was also and above all a refusal to die without issue. On her wedding day, the bride (and sometimes the groom as well) had to undergo certain rites with unmistakable sexual connotations; and through the first few months of her married life she would live in fear of not proving fruitful. And if she wished to avoid the prayers and pilgrimages which were the last resort of the childless woman, she would have to do all she could, from the beginning, to ensure that the fates would be kind.

The search for a husband

Even if she was not allowed to choose her future husband herself, a girl was always eager to know who it would be – and when. Ways of divining this were many and varied from region to region, but they all had the same primordial elements, elements which were meaningful for the community as a whole: stone, wood, running water.

Stones, large or small, were made use of everywhere by girls in search of a husband. But not just any stones. In the mid-nineteenth century girls living in

Porret, a suburb of Boulogne, used to pick up a 'lucky stone' on the beach: it had to be white and have a 'particular shape'. 'They believed it could give them children, deliver them from any danger and bring them a good husband at the time appointed.'[47]

Looking for such a stone was like looking for a four-leafed clover: you were unlikely to find one except by chance. Such was not the case with all rituals: some narrowly regulated ones even demanded a certain amount of physical effort from the girl. Near the Alpe d'Huez, in the Dauphiné, in the last century, there was an image of Saint Nicholas which was reputed to be able to bring about a marriage. In June, after the snows had melted, girls used to go up to the chapel of Brandes, which had been built by two aged spinsters in 1768;[48] there they would pray, kneeling 'on a sharp stone shaped like a flattened cone'. The folklorist Pilot de Thorey emphasizes the discomfort of the position: 'They then had to prostrate themselves, holding this same stone between their knees; the stone was believed to be able to bring them a husband. The most dedicated girls would themselves choose the sharpest stone they could find on their way up to the oratory, and would lay it with their offering at the feet of the saint.'[49]

Sometimes, the stone would be larger and require other feats from the would-be married woman. Near the chapel of Saint Eustace, at Saint-Étienne-en-Coglès in Brittany, there was a hollow rock onto which a girl had to climb, and then balance herself standing on the top. This ritual took place, unusually, in public, on the day of the local pilgrimage to the chapel.[50]

Even defying the law of gravity was sometimes not enough: the girl also had at times to give an exhibition of agility. In 1832 a Norman folklorist, Mangon de La Lande, described the fertility rites undergone some years previously by girls in the Bayeux region: 'Young virgins, hoping shortly to enter upon the married state, used until recently to lay their small coins upon the stone of Saint-Nicholas-de-La-Chesnaie; they had to be careful to put their fingers through a hole previously made in the centre of the coin so that it would have the necessary power.'[51]

This custom seems to have been quite widespread at one time in northern Normandy; it was still current in 1933 at the standing stone of Colombiers, about ten miles from Caen. Note here the habitual use of a coin with a hole in it, symbolizing the female genital organ and so the wish to lose one's virginity in marriage, and the hope of children; we shall see that stones with holes carry identical symbolism.

Those wanting to know when the marriage would take place would have recourse to 'talking' stones. Young men and women climbing the path to the Virgin's Tomb at Orcival would roll a stone down the mountain: 'As many times as the stone bounced, so many years would they have to wait before getting married.'[52] In Brittany, girls wanting to know the same thing would make offerings to the standing stones; around 1820 they used to lay 'tufts of pink wool tied with tinsel' in the cracks in a dolmen near Guérande, in the hope that they would find someone to marry them within the year.[53] Exactly the same rite was performed near the menhirs of Long-Boël in Normandy, and in the first years of the present century one would find 'in every hole or crack of the menhir of Pierre-Frite in the Lunain valley, in the *département* of Seine-et-Marne, a nail, or at least a pin, which had been put there by some young person of the region in the belief that by so doing they would be sure of getting married soon.[54]

Some late seventeenth-century accounts show that pins had an important part to play in fertility rites. In the nineteenth century, when the rite itself was fading, it was enough to place the pin in some crack in the sacred rock, or on a slab of stone, often a neolithic polishing stone. The custom of rubbing pins against it sometimes remained; but the zeal of would-be married women tended to be directed rather towards the wooden statues of the 'kindly saints'.

Sticking a pin into a saint's image is a very ancient means of divination which a girl would be almost bound to make use of, seeing how important the outcome would be for her future. Pricking a body, or an image of one, is a ritual practice found all over the world: to cure it, to harm it in course of an evil spell or sorcery – or to know when one's wedding day will come. In some places it is the nose, the neck or the head which is pricked, elsewhere the heel or leg.[55] There is always the idea of a test, because the way the operation is carried out has an influence on the result: if the correct spot is missed, the eagerly awaited union will be delayed.

Was this ritual a 'prayer by signs', as the folklorist Henri Gaidoz suggests? It was a sort of reminder to Saint So-and-so not to forget someone. The pricking operation must certainly have had some kind of phallic significance. It is no coincidence that most of the saints involved were male: in Brittany, Saints Nicholas, Christopher or Lawrence, or the local Saints Guénolé or Gildas, though Saint Barbara was the target at Guimiliau. In the nineteenth century the developing cult of the Virgin drew attention to the favours which Mary's intercession might confer; but the clergy was on the watch to make sure that it was only the dress of the venerable statue which received the pins on the day of the local festival.[56]

The rite being accomplished, the saint had to come up to expectations, or it would be the worse for him. Every time a wedding took place in a certain parish of the Minervois region, at the turn of the present century, the unmarried girls would file before the statue of Saint Sicre in the church porch and threaten him with hatchets:

> Great Saint Sicre, you have one year
> To give us all good husbands here,
> Or this my axe you may well fear![57]

In the same way, girls in the Ain region would threaten to throw Saint Blaize into the Rhône unless he got them married within the year.[58] Such marriage-broking saints were expected to live up to their reputation. Behind the figure of the patron saint we can discern the eponymous guardian of the village, the mythical ancestor, founder and perpetuator of the community, only thinly coloured by the Christianity superimposed by the Church.

Of all these rites, the ones which most persistently escaped the Church's control were those connected with sacred springs. Such springs, often tucked away at the side of a valley or hidden in a grove far from any trackway, were well suited to solitary devotions. Here one dared perform gestures and words with a contractual value: the girl was making a pact with the living forces of nature.

The water, welling up with greater or lesser abundance according to the time of year, symbolized the breathing of the earth: looking into it, throwing in a pin (or originally, a thorn), one was in communion with the earth, source of all renewal. If the pin floated up to the surface, the wedding would not be long delayed, but if it sank straight away it was a bad sign. No use planning for the honeymoon yet!

Those wishing for a happy outcome to a love affair were sometimes directed to a particular spring: that of Saint Baume in Provence, of Saint Abraham in Beaujolais, of Saint Anthony at Bussy-la-Côte in Lorraine.[59] Elsewhere the ritual would only work if the girl put her left foot in the water; at the spring of Saint-Martin-aux-Tourailles, in Lower Normandy, the rite had to be accompanied with a suitable prayer to Martin, who converted the Gauls to Christianity.[60] But the Christian colouring remains thin: in some cases it is certainly the spring itself which is considered divine, and if they are 'speaking springs' they are also springs to which many things are said. At Jussy, in Morvan, a girl disappointed in her hope of a husband would kneel before the spring and say to it: 'I bring you my misfortune, give me your good fortune.' Then she would get up, turn round, and throw a small coin, a cheese, or a pin over her shoulder into the water.[61]

Fertility rites involving young men are much less common; they normally occur only after the couple are engaged, the engagement being sealed by an elaborate ceremony. In the last century, at Braye-lès-Pesnes (Haute-Saône), betrothed couples would go at Candlemas to a spring where they would exchange cakes representing the two sexes; they would soak them in the spring water, then eat them at a symbolic repast which substantiated the betrothal vows.[62] Young couples in Draché (Touraine) were content with verbal promises exchanged through a ring-stone which symbolized their community.

It was advisable for the girl to continue her devotions right up to the wedding. Near Cravant (Morvan), a spring near Notre-Dame-d'Arbaud had the virtue of making a girl fertile; girls 'would therefore come and drink the water and pray to the Virgin, six months before the planned date of the wedding'.[63] And so to the wedding day itself . . ..

A kick from the bride

A wedding was the most suitable time of all to celebrate fertility rites. The exact moment and form of the ritual might vary, but the couple's expectations of it remained the same: protection and numerous progeny. Protection was most necessary during the religious ceremony, when the union was sealed before God and man. There was fear of the evil eye, or of sorcerers who might well be out to attack the young man's sexual energy by tying knots or driving in pegs: 'binding' (the *aiguillette*) or 'pegging' would make the husband impotent and the marriage childless.[64] Priests waded into battle against those who called upon dark forces, even at times using methods which were not strictly orthodox. For example, during a pastoral visitation of his diocese in 1650, the Bishop of Mende was indignant to discover an aged priest 'untying the lace' by a method which savoured of heresy.[65]

To 'set free' a husband who was taking his duty too lightly, a wife might well make use of certain fertility-inducing plants which were known to be effective against the *aiguillette*: 'sundew gathered at sunrise on 23 September' or mugwort gathered likewise on 24 June and 'worn around the neck together with mistletoe from an oak tree',[66] or alternatively, house-leeks.[67]

By the dawn of the present century, the fear of the *aiguillette* had not yet completely disappeared from the countryside, but the means used against magically induced sterility had changed considerably: it was now seeds which played the central role in the ritual of disenchantment. Around Bordeaux, if a couple was anxious to avoid the *aiguillette*, the bride had to put millet-seed in her shoes before setting out for the church;[68] in Périgord, she would fill her right pocket with millet so as to ensure that no spell cast by the 'binder' would impair her husband's virility on the wedding night; sometimes, as in Provence, it had to be the man who had the seed in his pocket,[69] and the 'binder' would not be able to work his evil spell unless he could count every seed without making a mistake. There is nothing surprising about the importance of seeds in these rituals of disenchantment, for grain-seeds were the very symbol of fertility. They were a normal part of the betrothal ceremony, and the handful of rice commonly thrown nowadays over newly-weds as they leave the church is the modern, usually purely ceremonial version of a rite whose powerful symbolic significance lasted down to the end of the nineteenth century.

Usually it was only the wife who received offerings of grain: this pouring of the fruits of the earth over her head or into her hands constituted a propitiatory rite. By it the wedding guests, and sometimes the whole community, were wishing her to bring the seed to germination and then to harvest, the harvest of the 'precious fruits of married life' which were to be formed in her womb. One of the most striking illustrations of this association between female fertility and the fruits of the earth is to be found in a Corsican ritual from the last century. After the ceremony, but before the wedding breakfast, the women chased away the men and the children; then each woman took a handful of wheat and poured it over the bride's head, singing a verse wishing her many sons born without pain. After this the bride had to sit on a bushel of corn, her body in direct contact with the seed.[70]

This sprinkling of seed over the bride, common in the Morvan region around 1840, used the different shapes of the various grains to represent a wish for male or female children: round grains, like millet or rapeseed, for boys, long or cloven grains, like rye or oats, for girls.[71]

In Lorraine and Haute-Provence, a near relation would present the grains of corn to the bride, who would immediately toss them over the wedding guests. It was in fact normal for the wife not to keep the proffered seeds to herself, and this was a mark of her dependence on the community: she made the most of what she was given, but she also spread the benefit among the members of the community there present. In Luzy and Lormes, in the Nivernais region, the *époigne* ritual showed the same reciprocal movement: the married couple had both to take a good bite out of a round, salty cake stuffed with garlic and hempseed; after that the other young people present fought for a share of the cake 'so as to get married soon';[72] its remains were returned to those who were about to take their turn in the perpetuation of the community. It was like sharing a fertile stem, or a sort of communal placenta, usually after the newly-weds had had their share.

Rites aimed at securing the fertility of the married couple took place during the wedding breakfast, creating a close association between celebration, eating and reproduction. The connection was made abundantly clear through the choice of morsels offered to signify the analogy between food and sex. In 1897, in the Gerzat region of Auvergne, 'to the bride was passed, between two plates, the tail end of a leg of mutton, or the hyoid bone of a chicken, known locally as the "horns" '.[73] Sometimes the sexual symbolism was accompanied by explicit references to children; at Charbonnières-les-Vieilles, and in the Ambert and Puy-en-Velay regions, the young wife was offered a doll in a little shoe: a powerful image, evoking both the end of her virginity and her wish for children, the shoe being a symbol of 'female sexuality, in its erotic and its reproductive aspects'.[74]

Some of the rites to which the bride was subjected on her wedding day were in fact intended as tests of her virginity. Around Soissons, after the wedding breakfast, the guests would go in procession to the 'Bride-stone', on to which the bride had to climb. She then sat on a shoe and 'slid down the stone; accordingly as she landed to the right, to the left, or in the middle, appropriate conclusions were drawn ... if the shoe happened to crack when it hit the ground, people would cry: "She's broken her shoe!" And the bridegroom knew what that meant.'[75] There, and also in the Bourbon region, 'breaking one's shoe' meant losing one's virginity. This symbolic tear or breakage did not have to apply to a shoe. In Armagnac the bride was taken to a spring the day after the wedding, and halfway back a water-jug was broken over her head.[76]

Men often took part in rites near a 'wedding-stone', then more commonly called a 'groom-stone'. Such stones were always some distance outside the village, generally on high ground, and were sometimes menhirs, or what remained of them; the activities of the Church in the seventeenth and eighteenth centuries and the depredations of nineteenth-century quarrymen had sometimes reduced them to a stump which now supported a cross, as at Albepierre, near Murat. Sometimes the stone had actually disappeared altogether and been replaced by a statue of the Virgin. On the plain of Puy-de-Mouton, in Provence, the guests would form a circle and the happy pair would dance three times round the statue which now stood in the place of the 'Bland-stone', 'so that their union should be fruitful and the wife suckle her children well'.[77] If the original stone was still in place, as at Graçay near Bourges, the couple would dance on top of it.[78]

In Poitou, the bride on her wedding-day would infallibly dip her clog or shoe in the water of a fertility spring such as that of La Roche-Rufin, near Pamproux; the company would make sure that she put her foot right in (such rituals always have an element of constraint, though it may be purely symbolic). They would cry:

> Now the bridal kick is done,
> Within the year the child will come.[79]

Sometimes, the wife would merely walk round the fountain, or jump over the streamlet which ran from it. Thus at the spring of Saint-Arnaud-Tallende, in Auvergne, whose ritual is reported and interpreted by Van Gennep: 'The jump has magical value; the bride shows her legs; the water symbolizes another fluid.'[80] At times both bride and groom had to undergo this ordeal by water: together they had to jump over the little pool beside the spring. At that moment, at Exoudun in Poitou, the boy and girl attendants would proceed to splash the happy couple, 'doing their best to throw water between their legs'.[81]

In many places the ritual of the white hen was performed on a wedding day. In the morning, the young men, or 'chicken-boys' as they were called, would go and steal (the ritual demanded this) a white hen, preferably from relatives of the bride. This unfortunate bird was then paraded round the streets throughout the day on the end of a pole. In the Vosges and some parts of Berry, one of its wings was decorated with ribbons, which were pulled on from time to time to make the creature squawk, this being an expression of the bride's regret at the imminent loss of her virginity: this ritual of the 'wedding hen' was in fact intended to focus attention on the end of her virginity and her desire to bear children. On the wedding night, the wedding hen was tormented until it died. In the La Marche region the guests hit each other with it; around Bordeaux, young men, blindfolded, threw stones at it in a public display.[82]

The new wife might consider the loss of her virginity to be compensated for by the hope of a large and blooming family. In Berry, the wedding hen was brought into the church during the nuptial mass to ensure that the couple would have many children. After killing, it was cooked and served to the happy pair in bed. Around Castres they would stew it along with a cabbage, also stolen, and which had served to give it the *coup de grace*. These rituals maintained a close association between virginity and fertility, the latter's part in the couple's future being symbolized by the cabbage.

The uprooting of the 'wedding cabbage' was a ceremony in itself. In Anjou it was done the morning after the wedding: all the farm oxen were yoked to the best available cart and everyone went off to the cabbage patch. The best cabbage, with the biggest head, was chosen and a trench was dug around it, everyone helping with a great display of zeal; but the honour of uprooting it naturally fell to the husband. Then the rest, armed with ropes and levers, would hoist it into the cart and return it in triumph to the nuptial home, where the women would take charge of it.[83]

The shape of the cabbage made it into one of the symbols for a fertile womb, swelling with new life 'leaf by leaf'. This allows us to understand why, in the last century when morality began to impose a decent reticence over the mysteries of birth, children, who had hitherto been seen to emerge from a womb symbolized as a cabbage, were now said to be found . . . in a cabbage patch!

3

What if No Child Appears?

That uncertain awareness of a mystic communion with Mother Earth . . .

Mircea Eliade

A young wife worried at the non-appearance of children after several years of marriage might well repair to sacred trees, blessed springs or old and venerated stones. The rituals she performed there would have strong sexual connotations and would always involve a part of the body, for some contact with the primordial elements of nature was indispensable. Behind them all we can discern a belief in the mythic origin of children.

Nature Reawakened

For country people, the sacred grove or stone 'image' was, if not the actual source of the community's life, at least the distributor and mediator of its vital forces. Through the image they sought contact with the living forces of nature, entering the realm of cosmic Time. Hence it was only primordial elements like stones, trees, water and wind – the bones, muscles, blood and slow breathing of the Earth Mother – that could put an end to a stubborn infertility which was seen as opposed to the very nature of womankind. By coming close to the great body of the mother of all things, the woman hoped to share in its abounding fertility: all the rituals were intended to encourage that symbolic transfusion.

Water bears the seed

Water is a sign of life: we have already seen its importance in the fertility rites undergone by girls in search of a husband and by brides on their wedding day. Water was believed capable of calming an overactive womb, or alternatively of reinvigorating one which had lost its vigour; but it was also thought to carry with it the germs of life which the woman had to get hold of. A childless wife would bathe in the 'living waters' of a river or spring; no benefit would come to her from the 'dead waters' of a standing pool or pond.

Treatment of infertility by external application of water was not common in France; it was, apparently, much more so in Spain, especially in Andalusia.[1] Is this because climatic conditions were more favourable there? There was, none the less, a certain number of springs where barren women would bathe in a sitting position. At Plombières,² in the Vosges, where the water sprang from a rock, specially shaped chairs would be placed over the running water 'in such a way that the rivulet of water would fall upon the genital region of the woman'. But the commonest sort of rite involved drinking a certain quantity of water from a wonder-working spring. Water oozing from a rock wall in a cavern would stand for the dark dampness in the vagina of the Great Mother.

Women tended to favour springs where the iron in the water turned it red, like diluted blood springing from the womb of Earth. These 'rust fountains' were 'founts of life'. Often the water would be covered by a bubbling scum which exhaled a strong odour of sulphur, and it was reputed a sure cure for barrenness in both women and animals. That women and female animals should go through the same rituals in the same place might appear shocking to us today, but people in times past saw nothing untoward about it.

Kissing the tree

Trees have always been a fertile source of myth. A tree's roots go down to chthonic depths, to the world of the dead, whence comes its vitality. The trunk is a powerful symbol of vigour and serenity. The yearly growth and fall of its leaves make it into a sort of abstract of all existence: the thrusting vigour of youth, the fullness of adulthood, the withering of old age, the nakedness before approaching death. And the expectation of renewal, of eternal new beginnings.

Trees figure in countless fertility rituals, usually with the idea of ensuring fruitfulness. At Les Brandons the local people would parade under the trees with lighted torches, begging them to give a good harvest – and threatening them, shaking them violently, beating them. Trees had a 'language' which assumed a great importance in dreams and foreshadowings, in the seeking of a husband, and on a wedding day. Dancing round the maypole was a common event, even in towns.

Hollow trees were given particular attention by newly-weds from their wedding day onwards. By climbing through such a tree, they showed their wish for a fertile union. Those desirous of children would also shake a tree at a given time of year. In Champagne, certain trees were ritually shaken on Christmas Day by those hoping for a child. Such a desire could be expressed by a sort of intimacy with the tree: the custom of 'kissing the tree', i.e. embracing it, was very widespread.

Not every tree could be the object of such attentions. It would be singled out for its exceptional age, the strength of its branches, or the thickness of its trunk, or perhaps for its situation: a tree at a crossroads or at a high point might be part of a mythic geography known only to the natives of the locality.

Sliding stones and rubbing stones

For many centuries, men and women worried at having no children have had recourse to the solidity of the mineral kingdom. Even more than a tree, a standing stone, or a rocking-stone perched on some rocky hilltop, seemed to defy the passage of time. Even more than a spring, a rock could strike one with awe: its strange chinks, swellings, rounded domes and veins seemed to lead one into an unknown and fascinating world. A complex of past beliefs, which present beliefs had never quite eliminated, ensured that stones would have a major part to play in fertility rituals.

Rock-sliding, a rough and 'primitive' activity, was certainly a very ancient rite. Childless women would climb to the top of a more or less flat and steeply sloping rock. Tucking up their skirts and petticoats, they would slide on bare buttocks to the bottom of the stone. For evident reasons of decency, but also because it was important for the rite, no outsider could intrude on what must be seen as a sacred ceremony; women normally acted alone, for only the stone must know . . .. And before leaving, they would make a point of depositing a small scrap of material or ribbon on the sliding-stone.

There were a good many of these sliding-stones or 'Rutschfelsen' on the Alsatian side of the Vosges. The most famous of all was the 'Gailer Liss' or 'Grande Lise', situated in a wood on the slopes of the Gross Wintersberg, near Niederbronn. A huge block of the local sandstone, it was frequented for centuries by the barren wives of Alsace. And it is still there:

On the south-east wall is a relief carving, almost life-sized, of a seated woman, naked from the waist up, her legs covered with draperies. Her hands, which are much damaged, hold on her knees a sort of cup with concentric grooves, considered to represent the female reproductive organs. This cup or dish goes down as a wide channel between the stumps of the arms and gradually vanishes as it nears the edge of the stone. Another channel, very wide and worn smooth, proves that the stone was used for sliding.[3]

It was common for women to rub their navels or bellies against a stone. Wide-sided menhirs looked from a distance like a round or oblong shape reminiscent of a phallus, and women would come to simulate the sexual act against these stones, erected by the hand of man, but believed to have 'fallen out of the apron' of some fairy.

Sliding and 'rubbing', both simulations of the sexual act, were attempts to stimulate an inactive womb. However, not all such rites demanded such agitation of the woman's body; in some cases she had to abandon herself passively to the stone. This meant stretching out on the stone and remaining thus for one or several nights. This nocturnal communion with the sacred stone must certainly have been the 'original' form of the rite of 'incubation', so frequently practised in the Middle Ages on the tombs of the saints by those seeking bodily healing. At bottom what the woman was really doing was entrusting her body to the 'heat-stone' so that the mysterious fluids within the rock could bring down the wall which had hitherto barred the advent of a child, making conception easier.

Water and stone, water and tree, tree and stone, often came together in one and the same fertility rite. There were even some notable places where all three of these fundamental elements were found together. From earliest times, these cosmic sites, where the sacred entered into immediate communion with mankind and 'one could contact God directly without going through the priest', were a favourite resort of childless couples.

Can a herb make a child come?

Certain herbs, either because of their natural properties or because of the weight of symbolism they carried, were thought to have the power to aid conception. Year by year, the plant world yields its tribute and bears witness to the inexhaustible bounty of earth.

Popular belief always inclined to blame sterility on an incorrect temperature in the womb. A womb that was too hot burned up the seed, just like soil scorched by too much sun. 'This defect is fairly common among lubricious and sexually insatiable women', according to Primerose, a late seventeenth-century doctor; such women should sedulously avoid hot baths, which would only increase their ardour. But a womb that was too cold was no good either: like earth that was too cool and damp, it impeded the germination of seeds, which rotted in it or 'leaked'. In either case, 'the barren womb is like sandy soil incapable of bearing crops'.[4]

Herbs which are supposed to control the temperature of the womb have always been popular with women; childless women placed great reliance on their 'simples'. On Saint John's Eve women would go to pick herbs from around a spring, near an ancient sacred stone or on a hill between two properties or two regions – among them, herbs whose virtue in aiding conception had long been known. One of them was artemisia, known as 'the mother of all herbs'. Besides its use as an aid to conception, it was also believed to speed menstruation, help in childbirth, or even prevent miscarriage.

Agnus castus was also reputed to be an aid to conception. Some ancient authors, such as Leo Africanus, attributed to it 'the property of revitalizing the male member and facilitating intercourse' and advised its administration in food; in the sixteenth century it was claimed that women would become pregnant after drinking the juice of this 'hot and bitter plant'. *Agnus castus* could have some peculiar effects: it was a treacherous sort of herb of which it behoved young girls, in particular, to beware. 'We are assured,' writes Leo, 'that by urinating on this root, the member immediately becomes erect, and that many maidens have lost their virginity simply by urinating upon it.'[5]

Women would bathe in a brew made from 'all the heating herbs of Saint John's Eve'; some of them would also wear a girdle of such herbs round their loins on the day they were gathered. These herbs were in fact supposed to 'make or keep a woman fruitful, even if worn under her dress'. This was one way of warming the womb, which was often seen as a sort of oven. Others preferred to rely on potions and unguents.

Mandragora

Mandragora was both a herb and a root. Its very name is redolent of the world of magic. Man-shaped, talisman of mickle might, favourite recourse of sorcerers, the mandragora has nourished centuries of Western imaginings about birth and about life.

The mandragora owes its fame above all to its shape. Its stumpy roots resemble those of beet or chard: 'they are forked from halfway down, so that they seem to have thighs like a man's', or they are 'like a man with no arms'. Over this 'trunk' and these black and hairy legs grow, in season, huge leaves and big fruiting pods. The whole is indisputably similar to a human figure, and it is easy to see why the analogical habits of Antiquity endowed it with special status. Some saw in the mandragora a resemblance to a human head:[6] it was 'the man-faced tree', the 'plant with a man's countenance', 'Adam's head'.

In the Middle Ages its aphrodisiac, hypnotic and narcotic properties made it a favourite ingredient in philtres and sleeping draughts: it was 'the magicians' herb', 'the sorcerers' herb'. The very name 'mandragora', or 'mandrake' (*drake* = 'dragon' in Anglo-Saxon), implied a link with the underground world of spells. In the highlands round Pistoia, in Italy, it was called the *erba mandragola, la maestra della stregoneria* (mistress of witchcraft); the Goths called it *alruna*, a word which could also mean 'witch'. In France it was *la fée* (fairy) *Maglore*, the *mandragole, mandagloire* or *main de gloire* (hand of glory).

Because of its strange shape and its hallucinogenic powers, the mandragora became a mythic plant belonging to two worlds, the chthonic and the terrestrial; but it also constituted a strange synthesis of elements from the three kingdoms, animal, vegetable and human. It was a creature of darkness. But certainly its 'human' nature must predominate: the fact that there were two varieties meant that it was even possible to distinguish the male mandragora, which was white, from the female, which was black.

In the seventeenth century the humanlike appearance of the mandrake was explained by its weird origin: it sprang from the sperm of hanged men which dripped on the ground below. Thus, in German-speaking countries, the mandragora was long known under the name of *Galgenmoenlein* or 'little gallows-man'.

Another increment to the myth of the manlike plant came from the ritual used in uprooting it. It was drawn forth like living flesh, in a sort of Caesarean operation; as it was torn from the earth it gave a terrible cry. In their account of German folk traditions, the Brothers Grimm report that 'It is very dangerous to pull it from the earth, for once uprooted, it moans, cries and screams so hideously that the person who has removed it dies on the spot.'[7]

An uprooted mandragora was revered like an idol: it was washed with red wine, then laid in a coffer. It was bathed every Friday and given a fresh white petticoat every new moon. Eighteenth-century peasants believed that 'the finder was obliged to feed it, either on bread, or on meat, or on any other food'. In exchange, the mandragora would make its master's fortune and ensure his happiness; it would reveal the secrets of the future and ensure him success in all his undertakings.

The mandragora, the 'little magic man', was above all known for its influence on reproduction: it 'aroused love' and so encouraged conception; it was well known to encourage fertility. 'Its possessor,' people averred, 'if he has no children, sees his marriage blessed and made fruitful by Heaven.'[8] This is an ancient belief; a comedy by the ancient Greek author Alexis mentions the incomparable aphrodisiac qualities of mandragora. It was quite possibly this play which inspired Machiavelli's *Mandragora*, in which once again that marvellous plant is recommended for making a barren woman fruitful.[9]

Where do Babies Come From?

Country children, living close alongside the animals and crowded with the rest of the family in a small house, very soon learned the facts of life. They saw farm animals copulating, and no-one thought to hide such natural scenes from their eyes. But it must not therefore be thought that young countryfolk made no distinction between human and animal births.[10] The child knew that the animal 'made its young', but readily believed that human parents found their babies in some hidden corner of the landscape. And everyone, young or old, was intrigued by the mystery of the origins of life.

It is a belief common to many peoples that the Earth is like a womb or crucible. In Estonia it is said that man is 'born of the earth'; in central Europe, he 'comes' from the depths, from springs or lakes, caverns or cracks in the rock, or perhaps from a tree or wood.[11] Even in modern Germany, in the Vosges and in the Valais region of France, this belief that man comes from earth survives in the form of legends and metaphors.

Children from wells and springs

Children came from water, from a spring in the heart of a wood, far from human habitation but reachable by a known path; or from a well so deep that it went down to the 'bowels of the earth'; or again, from a lonely pool or lake.

This belief in wells and sources which brought forth children was widespread in northern and north-eastern France, and indeed in the whole of north and central Europe, until the beginning of the present century. Alsace was dotted with *Kinderbrunnen* (child-springs) where mothers used to say they had found their children. These springs were in fact considered to be the place of origin of all the children in the village. They are so numerous in some cantons of Alsace that it is tempting to believe that villages there constituted themselves by reference to their 'ancestral spring'. Such springs or wells were, indeed, sacred fountains (*heilige Brunnen*).

Unborn children could also reside in lakes, reed-fringed pools, waterfalls or streams. The famous Titisee, the 'child-lake' near Freiburg im Breisgau, was considered to be the cradle of all the children in the region.[12]

The 'mother rocks'

The Earth Mother was a great oven or incubator, and rocks were embryos which gradually changed their form under the effects of her heat. This image of a mineral world in a state of perpetual ferment lingered long in the Western European mind. Over twenty or thirty years it is possible to witness the slow crumbling of rocks on the surface. Even in our own country there are country people who firmly believe that stones have life: a slow, sluggish kind of life, but life none the less. Springing from the beginnings of the world, stones live with a mysterious life which appears only in certain signs.

Peasants tilling their fields know that stones always 'come up again', that they have a power to move which brings them remorselessly up to the top of the field. This must be so, because every year the ploughshare grates against a new crop of them. But as well as these ordinary stones, signs of the living forces lower down, there are others, much more significant. Local people are always intrigued by sandstone or granite blocks which, perched on a hillock or on the side of a lonely slope, seem to take on human characteristics. Legend is full of these round or arched or humpbacked stones which grow magically, like mushrooms, in a single night.[13] Traditionally they are believed to be set up by the fairies, to grow bigger every year, and even (sometimes) to be able to speak. They are grey, or more commonly red, and they are sometimes close to a spring of reddish, iron-bearing water, which is supposed to be good against rheumatism and rickets in children. The Lia Fail (Fail's stone) in Ireland secretes milk in the presence of a woman destined to become a mother, but if the woman is to remain barren, it sweats blood: the bones and blood of Earth.[14]

If the villagers paid honour to the 'child-stone' it must have been because they believed that they had all come forth from it. The pregnant stone took care of the infants which it carried in its womb, and every day it went down to the stream so that they could drink; when one of them was ready, a woman (the midwife) went to fetch it for the waiting family, in exchange for a fair reward.[15] Most of these 'womb-stones' seem also to have been 'wedding-stones' for young people, 'sliding-stones' for childless women, and 'healing stones' for sickly children or those with rickets. They were also honoured by those hoping for a good harvest and an increase in their flocks, for they could guarantee the continuance of the cycle of the seasons and the endurance of living species. All manner of rituals converged on these 'good stones' in an ensemble bearing on the essentials of life.

'Hollow stones' were usually isolated, either amongst fields or in uncultivated heath or woodland on the boundary of several villages. They were almost always boundary stones, 'limiting' stones, 'stones of justice' or 'sarsens': rough-hewn, square or rectangular blocks, one-and-a-half to two metres tall and twenty or forty centimetres thick, upright, with a slightly oval hole in them, some twenty to twenty-five centimetres by thirty to forty centimetres. Very few remain of these 'hollow stones', which must have been abundant in Western Europe; the survivors are scattered from the Swiss frontier to Brittany and Ireland.

When a child was born, the parents would bring it to the hollow stone and pass it through the hole. This rite of passage, the 'stone baptism', re-enacted the birth and had a threefold purpose. The stone would ensure the child's body was normal and healthy, and protect it against the ill will that was bound to dog it. Finally, this passage through the hollow stone was a rite of recognition, of acceptance by the dead: the socialization of the child was not complete without a public presentation before the ancestral stone. It was there that a physical link was created between generations, between the past and the future. In this cosmology, the parents' task was to ensure that the junction was made: they were the guardians of the tradition.

Collective memory long retained the belief that these hollow stones were tombs, 'gateways to death'; the idea complements the image of a powerful link among the individuals of a single lineage or a single community, and of the close intermeshing of two worlds, which at that moment met and mingled.

4

The Cycle of Life

'Is', 'was' and 'will be' ... are generated forms of Time, which imitates
Eternity and circles round according to number.

Plato, Timaeus

The village stone (or cave or cavern) presided over the two great rites of
passage, birth and death. All the villagers were convinced that they had come
from it and would return to it in death. Even in the eighteenth century, when
burial in the local cemetery had become the norm, memory of the ancient burial
place, near the stone or the cave, had not faded away altogether.[1] Thus it was
that the stone saw the manifestations of an awareness of living forces which
remained with most of the rural populations of Western Europe until the
nineteenth century. An awareness of life which is indissolubly linked with an
equal awareness of death: awareness of a cycle in which all things are
interlinked, in which life ends in death, but death is easier to accept because it is
not 'really' death, and certainly not extinction, because from death, new life is
born.

The Span of Life

The most familiar image of human destiny is the span, or curve, which
individuals follow through life, and which is longer and more sustained for
some than for others.

Birth was an emergence into the light. A treatise published in 1655 in Danzig
by Jean-Claude de La Courvée, court physician to the queen of Poland, and
entitled *De Nutritione Foetus in Utero Paradoxa*, supplies some curious evidence
for the persistence of the ancient cosmological beliefs in learned works down to
the seventeenth century. The frontispiece of the work is by the Dutch engraver
Franz Allen, and it is divided into three sections: on the top of the print is
inscribed the title of the work, bordered by two seraphim; in the middle is a
cloudy sky crossed by a chariot drawn by doves and driven by a cupid; to the
right and left, the sun shining on a bird (the phoenix?), doubtless a way of
representing the eternal cycle of day and night, the passing of time; under this
scene, the legend *Ubicumque* (everywhere). On the lowest level there is the
surface of the earth, shrouded in semi-darkness: a sleeping child, curled up in

34

the foetal position, seems to merge with the rocky mass on which he lies; nearby we can make out a flower-covered hill. The legend is *Qui quasi flos egreditur* (Who cometh forth like a flower). The child, like all things born into life, comes out of the darkness of the underworld to go through his lifespan upon earth.

This iconography became quite popular in the seventeenth century: it is found, for example, as the frontispiece of the second edition of Hendrik van Roonhuyse's textbook of midwifery (1672).[2] In the foreground, a baby, lying among flowers, seems to emerge from a womb half-hidden in darkness; in the background are mountains; on each side, two women with their wombs revealed, one of them being pregnant. The stony covering from which the child seems to be struggling to escape is vascular, as if to give it some resemblance to the infant's 'nourishment', the 'secundine' or placenta.

These representations of the newborn child emerging from the Earth Mother may be compared with the imagery of the 'ages of man'. From the fifteenth century to the nineteenth, this theme was enormously popular in all European countries: the first illustration of it came from a Basel press in 1474, and from 1482 onwards there were coloured engravings of it circulating in the German-speaking countries. The schema is a familiar one:[3] the span of life has become a broken arch, a stair which rises and falls, as does every existence, and each step represents a decade. On each level appears a man, a woman, or both, or a symbolic plant or animal, together with a suitable sentiment. The most striking thing is the absence of any life under the earth: the span of life is now rarely prolonged into the underworld. There is often some architectural feature or some suggestion of a rocky floor which cuts mankind off from all contact with the dark womb of the Earth Mother, as if to emphasize that life belongs to earth and heaven, and not under the earth. For this image is the reflection of a new, urban, attitude to life.

Time of Year, Time of Life

If human existence was seen as cyclic, so too was the progress of time. In rural society, the brief span of the farming year was as it were a microcosm of the life of a man. As the seasons went by, the countryman saw the buds open and the young shoots appear; the flowers came out, the leaves turned, branches spread wide; then he witnessed the fall of leaf and fruit, the long-drawn death agony of the plant world. In the same way, but more slowly, 'the strength of his own body flowers in his vigorous youth, then fades once again as he reaches man's estate, diminishing to the point when death will come for him, this death which "cannot be healed by any herb" '.[4]

Childhood, adulthood and old age: a long spiral, a constant renewal. Day following night, the cycle of the seasons, life engendering life: the great universal mechanism, like a water-wheel whose integral system brings a never-ending gush of water to the fields.

One of the most important moments of the year was the Feast of the Purification of the Virgin, or Candlemass, celebrated on the 2nd of February.[5] This marked the end of the forty days of Mary's isolation after the birth of

Jesus, but for country people it was above all the end of winter and night, the beginning of renewal and the new agricultural year, as the life of nature gradually quickened once again. The candle which would be lit in every home symbolized the return of the light: its propitiatory value was recognized all over Western Christendom, at least from the seventeenth century onwards.[6] The blessed candle was supposed to be able to keep away both night-demons and thunderstorms, and helped with all the difficult rites of passage: its help was looked for by those in childbed – or death-bed.[7]

The year itself had its own microcosm. Each of the twelve days of Christmas was supposed to correspond to one month of the coming year, and for this reason, divination was often practised at this season. In 1850 at Illzach, in Alsace, pregnant women sought an answer to their anxieties at this time. If three days after Christmas the sun was still shining and a child died, many more would die during the coming year – or so it was said.[8]

But Christmastide, the most holy of the 'four tides', was also the time of the 'wild hunt', which caught up in its crazy ride all those who had died before their time: those whose lives had been brutally cut short by murder or death in battle, accident or sickness, 'before they had lived out their allotted span'.[9] Among them were some innocent victims, in the form of very young children: babies who had died before even seeing the light of day. For centuries people lived in terror of this troop of wandering ghosts, led in the German-speaking countries by the triple goddess Freya–Frouve–Holda – especially the last, the goddess of both the souls of the dead and those of unborn children. The reason was that premature death disturbed the succession of generations and broke off the cycle of nature, within which young children ought normally to carry on where their dead ancestors had left off.

Reception and Conception

We moderns find something astonishing in the image of the woman whose quest for children is guided by naturalist cosmology and fertility rites. Centuries-old peasant notions about the origin of the seed and the conditions under which it grew tended to overestimate the role of women. It appeared that conception was a two-stage process. Before the human intercourse which would humanize and 'familiarize' the future offspring came a coupling of the woman with the forces of nature. A woman paying her visit to the blessed spring, the sacred stone or the holy tree was attempting to capture the essence, the principal of the child, the human seed which dwelt in the womb of nature.

'The orchard of the human race'

The woman's body was like a field, cultivated earth opening to receive the seed of the child; it was the 'orchard of the human race', and the planting was done by mysterious forces; 'the mother did no more than *receive* the child'.[10] The woman received it from the womb of earth into her own womb, within which it would attain to human form. At this stage, the man still had nothing to do with the process. It was, of course, known that there was a connection between sexual intercourse and conception, but the biological origins of conception were held to be of little account. The father's role was indispensable, but secondary: he helped to fix the seed and went on to 'fashion' it by continuing to 'know' his wife during her pregnancy; this was doubtless the time when he endowed the child with its family resemblance.[11] Even the woman was no more than a carrier, a receptacle, an incubator for the seed or foetus. Her motherhood was more important than the fatherhood of the father, because by 'lending' her body she made it possible for the embryo to develop and be born into the world. But all in all one might well think that men were the children of the soil, of their ancestral earth, rather than of their parents.

Though it later became diluted, and progressively weakened by the idea that the man and woman were indeed the biological progenitors of the child, this ancient concept of the origins of life went on influencing many attitudes in the countryside of Western Europe until the middle of the last century. Certainly it allows a better understanding of the *couvade*, a curious rite which, after coitus and shaping *in utero*, constituted the last attempt of the father to assert his identity as such.

The couvade, or the importance of being father

Travellers and folklorists have often been inclined to see in the couvade nothing but a parody: there was not a woman among them, and what intrigued them was the comical or 'bizarre' side to the custom. However, it would be wrong to think that the ritual of the 'man in childbed' is nothing more than an amusing illustration of the theme of 'the world upside down'.

A woman is brought to bed, but rises again soon afterwards; the man then takes her place in the bed and 'lives through' the birth: he writhes and moans; his face is distorted with pain; when the 'labour' is over, the baby is given to him to cuddle and soothe; sometimes he pretends to suckle it, and among the Arapesh, in New Guinea, he undergoes the same dietary restrictions as his wife in order not to endanger the health of the child. It is he who receives the congratulations of visiting friends – and the presents too. While his wife is in retreat – or simply doing the housework – people would 'Be nice to Smith, his wife's in labour!' as eighteenth-century jesters would put it.

The couvade rite is an ancient one.[12] Strabo mentions it as being current in Spain, and Diodorus Siculus in Corsica; Apollonius of Rhodes noted it in Pontus, on the Black Sea, and Plutarch in Cyprus. And it is found all over the world: in the seventeenth century, it was known to be practised in the Antilles and in Brazil;[13] in the nineteenth and early twentieth centuries it was described among the North American Indians, in Tartary and in the Indies. Survivals of it were noted in the Basque Country, Navarre and Bearn less than a century ago,[14] and near Nevers as recently as 1905.

This ancient and widespread custom has been variously interpreted by anthropologists. We now know that it is not a reflection of the 'change from matriarchal to patriarchal society', as Bachofen would have it, nor yet a sign of 'the advent of paternal power', as von Dargun claimed. But it is much harder to agree on what it really is. Frazer thought it showed the father's willingness to share in the mother's sufferings by a kind of sympathetic magic; and indeed, among the Arapesh, the man used to share with his wife the period of sequestration *post partum*.[15] Zmigrodski and Bastian believed that the man took his wife's place in order to avert the dangers which threatened her and her baby during the uncertain period after the birth: thus, the better to 'deceive the demons', the woman would assume the hat and trousers of her husband and walk ritually round the house.[16] Claude Lévi-Strauss holds that it is not the mother's part which the husband is playing, but the child's, the latter being the one in need of protection.[17] Psychoanalysts see in the couvade a 'direct link with the man's anxiety to procreate'.[18] As early as the seventeenth century the doctor Primerose mentioned the assumption that 'during the wife's pregnancy the man suffers the same indispositions as does she'.[19]

It is possible that all these diverse interpretations have some validity: so many different peoples have engaged in the rite of couvade that it is unreasonable to expect a single interpretation to do for them all. In Western Europe at least, the ideas on the origins of life which were current in the old rural society led logically to a ritual of recognition of the father. 'In origin, the couvade is a rite of adoption in which, by engaging in symbolic or mimetic action, the father solemnly pretended to have borne the baby himself, and thus publicly and mystically recognized and adopted it'.[20] From this viewpoint it is clear that the couvade was actually a socialization rite, of the man as father.

All things swell with the moon

Just as there were places, so also there were times particularly suited to conception; and since nature was profoundly under the influence of cosmic forces, it was important to know the most favourable moments and make the most of them. The moon was an essential factor in this. The sowing of the seed of man, like that of plants, depended on the great determiner of the forms of species. The moon was believed to have an influence over all life on earth; the germination of plants, the growth of animals, depended on this luminary of the night.

The moon was widely thought to have a power of attraction not only over the tides, but also over the shoots of plants as they thrust through the earth. She made all things swell. The female womb was no exception to this universal dilatation, and as the attraction was supposed to be strongest and most benign when the moon was new, it was at that time that childless wives performed their fertility rites.

Farmers and gardeners were scrupulous in following the lunar cycle: they sowed and planted at the time of the new moon, which ensured good growth in 'outside' crops (i.e. not roots) and helped them set seed. The old moon was good only for plants which developed underground, tubers and roots; it also helped with the conservation of products which were 'dead' or about to become so: thus trees ought to be cut down 'when the moon was on the wane' so that the wood would keep better, and a tree that had been cut down at this time was said to be 'well mooned'.[21] It was at that time also that bodily excrescences, hair and beard, must be removed, because they would then grow again more slowly. And to save 'preserves' of pork and goose from going rancid quickly, the animals had to be killed when the moon was on the wane; so deeply ingrained was this precept that even around the year 1930, meat markets in south-west France were deserted at the time of the new moon.[22]

The foetus, although it matured slowly for nine months in a damp, dark enclosed space similar to the womb of the Earth, was considered to be an 'outside' plant because it went on growing after birth.

If the new moon was thought favourable to conception – as it was – it was above all because it favoured the birth of boys. The moon was a male star which had its effect on sexual differentiation. The new moon was positive, the old moon negative, bringing girls, i.e. second-rate products. 'It is commonly believed', wrote Salgues in 1811, 'that the woman who conceives under the new moon bears a boy, and *that she has only a girl* if she receives her husband's attentions in the moon's last quarter'.[23] Boys belong to the outside, to the light; girls to the inside, to darkness, to Earth.

Souls of Ancestral Children

According to an ancient belief, reported from various parts of the Vosges highlands in the nineteenth century, newborn children bring back to earth the souls of their ancestors.[24] The tradition was not limited to that region: in Switzerland and Germany, hollow stones were supposed to house the souls of ancestors awaiting reincarnation.[25] Thus, just as in nature the decay of plants under the surface prepares for future harvests, so human ancestors waited impatiently for the moment when the body of a newborn baby would be available to ensure the continuance of the family line. There are numerous indications of the existence of this concept of the cycle of life; though the influence of Christian belief and the unceasing vigilance of the Church did a good deal to erode its overall coherence, they were unable to eliminate all expression of it.

It often seemed as if the destiny of the 'ancient' and that of the newborn child were closely connected; there was a sort of automatic mechanism by which, when one appeared, the other departed. The changeover was initiated by one or the other, according to region. In highland Alsace, it was generally believed 'that there will be a birth in the family, since there's just been a death'.[26] In Lower Normandy, the child appeared first; its birth would shortly be followed by the death of some old person from the same family. If the 'ancient' refused to take his departure, the child would die instead; hence the saying that 'the old must make room for the young'.[27] 'They're pushing us on!', as grandparents still say of their grandchildren, as if to pay recognition to this complementary link inherent in the cycle of life. It was a good omen if a child was born on the same day that a very old person died: in the *département* of Loir-et-Cher, around 1900, it was thought that the life of the baby, far from being short, would be as long as that of the dear departed.[28] The same background of thought accounts for some apparently aberrant practices reported in the mid-nineteenth century in Lorraine: when someone met a pregnant woman in the morning, he would unfailingly consider it to be 'bad luck', which could only be evaded by an insult, as if the child to be were a direct threat to his own existence.[29] These very simple facts deserve particular attention as survivals of a very ancient belief in 'the transmigration of souls from one body to another'.

It was on All Saints' and All Souls' days, and especially the night of the 1st of November, that the periodic rebirth of the world and of living creatures was given its most specific recognition. It was then that every family or extended family celebrated the ancestors whose disappearance could and must be only temporary: for death was only a change of state, a new life. This is why the death of a young child was fairly easy to accept so long as it had been baptised; in the valley of Ajol, in the nineteenth century, the church bells rang out joyfully at such a time, announcing the *Renanaio*, the new birth.[30]

Certain turns of phrase whose deeper meanings have been lost to us are a sort of echo of these lost beliefs: thus we speak of 'a soul in torment', and when someone dies he 'gives up the ghost', which originally meant that he restored his soul to the pool of souls where it would await its future reincarnation. Behind such sayings and such attitudes we can discern the idea of a world complete, a great family of the living and the dead whose numbers never varied; of a 'constant rolling capital of souls' divided between the two worlds, between which exchanges were made 'life for life, soul for soul'.[31] A humanity forever changing but forever one, doubly clad in life and death, just as nature is one in the winter sleep that comes before and after the abundance of her harvests.

The hollow, basin or hole in the sacred stone represented the birthplace of men and symbolized the dwelling-place of non-incarnate souls. And from this 'stone in the middle of the world', this *omphalos*[32] of the community, this 'reservoir of souls', there came forth periodically a vital force which could regenerate all creation.[33] For such a holy stone could also be a burial place; to lay the dead man in his tomb was to return him to the womb, and the dolmen, as tombstone, was the place of passage whence would come the new life which would ensure the eternal continuation of the cycle. Now we can understand the real meaning of those fertility rites near the ancient stones: the women who slid down the stone or rubbed their bellies against its sacred surface were seeking to capture the soul-seeds awaiting reincarnation. We can also understand the disappointment and grief of parents whose child was stillborn: the cycle was broken and their offspring could only bring misfortune. For this child was nameless, and so all the more dangerous. The tenacious country tradition whereby children bear the Christian names of their grandparents witnessed to the desire to link past and future and do something to guarantee the closing of the circle which constituted the mental universe of the rural population.

A human life was divided into three parts: mature adults were the link between the ancestors and the newborn, between old traditions and the future, between humanity past and humanity to come. Theirs was the enormous responsibility of maintaining the cycle through the troubles of time. In this sense the present hardly mattered, it existed only in relation to what came before and after; adults capable of procreation were carrying on a task, taking on a responsibility which excluded the bare thought of any control over their fertility. We might even wonder if some beliefs that are still current, like the idea that grandchildren tend to look like their grandparents, are not a surviving trace of that ancient chain linking past and future. As a conception of the dynamics of life it was fundamentally opposed to the 'populationist' ideas which were adopted by the State in the course of the eighteenth century.

PART II

Pregnancy: A Time of Hope, Suffering and Anxiety

Children in their mother's womb are like tender plants rooting in a garden . . . . They are forced to draw their nourishment from the sap that comes to them there.

Jacques Duval, 1612

Being with child was part of the scheme of things. In the life of a married woman in former times, pregnancy occurred more or less regularly. Its harvest depended on the quality of the vessel, but also on the nature of the season: as in the fields or orchards, there were good and bad years. Thus 'being with child' was a state of normality which it would not occur to a woman to avoid. A newly married wife so feared barrenness that the first signs of pregnancy were welcomed as a blessing. Successive pregnancies throughout the fertile period were a guarantee for the future: the more births, the less risk of dying without issue. Women, by nature's law, was the depository of the species: a heavy responsibility which allowed of neither imprudence nor error. The mother-to-be must constantly be on her guard: she was anxious every minute of the day. In this, Judaeo–Christian religion did no more than reinforce a very ancient guilt feeling which undeniably reached its height in early modern times.

It is often hard for us to understand the real experience of pregnancy in past times. Through modesty and through the fear of doing harm to the child, the woman, be she from town or country, said little about her state: her hopes and fears and everyday attitudes are revealed to us only incidentally by doctors. Nor is that the only paradox of pregnancy: like childbirth itself, it was 'women's business' – but it is men who talk about it and inform us about it. And men from the towns, moreover, with their knowledge, their caution, their frequent lack of understanding, their desire, ever-growing from the seventeenth century onwards, to impose their own way of seeing things.

But while little was said about pregnancy, it could scarcely pass unnoticed. Few women could conceal their 'interesting state of health': before very long, all the neighbourhood would know. The pregnant woman was never alone: pregnancy was a collective experience, for several women – perhaps dozens – would be pregnant at the same time in the same village or the same part of the town. This simultaneous and permanent presence of pregnancy was an essential element in the 'human landscape' of past centuries. The community was perpetually pregnant with itself.

5

The Body in Pregnancy

The midwife may touch gently, to see if the womb is tightly shut, like a hen's rear into which one could not introduce as much as a grain of wheat.

Louise Bourgeois, 1626

Signs of pregnancy might sometimes be so ambiguous or hard to interpret that a woman was wrongly believed to be pregnant when she was not, while an actual pregnancy was not discovered until it was quite well advanced. It was not only women and old wives who made such errors: doctors were not much better until the eighteenth century, committing many errors under the persistent influence of Hippocrates and Galen; however, the wisest of them readily admitted that 'it is difficult to discern a true pregnancy at the very beginning'.

When a Woman is With Child

In his *Observations on the Practice of Childbirth*, published in 1674, the surgeon Cosme Viardel does no more than repeat the centuries-old shibboleths of medical tradition. The signs of pregnancy are four in number: 'The little shiver' which the woman was supposed to feel during the fertilizing intercourse; the tight closure of the neck of the womb immediately afterward; then the cessation of the 'monthly purgation', and finally the 'swelling of the breasts'.[1] Some of the same signs were also noted, but with vastly more detail, by the midwife Louise Bourgeois in the early seventeenth century. She opines that the first thing to look for is the cessation of the monthly flow: 'One must enquire how long ago it was that she had her period and if the last time she had it it was in the same quantity and of the same colour as usual.'[2]

The cessation of menstruation was the essential sign of pregnancy for women.[3] But it was important not to jump to conclusions, for some lost their periods through illness, and others through 'fear and annoyance'. Moreover, women in former times would suckle their children up to the age of two, and sometimes three, and so did not always menstruate between pregnancies. In Languedoc, women of childbearing age were said to be 'always producing milk and eggs'. Loss of appetite ('appetite for the foods she was accustomed to love'),

46

nausea ('either they vomit in the morning, or they feel the need but are unable to do it'), irritability ('they feel more angry and easy to annoy than usual'), changes in the breasts ('if their breasts are enlarged and hard, if the tips change colour, so that they become red in white-skinned women and brown in others') or in the abdomen ('rounder on one side than the other'), indigestion ('if after eating she feels distended and sleepy'): all these, according to Louise Bourgeois, are signs of pregnancy.[4]

A woman might be induced by modesty or self-interest to keep quiet about her state as long as possible and hide the signs from the public eye; but her 'mask of pregnancy' often gave her away. 'In the second month', says the obstetrician Jacques Guillemeau, 'her eyes are sunken and dull, the pupil contracted, the eyelids slack, bruised and limp, the veins in the corner of the eye fuller and more swollen than normal.' Above all there was the look in her eyes: 'If you have no other way of telling if a woman is pregnant, the eyes will show you.'[5] The eye was the mirror of pregnancy.

Country women often made use of other tests. They used to say that the surest was to measure the waist: a cord around it was usually enough to show the slight rounding of the abdomen. Caution was needed, however, because it was popularly believed that the first weeks of pregnancy actually caused a shrinkage of the organs. At that time the womb 'hugs the seed, which it does not want to escape, so tightly that the stomach decreases in volume'. Hence a saying common from the seventeenth century onwards: 'Flat stomach, child inside.'[6] The garlic test was also frequently employed. The woman's body was thought of as a sort of sheath, open to the outside at top and bottom. Before going to bed, a woman who thought she might be pregnant would slip a clove of garlic into her genital organ. In the morning, if she breathed out the characteristic odour, she was assuredly not pregnant. An embryo, if present, would certainly get in the way of this diffusion: sweet breath proved conception.[7] The idea was strengthened by the fact that the shape of a clove of garlic is usually similar to a curled-up foetus.

Some sorts of bird-song could also give warning of an impending birth. Round Nevers, in the eighteenth and nineteenth centuries, it was said that if the cock answered the cuckoo, the woman of the house was pregnant – or was deceiving her husband. From Savoy to Saintonge and Poitou the herald of pregnancy was an owl of some kind. The hooting of the nocturnal predator, perched on a nearby tree or roof, pointed out the woman whose interesting state had hitherto been unknown to everybody.[8] The tone of the hoot was carefully noted, because the owl could be both lucky and unlucky. In Saintonge, its 'laughter' spoke of life and its 'weeping' foretold death;[9] nearby, in Limousin, it was said to 'sing for the chrism and for the shroud', for birth and death.[10] The theme of the night-bird which announces new life is a very ancient one. In nineteenth-century Perigord women would seek confirmation of its message from the discoverer of hidden life – the sorcerer. The folklorist Rocal describes the talents of a peasant who died about 1820, who was unbeatable at water-divining, and 'claimed he was never wrong about the pregnancy of a woman and could even discover the sex of the child from the very beginning'.[11] There is an unmistakable symbolic correspondence between the hidden life-giving waters under the earth and the dark and hopeful waters of the womb. But if 'waters' were to be examined, it was usually the water voided by the woman – her urine.

The urine test

Uromancy enjoyed considerable popularity in early modern Europe: not a province, not a canton but had its 'seer of waters'. These empiricists were expected to be able to learn the cause of their clients' maladies just by examining their urine; women frequently consulted them over diseases of the womb, obstruction of the milk-flow or suspected pregnancy. A 'well-cooked' colour and a residue 'like carded cotton' were normally considered as sure signs of pregnancy. We now know that the urine of a pregnant woman contains an abnormally high level of albumen, so we cannot *a priori* deny that such 'uromancers', with the help of experience, may have been capable of detecting signs of conception in 'troubled waters'.

Painters and engravers of the seventeenth and eighteenth centuries drew inspiration from this theme of the 'urine doctor'. Genre paintings with titles like *The fainting woman*, *The consultation* and *The doctor's visit* bear witness to their interest in such scenes, which were often treated ironically, showing the patients in a poor light. Elegant young 'seers' primp and parade with their urine-bottles in front of their swooning clients. Explanation for the latters' strange indisposition comes from the title of the picture: the apparently 'love-sick' patient is no platonic lover, for her malady is caused by her 'delicate state of health'.[12] Doctors disagreed about the question of divination from urine. The sixteenth-century authority Rondelet gives it his approval (*Tractatus de Urinis*, Chapter XV, 'De urina praegnantium'); so does Davach de La Rivière in his *Miroir des urines*. But Guy Patin's 1626 thesis on the question 'Whether it is possible to find a certain proof of pregnancy in the urine' concludes that it is not.[13]

It moves!

In the fourth month the child begins to move in the womb, confirming what the mother had hitherto only suspected.[14] This movement was indeed incontestable proof of pregnancy. There are movements and movements, however, as Louise Bourgeois points out: 'A child can make a little movement, like the beating of a small bird's wing or a mild pinching at the beginning of the sensation, which becomes stronger as the child grows.' In a case of false pregnancy, by contrast, when 'the blood retained sends strange vapours to the heart', the womb was disturbed by an arching movement like 'a cat arching its back and stretching out when it feels the warmth of a fire'. To resolve any doubts, the wise midwife would have recourse to the sense of touch.

To make absolutely certain, the midwife may touch gently, to see if the womb is tightly shut, like the rear of a hen into which one could not introduce as much as a grain of wheat, touching only the exterior orifice, without trying to touch the interior, and taking care that the neck of the womb is not calloused and hardened.[15]

Hippocrates held that male children began to move in the third month and girls in the fourth, for males formed earlier than females. This principle, that girls developed more slowly, brings in the idea of male superiority right from the first months after conception. It was taken up by Cosme Viardel (mid-seventeenth century), whose works constitute a compendium of contemporary commonplaces. 'Males,' he says, 'being formed from the thirtieth day, must have the power of movement from the eighty-second day, which is within the space of three months; girls, on the other hand, are formed only after forty-two days, and thus they can have no movement before the hundred and twentieth day, which is exactly four months.'[16] This idea that the foetus did not receive life until the third or fourth month was very widely and commonly believed.

'The heart is going like the clappers!'

A pregnancy can be confirmed when the foetal heartbeat becomes perceptible. This more refined test was not unknown in earlier days. In his *Memoir on Auscultation as Applied to the Study of Pregnancy* (1822), Lejumeau de Kergaradec tells how he became aware of this indication of pregnancy:

Madame L. was nearing the term of her pregnancy. One day, as I was carefully examining the movements of the foetus, I was suddenly struck by a sound to which I had hitherto paid no attention: it was as if a watch had been placed so close to me that I could hear it ticking. I moved my ear away from the abdominal wall; immediately the sound ceased entirely. At first I thought it was a trick of the ear; but, when I again applied my ear to the womb, the same sound became audible. The experiment, several times repeated, gave the same result each time. Resolving to analyse this phenomenon, I very soon recognized the regular double beat produced by the contractions of the heart. Astonished as I was, I hesitated to pronounce judgement on the cause of this beat. However, I counted it for a while, and found that it recurred from 143 to 144 times a minute. The pulse of Madame L. was then beating only 66 times in the same space of time. Such a lack of isochronicity, and the place itself where the beating was heard, made it impossible for me to consider it as coming from the heart of the mother. Thus I was obliged to recognize that it was produced by the contractions of the foetal heart.[17]

Back in 1818, Doctor Mayor of Geneva had already drawn attention to this physiological phenomenon. Lejumeau, a pupil of Laënnec, did no more than use his stethoscope to confirm its usefulness in obstetrics. So, at least, we learn from the history of medicine. But many midwives had long been accustomed to recognizing the beatings of the foetal heart; and as far back as 1630–40 Lussaud, Marsac and Le Goust, doctors from near Limoges, had been capable of making out the 'uterine breath' through the abdominal wall of a pregnant woman.[18] Living in close contact with the rural world, they compared the heartbeat to the clacking of a mill: 'The heart,' they say, 'gallops along like a clapper' – that is, the vertical spindle of wood which moves the small box or trough containing the grain, so that it falls evenly into the hopper.[19] The beating of the two pieces of wood on each other commonly reaches three hundred strokes a minute, which is indeed much the same as the foetal heartbeat, which averages 140 double beats per minute. The sound metaphor was the one which came most naturally to the doctors of Limousin.

The Seed Within the Body

Once fertilized, the woman must shelter the maturing foetus. The child in its mother's womb is like a flower in a vase of life-giving water, like a plant pricked out in a good tilth: from it comes the vital juices which allow it to grow.

The infant lodger

Just where is the child to be found in the mysterious depths of the womb, the moist labyrinth of the viscera which enfolds it? In the first months of pregnancy, no doubt, the child has plenty of room; but as time passes and it grows in size and weight, its horizon narrows; more and more it feels itself a captive; that is why the foetus, the 'lodger in its mother's womb', is impelled to escape from its prison of flesh.

Generally speaking, the taller and more upright a woman was, the more she tended to 'carry high'. This was not an advantage during labour itself, for since the child had further to travel, 'the mother must needs suffer many pains before it comes there', that is, before it was born. Conversely, when a woman was ill-made, even so that 'the parts below the waist (as it were) widen out, while the higher parts narrow down', the child had more room and was placed 'very low'; it was then born more easily, for 'from the first pain, it throws itself into the siege and urges its mother to help it and labour mightily'.[20]

The foetus in its mother's womb was represented in two types of illustration in medical textbooks. More commonly, the child is shown at the moment of birth: in the earliest manuals of obstetrics, printed in the sixteenth century and modelled on Rösslin's work, the foetus is shown to progress as if in a state of weightlessness, inside a womb shaped like 'a powder-horn used in hunting' – a concept which had not fundamentally changed since Antiquity, when it was developed by Soranus of Ephesus. The second image shows the child in process of gestation; it is asleep and resting.

The two images have one thing in common: they show a finished child which has come to term. Indeed, until the eighteenth century there are few plates showing the embryo at different stages of development. The child in its mother's womb was imagined as a completed, presentable, human infant – not an unformed monster.

The sleeping child

Through the months of gestation the child lives in darkness, in a long night-time of waiting. Slowly, silently, it matures. Exactly the same mental image of the foetus occurs in modern popular thought and in the ancient medical tradition stemming from Hippocrates: the child sits in its mother's womb as if resting, with closed eyes, asleep. Jacques Duval (early seventeenth century) gives a would-be scientific description which in fact reveals his ignorance of life in the womb:

The situation of the child . . . is such that the head is bent downwards, with the chin very close to the chest, the face inclined towards the navel, as if it were curious to see the place whence its nourishment is obtained. The spine is curved, the right arm so bent that the elbow is against the flank, the hand stretched over the neck, the fingers pointing towards the left eye. As to the left arm, the elbow is in almost the same situation *vis-à-vis* the flank on that side as is the right arm. But the hand is situated between the chest and the throat, the thumb being bent inwards. The right leg is so situated that the heel touches the left buttock, and the end of the foot is raised towards the genital area.[21]

Between the fourth month and term, the child goes through alternate periods of quiescence and activity; like a little tired animal, when full-fed it needs quiet and sleep; then suddenly it awakes and launches into ill-regulated movement, before falling asleep once again. This belief in foetal sleep is not confined to Western culture; even today, in Morocco, a barren woman refers to her imagined 'sleeping' foetus in an attempt to escape repudiation.[22]

For the child's body the resting position, the 'spherical or oval situation', was the best preparation for adult life: even within the womb the child was acquiring the good constitution of the man it would become – vigour, dexterity and (notes Duval) primacy of the right side:

This is the cause of the strength, agility and dexterity which are ordinarily found more in the right arm and leg than in the left because the former lay straighter and in a higher position from their initial formation. Hence tailors often notice that the right shoulder is ordinarily higher and better formed than the left.[23]

Christian tradition has its own version of this idea of shaping within the womb: Erasmus, in his *Discourse on the Duties of Mothers Towards their Children During Pregnancy*, states that qualities of both mind and body are developed in the womb, and that education begins before birth: 'This care for children, when they are still carried in the body, is the first part of their education. For, although they are not yet born, one should, as far as in one lies, not neglect to prepare and school them, even in this state, in honest Christian behaviour.'[24]

For a mother, this image of her child sitting and sleeping was not altogether a reassuring one. She knew that such a situation must be unstable; she constantly feared lest the child's head, which was 'bent towards the navel', should drag the rest of the body after it. It was her duty to prevent the foetus from taking an untimely dive into the world. Hence she might have recourse to amulets worn round the arm or neck to keep the child's body, and particularly its head, 'upright'. Such an amulet might be an eagle-stone, a metal ring or a magnet.

Wonders in the womb

Thus the commonest image for the foetus shows it sleeping in the mother's womb like a cockchafer grub lurking deep in Mother Earth, or a bear curled up in a cave and waiting for the spring awakening. Therefore the child which remained awake, or spoke, must indeed be something exceptional. Even before birth, it made its presence felt and so revealed to its mother its uncommon destiny. Transgression maybe, but in this case the omens were good.[25]

The announcement, to a mother or to both parents, of the birth of an exceptional child is a common theme in the Old and New Testaments; the best-known case is of course the Annunciation.[26] As is well known, the child in such a case is often born to an old couple who had despaired of having offspring. This tradition of the announcement of babies destined for a brilliant future is perpetuated in hagiographic legend; Father Delahaye even considers that 'the Annunciation was a necessary element in a well-constituted saint's life'.[27]

The circumstances of the announcement may belong to one of a number of stereotypes. At some stage in her pregnancy – immediately after conception or shortly before the birth – the mother to be is told of the honour which is being done to her. This revelation often comes to her in sleep: the mothers of Saint Eucher of Lyons, of Saint Samson of Dol (in Brittany) and of Saint Taurin of Évreux all hear angelic messengers predicting the destiny of the fruit of their womb. Sometimes the child itself appears to her: Aeneas Sylvius, later to become pope under the name of Pius II, appeared to his mother wearing a mitre; another child, destined to be a king, appeared sitting on a throne.[28] There were cases of pregnant women dreaming of giving birth to torches or flames: this meant that their child would become a leading churchman.[29] A barking dog, found as a theme as far back as the Book of Isaiah, foretells a great preacher:

The blessed Joan of Aza dreamed that she bore in her womb a little dog holding a torch in its maw, and that when it was born, it set the whole earth on fire. She gave birth to Saint Dominic, founder of the order of friars preachers. The mother of Saint Bernard dreamed that she was giving birth to a white dog with red markings which barked with a great voice, as a sign of his future role as a scourge of heresy.[30]

An identical vision was vouchsafed to the mother of Vicente Ferrer in the fourteenth century, and to the mother of Monsieur Olier in the seventeenth.

A final theme from hagiographic legend is the woman who sees emerging from her womb a tree bearing magnificent fruit. In the case of Saint Fulcran's mother it is a tree of unknown species, but green and covered with fruit; in other cases the tree is huge, or, if small, it has a sweet scent: the mother of Roseline of Villeneuve learns in a dream that she is to give life to a sweet-scented rose without a thorn.[31]

Pregnancy causes deep-seated changes in a woman's body whose effects are felt even in sleep and in dreams, especially in the ninth month, when the size and weight of the foetus compress the organs in the lower abdomen. And

what mother has never sometimes dreamed impossible dreams about the creature she carries in her womb? ... Dreams soon forgotten, wild thoughts swept away by reality! But if one day the child she has borne were indeed to achieve a noble, a holy pre-eminence, would not that dream return to the memory of the mother or the father in whose imagination it once formed?[32]

The announcement did not always come through a dream of the mother. An exceptional child could call attention to itself by moving about or speaking in its mother's womb. The theme of the child making significant movements in the maternal womb is clearly present in the story of the Visitation: when the two holy women greet each other, St John the Baptist leaps in the womb of Elizabeth; the movement is not random, but shows the recognition of Jesus' divinity by his Precursor.

This theme of the child speaking in its mother's womb is also very ancient: Isaac made himself heard three times in a single day. It persists up to the end of the eighteenth century, when there are even cases of unborn children singing: in the *Luciniade* the doctor Sacombe tells the story of a seven-month foetus which sang the revolutionary song *Ça ira* in its mother's womb! Talking foetuses have a big place in hagiographic legend, especially if, as in the 'Life of Saint Fursy', a seventh-century Irish saint, the episode contributes to the dramatic or moral impact of the story. His mother, Gelges, was a king's daughter; she married without her father's consent, and he condemned her to be burned alive in punishment, when she was pregnant with Fursy. 'At that moment,' says the eleventh-century biographer, 'the child whom Gelges carried in her womb spoke in a clear voice and sternly reproached his grandfather for his cruelty towards his mother and himself.' Gelges' tears changed into a miraculous fountain, which extinguished the faggots, and both lives were saved. Saint Fursy grew up to be a monk, and later a hermit, and several times brought dead children back to life. At Saint Peter's Church in Lagny his cult was associated with that of the Holy Innocents.[33] The child of destiny, who had spoken in his mother's womb, kept all his life – and after it – a special link with the world of early childhood.

Cravings and Imaginings

It was generally believed that during the pregnancy the child saw what the mother saw, heard what she heard and felt what she felt. Any unpleasant sight or unsatisfied desire was echoed, with greater or lesser intensity, in the body of the foetus. Thus the mother's body had a dual function. Part screen, part filter, it protected the child from excessive heat or cold; but it was also a conductor which transmitted to the child various influences, some of which were far from beneficial. The mother's dreams and fantasies could make a harmful 'impression' on the foetus.

'The virtue of imagination'

Not everyone attributed the same meaning to the word 'imagination'. If a woman dreamed repeatedly one night of a monstrous or deformed being, that was 'imagination'; but so was the very concrete spectacle of a man broken on the wheel in a public execution, or one who had lost an arm or an eye in an accident. In each case the result was the same: the child the woman was carrying was at risk of being born with broken legs, or with no legs at all, or minus an arm or an eye. And the appearance of a ghost or the sight of a corpse could so upset a woman's mental balance that the child would perforce be stillborn.

In truth, a pregnant woman had, as many people would say, 'a melancholy cast of mind, full of sorrowful ideas'. That is why her womb and its contents could be adversely affected, as Claude Quillet insists in his poem *The Callipaed, or the Art of creating fair children*: 'The spirits descending from the brain mingle in the womb with the prolific [child-making] essence and penetrate it through and through; there they imprint with invincible force the same images by which they have themselves been struck.' He makes a comparison with baker's dough: 'Thus in a baker's trough, the flour mixed with warm water and set in motion by the yeast, swells up into one single mass; if the baker sets a hand to it, he can make all different kinds of cake of many different shapes: so in women, ideas make the same sort of impressions on the foetus.'[34]

At certain stages in the pregnancy, moreover, the mother was more receptive to the influence of imagination. Ambroise Paré thought that there was a risk only before the child was properly formed, that is (according to earlier medical belief), before the thirtieth day in males and the fortieth in females; at a later stage, the human 'dough' was already moulded and was less receptive. It was important for parents to know that the most dangerous moment was that of conception. Paré cites an example which the reader will certainly find convincing, so great is its appeal to *his* imagination! In 1517, at Blois-le-Roy in the forest of Bièvre, there was born a child with the face of a frog. A surgeon and various officers of the law were called and attempted to 'discover the reason for this monster'. The father explained that

his wife suffering from a fever, one of her neighbours advised her that, in order to cure her fever, she should take a live frog in her hand and hold it until the said frog was dead. That night she went to bed with her husband, still holding the said frog in her hand; her husband and she embraced together, and so it was that, by the virtue of imagination, this monster had been produced.[35]

Doctors who told such tales in all seriousness were doing little to disguise their ignorance; they fell back on the power of imagination when they were unable to explain an unusual event, the pathological problems of a birth. But behind them, up to the nineteenth century, was a long line of enlightened people who gave credence to these beliefs. Even Voltaire acknowledges, with a touch of scorn, that 'this passive imagination in easily disturbed minds can sometimes pass on to children the clear signs of an impression received by the mother. There are innumerable examples of this, and' – he adds – 'the author of this article has seen some so striking that he would be denying the evidence of his own eyes if he were to doubt it.'[36]

No-one was exempt from the anxiety aroused by the mysteries of pregnancy. In 1810 Napoleon, on a journey through the Low Countries with Maria Louisa, saw coming towards him a procession of grotesque forms, the 'giants' of Wetteren. Fearing for the Empress, who was then with child, he cried: 'No monsters! No monsters!' And he sent his hussars to slit their bellies, which were made of willow-twigs ... to the terrible disappointment of the authorities, who had intended to give pleasure to the Emperor![37]

It could happen that this power of the imagination had beneficial effects, but in that case it had to be properly guided. Of all the senses which could come into play, that of sight was unquestionably the most influential. A woman's gaze was like an object lens focusing on a particular scene; what could be easier, if she ardently desired a handsome child, than to gaze fixedly, during the act of generation, at a picture of a handsome man, or at a beautiful doll attached to the bedpost or to the ceiling?[38] But it was vital to eliminate every detail which might attract too much of the woman's attention, every physical oddity in the model, and, as Montaigne believed, anything unusual about its dress. Once Charles, King of Bohemia, was presented with 'a girl from near Pisa, all hairy and bristly, who according to her mother had been conceived because of an image of John the Baptist which hung over her bed'.[39] But in the popular mind the negative aspects of the power of imagination unquestionably took precedence over the positive ones. Had the new baby a feeble constitution, or was it seriously malformed? This had to be explained and a cause be found. How could the mother not believe herself to be to blame for what has happened? She was helped to retrace the aberrant thoughts which had disturbed her mind during her pregnancy, in the hope that they would explain what had happened – to the great relief of all concerned.

Sometimes the father was also given a share of the blame. Had he indulged, at any time during the pregnancy, in some sort of bestial sexual behaviour of which his wife disapproved? She could be so upset by it as to produce a monstrous child. 'On 21 September 1677 Elisabeth Tomboy, midwife, helped deliver a woman who brought forth a bitch enveloped in her membranes, and alive. It had no hair, had well-formed limbs, and was as long as her little finger.' Planque, the surgeon who recorded this event, suggests an explanation:

This is what happened, as far as I could discover from disinterested persons who told it me, and also from the mother, whom I do not suspect of trying to impose on me: the father was a low sort of fellow, rough and a drunkard. One day when he attempted to approach his wife after a fashion which she found repugnant, this unpleasant man did as he had proposed, leaving clearly in her mind the idea of the animal whose practices he was imitating. The impression remained profoundly fixed in her mind, and her lively imagination produced the animal of which we are speaking.[40]

The imagination of a pregnant woman could confound the man who had abused her and 'refused to acknowledge the title of father'. In 1817 a girl from Galloway, in Scotland, realized she was pregnant and at once accused the guilty man, John Woods, a respectable man of the town. The latter, brought before a tribunal, denied it most energetically: 'Never will I acknowledge the child unless my name is written on its face!' he exclaimed as if in jest. The young woman, who was present, was deeply affected by his behaviour; all through her pregnancy she thought incessantly about this scene. The child was born with the name of his father legibly inscribed on his right eye, with the information 'born in 1817' on the left eye. As soon as he heard the news, the supposed father hastily disappeared; he was never seen again. Doctor Munro of Edinburgh, who reported this event in 1825, declares that he several times presented the child to the professors and scientists of that city; all saw in it an astonishing manifestation of the workings of providence: the case must serve as a warning to young persons of both sexes, and dissuade them from evil behaviour and perjury.[41]

Thus, seeing a thing, animal or person, or hearing a story, could cause a fright or an anxiety that would rebound on the body of the child. Another essential element was the mother's hand: its place at the moment when the mental upset took place decided the precise position of the mark. In Lorraine, a pregnant woman who encountered a hare – an unlucky animal – after sunset must not touch her face, or her child would be born with a hare lip.[42] Any abnormalities in the baby were a consequence of some sort of panic in the mother.

All mothers could be afflicted by fear of animals. Witness this example from the eighteenth century, reported by Van Swieten:

A pregnant woman was frightened by a monkey, because she thought it was going to bite her. This terror tormented her for three months. At the time, however, she had fled, rubbing the part which she thought the animal was threatening to bite. In due time she was delivered of a very healthy daughter. The outside of her right hand was brown in colour and covered with bristly hairs. Some years after her birth, this mark was rubbed with soapy water and the hair was cut off with a razor; soon afterwards that part became covered with pustules, the arm was considerably inflamed, and there was even a fear that it would become gangrenous. The trouble was cured by suitable remedies; the hair subsequently grew again, and this unpleasant mark, which certainly bore witness to the power of the mother's imagination, reappeared in its original state.[43]

'Women with strange cravings'

The idea that marks appearing on the baby's body were the results of maternal imagination was not automatically accepted. Such a 'naevus' tended rather to be attributed to the cravings of the mother.

Until the nineteenth century it was very commonly felt that the desires of a pregnant woman ought not to be opposed. Not to respect this rule was a very serious matter, for the unsatisfied desires of a pregnant woman were supposed to reappear on the body of her child in the shape of birthmarks; the connection is very apparent in French, for the word *envie*, meaning a birthmark, can also mean 'craving'. The doctor Chambon de Montaux, writing in 1785, said that

Women call 'craving' an immoderate desire to satisfy a taste, a passion, an impulse of hatred or anger, etc. The common people are still persuaded that one must not permit oneself to show the least irritation or the slightest resistance to any inclination which they may show, without exposing the foetus to the risk of bearing the marks of the thing desired, or of being born with monstrous vices of confirmation.[44]

In fact such beliefs were not confined to the common people; the 'woman with a craving' was handled with care in every social class. The diarist Saint Simon reports that on the occasion of a grand public dinner given by the Cardinal of

Noailles to the Dauphin in 1711, the Prince insisted that good care should be taken of 'a pregnant woman who had insinuated herself on this occasion, and he sent her a dish of which she desired to eat, with an intensity which she could not disguise'.[45]

These cravings were indeed most commonly cravings for food. If the pregnant woman wished to eat some exotic fruit which was unobtainable out of season, or to taste some expensive dish which her entourage could not procure for her, then the child's body would bear the trace of it. Ambroise Paré says that the 'signs and marks on children' are shaped sometimes like a cherry or grape, sometimes a fig or a melon. In the eighteenth century there was a sudden plethora of frustrated cravings for coffee or chocolate.

A curious thing about marks on the body shaped like fruits or vegetables was that they altered with the seasons; each year the colour changed as the fruit the mother had once desired changed on the tree. On 7 November 1862, the newspaper *Le Siècle* reported the following example in all seriousness:

A rather odd case of maternal craving came to light a few days ago at Château-Thierry. A woman gave birth to twins, both of which bore the mark of a beet, one on the stomach, the other on the face. Science tells us that this kind of birthmark has a curious property: when the actual plant reaches maturity, that part of the body which resembles it goes through the same process of maturation; thus the skin becomes dull and greyish, and would ultimately rot and infect other parts of the body if the affected part were not cauterized with a hot iron, and by this extreme method new skin were made to form.[46]

Such cravings could sometimes become pathological. Guillemeau, an obstetrician, reported that 'Some women have an appetite so depraved, because of some bitter or salty humour which is contained in the stomach lining – such as eating coal, chalk, ashes or uncooked salt fish which have not even been soaked, or drinking verjuice, vinegar or even wine-lees – that it is impossible to stop them tasting and eating them.'[47] Some reports even mention cravings for freshly killed meat, which immediately makes one think of old myths of savage hunger, or cannibalistic rituals – for at times the desire was actually translated into action.

The sixteenth-century moralist Vivès reports having seen a woman bite a young man in the neck, causing him unbearable agony. 'It seems that her paroxysms of anger would have brought on an abortion if she had not satisfied this unbridled desire.' And the doctor Langius speaks of the horrid cruelty of a pregnant woman living near Cologne, who wanted to eat her husband's flesh. 'She murdered him in order to satisfy her savage appetite; she had salted a large part of him so that this pleasure would last longer. Once sated with this barbarous ragout, she confessed her crime to friends of her husband, who sought in vain for the place where she had concealed him.'[48]

The symbolism attaching to birthmarks also tends to respond to great historical events. Come the French Revolution the fleur-de-lys went out in favour of the Phrygian cap of liberty, and the cornea of newborn babies, instead of bearing the words *Sit nomen domini benedictum* ('Blessed be the name of the Lord'), as they had during the apogee of catholicism, began to bear the words 'Napoleon, Emperor'. Sign of the times!

Medical opinion has long since rejected the popular interpretation of birth-marks. Vascular or pigmentary 'naevi' cannot really be attributed to the unsatisfied cravings of a pregnant woman – unless one admits that the same phenomenon, which can be observed in animals and even plants, is in their case also the result of imagination and unsatisfied desires! Moreover, it is quite common for children to be born with so-called port wine stains, in areas where nature does not allow the production of that commodity.

Ambroise Paré did, however, believe that the woman was the cause of birthmarks. But they merely meant that she had conceived during menstrua-tion; was not this proved by the usual colour of most naevi – bright red or wine-red? Seventeenth and eighteenth-century doctors were inclined to wonder if they were not a consequence of the evil inclinations of the female sex. Perhaps women were seeking a pretext to satisfy their natural inclinations with impunity, and kept up the belief in cravings 'so as to enjoy a freedom which they could not be granted without some such convincing pretext' – complaisant husbands being resigned to suffering in silence! Such antifeminist remarks betray a desire to reduce the margin of freedom accorded to the pregnant woman. Louise Bourgeois suggests quite a different interpretation: drawing on her own experi-ence as a mother, she believes that a woman's body is naturally disturbed by pregnancy; the consequences include 'loss of appetite, weakness, a desire to eat unusual things, which [she emphasizes] a woman is much ashamed to mention'.[49] Much ashamed to mention . . . .

A pregnant woman is very aware that she is not in control of her own body. She fears anything which may injure the child-to-be; behind the 'power of imagination' and the 'cravings' lies hidden, in fact, the fear of abnormality.

The Womb, Rind of the Fruit

'The child is a fruit which, being made from a seed, ripens in the womb as if in a pod which splits when it is ripe and ready to fall.'[50] Pod, pocket, horn or bottle; black hole, sewer, place of darkness and horror; mother, anchorage or fertile field of nature: metaphors for the womb which relate to its form, its function or its place within the woman's body. Hidden away in the depths of that body, it is the magic crucible, the mould, the form in which the human race is constantly being renewed, the secret place which is the source of life.

'The orchard of the human race'

The womb is both intriguing and menacing. Its power to turn a few drops of semen into a little creature a-quiver with new life has always aroused astonish-ment and wonder: 'Here is the place where mankind is first formed, nourished and sustained! . . . Between the regions occupied by the most filthy and vile excrements which exist in the body . . . between the lower intestine or entrails near the rectum and the bladder used for urine!'[51] What a neighbourhood! But was not the womb itself like a foul drain? Was it not the womb that regularly sent forth impure and corrupted blood when it was not carrying a child? Could it be that mankind entered the world from out of a sewer? Was Aristotle right to dismiss this part of the body as a servile and abject thing? Not unless we forget that 'the great architect of nature honoured it with his creating hand'. The womb had 'the honour to be the first dwelling-place and home not only of the greatest, noblest, most signal and holy persons who have ever been among the living, but also of the Saviour and Redeemer of the world, who dwelt and resided there for the space of nine months when he deigned to begin the work of our redempton.'[52] Thus we should not believe 'those who rashly term it a shameful and dishonourable part' and who forget that man may be born of filth, but is nevertheless the fairest of all created things.

According to Laurent Joubert, a good womb was 'well complexioned, of a good heat and not excessively moist', in which case it will be 'a very fertile field for the propagation of the human race'.[53] But the 'temperament' of the womb is generally inconstant, like the weather. When the woman is about to have her period, it is 'cold and very moist because of the humour which is stagnating round it, like a pond';[54] at the end of the flow, 'it becomes dry and hot, the blood being then like the blood in the rest of the body': that was the ideal moment to conceive. Thus 'nature's field', like other fields, had its good and bad seasons; and it also had its secret urges.

'The womb is an animal'

Because pregnancy induces such great changes in the woman's behaviour, the womb is often considered as an organ apart, with its own autonomy, capable of imposing its desires. Ever since Antiquity, philosophers and doctors have wondered about its real nature. Jacques Duval and his contemporaries in the seventeenth century still believed that it was particularly sensitive to smells:

Plato and Theophrastus Paracelsus called it animal, because they saw in it movements which seemed to be voluntary. So that, if one brings some strong-smelling thing close to a woman's nose, this part creeps and rises up; if you put it to her oval [the vulva] it sinks down; if you put it to one side of the belly, it can be felt to be inclining towards the side to which the thing has been applied. It summons the vivifying seed like an elixir of life, for the purposes of conception.[55]

It rejected bad and useless seed and drew to itself that which was good and useful. It was risky to frustrate its appetites, for it then 'becomes discontented and causes irritation and even fury'; it was disturbed by 'strange and violent movements which are harmful to the woman'; indispositions, often serious ones, could result: 'a kind of jaundice called the pale colour [chlorosis?], suffocation of the womb, fever of the uterus, and other similar things'.

Such disturbance could only be caused by an animal, an animal which was invisible and so all the more alarming. In both vulgar and medical parlance there are constant animal references: the vulva 'is shaped like the mouth of a little newborn puppy'; it is sometimes called *rictus caninus* or 'dog's muzzle'; it is supposed to resemble 'the mouth of the fish commonly known as a tench'; and the expression 'tench's nose' is still found in modern medical jargon. It is during sexual intercourse that the voracity of this animal is most clearly shown:

This mouth opens easily, freely and voluptuously when it has a chance to receive the male sperm, which it loves and enjoys most marvellously. This is the reason why, during coitus, the man feels it fluttering like a butterfly or moving like a tench, coming at intervals to kiss or suck the extremity of the balanus, eager to gain its natural balm.[56]

In north-eastern France and the Germanic countries, the womb, hidden away as it was in the depths of the entrails, was symbolized by that creature of darkness, the toad. 'Gloomy, mysterious, surrounded by mystic superstitions, arousing anxiety in the popular mind', the toad was supposed to be in contact with the underworld, with the inexhaustible fecundity of the womb of Earth.[57] A vague resemblance of its form to that of the womb and its connecting organs probably helped to cement the analogy. From Antiquity to the present century, in Alsace, barren women and women with child or suffering from some affliction of the womb have been accustomed to leave ex-votos in the shape of toads in sanctuaries, at the foot of crosses, or in caves. These images, carved of stone or moulded in clay, or (from the nineteenth century onwards) cut out of sheet metal, witnessed to the hopes of these women or to mercies received. They were often to be seen side-by-side with ex-votos in the shape of pregnant women.[58]

This image of the toad as representing a womb must have been exceptionally powerful, since it indicates an unusual willingness in the popular mind to assimilate a human organ to a living creature considered so repugnant; with its staring eyes, its slow, often jerky movements, and its hatred of light it is still disturbing: people hate and fear toads. 'Together with the flesh of a hanged man and the heart of a newborn child, its quivering body, firmly believed to be venomous, is a customary ingredient of witches' brews.'[59] It is a denizen of the underworld, and as such appears, crouching on a skull, in fourteenth and fifteenth-century *memento mori*; moreover, since the Middle Ages it has been a creature of evil will, companion of witches, seducer of foolish virgins, incarnation of Satan, familiar of wanton women whose breasts and genitals it devours.

'Woman is made for the womb'

The state of pregnancy has a profound effect on the behaviour of the womb. Temporarily appeased, it devotes itself to the nourishment of the foetus; its size and shape both change. 'It grows and stretches in a miraculous way, as if to contain nine or ten children with their beds or afterbirths; then, it falls back on itself, confined and restricted, so that it seems no greater in size than the root of the thumb.'[60] So spectacular a change reinforced the idea that this organ was altogether exceptional. Paracelsus admires its 'properties and virtues' and talks of it as 'a pefect animal'; he has it that the whole body of woman, that inferior microcosm, was made exclusively for the womb; 'it is a world shaped for that animal' and is under its control. 'The health and good condition [of women] depends on the contentment and healthy state of that animal.'[61] Thus, when the womb is in a healthy state, the woman is also in enjoyment of perfect health.

Tota mulier in utero – 'the whole woman is in the womb' – is a saying often repeated since the time of St Augustine, who was already inclined to see the 'mother' as a beast lurking in the dark lair of the entrails. Woman, unlike man (who, being guided by reason alone, is more constant and more sensible), is easily influenced, changeable, unstable, puzzling . . . . In woman, matter, the forces of darkness, the baseness of the flesh, triumph over spirit. The idea that the womb is indeed an animal within an animal persisted until the nineteenth century. In 1856, Du Chesnel, in his *Dictionary of Popular Superstitions*, declared that it was 'both exaggerated and eccentric' to consider the womb as a perfected animal, he hastily adds that 'it is, however, incontestable that it plays an important, directing, dominant role in the life of the woman. And,' he adds, 'it might be considered that there are two nerve centres: one, the brain, deals with the motions of the intelligence; the other, the womb, deals with sensual passions and aberrations of the soul.'[62]

The Duration of Pregnancy

Up to the end of the eighteenth century, the duration of human gestation was believed to be indeterminate. A term of 270 days was merely an ideal which nature could sometimes ignore; there was much talk of premature or advanced, tardy or retarded births; this advance or delay could sometimes stretch to several weeks or even months.

This elasticity in the period of human pregnancy contrasted with the immutable duration of gestation in other viviparous animals, which (as eighteenth-century doctors remarked) had always been well-known to country people.[63] The latter were therefore more inclined to compare human gestation with examples from the vegetable world, pointing out the observable differences in the germination of the same seeds sown in the same ground, in the sprouting of flowers and the ripening of fruit on the same plant or tree; they concluded, by analogy, that babies must arrive sometimes earlier, sometimes later, depending on the amount of growth they undergo in the womb; and on this amount, they say, depends the date of the birth.'[64]

Since Antiquity, experts have been taking up the same metaphors and using the same concepts of the duration of pregnancy. Even Aristotle considered the elastic duration of pregnancy as an essential element of the human condition. The sixteenth-century author Laurent Joubert, in his *Popular Errors*, asks 'if a woman can carry for more than nine months and what one should consider to be the term of pregnancy'; he acknowledges that 'women have no fixed time for carrying their children, as other animals have. For they sometimes give birth at seven months, commonly at nine, sometimes at ten or eleven months; and all these terms', he adds, 'are good and viable.'[65] Pythagoras distinguished between two types of gestation, 'The lesser, which is called the seven-month carriage and comes to term on the 210th day after conception; the greater, called the ten-month carriage, which ends on the 274th day.'[66] Hippocrates, for his part, believed that the really important date was that of the child's first movement, which one simply multiplied by three: if it moved at seventy days, it would be born after 210 days; if at ninety days, it would be born after 270 days.[67]

Late births: a persistent belief

Premature birth, despite its frequency, attracted little interest from obstetricians. Textbooks are cautious in approaching it, often tackling it alongside miscarriage. Late birth, on the other hand, attracted a good deal of attention from both doctors and lawyers, for it might endanger the family honour or cause a disputed succession. Hence the abundance of documentary evidence available to us, especially from the eighteenth century – a time of particularly heated debate between those who (like Antone Petit and Bertin) thought there was no 'fixed term', and those who (like Louis and Bouvard) believed the opposite. Doctors in the eighteenth century who believed there were no such things as late births were swimming against the tide, though they were cautious enough to rely on observation and even their own experience as fathers. One of them, Chambon de Montaux, reports that a practitioner who was often obliged to be away from home for several days at a time desired 'to gain a certain knowledge of the duration of pregnancy . . . . To be sure of avoiding error, he scrupulously noted down the dates on which he had seen his first wife, by whom he had had five children.' The results, says Chambon, were conclusive, for while 'the birth of the first was uncertain as to the number of days' (his colleague had not yet thought of his plan), 'the fourth and fifth children were born after a fixed time of precisely nine months.'[68] A deviation of a few days often results from a passing indisposition of the mother; this happened to the experimenting doctor's wife, who had suffered a fall – not a serious one – during her third pregnancy.

Eighteenth-century practitioners also discovered that the previously much-vaunted regularity of animal pregnancies could also be subject to advances or delays. In 1766 the Paris doctor Darcet made some statistical observations on clutches of chicks and concluded that they certainly hatched in succession.[69] And in 1817 Tessier made a long series of observations on 575 cows, 277 mares, 7 buffalos, 2 donkeys, 912 ewes, 25 sows and 172 rabbits, which led him to exactly the same conclusion: 'The duration of gestation is very variable in all these species.'[70]

One thing emerged very clearly from these observations and those made on pregnant women at the turn of the nineteenth century: late births were very rare. Thus J. F. Lobstein, chief obstetrician of the civil hospital in Strasbourg, observed that of 714 births which took place in his hospital between March 1804 and December 1814, only one could be considered as late, while 630 women were at the normal term of nine months, 16 had miscarried and 67 had given birth prematurely.[71] Evidently the real problem was not late birth, as had been said and believed for centuries, but premature birth. It is hard to explain how such a misapprehension can have persisted for so long, both among the experts and in popular belief. But was it really such an error?

Pregnancy and the moon: measurement of time

Women's own perception of the duration of pregnancy certainly did a good deal to bolster the idea that it lasted ten months: they were in fact referring to the lunar month, of twenty-seven days. Thus ten lunar months were equivalent to nine solar months. This reference to the lunar cycle implies a fundamentally different way of measuring time. It is well known that time used to be measured by nights, by moons and by winters before it was measured by days, suns and years: more emphasis was laid on darkness than on light.[72] The Sanskrit word for the moon, *mas*, comes in fact from the root *ma*, 'measure'. The moon was the heavenly body which gave the measure of time. There can be no doubt that the custom of counting ten lunar cycles as the duration of pregnancy was in full accord with natural observation: 'A woman could note ten or even eleven successive moons (including the one which was shining during the last menstruation before she conceived) before she was delivered of her burden.'[73] This custom was part of a whole way of thinking; in Ancient Rome, for example, the duration of pregnancy had become a yardstick for time itself. In several passages of the *Fasti*, Ovid alludes to the custom of counting ten months in a year, and explains it by the duration of gestation. Later, in many modern languages, the same word was often used for 'moon' and 'month', or the two words were interchangeable. The two are obviously closely related in modern English, as are *Monat* and *Mond* in German, while *luna* in Rumanian means both. And not so long ago, in France, a woman who was 'having her monthlies' or 'menstruating' was referring by implication to the phases of the moon. So there is nothing astonishing about the fact that until the nineteenth century a ten-month pregnancy was considered the norm: the months were lunar months. It had been known since Antiquity that they corresponded to nine solar months, but the habit of perceiving and reckoning time from the lunar cycle had persisted.

We can now comprehend the real import of the great eighteenth-century debate on late births; questions of law – of legitimacy and the conservation of inheritance – were not unimportant, but they were not at the heart of the matter. The real debate was over the perception of time; the old concept, which had come under fire in France as early as the end of the fourteenth century, was giving way to the modern concept: the sun's time and the clock were ousting the phases of the moon and the hour-glass. And so pregnancy was henceforward reduced to a period of nine months.[74]

The mother 'cooks' the child[75]

The idea that the date of the birth could be advanced or postponed found further support in the notion of the foetus freeing itself by its own efforts from its imprisonment in the womb. Lack of space within, and also an insufficiency of heat and nourishment, were believed to cause premature birth. A seven- or eight-month-old foetus which had already reached a respectable size felt squeezed from all sides and uncomfortable: it felt an irresistible need to escape to the outside world and there seek the nourishment which its mother's womb and placenta could no longer supply in sufficient quantities. A fruit is no more than fixed *to* a tree externally, but a foetus grows *in* the womb. A premature foetus was literally un-ripe, *prae-maturus*. Moreover, it was 'uncooked': the metaphor of the tree and the fruit was replaced by that of bread in the oven, the womb as the oven and the foetus as the dough, which gives a still more fundamentally accurate rendition of the notion of pregnancy current among country people in past ages. Obstetricians also used the same image up to the seventeenth century: 'They say that, as the temperaments of men are almost infinitely varied, so the children with the most choler (heat) form more rapidly in their mother's womb and are born earlier: thus there are some who come into the world after six months.'[76]

The foetal 'dough' takes shape slowly in the womb: it rises and swells within its sealed and rounded space; eventually the 'loaf' is well cooked, perfectly formed in all its parts and with a skin – or 'crust' – adequate to allow its arrival in the world. When considering the question of the duration of pregnancy, Louise Bourgeois, like all other authors since Antiquity, believed that children are viable from seven months onwards: if they remain another two months in the womb it is because they 'are retained by nature so as to form their hides'.[77] This image of a well-cooked child, able from birth to endure the onslaughts of the outside world, has persisted right up to our own day. People in the Vivarais and Forez regions of France say of an immature person, or one with poor judgement, that he 'isn't well-cooked', or 'there wasn't enough fuel on his fire'.

The foetus: viable at seven months, but not at eight

This image of the mother's womb cooking the child explains why a child was thought to be viable after seven months but not after eight. Hippocrates observed that 'few seven-month children survive', but acknowledged that at that stage foetuses are complete in all their parts and capable of life: 'The time during which they have been nourished within the womb gives them all that is possessed by the most perfect foetuses, those most capable of life.'[78] It is at this stage also that children began to kick. They were making a first attempt to escape, which was only to be expected since they were already as strong as a nine-month child. If they did manage to be born, they could escape the dangers to which they would normally be exposed if they remained within the womb.[79] If they did not succeed in being born at seven months, they would be so weakened, and their whole organism so enfeebled, by their struggle to escape from the imprisoning womb that they would have to wait until the ninth month before they could regain enough vigour for a second attempt. The child had to 'go back in the oven' for further cooking, as Ambroise Paré observes: 'The child, being further enfeebled by the combat and efforts which it has made in vain, needs as it were to be cooked again, retained within the womb.'[80] If by some unhappy chance the womb, convulsed by the movements which it had undergone during the seventh month, cast off its burden in the eighth month, the latter would have no chance of survival: 'During these maladies of the eighth month, if it then happens that the child comes to birth, its conservation is impossible.'[81] This idea that a seven-month child is better off than an eight-month child was already current among the Greeks, Romans and ancient Germanic peoples. Apollo and Dionysius were born in the seventh month. The magical meaning of the number seven and the influence of Pythagorean doctrine may also lie at the root of this belief in the happy auguries attendant on a seventh-month child.[82]

The quality of the oven – the temperament of the maternal 'cook' – naturally had a great influence on conditions during the cooking. The foetus was like a meat roast or a chicken: the bigger it was, the longer it had to cook – an elementary principle of the culinary art! 'There are,' explains Laurent Joubert, 'children of great girth and corpulence which require a longer sojourn to reach maturity.'[83] The animal kingdom, indeed, offers many an illustration of the principle; Aristotle had pointed out that 'elephants, by reason of their great size, must remain two years in the womb'. It now becomes obvious why girls must remain longer in the uterus: 'If a child is thin and frail from its conception or first shaping, with a complexion hot and dry, active and much given to kicking, it will mature within nine months and sometimes within seven; but another will require ten or eleven. Thus we commonly see that girls arrive at the end of the ninth month and boys at the very beginning.'[84]

To the country mind, in times gone by, men had to wait for nature to accomplish her work within the time she herself had set. Its course should be neither hindered nor precipitated. In a word, nature must go at her own pace, and the child come 'in its own time'.

6

The Experience of Pregnancy

Nature takes good care of her precious burden.
F. A. Deleurye, Treatise on Childbirth, *1770*

The evidence available to us allows us to guess at the pride women felt in being pregnant, but it is seldom expressed directly. Women expecting babies were discreet about it; they were often even ashamed of it; they concealed their state as best they could.[1] Being pregnant means losing one's freedom of body and mind: every gesture, every word spoken, every movement of a pregnant woman also involves the child. She has to live for two. As intermediary between the foetus and the outside world, she has to ensure that her offspring is protected from every harmful influence, whatever its source. She has to think, calculate, keep herself under close supervision and constraint.

Fears of the Pregnant Woman

A pregnant woman lives in terror of an accident: she is in constant fear of tripping on a stair, spraining a knee or an ankle, or falling heavily; her abdomen could bump against a table-edge, a root or a stone; to be jostled in the crowd on market-day or to fall over could have the gravest consequences – not uncommonly, haemorrhage followed by miscarriage. Fairground charlatans and chapbooks sold or recommended lotions and poultices which were supposed to save a woman's baby after she had 'hurt herself'. Many of them resemble the following recipe from *Charitable Remedies*, by Madame Fouquet (late seventeenth century):

If often happens that pregnant women are at risk from falls, often in the last months of pregnancy, and in consequence that there is a risk of abortion. To prevent such falls they must make use of the following remedy: take three ounces of oil of St John's wort, or of hypericon (to be found at any apothecary's) and an ounce of brandy; mix; rub it vigorously on the fleshy part of the thighs and legs, morning and evening.[2]

Uterine haemorrhage was not the only worry. As is well known, pregnancy often causes loss of calcium, which affects the teeth. Caries and toothache seemed to call for an extraction, but the doctors sometimes refused to perform it: better to let the woman suffer than to endanger the foetus and be blamed for it later![3]

However the accident happens, the woman knows that she will always be held responsible: 'Why couldn't she be more careful?' 'What was she doing there, anyway?' The pregnant woman, thus accused, feels guilty. A premature birth, a deformed child, will set her asking what rashness, what error she has committed during her pregnancy.[4] In such circumstances the habit of thinking in analogies could lead to some startling conclusions. The early seventeenth-century midwife Louise Bourgeois reports the case of a woman who suffered from hydropsy during her pregnancy and bore a child with the same complaint; she was accused of being responsible for her child's affliction because she had drunk too much at a meal while she was expecting him.[5]

Symbolic taboos

To safeguard her child and herself, a pregnant woman was banned from certain attitudes and actions, most often those which could complicate the birth or cause physical harm to the baby. The mother-to-be had to 'avoid sitting without her feet touching the ground, or with her legs crossed, because it made children deformed and lengthened labour'.[6] Nothing on her body must constrict or enclose: no unnecessary ties or necklaces. The medieval Latin and French words for pregnancy, *incicta*, *enceinte*, both mean 'ungirdled', perhaps referring to the girdle which young women used to wear just over their hips.[7] In the Vendée, in the last century, peasant women would wear their scapulars and medallions in a little bag sown into their corsets or in their bosom:[8] without this precaution 'the child-to-be would have the cord round its neck, twisted as many times as the mother had worn necklaces or neckties'.[9] Fear of strangulation by the 'circles of the cord' was universal. A pregnant woman had to avoid anything to do with movement in circles. In the region of Les Landes and in Baziège (Languedoc) she had to be careful not to grind coffee or unwind skeins of thread or wool.[10]

Also banned was a series of things which could get in the way of the natural progression of events: for example, it was not a good idea for a woman to work on the baby's layette during her pregnancy, as she would be anticipating the time of the birth, which was dangerous and might cause it to turn out badly.[11]

A pregnant woman kept away from death and anything symbolical of death. Around Nevers, in the last century, she 'must not attend a funeral, for the baby would be born as yellow as death'.[12] In the Valdaine region (Dauphiné) she must not see a dead child, 'for her own child would be born as pale as a corpse'.[13] It was not only a corpse which could raise fears of evil influences: any 'doubling' of the woman's situation could be equally malefic. Around Cambrai, 'a pregnant woman should not be a godmother, or the child she is to bear will die'.[14] A variant from Limousin and Périgord has it that the woman ought not to be a godmother, or one of the children involved will die. Carrying a child cut one off from any other aspect of reproduction, even in animals: in Languedoc 'a pregnant woman will never put a hen on a clutch of chicks'.[15]

All these fears and forbidden actions go to explain why outside help was considered so important, why women constantly sought protective measures which would ease them through this difficult time.

Helpful and Protective Measures

Prayers and vows were used by the pregnant woman in an attempt to reassure herself and protect her fruit. If forbidden actions and dangers were numerous, so were the measures which could be taken against them. Some of these practices fitted in with the rituals of the reformed Catholic Church, which accorded a special importance to the Virgin; but others betray the survival of ancient beliefs based on the idea of the body's closeness to nature.

'Pregnant stones'

Pregnant women often carried a symbolic object which was supposed to ward off accidents and bad luck. Certain gemstones, such as agate, were much sought after, particularly those whose 'flesh' bears brownish or reddish lines strangely reminiscent of the shape and colour of a foetus. In Provence, these stones were replaced, after the birth, by others called *pater de la* or *gardo la*, which had a milky colour and were supposed to encourage the flow of milk.[16] Since Antiquity, however, the favourite amulet had been the eagle-stone, known as the 'pregnant stone' because inside it rattled a concretion which made one think of the foetus within the womb. It was simple to use: it was tied round the neck, against the skin, on a thong, ribbon or necklace; it could also go on the left arm. Carried on the upper part of the woman's body, rather than on the abdomen, it helped to hold back the child from being born before the proper time.[17] Like all amulets, the eagle-stone had a purely psychological effect: a magic object made one feel safer, it was reassuring. Up to the end of the seventeenth century doctors made no attempt to cast doubt on the virtues which women assigned to such topical remedies, though they feared the excessive trust put in them and railed against the rash actions which women might consequently take. The obstetrician Mauquest de La Motte declared that he always feared 'lest a young woman take part in wild amusements, such as riding, running, jumping, dancing and other kinds of violent exercise ... because of her faith in the supposed specific qualities of this eagle-stone'.[18]

'False cults'

In the seventeenth and eighteenth centuries there were still some practices around which had a strong overtone of paganism, as is shown by the pastoral visitations of certain bishops. The Church tried more and more to channel superstitions and limit their excess, but it was extremely difficult to eliminate centuries-old practices rooted in everyday life and passed on from woman to woman with the complicity of the midwives: 'old wives' tales' were a many-headed hydra which was always deforming and turning aside the belief-systems of peoples who were supposed to be thoroughly Christian. For a pregnant woman will do anything to overcome her tormenting anxiety and to avoid pain during the birth – even if the Church does condemn what she herself sees as a saving precaution, as here through the pen of the Abbé Jean-Baptiste

Thiers:

Most certainly it is also [a superstition] that a pregnant woman will give birth without pain if she remains seated during the Gospel at Mass a few days beforehand. For however could such a posture contribute in any way to making labour easier?

This custom, commonplace in the countryside, had to be condemned as 'a false and unnecessary practice, a vain observance and an attempt at divination of future chances and events'.[19] There was always the fear of an unforeseen accident which might prove fatal to the foetus, and above all the fear that it might then die before it could be baptized. While such concern for the child's spiritual destiny was praiseworthy in the eyes of the Church, it could also lead to reprehensible actions. Abbé Thiers denounces the 'gross error' committed by some people 'who believe that when a pregnant woman receives the Host, the child she carries is so sanctified by receiving this divine sacrament that it has no need of baptism'. Parents thought this to be axiomatic, since the foetus was constantly under its mother's influence: why should not the principle that 'what's good for the mother is good for the child' hold good in this case, for so important an issue?[20]

The Virgin and the saints

It is no new thing for mothers-to-be to entrust themselves to the Virgin: they often did this back in the Middle Ages. Some of her shrines had a miraculous image which was supposed to guarantee a trouble-free pregnancy and the birth of a healthy child. One of the most famous of these, the 'underground Virgin' in the crypt of Chartres, was invoked by women in this dual hope.

The emphasis on Mariology, the cult of the Virgin Mother, in the seventeenth century tended to make the Mother of Christ into the pattern for all mothers. She was first and foremost the protectress and helper, Our Lady of All Succour or Our Lady of Good Help. She never failed to answer those who called on her. Sometimes the image itself was symbolic of her role as protectress: the Virgin of Good Help which was famous in and around Nancy in the seventeenth and eighteenth centuries was shown sheltering people under her mantle.[21] But what the pregnant woman fears above all, to the point of obsession, is the end of her pregnancy, the birth itself: it was only natural to ask the Virgin for a happy outcome, since she was the mother above all mothers, and gave birth without pain. In the Perche region women turned to Our Lady of Deliverance at Saint-Denis-Du-Perche; in Savoy they placed their hope in Our Lady of Delivering, who had several shrines.[22] Sometimes a chance coincidence of language helped to fix the cult in one particular place: thus at Mosnac near Châteauneuf, in the Charente region, pregnant women came to the shrine of Notre-Dame-du-Liège to ask for a 'lightening' of their burden: they interpreted 'du Liège' as 'de l'Allège' (*alléger*, 'to make lighter').[23]

Shrines to the Virgin, ever more numerous in early modern Europe, did not however displace all other sources of help: they could even be, as it were, arranged in a hierarchy, or a mesh over the landscape.[24] As can be seen, for instance, in the case of Brittany, the fame of such saints was limited to a single

canton. Montcontour had its Saint Eugenia and its Saint Mamert, Lanloup its
Thouine, Saint Pever near Guingamp its titular saint: all were invoked only by
the women of a small area round about,[25] but for such women their own
familiar 'good saint' was none the less helpful for that. In any case, devotion to
some local saint did not prevent one turning also to another more prestigious,
more distant saint, or to the image of the Virgin. Women were happy to take
more than one precaution when they could.

Notre Dame de Quintin is a good example of this second type of 'image'
which attracted a following from a wider area: the women of North Brittany had
been looking to her for protection since the seventeenth century; in the next
hundred years her reputation spread throughout the province; by the eve of the
Second World War women all over France were calling on her during their
pregnancy. In 1926 the poet Paul Claudel mentioned the Virgin of Quintin to
his friend, Jacques Rivière, whose wife was pregnant at the time: 'In my family,'
he wrote, 'all women in this state ask for a blessed ribbon from an old convent in
Brittany (I could give you the address), and none of them has ever come to
grief.'[26] In every region there was some such well-known shrine to which
pregnant women made pilgrimages: round Laon and in parts of Picardy they
went to Notre-Dame-de-Liesse; in Flanders to Bollezeele; from Velay, Viviers
and the Auvergne to Le-Puy-en-Velay; from the Montpellier region of Languedoc to Gignac; and from the Toulouse area of Languedoc to Notre-Dame-
de-la-Daurade. Women from round Albi and parts of south-west France went
to Sainte-Foye-de-Conques; in Limousin they went to Saint-Leonard-de-
Noblat.

These big regional shrines presented certain problems to women with child,
especially that of distance. The time of year had to be taken into account, and
also the woman's condition: the more difficult the pregnancy, the more
important the pilgrimage, and it was then that women could be imprudent.
Obstetric textbooks have much to say about indispositions, often serious,
caused by the fatigues of the journey and long hours spent standing up in a
damp, chilly church. Thus some women preferred to rely on a 'travelling girl'
who would make the trip on their behalf; or they would vow to go and give
thanks to the relevant virgin or saint after the birth, and with the baby.

In the hierarchy of saints helpful in pregnancy, Saint Margaret held a special
place: her cult covered the whole of Western Christendom, where she had
displaced the Illythias, Dianas and Lucinas of Antiquity. On 20 July many
women gathered at her shrines. Her statue was a focus for local devotion: she
has numerous shrines in Brittany (despite being in 'competition' there with
Saint Bridget), most notably, at Collorec, Plomeur and Bannalec. She was very
popular in Paris: her girdle, kept at the abbey of Saint-Germain-des-Prés,
generated a cult which remained vigorous until the Revolution. In the seventeenth century Thomas Platter reported that every year a great feast was
celebrated, 'during which, to make barren women fertile or to aid those who
have difficult births, the priest drapes a girdle round their shoulders and body;
this ceremony,' he adds, 'is carried out with the greatest fervour.'[27] But it
remained confined to Paris and its immediate environs. Widespread as it was,

the cult of Saint Margaret did not give rise to any great shrine with at least a local reputation, as happened with Saint Foy at Conques.

Pregnancy and virginity

The theme of virginity is a feature of the lives of most of the female saints invoked during pregnancy: it is almost always connected with their martyrdom, for they die in order to defend their virginity. In the *Golden Legend* Jacopo da Voragine explains that

Margaret was so called after a precious white stone, small and replete with virtues [*margarita*, the pearl]. Thus Saint Margaret was white in her virginity, precious in her humility, and full of virtues by reason of her miracles.[28]

So as to remain a virgin she refused the marriage forced on her by the Prefect Olibrius; she was tortured by the Devil in the form of a hideous dragon, but held to her vow. Saint Foy was likewise martyred because she refused to surrender her virginity. And the virgin girdles of these two saints played an important part in the devotions of pregnant women. Even more revealing is the case of Saint Nonne of Dirinon, in Brittany. In his *Lives of the Breton Saints* (1725), Father Lobineau used her as an example to show that all young girls should be discreet and restrained: 'The misfortunes of Saint Nonne,' he wrote, 'should be a lesson to Christian virgins and turn them away from all outward and outlandish devotions which entice them to appear unnecessarily in the world. Living secretly and in retirement is their best safeguard.'[29]

Both in learned works and in popular belief, the preservation of virginity was closely associated with a healthy pregnancy. Women who had given their lives in defence of their honour seemed best equipped to protect the fruit of the marital union. But only the Virgin, the chosen mother of God, had achieved the impossible and conceived, carried and given birth to a child without having known a man. In the late nineteenth century the dogma of the Immaculate Conception produced a rich iconography which could scarcely have gone unnoticed by women. There is a stained-glass window at Montluçon showing the child Mary instructed by Saint Anne, with a legend emphasizing her unattainable perfection:

> Over many a hundred years virginity and motherhood
> Have been allied in Mary's womb.[30]

No wonder, then, if the Virgin outstripped all other intercessors to become the great protectress of women in pregnancy and in childbirth.

'The pregnant statue'

In some rites aimed at protecting pregnancy there is allusion to the stomach. Saints known to be expert in the curing of stomach ailments were often invoked by pregnant women: for example, Saint Mamart, who in western France was believed to cure colics and fluxes. He was often protrayed with his abdomen cut open, holding up his own intestines; at Montcontour, in Brittany, he was (as we have seen) asked to grant a short and pain-free labour. The mothers-to-be of north Finistère called on Saintez Gwentrok or Wentrok (Saint Ediltrude); this cult surely originated in the old Breton word *gwentr*, meaning rheumatism or stomach-ache.

The favourite image for pregnancy was that of the womb as a container for the 'fruit': thus a 'miraculous statue' was often itself shown to be pregnant, with a stomach protruding so emphatically that there could be no mistaking it. Saint Margaret, despite her reputation for virginity, was shown pregnant at Collorec and Bannalec. Even, astonishingly, the Virgin herself was subject to this symbolism of the pregnant body. There are statues and pictures painted on wood or stone which show the Mother of God as being with child. In sixteenth-century 'images' she is often alone. On an enamel from the Limoges region, from the end of the sixteenth century, we see her 'wearing a white robe, kilted up in places to show an under-robe of red and gold . . .. On the womb of the Virgin a tiny human figure, naked and with its hands joined in prayer, appears inside a golden halo.'[31] The same image figures in a stained-glass window in the church of Jouy, near Rheims; on a painted panel in the church of Chissey, in the Jura; and in a statue now in the Public Library at Amiens. This iconographic type, known as 'the virgin of the incarnation', is an ancient one. It may well have been the Virgin in a thirteenth-century stained-glass window at Chartres which served as a model for the glass-painters, painters and sculptors of the modern period.[32]

The scene of the Visitation may be pictured in exactly the same way. In this case there are two characters: the Virgin and Elizabeth, both pregnant, greet each other with a reverence or with the kiss of peace. The painter or sculptor will leave an opening in Elizabeth's robe to show the infant Saint John bowing before the Jesus, shown in the Virgin's womb, his right hand raised in blessing. The same iconography appears in a fifteenth-century painting of the German school, now in the museum at Lyons, and in a sixteenth-century stained-glass window in the church of Saint Nizier in the same city.

In a final model for the 'pregnant Virgin', Saint Anne also appears. Here, two or three generations are seen, as it were, one within the other: Saint Anne and the Virgin, or Saint Anne, the Virgin and the infant Jesus. The first type is illustrated by a window at Bennilis, called 'the Holy Conception', and by a statuette at Morlaix, probably of the early sixteenth century. This threefold 'holy relationship' is well represented in western France (Brittany and Anjou) from the fifteenth to the mid-sixteenth century; in the *Book of Hours for the Use of the Diocese of Angers* (1510), Saint Anne is shown standing, her mantle partly open to show the Virgin seated in her lap, and holding on her own knees the infant Jesus, wholly naked. This type is also found in Italy, where it may have originated.[33] The creation and diffusion of such images was rudely interrupted by the Council of Trent, which decided that they were too ambiguous to fit in with sound doctrine. However, the cult of some of these 'opening Virgins' has persisted up to the present day. Thus, for centuries the women of the Morvan region have venerated an 'image' in the church at Reclesne, which they used to ask for a happy delivery. They would have a mass said and would have the chest of an ancient wooden statue opened up so as to marvel at the infant Jesus in his mother's womb.[34] In the nineteenth century the Church 'finally forbade this pilgrimage and had an iron railing put round the statue to put a stop to such practices'.[35]

These representations of the Virgin constitute a type for pregnancy whose origins must be very ancient. The stone statue of the 'Quinipily Venus', in Morbihan, known in the seventeenth century as the 'Cowardly Old Woman' (in Breton, *Er Groach Couard*) or as the 'good woman', represents some ancient pagan goddess: a Graeco-Roman Venus? The Irish Dercith? Isis? It is extremely hard to be sure. Be that as it may, this statue, which in the mid-seventeenth century stood proudly on a grassy mound above Blavet, at Castennec-en-Bieuzy, was the object of an impressively continuous cult going back at least to the medieval period. Pregnant women from the country round would come to put themselves under her protection. The pilgrimage became so well known that the Bishop of Nantes took fright and decided to put an end to it, on the grounds that its practice was indecent. He did not succeed. Some time later, missionaries who had come to preach at Baud had the ancient idol flung into the river and raised an expiatory cross in its place. The 'Cowardly Old Woman' was secretly pulled out again, and three years later it was lying on its side on the river bank. This did not deter the peasant women, who once again flocked to it from all sides! In 1670 it was thrown back into the water; finally, in 1696, Count Pierre de Lannion had it transported to the park of his château at Quinipily, where up to the present day women have been coming secretly to implore its protection.[36]

Rituals of devotion

Pregnant women often made their way to a sanctuary at some special moment in the liturgical year. On the particular saint's day, or on the great feast days of the Virgin (15 August and 8 September), great numbers of expectant mothers would congregate – so long as their condition would permit it. A woman was not always able to wait for such a special day; in that case, ignoring the liturgical calendar, she would make at a suitable time the pilgrimage which, as she firmly believed, was sure to be for her good.

The journey could also be taken at the time of some great agricultural feast day – which incidentally shows how ancient the practice was. Above the principal gateway of the Commanderie at Braux, near Ancerville on the River Meuse there was, up to the nineteenth century, an old statue of Saint Crispin whose protection was requested by pregnant women coming from that part of Lorraine. The pilgrimage took place at Rogationtide and the women took good care to pass through the gate: it would be no surprise to learn that at the season when the fruits of the earth were being blessed, they were hoping that this symbolic passage would ensure the birth of a healthy baby.[37]

As in the case of fertility rites, the 'journey' to the image or fountain was sometimes followed by a circumambulation. Breton women from the Finistère region were assured of a trouble-free pregnancy and birth if they went to Collorec and walked three times round the tower of the chapel of Saint Margaret before sunrise or after sunset. Each time round, they must go into the chapel and recite five Paternosters and five Aves. This having been done, they must touch their naked navel against the statue of the saint (shown as being pregnant), make their confession, and leave an offering.[38]

Touching, direct and indirect   The example of Collorec makes it sufficiently clear that touching was an essential part of the ritual. Pregnancy relates to the abdomen, so it was by contact with this part of the body that the virtues of the protecting statue must act. The Church struggled to suppress such practices, which took place in public and which it considered to be indecent. In the last century, at Saint-Péver, the priest finally had to get rid of the statue of the 'good saint' altogether before he could put an end to the licentious behaviour of his female parishioners.

Thus women normally had to be content with brushing the saint's robe with their hands; sometimes they were allowed to kiss the wooden or stone body of the protecting saint. They would depart happy in the conviction that they would carry their child to full term and have an easy birth. Sometimes they would bring the linen they intended to use during labour. By having it blessed, or even better, by bringing it into contact with the wonder-working image, they were convinced that they would be safely delivered when the time came. This was particularly likely if the name of the statue could easily take on a different meaning which reinforced the idea of protection from its clothing. Women from around Domfront, in Lower Normandy, came to seek the protection of Notre Dame de l'Abie, who became (the pronunciation being identical) Notre Dame de l'Habit – Our Lady of the Garment. In accordance with local tradition, the pregnant woman would make a package of the linen which she was going to need; she would offer it to Our Lady of the Garment in her sanctuary for it to be consecrated, and then go home with her precious burden. Her pilgrimage would give her the feeling that from now on she was protected: it perfectly fulfilled its role as a therapy.

Often the pregnant woman would bring a 'cord' back with her: a piece of ribbon which (as she had taken care to ensure) had touched the holy relic. Tied round her waist, it would give permanent protection during her pregnancy, and be a material token of that protection. The link with the miraculous girdle could sometimes be kept up in a more subtle way: until the dawn of the present century the women who came to call upon Our Lady Of Deliverance at Neufchâtel-en-Bray used to tie half of a ribbon to the statue and keep the other half on their persons until the birth.[39]

From this ritual, the mother-to-be expected protection for herself alone; but surely the fruit of her womb must have its own protection against any accident or ill will? Many were the women of Picardy who went to Gamaches to worship the statue of Saint Vincent, being careful to bring a robe intended for the coming child, and a silk ribbon. The robe was held against the statue, and half of the ribbon was 'hung from the saint's arm by way of a memento'. When the child was born, it would be clad in the robe and would wear it for nine days; then its mother would put the piece of ribbon which she had brought back with her around its neck, and she would keep it on him for eight days.[40]

Miracle-working girdles The girdle of the Virgin or of a female saint, the cord worn by a male saint, had a symbolic value which made them essential in the ritual of protection during pregnancy. The girdles of Saints Margaret, Foy and Honorine, and various girdles of the Virgin, conferred fame on some principal shrines where hundreds, even thousands of pregnant women flocked each year. The cords of Saint Dominic and Saint Honorat, for their part, were revered in particular by pregnant women in the south of France, especially in Provence.

The rich fund of legends which surrounded these relics helped give them even more prestige. In the eighteenth century the people of Niègles, in Haute-Languedoc, attributed the foundation of their village to an eagle which was supposed to have brought a girdle belonging to the Virgin back to its nest: hence the name Nids-Aigle (Eagle Nests), which became Niègles. 'The parish,' wrote the village priest, Malosse, 'is under the invocation of the Nativity of the Virgin, and what with the legend of the miraculous eagle, it attracts many pilgrims who come several times a year from neighbouring parishes . . . to touch the Virgin's holy girdle, which is supposed to protect them against miscarriage.'[41]

Some shrines possessed only part of a girdle: for example, Notre-Dame de Quintin. Their reputation was none the worse for that. The size of the piece of girdle was almost immaterial, since where relics are concerned the part is equal in value to the whole. However, the possession of a girdle did not automatically mean that a shrine had an extensive public. The reputation of Niègles did not spread particularly widely; nor did that of the Benedictine abbey of Saint Paul, near Auteuil, which in the seventeenth century possessed a piece of the Virgin's girdle, but was visited only by pregnant women from the Bray region.[42]

Water rituals There were some 'blessed springs' which were endowed with the same beneficent powers as saint's images or girdles of the Virgin. Until the beginning of the nineteenth century the spring of Aiguevive, in Touraine, was frequented by all the pregnant women from the country round. It was dedicated to Saint Gilles, a patron of little children; the child-to-be would be consecrated at the fountain. Normally the women did no more than drink water from the spring, thinking that this would keep the foetus in good health and give it the strength to be born safely. Sometimes, however, they also washed themselves.[43]

Pregnant women bathing in a spring was part of an ancient ritual which it was always hard to extirpate. When in 1660 the Bishop of Vannes decided to put an end to the cult of the 'Cowardly Old Woman' at Castennec, he was largely influenced by the scandalous aspect (as he saw it) of what used to happen by the statue: naked women bathing in a sarcophagus fed by the spring. This bathing custom persisted until the last century at Bonnamour-en-Trevé, where the spring of Saint Eutropius was still favoured by mothers-to-be.

After it was forbidden to strip naked and bathe in the spring, substitute practices arose; they always had some bearing on the essential symbolic values. In the eighteenth and nineteenth centuries, pregnant women would come to the spring of Saint Thouine at Lanloup, in Southern Brittany, and dip in it their underlinen, girdle or just a ribbon, hoping thereby to benefit from the virtues of the holy water; they would put the pieces of material round their waists and thus be sure of bearing a good, strong child at the time appointed.[44] Sometimes, to bring the protection down on the child as well, the tiny garments of the layette would also be dipped in the water.[45] This ritual had some local variants, but it was always underlaid by the symbolism of the pregnant body which must be delivered; since one of the outward and visible signs of pregnancy was the swelling of the abdomen, it must perforce shrink again if all went well at the birth. This is illustrated by some practices of sympathetic magic. Pregnant women bathed in the spring of Bonnamour-en-Trevé in the hope that Saint Eutropius, patron saint of the fountain, who was supposed to cure hydropsy (his name could be read as *eau-trop*, 'too much water'), would show his favour to women whose figure had temporarily thickened. At Moncontour women would call on Saint Maudez and Saint Adrian; they would 'measure the size of their abdomens exactly so as to offer a candle of the same length'.[46] Water is replaced by wax, but the symbolism is comparable: the candle will melt, and in a few weeks or months the waist measurement will do the same.

Hygiene During Pregnancy

A woman had to make sure that the child she carried had 'the strength and good constitution which he will need to withstand the efforts he must make, and endure, in order to escape from his strait prison and make his appearance in a new world'.[47] Eighteenth-century doctors were interested in 'the regulation of the life of pregnant women', and were free with advice and criticism. In particular they came out against the latest fashions, which, it seemed to them, endangered the health both of the mother and of the unborn child, especially in towns; no less violent were their denunciations of 'popular misconceptions' which were unworthy of an enlightened age. People must, they said, get rid of prejudices and stay close to nature – a nature which, however, was still little known, ill-defined and idealized.

Moreover, practitioners did not, on the whole, take account of differences in social condition: their advice was addressed primarily to their better-off clients in the towns, to women who had the means to 'govern themselves well'. How could an ordinary lower-class woman go in for a 'regulation of life' which required some resources and some free time? Could she take walks, take a rest, turn her house into a 'well-aired and agreeable dwelling place', avoid unhealthy food, 'partake of nourishment in moderation' . . .? Was that all?! Poor women compelled to work right up to the end of their pregnancies, never knowing today what would become of them tomorrow, could hardly benefit from suchlike advice. The choices made by the professional doctors, and the contradictions they fell into, are nowhere better illustrated than by the way they tackled the question of hygiene in pregnancy.

'Good air is very proper to pregnant women'

In the seventeenth century, and more especially in the eighteenth, doctors often drew attention to the hygiene of particular places, creating a sort of medical topography of town and country; they took particular care to mention the quality of the air, and would declare that in a certain parish the soil did not everywhere offer the same assurances of health to a pregnant woman. Thus they advised avoiding riverbanks and marshy areas, because the miasmas which issued from them were supposed to provoke miscarriage. Town slums presented the same dangers, added to those consequent on a shortage of sunshine. Everybody knew this to be true – the people who lived in such places knew it for a start – but what could they do about it if their home and jobs were there?

Expectant mothers had to be wary of the wind: winds blowing from the south were, it seems, exceedingly dangerous because they could bring a pregnancy to an abrupt end[48] – just as they could make a green fruit, scarcely yet formed, wither on the tree. The north wind was no less to be feared: it caused coughs and could, again, bring about the loss of a baby; moreover, it often brought 'bad smells and mists' which were most injurious to the health of pregnant women.

It was not only winds which had to be attended to. Day by day women were under threat from 'harsh and nauseating smells': textbooks, following Aristotle, warned that 'the smell of the smoke from an extinguished candle can cause abortion'.[49] Advice follows: 'A pregnant woman must, as far as possible, dwell in a pure and temperate air'; above all she must avoid doing what was done by the woman in the Dauphiné, who, in cold weather, would 'squat on earthern vessels filled with hot coals. In 1775 Dr Nicolas reported that

This abominable habit, is prevalent especially amongst poorer people and in the countryside, where women retire into stables during the day; there they breathe in the stench of animal urine and excrement . . . .. Sitting almost motionless on a chair, moving no other limb except their arms and tongue, they sniff for long periods the putrid miasmas with which the air of these stables is laden, and take in through the pores of their skin the smoke from the coals, which cannot escape and disperse outside because of their skirts. I am convinced that all these dangers bring about a great number of abortions.[50]

This idea of blaming bad smells and the heat from braziers for the loss of unborn children is an ancient one which this doctor of the Enlightenment was quite willing to make his own. But there is nothing surprising in a town-bred doctor being taken aback by a whole world of smells so alien to his own experience. 'On entering these hovels, which the people call "watch-houses", one has to hold one's nose for a few moments and one feels as if pushed back by an invisible hand, so foetid is the stench and so abundant the miasmas within.'

'Exercise nourishes good health'

The good doctor from the Dauphiné was particularly opposed to inactivity in pregnant women: 'Pregnant women must take exercise.' Indeed it was customary for women to remain as inactive as possible during early pregnancy, when the foetus's hold on life was so fragile. In any case, observation of nature confirmed the idea: a fruit is never in greater peril than when it is forming or when the tree is in flower; a sharp shower of rain, a late frost, an ill-timed shaking of the trunk, and the hopes of a whole year can be endangered in a few minutes.

In the early stages of her pregnancy a woman was supposed not to travel by carriage and not to tire herself unnecessarily. Such was Madame de Sévigné's advice to her pregnant daughter when the former heard that the latter was to accompany her husband, Monsieur de Grignan, on a tiring journey across Provence. 'Do not agitate yourself at this early stage by a journey to Marseilles,' wrote Madame de Sévigné; 'let things become more settled; think of your delicate condition.'[51]

All doctors agreed that walking was by far the best exercise. 'If a woman wishes to keep in good health during her pregnancy and know the inexpressible joy of bringing a thriving child into the world, she should go on foot .... Pedestrian travel is the most fitting for pregnant women; it is the most useful to their health.'[52] Dancing, on the other hand, was the worst kind of rashness; how many newly wedded wives had had the cruel experience of a miscarriage after an evening's entertainment? Was that not the reason why 'we see so few dancing girls carry a child to the normal term of pregnancy'?[53] It was necessary to 'refrain from extremes, either too much or too little'.

Total immobility was not to be recommended either. Well-off women from noble or bourgeois families in the towns took too much care of themselves; they lived without stirring themselves at all and so were in danger from the slightest stumble. Why not do as the village women did? Work got the body moving and was an aid to health!

Country women do not cease working even if they know that they have conceived; being accustomed to hard work, they are safe from mishaps incident on idleness; their sinews are stronger, more elastic, more resistant to fatigue than those of wealthy women who, lying voluptuously on soft beds, find it hard to believe that healthy babies can come into the world upon straw, or even on bare earth.[54]

Here we find a gathering of all the images cherished by the 'ruralism' of the Enlightenment: an idealized vision of country life; the virtues of hard work; the happiness of the poor.

Cleanliness day by day

The documents rarely mention the toilette of pregnant women; even the doctors often pass in silence over the topic of day-to-day cleanliness.

Mothers-to-be took no more thought for bodily hygiene than they used to do during menstruation. It is not sufficient explanation to talk about the shortage of water supplies in towns and in some country districts. We are in fact talking about a society in which daily ablutions tended to be extremely sketchy in any case. Why should expectant mothers be any different? Until the mid-nineteenth century, personal hygiene was considered rather suspect from a moral viewpoint; only 'women of pleasure' washed and bathed with any frequency!

But people thought equally badly of a pregnant woman who took a bath, for they were suspicious of her motives. Bathing was supposed to dilate and relax the muscles; it might bring about an abortion. And 'The first doctors to propose bathing as a way of aiding the development of the womb during pregnancy ...

were looked upon as murderers out to kill both mothers and children' – so said a doctor from the end of the seventeenth century.[55]

The dirty and neglected aspect of country women was sometimes remarked upon by practitioners: Doctor Nicolas, he of the sensitive nose, made special mention, in speaking of the women of the Dauphiné, of 'the smell which issues from each and every one of them, because of the dirtiness of their bodies or their clothes'.[56] True, they did live in astonishingly crowded conditions and had no access to the scented toilet waters used so abundantly by their better-off sisters in the towns.

At every social level the most important part of the toilet was the coiffure. Combing and styling one's hair was a necessity: it got rid of vermin. But it would be wrong to underestimate the symbolic importance of a ritual subscribed to by all women: to confirm this one need only read what Pierre-Jakez Héliaz wrote about the way his mother did her hair.[57] A woman with properly styled hair was a decent, 'presentable' woman. In the towns coquetry and fashion also played their part: in the doctors' opinion, 'women of the world' spent far too much time before their 'dressing tables', that piece of furniture so highly prized in the eighteenth century; thus 'their toilet was a dangerous thing'. 'I have known women who spent two or three hours doing their hair,' declares one such doctor. 'This task, so "important" for women with any social ambition, is excellently suited to provoking abortion.'[58] Once again we note the fear of losing the fruit of the womb.

'Taking care of breasts and belly'

Pregnant women may have taken little thought for cleanliness, but they did take care of their bodies, and in a surprising way. They made generous use of 'oils and liniments' intended to make the flesh of the bosom and the abdomen more elastic during pregnancy. These ointments were supposed to act over time so as to prepare the belly for labour and the breasts for suckling the child; all of them were white in colour.

Bourgeois ladies of Paris anxious to keep their abdomens in good shape used to anoint themselves with 'pomades', which they prepared themselves or got their maidservants to prepare for them. Alongside the 'pomade of melted pork fat purified with rose-water' favoured by Louise Bourgeois there were others made from 'calves'-foot marrow, the caul of a kid, the grease from a fat chicken, goose, linseed oil, almonds, marshmallow and March stocks, also very good'. As for Flemish ladies, they 'never use anything but oil of lilies, and so preserve their bellies very well so that they are not spoilt'.[59] Through the sixteenth and seventeenth centuries this growing anxiety to preserve the abdomen probably had something to do with the changing attitudes of better-off women towards pregnancy and towards children: a point to which we shall return.

Regular use of liniments of animal or vegetable origin could profitably be supplemented by bandaging: wide linen bandages helped to hold up an abdomen which in the last months of pregnancy would have become as fat and heavy as a stuffed sack.[60]

Women also held up their abdomens by means of a pregnancy girdle made of dogskin, 'or some other skin suitable for making gloves'; but the skin had to be carefully prepared. At the beginning of the seventeenth century, the obstetrician Jacques Guillemeau advised 'washing it several times in ordinary water, then in rose-water' and drying it in the shade for two or three days, then softening it by soaking it in the 'oils and greases' from St John's wort or sweet almonds, or in a white-rose unguent, fresh butter, or spermaceti; finally it should be taken out and dried in the fresh air. Then 'it can be cut to the size and shape of the belly'. Women who used such girdles 'changed it every fortnight more or less, when they became spoiled, and only adjust it every two or three days when it wrinkles and becomes crumpled.'[61] Such girdles remained the perquisite of the well-off. Ordinary women stuck to bandages up to the nineteenth century.

Bandages and girdles held up the abdomen and made the burden less hard to bear; moreover, they prevented some infections of the urinary tract, as a doctor pointed out at the end of the seventeenth century: 'If the belly falls too low, as often happens; if the bladder is compressed and the flow of urine constricted, this discomfort can be stopped by holding up the lower part of the abdomen with bandages and draw-sheets, which any woman can make, and so increase her comfort.'[62] Fear of a 'fall of the womb' haunted all pregnant women of modest means who often had to work hard right up to the end of their pregnancy.

Bandaging the abdomen, and sometimes also the bosom, was the only notable change made to one's attire. Doctors were generous with their advice on clothing for a pregnant woman, but they were seldom listened to. They advised the expectant mother to 'dress in light rather than heavy clothes', to wear 'sober but widely fitting', 'free and easy' garments. Dress, they said, must not impede 'the expansion of the womb, and in consequence, of the foetus'.[63] Some maintained that the fastenings of the dress should be modified 'by holding up the skirts by means of cords passing over the shoulders'. Thus, they said, 'one could get rid of the harm caused by the tightness of fastenings round the loins'. Practitioners condemned with one voice 'shoes with excessively high heels which disturb the balance of the body and cause sprains'.[64] When they speak of the right clothes and shoes to wear during pregnancy, the doctors are evidently addressing women of the wealthier classes: ordinary women could do nothing to change their manner of dress, and just had to adapt their poor everyday garment to the exigencies of their new state, in particular by adjusting the stitching at the waist. And they went on walking about in their clumsy sabots – if they had even those.

'She must sleep at night'

A pregnant woman must 'seek repose and take it when necessary'. All the textbooks for midwives and obstetricians counsel prudence and emphasize this need for rest: good sleep means a successful pregnancy. The expectant mother needs a little more sleep than usual, especially if she is working and taking a lot out of herself; an extra hour or hour and a half of sleep is desirable in such cases. But 'a woman who lives in idleness' has no need to prolong her night's rest, since 'inaction is a kind of night'.[65]

Pregnant women had to pay heed to the rhythms of nature, more even than other people did: the best sleep was sleep at night, the only kind which aided digestion. Doctors also drew attention to the quality of the bed, criticizing not the uncomfortable and even insanitary paliasses which poorer people had to put up with, but the feather beds which were to be adopted in the countryside in the late nineteenth century, but which in the seventeenth and eighteenth centuries were still the prerogative of bourgeois town-dwellers. They must be treated with suspicion, it seems, because 'by causing forced transpiration and heating the loins, [they] can cause miscarriage'.[66] Late nights must be avoided because they 'overheat the blood and attack the nervous system'. Above all, mothers to be must not act like 'great ladies, who turn day into night and night into day'. They must realize that an ill-regulated kind of life would have immediate consequences for their offspring. Late nights produced 'indigestion and illnesses which produce stunted children instead of large and beautiful ones'.

'Her bowels will relax'

Constipation was one of the scourges of past ages, due to the diet: so many 'retaining' foods were eaten that it was necessary to have occasional recourse to purges or enemas. Molière, with his mockery of doctors who know nothing about anything except clysters, bears witness to the customs of his time. Pregnancy predisposed women to be 'hard in the bowels, unable to go to stool save with great discomfort and infrequency'. Thence came colics, aches and pains, and headaches. Constipation was all the more serious, for a mother-to-be, in that she feared the consequences for the fruit of her womb: retaining waste matter for too long could bring on premature labour, for 'by bearing down for a long time and with violence in order to do what she must, ligaments can relax, or some vein might open and cause an effusion of blood'.[67]

Obstetricians, having witnessed such unfortunate outcomes, gave helpful advice to pregnant women. Jacques Guillemeau (early seventeenth century) advised taking 'some suppositories, not too harsh', or 'clysters made of [the liquid from] a calf's [or] sheep's head, with a little aniseed or fennel, in which has been dissolved red sugar or violet oil'.[68] Eighteenth-century practitioners, however, counselled prudence, saying that they feared the way that some women in towns overused enemas. It was quite otherwise in the country: 'There is a prejudice against enemas during pregnancy.'[69] Women were afraid that the foetus might be dislodged by the enema and drawn out, expelled, at the same time as the waste matter. They also distrusted strong purgatives, thinking that they might 'dislodge the child' and push it out of the mother's womb. So they turned to gentler purgatives: in Lorraine, to 'relaxing substances, such as leeks, spinach, lettuce, fresh butter, veal, honey and cooked prunes',[70] or, again, 'senna leaves dipped in damson sauce'; or, in the Ile de France, to a brew made from 'borage, bugloss, lettuce, purslane, dock and a little mercury'.[71]

In truth, according to the doctors, the only effective way to combat constipation was to prevent it by a regular, well-balanced diet – often no more than a pious hope in a world at the mercy of bad harvests and of famine.

'Eating for two'

'It is only in recent times that pregnant women have paid careful attention to their diet.' In the seventeenth century, and especially in the eighteenth, the medical fraternity certainly made recommendations on diet during pregnancy and drew attention to certain dishes which they considered dangerous, but they had little effect on people's behaviour, except in some sections of urban society. But is it all that surprising?

It is commonly believed that what the mother ingests has a direct influence on the foetus: a pregnant woman shares her meals with the child she is carrying, which, like a parasite encysted in her womb, extracts what it needs; it is even the main beneficiary of the nourishment: 'the first morsel goes to the child', according to an old proverb. Pregnant woman yielded to the conviction that they had to 'do their best to eat a lot', even if they were not 'urged thereto by hunger'.[72] In short, they had to 'eat for two'. Doctors protested against the depraved appetite of women who ate too much, and seemed to be 'pregnant right up to the throat'! But the reason why pregnant women ate a lot was that they always feared 'weakness', and so, to 'keep their strength up', they ate more than usual and unhesitatingly partook of 'spiritous liquors'. This, declared the doctors, was a 'destructive preconception', for such a 'heat-engendering method' could not but lead to accidents; pregnant women must desist from ingesting too much 'hot and dessicating' food and drink, which were always likely to produce thick and melancholy blood: such foods were (according to Jacques Duval) beef, hare, eel and other similar things, especially if salted and spiced: venison pâté, saveloys, Mainz ham and so on. Also undesirable were vegetables, cheese, garlic, onions, quinces both wild and cultivated, hazelnuts, walnuts, medlars and hard-boiled eggs.[73] Guillemeau also advised against salted foods and spicy dishes, following Aristotle and Pliny in saying that 'if a pregnant woman eats foods which are too salty, her child will come into the world without nails, which is a sign that it will not have a long life'. It is also necessary to avoid all 'diuretic foods' which 'increase the flow of urine and bring on menstruation; and foods which cause flatulence, such as peas and beans'.[74] Women must abandon such foods, which could imperil the existence of the foetus, that 'tender sprig of humanity', in favour of a cooling diet. 'At such a time, therefore, their solid food should consist of veal, lamb, capons, chickens, partridges and other such things, preferably boiled and mixed with lettuce, sorrel, bugloss, borage, spinach and other garden herbs of that kind: they should frequently partake of a broth made from these, and this will be better for them than if the meat were fricasseed, grilled, roasted or baked in a crust'.[75] It would also ease digestion, for 'one is strengthened not by what one eats, but by what one can digest properly':[76] it was bad food which caused the nausea and vomiting that afflicted so many pregnant women.[77] Finally, some attention must be paid to the frequency of meals: it was better to 'eat little and often, than to eat too much at a sitting'.[78]

From the sixteenth century to the eighteenth, doctors continued to fight against popular patterns of behaviour and tried to define the ideal diet for a pregnant woman. Their recommendations – eat plenty of healthy, cooling foods at regular intervals, drink claret and sometimes red wine, in 'reasonable' quantities – give us some idea of the gulf which then existed between medical theory and the day-to-day existence of the majority of women. However judicious, the medical men's advice seems singularly ill-adapted to actual conditions at the time.

The diet of pregnant women in olden times was mainly characterized by monotony, insufficient protein and seasonal variation. 'Eating for two'? It was rather a case of sharing an already meagre repast. How could the child benefit if the mother could not get enough to eat? The problem of undernourishment sometimes emerges in the texts: Doctor Nicolas, for example, mentions the case of 'country women and others, forced to do heavy work and without the wherewithal to procure foods which are always expensive'.[79] In such cases the quality of what they ate was of secondary importance: what mattered was getting enough to eat. In the supply gap just before the harvest, when barns and purses were both empty, orchard fruits could be a boon; but while green fruit could satisfy hunger, it was highly dangerous to women who ate too much of it, without taking the precaution of cooking it first! 'Fluxes' were always to be feared; it was in summer that miscarriages were most frequent.

'She should be merry and gay'

A pregnant woman, said the doctors, was not always able to control her feelings – which was not good either for her or for the child. 'She is naturally inclined to anger and bad temper, more so than at other times', as the obstetrician Deleurye insisted in about 1770; consequently, anything which could provoke such passions must be avoided.[80] All excess was dangerous: 'immoderate shouting and laughing is bad for her'. She must also beware of 'loud sounds and noises, such as thunder, artillery and loud bells'. Pregnant women had been known to die of fright on hearing thunder.[81]

'These mental passions' were always bad for the child, for they 'often cause miscarriage' . . .. Fortunately the outcome was not always so dramatic: the mother must not, however, forget that passions 'are perceptibly communicated to the foetus. It is very common to see children stained from birth with a thousand defects that they have brought from the womb of a dejected, quick-tempered, capricious or intemperate mother. Vices', says Nicolas, 'are infectious, like diseases.'[82]

Above all, the pregnant woman must be even-tempered. Nothing was more harmful than the 'melancholies and unpleasant things which may pass through her mind'.[83] 'You know that one cannot always be laughing,' wrote Madame de Sévigné to her daughter in 1671; 'however, be careful not to make any black bile'.[84] An expectant mother must be light-hearted: 'she should be merry and gay'. But this did not depend on her alone. A good environment also helped to make a good pregnancy.

The Pregnant Woman and Other People

Nowadays, a woman expecting a child is the object of consideration: as far as possible she is spared fatigue and annoyance; she is not expected to do tiring work; people willingly make way for her. In former times, nothing really changed for a woman who became pregnant, and among working people, where her life was always rather hard, she had no-one to rely on but herself. However, in the eighteenth century voices were raised in favour of a more considerate treatment.

'Treat her more kindly than ever'

Society in those days was harsh for everybody. Each and every member of the family took risks in the course of his or her daily round, from the shepherd-boy sleeping amidst his flock under the threat of attack by wolves to the grown man thatching a roof, risking his life without any insurance; or venturing onto a lake although he could not swim. There was a constant danger of accident or attack. It was the destiny of a woman to be pregnant; why should she have escaped the general rule? Her state, however 'interesting' it may have been, did not free her from the necessity of earning a living – which could mean risking her life. Many are the descriptions of woman at an advanced stage of pregnancy helping with hay-making or the harvest, winnowing the corn or carrying heavy baskets. Doctors and country priests sometimes complained bitterly about the consequences of such overwork; but what hope had they of being listened to when for a working woman, a day-labourer, work was the very condition of her survival?

Women did help one another; they did so without extravagant words or gestures, mother helping daughter, or friends helping out at the place of work, the communal wash-place or the public well. Someone would carry the pregnant woman's heavy burden, or go shopping for her.

Men, on the other hand, did not always behave towards their wives as might have been wished; in the eighteenth century, priests sometimes took their somewhat uncultivated parishioners severely to task for forgetting their duties towards 'the carrier of so precious a burden'. In 1769 Froger, priest of Mayet in the diocese of Le Mans, asked them to pay their wives a little more attention and help them in the hardest tasks.[85] Most to be feared were quick-tempered husbands who threatened readily and sometimes lashed out. One brandished a sabre over the head of his wife when she was near her time;[86] another laid into her with a stick, and caused premature labour and the death of the child, which was born with the back of its head flattened and bloody! The grief-stricken mother told the story to Louise Bourgeois: 'She told me that six weeks before the birth her husband had struck her three blows on the lower back with a big stick from his bundle of faggots; to which she attributes the cause of this deformity.'[87] No doubt such were extreme cases.

'Making the beast with two backs'

The husband's 'approaches' to his wife during pregnancy drew various comments from the doctors; but such approaches certainly took place, as is shown by the pages devoted to sexual relations during pregnancy in diverse textbooks of midwifery. The husband's desire to continue enjoying his wife is sufficient to explain the persistence of such relations, but the cultural reasons for such conduct should not be underestimated: was it not in this way that the husband helped to fashion the child? The shapeless mass within the mould of the womb thus received the stamp of the father.

Up to the beginning of the eighteenth century, most practitioners remained fairly tolerant of sexual relations during pregnancy; many of them also thought that coitus helped to shape the child. In any case, was it not behaviour which made a difference between men and beasts? 'Some women being pregnant', wrote Guillemeau, 'disdain the company of their husbands; which could be said of brute beasts when they are in whelp, the like of which ordinarily flee from the male.'[88] And Laurent Joubert emphasizes the sexual appetite of the woman during pregnancy: 'Pregnant up to the bosom, [she] will often be more eager, indeed more hungry than if she were not pregnant at all'.[89] However, the doctors, while not proscribing 'conjugal relations', considered that they ought not to be 'made too frequent, because the womb can be damaged thereby'.[90] Guillemeau emphasizes that the woman should avoid 'making the beast with two backs' during the first four months of pregnancy, 'for fear of dislodging the fruit'.[91] Some, in fact, explained 'superfetation', i.e. the simultaneous presence in the womb of children of differing ages, by a fresh conception on the part of an already pregnant woman.

The change of tone which appears in medical discourse during the second half of the eighteenth century can be explained by 'populationist' ideas. On behalf of the future of the kingdom, doctors went into battle against anything which seemed likely to slow the increase in population. They fulminated against sexual relations in pregnancy as a threat to the survival of the foetus. And during the French Revolution, when the production of a 'healthy and vigorous generation' was urged as a condition for the regeneration of the State, they appealed to the father's conscience, as the obstetrician Nicolas Saucerotte does here:

As soon as there are signs of pregnancy, take care not to imperil, in the mother's womb, the existence of the fruit of your love. Husbands, be temperate in every way necessary for the state of an individual who, one might say, has two lives, that is her own, and that of the creature which she is to bring into the world.[92]

The Church, for its part, insisted throughout the eighteenth century on the moral implications of the sexual act in pregnancy. To the Church, a husband who took his pleasure at such a time was a brute doing outrage to his wife, a 'human monster whom everyone regarded with horror and who should be banished from society'.[93] The heated tone corresponds to the seriousness with which such an act was regarded – and to its relative frequency in the countryside up to the nineteench century.

The Longed-for Child

Until the birth, the womb held a secret: what would it be like, this child who grew day by day away from all curious eyes? Reverie fed on mystery. How could you know? How could you find out in advance?

For centuries, if not for millennia, Western society kept to the same archetype of the ideal child; it was still very present to the minds of countrywomen over almost the whole of France until a few decades ago. Strangely, it has received very little scholarly attention. Perhaps because our sources tend to pay more attention to the idea of determining the sex of the child-to-be: we have only to consult the innumerable editions of the *Grand Albert* and the publications of the popular chapbook series, the 'Bibliothèque Bleue', to see the truth of that. Girl or boy? Nowadays, echography and the testing of the amniotic fluid can give us the answer. There is no more room for reverie: we have to know; we are incessantly in quest of further certainty.

The imagined child

If the womb was an oven, the child that one wanted to see come forth from it was 'done to a turn', neither undercooked nor overcooked. An 'overcooked' child was one which had dull skin, a leaden grey complexion and a lot of black hair: such a child had been too long in the womb – unless the mother's temperament was too strong and the cooking had been too quick, or the water of the bath into which the newborn child had been plunged had been too hot.[94] In contrast, the premature child was too pale, too small, too thin, like dough which had been baked at the wrong temperature and so had not risen properly. Between the two was the pink, hale, 'blond, curly-haired' child of every expectant mother's dreams.

A curly-haired child is mentioned in the fertility and pregnancy rites of Burgundy, Bresse, Brittany and Touraine.[95] Places visited by women desirous of bearing a handsome child on this model often have a fertility-spring under the patronage of some saint. Thus, the women of Bresse went to the spring of Saint-Jean-des-Eaux, near Tournus, to call on the aid of John the Baptist.[96] But at the chapel of Beaumont-en-Dombes, which was near a famous spring, it was a miraculous virgin, Notre-Dame-des-Mouches, which received the women's prayers. Furthermore, this cult is often associated with boundaries: at Burgy, in the Mâcon region, the place where mothers-to-be came to ask Saint Barbe to give them a golden-haired child was a wayside cross on the boundary between the parishes of Péronne and Villé.[97]

Perhaps because of their isolation, such places of pilgrimage often escaped the control of the Church: they were the territory of 'bogus saints' like Saint Greluchon, asked to provide curly-haired children in Burgundy, Berry,

Touraine and Brittany, or Saint Freluchot in Morvan: obviously fertility saints, they bear witness to a stratum of belief which goes back to the Middle Ages – when women dreamed of a child who 'had fair curly hair'[98] – and perhaps even back to the Gallo-Roman period. At Saint-Sernin-du-Bois, near Le Creusot, at the confluence of the two sources of the River Mesvrin, excavations in the nineteenth century confirmed that such pilgrimages had taken place since the Gaulish period. The horned god Cernunnos, symbol of the meeting of waters, had been succeeded in Gallo-Roman times by Belen-Borvo, god of healing springs, represented 'naked, in the form of a young man with curly hair';[99] later, Borvo gave way to Saint Gervais; but even about the year 1880, women came every Friday to pray for the healing of sickly children or for an end to barrenness; and those who were pregnant voiced their desire for a 'child with fair curly hair'.[100]

Since Antiquity, hair has been seen as an essential element of beauty; in the mid-eighteenth century in France, people still talked about 'a beautiful head'[101] – i.e. of hair. The real significance of this image of the ideal child still escapes us, however. Is it a survival of the ancient solar cult of the Gaulish Apollo? And in that case, is not the opposite of the ideal child the 'little dark man with the bronzed face', the imp, the *korrigan* of Breton legend who lurks in the deep shadows of the underworld?[102]

But it is possible that 'curly simply meant "strong" '.[103] This is indicated by the kind of prayers addressed to Saint Greluchon or similar saints at certain sacred springs. Women came to pray to 'the good saint' for fine children, and girls asked for a faithful and vigorous (in the amatory sense) husband. This allows us to construe this quest for a fine child as a response to the deep-seated anxiety of a mother: a sickly, weakly, not quite 'human' child was perhaps a sort of evil enchantment, like the piece of sympathetic magic known as the *aiguillette* (whereby an ill-wisher rendered the husband impotent by tying a symbolical knot in a cord) which must be feared and guarded against.

Facial beauty was also a cause of concern. A woman always hopes that her child will have a good complexion. That is the only explanation for some food taboos in pregnancy and for certain fertility rites. In Lorraine the newborn baby's face would actually be rubbed with the placenta or cord, 'so as to give it a clear complexion, and if it has any blemishes on its skin, to get rid of them'. It was also believed that if the cord was drawn three times across the baby's eyes this would give it better eyesight. Eyes, and in particular their expression, were very important. Deep-set eyes were not popular: they 'said' something about the father. According to Laurent Joubert, 'Those who have deep-set eyes were engendered by an old man'; or, again, 'a child will have more deeply set eyes, and also its whole body will be frailer and less plump, if such has been its father'.[104] But the colour of the eyes was also important: in Alsace, where black eyes were preferred, pregnant women were quite sure that if they swallowed *Kirchwasser* during the first months of pregnancy, they would get what they wanted.[105]

It is true that everywhere, in the seventeenth and eighteenth centuries, there was some belief in the use of liqueurs and wine to help the arrival of a fine offspring. Drinking brandy before the birth apparently helped to 'ungrease' the child, to free it from the sebaceous covering of cheese-like material which was commonly believed to come from the father's sperm.[106] It was widely believed that stimulants like coffee, tea or chocolate also made babies healthy and strong, though not everyone had the same confidence in chocolate. Madame de Sévigné asked her daughter to drink it sparingly for the sake of her child: 'The Marquise de Coëtlogon, who took a great deal of it,' she wrote to her daughter, 'had a little boy as black as a devil, and he died.'[107] One had to be wary of anything which could 'taint' the foetus.

But why should not the mother, who helped to form her child by what she ate, try to act on it by eating particular things of proven virtue? It was not always greedy to gorge oneself with delicious firm, pink, quince jelly, as Primerose remarked towards the end of the seventeenth century: 'There are worthy women who, during their pregnancy, eat a great deal of marmalade, which, they say, is so that their children should be clever, having perhaps heard that it strengthens the retentive capacity of the brain by drying it out, because being yet tender like soft wax, it easily receives the impression and the virtue of the jelly.'[108]

Divining the sex

Is it a boy or a girl? The mother-to-be could not fail to ask herself that question. However, it was seldom the mother who initiated the rite of divination; as a participant in the development of the foetus, she was not qualified to judge. It was the people around her who conducted the inquiry on her body.

The pregnant body, jealous of its secret, nevertheless had to reveal the sex of the child to those who know how to make the correct observations and deductions. The mask of pregnancy was the best known, because the most easily accessible, indication: in Brittany or Touraine a 'marked face' or 'spots' invariably meant a girl.[109] The shape of the womb was also taken into consideration. A pointed womb meant a girl, a wide one a boy. But the essential criterion had to do with the two sides of the body. The right was always considered to be the noble, strong, positive side: it symbolized the masculine element; the left or 'sinister' side was weak, negative, which is as much as to say feminine. If the woman was carrying to the right she would have a boy; if to the left, a girl. But a part of the body could 'speak' for the whole: in Morbihan, towards the end of the nineteenth century, one heard about women who were sure to have a boy if their right leg swelled up during the pregnancy.[110]

Since observation was not always sufficient in itself, the body would be tested, made to react. If the woman, when told to move, set off on the right foot, she would have a boy; if she was made to sit on the ground, and used her left hand as a support when getting up, she would have a girl. One could also try the key test. A key was thrown to the ground, and the woman picked it up, unthinkingly using one hand or the other. Often the husband took an active part in the divination: his wife would sit on his knees, which were kept carefully horizontal, and a third person would look to see if the wife's right foot came down lower than her left. More examples could be cited. There may have been regional variations, but the idea was always the same. For the belief that the sex of the foetus conditions the behaviour of the pregnant woman had been universally accepted since Antiquity.[111] The child 'spoke' to the right or left according to whether it was a boy or a girl.

Sometimes the sex would be determined by the toss of a coin. The coin was habitually put into the top of the woman's bodice, between her breasts: if it fell tails it foretold a girl; if it was heads, a boy. Around Cambrai, in the nineteenth century, a *sou* was used; in Normandy, right up to 1914, a five-franc piece. Around Bordeaux there was a slight variation: the woman threw the coin behind her.[112]

Another possible criterion was the sex of the first person one met in certain particular circumstnces: when the woman felt the baby move for the first time, or when she was leaving the church after a churching. The latter gives an early indication of the idea that there was a link between the children of the same family, with the last-born announcing the next-comer, or allowing it to be announced.

The last-born could also show the sex of the next child by its speech. According to whether its first word was 'papa' or 'mamma', it was telling its parents that it would have a little brother or sister. Normally the connection between the word and the sex was analogous, but it could also be inverse, so that 'papa' foretold a girl and 'mamma' a boy.[113] The phases of the moon at the time of a birth also had an important part to play in determining the sex of the next child. If the new moon appeared in the course of the six days immediately following the birth, the next child would be of the same sex; otherwise it would be different.[114] In Touraine, if the new moon appeared within nine days, the child to be would *not* be of the same sex; in the contrary case, it would be.[115] In Morvan there was yet another formula: if the first child was born 'under a tender moon', i.e. under the first two quarters, the next child would be of the same sex; if it was born 'under a gentle moon', i.e. between the full moon and the last quarter, the sex would be different.

These regional variations in interpretation should not obscure the essential fact: everyone was seeking a rule for 'reading' the signs. Since the moon was thought to have an essential role in conception, it was only natural that it should be the preferred instrument for the divination of the sex. Here we find the temporal aspect intervening once again. Indeed, the 'time of the pregnancy' was also taken into account; the beginning and end of pregnancy were useful indications. A particularly close eye was kept on the mother's behaviour during the first month: if she was sick during this time she would have a boy[116] – which was perfectly logical, because it was believed at the time that only the male embryo was formed at that stage. A pregnancy which went beyond the expected term also meant a boy: did this mean that the 'cooking' of a male child took longer?[117]

Many other divinatory procedures were also tried. In one place, women went around the blessed springs and threw in two little garments, one for a boy, one for a girl; the one which floated longer showed the sex.[118] In another place the colour of the knots at the end of the afterbirth would be carefully examined: red meant a boy, white a girl.[119] In reality, it was impossible to be sure of anything and the best predictions were often proved wrong. In which case one had to turn to the doctors.

If the mother was	
Rosy and merry	Pale and pensive
Heavier on the right side and carrying high	Heavier on the left side and carrying low
Of cool and humid temperament	Of dry and hot temperament
If the mother had	
Pains on the right side of the womb	Pains on the left side of the womb
The right breast harder and firmer	The left breast larger
Red, hard, raised nipples	Paler, more drooping nipples
Thick white milk oozing from the breast	Pale, dilute milk
then	
It would be a boy	*It would be a girl*

In the towns, from the seventeenth century onward, the family often asked the doctor to pronounce on the sex, and according to Guillemeau, doctors ought not to refuse to answer: they must, he said, 'satisfy curious minds, who immediately ask the surgeon who confirms the pregnancy what child is to be expected' – but they must be cautious. Indeed, 'as it is difficult in the early stages to know if the woman is pregnant or not, it will naturally be extremely difficult to discern the sex, to know if it is a boy or girl. I know,' he adds, 'that there are those who boast of being able to tell it with certainty, but more often than not, it is rather by chance than by reason and knowledge.'[120] Practitioners normally parrotted the predictions of the Ancients, trying to give them some sort of coherence.

Always to be perceived behind these divinatory practices is the desire for a son, an heir to carry on the family name and lineage. The market value of a son was indeed twice that of a daughter, or so rumour had it in the Montauban of 1691. In that year, the women of the people rose in revolt because a notice put up by an attending physician had given them the idea that they would thereafter have to pay a tax on newborn babies: 'Ten sous for every boy they brought into the world, five sous for every girl!'[121]

Waiting for a Dauphin

Never, perhaps, was the hope for a boy so intense as when the queen was expecting. In a monarchy whose succession went through the male line, they lived in the hope of a dauphin. When the foetus began to move in the fourth month, the royal couple's hopes turned to certainty: the pregnancy was officially confirmed and all their subjects joined in the expectancy of a royal child. It was usual for the Archbishop of Paris to write to the sovereign, asking him to order public prayers.[122] Great was the fervour of those crowds which gathered throughout the kingdom to ask God's protection on the offspring and a happy deliverance for the queen. Because the queen's womb carried the hopes of the whole people, a royal pregnancy was a serious matter. Everything hung on that fearful and wonderful moment: the birth of the heir.

Naturally the king gave a good deal of attention to the choice of a midwife. In her hands, at the birth, would be the future of the dynasty and the destiny of its subjects. Was it not 'the principal element in the delivery, that the midwife should be pleasing to the woman whom she is delivering'? The desire of Marie de Medici, wife of Henry IV, for a young, alert and experienced midwife was a novelty at the time: it shows a change in custom and the appearance of a new image of the ideal midwife among the royal women of the early seventeenth century. It caused a quarrel between the Queen and King Henry, who wanted to inflict an elderly widow on her – until the King, having obtained proof of the competence of Louise Bourgeois, acceded to the desire of his wife.[123]

The post of queen's midwife was an enviable one which carried various privileges. Once engaged, the royal midwife had to be constantly in attendance on her mistress; she would advise her during the last days of her pregnancy, take care of her health, and watch out above all for unwise eating habits: 'In my heart I feared that the Queen might suffer from colic during the delivery,' Louise Bourgeois reveals, 'because I had been told that she had eaten a considerable quantity of ices, melons, grapes, apricots and peaches. I implored Her Majesty to stop eating melons; she promised me that she would not, so long as she was not offered them.'[124]

It was not until eight days before the birth that the King met Louise Bourgeois. 'I think that she will serve you well,' he said to the queen, 'she seems a good girl'; then, turning to the midwife, he impressed upon her the importance of her task: 'My dear, you must do it well: it is something of great importance which you must carry out.'[125]

Salic law, which confined the French succession to the male line, helped make the wait for a dauphin yet more dramatic. The hope for a royal son made the Queen's first pregnancy and labour an event of unequalled importance. For Henry IV, the birth of a son would safeguard the future of his throne and the continuance of his power; to the Queen, it was vital not to disappoint the hopes of a people which was in need of tranquillity and continuity after the dreadful Wars of Religion.

In her last months of pregnancy, Marie de Medici was visibly obsessed with the sex of the child she was carrying. In an attempt to find it out beforehand and be reassured, the Queen, who was very superstitious, fell back on the old fund of popular beliefs. Doctor Héroard tells us that 'She often asked what phase the moon was in, following the popular opinion that females are born under a waning moon.'[126] Feeling depressed one morning, she told her midwife 'that she thought she would have a girl, because people said that women pregnant with sons got thinner at the end of their pregnancy'. To which Louise Bourgeois retorted that the Queen looked 'so fair and with such a good colour, and such bright eyes, that according to the midwives' beliefs, it would have to be a son'.

A woman who bears within her the destiny of a State has a crushing responsibility, and we can easily understand that it was not easy to keep up her hopes. In an attempt to be more convincing, the midwife talked about the higher interests of the realm and God's own need to finish what He had begun:

The surest judgement I could make is that God was showing us that He wished to restore France, having made a good catholic of our King; the master being married and the Queen with child, before anybody had even had the time to wish for it, seeing that all of this was the great work of His hands, I thought that He would complete this work by giving us a Dauphin.[127]

We must surely see these words as evidence of a belief in a special protection accorded the French royal house.

As the time for the birth drew nigh, the general anxiety became more intense. Louise Bourgeois declared that they must not look to her to proclaim the sex of the royal child at the moment it was born; at such a time she must show 'neither joy nor disappointment', so as not to complicate the delivery. 'The King', she tells us 'replied that if it were a son, I would not say so quietly, but would shout it out as loudly as I could, and that there was no woman in the world who could keep silence in such circumstances.'[128] But Louise had her pride; she affirmed that she would be able to control herself, and when the time came, she kept her word.

Through the seventeenth and eighteenth centuries, the kingdom knew incessant anxiety over the future of the dynasty. The fear of having no heir was not new, in fact; Philip Augustus and Queen Isabella, Louis VIII and Blanche of Castille, Saint Louis and Margeret of Provence had, long ago, prayed loud and long to the Virgin for a son. But the recent memory of the extinction of the Valois remained vivid in the minds of the Bourbons, and circumstances several times reminded them of the frailty of lineages. The marriage of Louis XIII and Anne of Austria long remained barren; so, to a lesser degree, did that of Louis XVI and Marie Antionette; death struck again and again at the descendants of Henry IV and made them fear the worst.

PART III

The Woman Giving Birth

A young thing, scarcely come forth from the blood and the womb of its mother, still warm, asking only to blossom and flourish.

Jules Michelet

Birth is a break with the past. The child finds its way through the dark labyrinth of the womb and at last 'falls into the world'. It leaves its mother by passing through a symbolic circle. After the long drawn-out time of pregnancy, a time of hope and uncertainty, comes the short period of labour, a time of suffering and of deliverance for the mother and the child. The tree has nourished the fruit, which is now ready to drop away.

This separation was surrounded by an exceedingly elaborate ritual. Prior to the labour, laces and girdles were unfastened, ear and finger-rings taken off. To speed up the labour and help the action of gravity, the woman took up various positions. After the birth, the child was separated from its mother 'by the ceremonial severing of the umbilical cord'.

These rites of separation were completed by rites of accession to the group. The child was welcomed by the inhabitants of its new milieu, washed and put to the breast for the first time, which constituted its recognition as a 'human being'.

7

The Society of Birth

I think it good and reasonable that women should help each other with
their little traditional remedies, and that midwives should use their
experience and the dexterity they may have acquired.

Laurent Joubert, Popular errors, *1579*

In the last few decades, the almost universal practice of giving birth in hospital
has wrought a profound transformation in the circumstances of childbirth.
Women no longer give birth in the place where they live, and an ever more
refined technology has replaced the attentions of a familiar household. This
break with the old place and society of birth is the final outcome of a
development which began several centuries ago; it coincides with the disappearance of age-old values, a certain way of being and thinking, a system of
references which the industrial revolution first disturbed, then eliminated, but
without offering anything in their place.

A Place to be Born

Birth meant taking root. Between a man and the 'land which saw his birth' was
something resembling a blood relationship. People used to say of a countryman
that he was 'of such-and-such a village': this emphasized that the link was not
only between the community and the individual, but more fundamentally
between that earth which had belonged to his ancestors, the earth from which
he had sprung, and the individual himself.[1] The depth of this feeling allows us
to understand the sacredness of his native earth for a countryman, the love of
the migrant for 'his own country'. Men in former times attached a great deal of
importance to the exact spot where they were born: in the hamlet or the village;
in this house or that house; in this room, in this place.

The communal room

Normally, the birth took place in the woman's home, in the communal room. As
soon as the first contractions came, the womenfolk would hasten to stop up the

96

doors and windows, which had to remain tightly closed throughout the birth. For what they feared above all was a cold draught which might make the suffering woman shiver, and could even cause some flux. Cold was the mortal enemy of women in travail! They stirred up the fire and threw on some more logs: they had to be quick to create a warm, enclosed space where the woman would feel comfortable. Indeed, the atmosphere soon became suffocating in those low-ceilinged rural dwellings. Doctors in the late eighteenth century were critical of the 'suffocation method', which complicated labour and added to the woman's sufferings; thus they themselves would start by throwing the windows wide to let in a little fresh air, if they were summoned to the aid of a woman in difficulties.[2] These diametrically opposed kinds of behaviour are based on opposing conceptions of the development of labour.

It is not just fear of the cold which explains the shutting in of the woman in labour. Women greatly feared evil spells, and by tightly shutting all the exits, they thought they might save the child from the influence of some sorcerer or witch. At all costs they wanted to prevent the afterbirth and its attachments from being stolen away and later used to harm the baby. It is hard to be sure that this fear of sorcery was general, but it is at least to be found in a good many provinces. In nineteenth-century Alsace, for example, the moment of birth was considered 'very dangerous' for the child, because the devil, witches and the 'people of the waters' would try to hurt or even kill it, and its mother, so as to steal away their souls.[3] This is an amalgam of Christian and 'pagan' beliefs which were certainly very ancient, but remained alive almost within living memory. There was but one way of keeping off these evil spirits: to stop them entering the house where the confinement was taking place by bolting the doors. In the Sundgau region they even went as far as to caulk up any cracks in the doors to prevent a surprise attack. Thus the house was cut off from the world so that a human being could come into the world without trouble: the house became a womb, self-sufficient, kept free for a while from the evil designs of men and malevolent spirits.

The best place for the woman was actually before the hearth: very often she gave birth there, especially in icy weather. Straw was brought and scattered on the floor: it would absorb the excretions which accompanied the emerging child, and would then be burned. Exactly the same thing happened in the cowshed when a calf was born. If too much matter came forth, ashes from the nearby fire would be scattered over the floor of beaten earth, stone or brick, to soak it up. Poor people had their own way of cleaning up. And there was no floorcloth either: at best, in the nineteenth century, they would use an old sack to clean the tiling.

Between the ox and the ass

People were not always happy to foul up the living space where they lived. Convinced that blood shed during a birth was unlucky and that it would be dangerous to let it flow out in the communal room, they might try to find another harbour, especially if there were 'growing children' in the family whom they had not been able to send to stay with aunts or neighbours. Modesty thus drew the parents towards the only haven which offered both warmth and privacy: the stable. In any case, it might well have been the place where the child was conceived, since even at that stage the parents wanted to protect their children from the sight and sounds of their conjugal embraces. To give birth among the beasts – a questionable notion! For countryfolk in the seventeenth and eighteenth centuries it was as good a way as any to 'come into the world'. And when the village priest spoke to them of the birth of Jesus in the manger, between the ox and the ass, they didn't need to make any great effort of the imagination: it was a world familiar to them already. Their own.

Birth in a stable may well have been more frequent and persistent than is commonly thought. In Auvergne, one of the places where rural traditions lingered longest, it was 'common practice' in the nineteenth century. Even in 1906, in the Monts Dore region, 'some women, so as not to have to clean the house up, still give birth in the stable'.[4] At the same period, in other provinces, people who had more than one room used the kitchen as 'the place to give birth': it was, indeed, more practical than the bedroom, with its stove, its 'spring' of hot water, the sink to clean up and, last but not least, the table which could serve for the 'childbed'.

Born in the fields

Sometimes there was no roof over her head at all. Many country women used to work hard up to the last moment and some felt their first pains come upon them at the washplace,[5] or away in the fields and meadows. Perhaps the contractions were brief and the birth so swift that they had no time or strength to get home. In the eighteenth and nineteenth centuries priests and doctors report with surprise examples of 'child-shedders' who gave birth in the fields or by the roadside. In a book published in 1837, Doctor Munaret tells that he has 'known three of them who were taken with the first pains as they were walking along, and who bore away in their aprons the impatient fruit of their love'.[6] The stereotyped image of the healthy countrywoman, strong in the face of pain, sometimes prevented practitioners from grasping the pain, anguish and deprivation which lay behind such cases. Singular and isolated cases? But there are certain situations which tell us a good deal about the behaviour of the mothers. They sometimes voluntarily took the risk of giving birth in the fields: the realities of life meant that one did not 'look after oneself' much in the countryside. At Sainte-Gemme, in the Charente region, as late as the beginning of this century, a woman was working in the beet-field right at the end of her pregnancy: it had not made her let up on her work, only she took with her into the fields 'in her pocket, a pair of scissors and a reel of thread . . . then, in the evening, she came back with a new baby perched in her wheelbarrow on top of the beets. All her children were born in that way,' concludes the narrator.[7] A scene worthy of a genre painter such as Millet. Following the rhythm of the earth . . . .

Feminine Solidarity

The conditions under which childbirth took place ranged so widely among the different regions and milieux that it would be rash to attempt to create a model of childbirth for the France of olden times. However, there are some similarities and constants, and developments become perceptible over a long period.

The circle of women around the one in travail was one of these constants. One does come across the occasional solitary labour, and it did happen at times that only the husband was there to help; but that was not the general rule, because childbirth was women's business. Usually it was female relatives, neighbours or friends who surrounded the woman in labour: the birth was a public event.

A swirl in the hive

As soon as the first symptoms of labour were revealed, the women appeared at a run. A labouring woman needed help. Even when 'Nature was at work', when everything went as it should, there were mundane tasks to be done: keeping the fire up, drawing water and heating it, holding the woman down later if necessary, then washing, sponging, drying linen before the hearth, looking after the child, preparing a cordial or broth . . .. Spontaneously the women got organized, with the mother, mother-in-law or aunt taking the leading role, as was to be expected.

This material aid was much appreciated: women had no other resources to hand except what the community could provide. For centuries the idea of calling on outside help was totally alien to the minds of the village women. They 'got by' on their own. And the same applied to any activity, starting with the work in the fields, especially at harvest time, when for a few weeks all hands were at work with one accord. Why should the harvest of new human beings have been an exception to the rule?

'Women helping one another' or 'mutual assistance' are words which recur constantly in the writings of priests and administrators of the eighteenth century reporting on childbirth in the countryside. The inquiry into 'Midwives in the Kingdom', conducted in 1786 to discover the nature of the assistance which village women had at the time, shows clearly that whole regions had no other way of doing things: the remotest areas of the Dauphiné, Limousin and the Pyrenees, the lowlands of the Sologne and the Landes, the meadowlands of Brittany: everywhere, that is to say, where the local midwife did not, as a rule, yet exist. Which did not stop this kind of elementary assistance from continuing, on this eve of the French Revolution, in the provinces which seemed to be best supplied with midwives and obstetricians.

It was only natural to help a neighbour through her confinement. One day soon, one would need her help in one's turn. But if that was the only reason, what a shameful example of self-interest! In reality such things came from the heart. Bonds forged day by day, at the communal well or the washplace, at the communal bakehouse while one was waiting one's turn to do the baking, created a feminine solidarity which came out at the crises of life: the early death of a friend whose last-born one would take in, or, as here, the birth of a child. And the woman in labour would not understand it, or would consider it a grave dereliction of duty, if a relative or near neighbour failed to come and show her sympathy, bringing aid and comfort.

Normally four, five or six people would be present. Sometimes more, if there were complications, if the labour were prolonged. An unnatural presentation would baffle the wisest assembly: pity for the woman languishing for days in childbed, prayers, nothing helped. A part of the female population of the village would then process through the chamber which already 'was like a morgue'. Every woman would have a word to say, recalling – but without telling the sufferer – such and such a labour which, in similar circumstances, had ended tragically in the past. Above all, each had her own experience to fall back on: for, without doubt, this assemblage was an assemblage of married women who had borne children. It would not be thought proper for an unmarried girl to intrude into this gathering: the community's moral code imposed a significant divide in these circumstances.

Even ordinarily, when labour was progressing normally, a strange atmosphere would pervade the house. The coming and going of the women turned the room of the confinement into a buzzing hive. But there were meaningful swirls in this hive; everything spun round the mother-to-be: periods of tension and relaxation, pains and interludes, cries and whisperings, determined the rhythm of time as the confinement progressed. For those with ears to hear, a lot of talking went on as well. The Word was sovereign over all.

The seventeenth-century *Chitchat of the New Mother* is a sort of literary echo of this real-life phenomenon.[8] The anonymous author is writing for men, and he sees in woman an immeasurable degree of agitation and garrulousness, Indeed, this pamphlet, with its antifeminist tone, was a contribution to the contemporary campaign against midwives, against the circle of women present at the birth, against all those who clucked away like hens in a farmyard, against the 'gossips' who were supposed to assist the mother but could do nothing but talk. It was, above all, the practitioners of early modern times who inveighed against the excessively large number of bystanders. They thought all that noise and disturbance was intolerable: calm, they said, was vital to the satisfactory progress of the confinement. And their first instinct, when brought in, was to get rid of all those whose presence was not considered indispensable. Everything comes to a head in this difference of opinion over the value of the female presence. Behind the two attitudes there is a clash of two ways of doing things, two ethics, two cultures.

True: the woman in travail herself, amidst all those women, could be torn between contradictory desires. Often she really needed the presence of friends who helped her in her agony; but not all of them had the tact and self-control which were proper in such circumstances. A whisper could be as pernicious as a harsh or disobliging remark: it could well cause panic in a woman who would always be fearing the worst.[9] The most important thing, indeed, was to avoid frightening her. It was better to 'talk to her of pleasant things', as Madame du

Coudray declared, to encourge her, to tell her that everything was going well. If, for one reason or another, the child was slow to appear, the women present should be careful not to suggest any outside help! 'There are those,' says Louise Bourgeois emphatically, 'who, suffering in childbed, if it is not their own idea to call in the doctors, and one speaks to them of it, will take such a fright, that they think that their life is in danger.'[10] Calling on outside help only slowed the labour still further by its pyschological effect on the woman. And there should be no talk about 'forceps' either, because a mere mention of them made the woman's world rock on its foundations and triggered a panic reaction.

Labour was an act demanding modesty and secrecy. If the woman needed some comfort, it could distress her to be stared at and overheard by all those women who were none of her choice. Some presences were indeed undesirable: the 'nasty neighbour', for example, drawn by mere curiosity; the mother-in-law; or, more astonishingly, a close friend. In 1698 La Motte was called to help a woman whose labour had begun well.

One of her neighbours, seemingly a good friend of hers, had come to visit her and entered unceremoniously into her room to offer her help; but on this occasion, the services of this good friend were ill-received by the suffering woman, though she did not dare explain why either to me or to the others present; after which the pains ceased.

As it was getting late, the obstetrician advised all the women to go to bed and said that he would let them know if anything changed. 'Which happened a moment after the neighbour had gone to bed. But the sufferer, far from allowing us to go and rouse her, seemed very annoyed that she had come without being asked. In a short time I delivered her of a fine boy.'[11]

There are some strange kinds of behaviour, whose motives remain deeply buried . . ..

And what about the father?

The man was not always absent. For obvious reasons initially, if a couple lived in a lonely spot, the husband naturally came to the aid of his wife. This happened frequently where the population was scattered, but also in areas of more nucleated villages if the farm was far from the centre of the parish, and so from all nearby female help; the husband could not leave his wife to go for help and leave her to the danger of having the baby all alone during his absence.

His presence was considered indispensable when the labour turned out to be difficult, not so much to comfort his wife as to help bring forth the child: as the ethnologist Françoise Loux has rightly remarked, his strength was needed to hold up the wife.[12] This was in fact recommended, from the beginning of the eighteenth century, by some obstetricians, including Mauquest de La Motte, when it was a case of delivering a dead baby or performing a caesarean.

Finally, it was often the husband who carried his wife from the straw mattress on which the birth had taken place back to the conjugal bed; it is true that in that case he was called upon only when all was over. As a rule, the man's presence was unusual and not much desired. And in many cases, his presence indicated a particularly hard labour, even a fatal one: it was not a good sign.

Things may have changed, however, in the nineteenth century, a period for which we have more information, and in which the man was more often present. Perhaps this increased frequency meant that families were falling back on their own resources and that medical control was increasing, with the doctor and midwife preferring to be aided by the husband rather than the neighbours. However that may be, in early nineteenth-century Brittany, Alexandre Bouet tells us that 'no-one is admitted to the sanctuary of maternity except the father, the midwife and a few special female acquaintances'.[13]

However, even if he got no further than the doorway, the father was not inactive: he had his part to play. He would go for help if necessary; he would go and fetch water if asked; he would go and rouse up another midwife, or – in the eighteenth and especially the nineteenth century – he would go for the doctor in the nearest town. When people were really at their wits' end, when the woman's state was so bad that they feared for her life, it would again be the husband who would go and hammer on the presbytery door, and bring the priest hastening to administer the last rites.

It is not surprising if the husband was generally excluded from the place of birth. Giving birth is women's business. A countryman would immediately perceive his own uselessness if his wife started to scream, or, worse, if she had been stripped half-naked before the onlookers, so that the labour could be monitored more easily, giving them a view of her private parts. Such situations inevitably caused mutual embarrassment at a time when the expression of feelings, especially 'at a moment like that', was still narrowly restricted by modesty. The presence of the man at the birth, traditional in other cultures, was not popular in Western Europe in the modern period. With one exception, admittedly an important one: the king of France was always present at the confinement of the queen.

Tasks were, in fact, shared out, so to speak, in a village, where relationships were often more subtle than is generally thought. While women took on the most important tasks during a confinement, it was the men who took over when farm animals were concerned: the birth of a calf or lamb was men's business. Doctor Brieude, discussing stock-rearing on the plains of the Auvergne in 1785, noted that 'almost all the cowmen on the big farms have of necessity acquired some ideas about birth: if they see that the animal is in difficulties they smear their arms with oil, butter or grease and rotate the foetus in the womb'.[14] Within the family and in rural society, where there seemed to be a chaotic confusion of roles which was repellent to the superficial judgement of urban minds in the eighteenth and nineteenth centuries, there existed 'of necessity' (as Brieude has it) a certain distribution of tasks which ensured that that society continued to function. The women took care of newborn babies; the men were more inclined to look after the increase of their flocks and herds.

However, such arrangements did not preclude 'exchanges' in both directions, from humans to animals and vice versa. Thus a woman 'animal doctor' accustomed to calvings became obstetrician to a community in the Laon area in the latter half of the eighteenth century. In the nineteenth century, the blacksmith, that repository of secrets, was equally capable of birthing the village livestock and of symbolically 'hammering' women in childbed. For countryfolk accustomed to live at close quarters with their animals, such activities were perfectly natural. Nor was there any reason for enlightened spirits of the eighteenth century to be shocked at such things, seeing that they had set up a course in birthing techniques at the veterinary school at Alfort which were intended for animal doctors – but if the occasion offered, they would also be able to lend assistance to peasant women in difficulties! A confusion of roles which was not, in fact, to last long, because the young vets preferred to become obstetricians for the sake of the reputation and money which this career offered, rather than tending the animals.[15]

The 'Good Mother'

Among all those women who came running, when summoned, to attend their sister in distress, there was often one who showed greater patience and dexterity, and whose advice was more readily followed. Having had a chance successfully to show off her skill at a difficult confinement, she would be adopted by the women as their recognized midwife: she had become the 'good mother'. Confidence would be gained at the first confinement at which she offered her services.

The priest sometimes encouraged these favourable impressions and lent his support to a dawning vocation. In 1772 the priest of Vouzy, in Champagne, wrote: 'There is a woman of thirty-two, named Marie Cellier, wife of Pierre Bare, who has already attended several confinements with the intention of taking up the profession, for which she seems to me to have some ability.'[16]

Thus it is an easy step from mutual assistance to the idea of the village midwife: she represented the security and comfort which every woman would need when she went into labour. But this 'function' was not, alas, guaranteed for ever. A few years later the midwife might die and force the women to rely on one another again until another appeared whom they could trust, and who would in her turn take on the responsibilities of the village midwife.

This role sometimes passed from mother to daughter. At Lapeirouse, in the subdelegation of Toulouse, in 1786, there was a midwife called Antoinette Martin, married to a domestic servant, who 'learned her trade from no-one other than her late mother'; and at La Madeleine there were two women doing the job, of whom one 'had learned everything she knew from a sister she had', while the other, who had years of experience, was starting to train her daughter, 'who has some ability, following the precepts of her mother'.[17] The daughter followed the mother wherever she went and assisted her until she retired through old age, when the daughter carried on alone. In other cases, the ageing midwife adopted a 'helper' who would carry on after her. In Languedoc she was called the *servicial*: she made the necessary preparations for the birth, heated the water, made the bed ready, and if necessary helped the midwife at a difficult labour; and it was she who would come to give the necessary care to mother and child after the birth.[18] From the sixteenth century, around Dijon, the same function was performed by a *chambérière*.

Thus the training of such women was purely empirical, as it would be for a son learning to plough from his father, or for a daughter advised by her mother on how to cook and keep house. These midwives had no book learning at all: 'They are the kind of women who become midwives in villages without ever having learned anything of the art,' as an eighteenth-century administrator pointed out; 'they have seen women give birth and they help them, and that is all.'[19] They were content to pass on their 'ways of doing things', their 'little secrets', so much despised by surgeons and priests.

So who is the midwife?

Certainly not a virgin! A virgin midwife would cause a scandal in the community; in any case the women, one and all, would reject her services. The obstetrician Pierre Dionis thought that propriety was against it: 'It would scarcely be fitting in a virgin to undertake to help others give birth, since she must be wholly ignorant of all that is required to make a child.'[20] And the priest of Saint-Aubin de Vitrezai, near Bordeaux, called on both decency and custom when he wrote in 1782: 'In the countryside, no virgin practises this profession: it is not even decent for them. Only aged women and widows undertake it.'[21]

Up to 1770, or 1780 in some provinces, it was married women who qualified; then some development took place under the influence of the nearby towns,[22] but slowly and reluctantly: the daughter of the old midwife could take her place after her death. She was well known; she had been seen with her mother. And after all, women did need help! It was often in this way that a gradual change took place, at the end of the eighteenth century. But not everywhere did one find the same tolerance. Some communities could find it very hard to make the choice, 'as if it were necessary to have felt the pain of childbirth before one was equipped to mitigate it for others, or preserve them from it'.[23]

However, that was still very much the feeling in the countryside. Normally, the women chose the midwife from among those who had the largest number of children, 'because that implies more experience'. A woman who had negotiated several confinements without major upsets must be capable of dealing with other births in her turn. In a village near Fère-en-Tardenois, in 1772, all the women were accustomed to trust in a midwife aged seventy-two, who 'learned her skill by delivering herself of the twelve children she has had'.[24] The midwife's sole qualification was her own fertility.

This makes it rather astonishing that so many midwives had no children of their own; being barren, they did not know what pregnancy was like, nor had they suffered in their own flesh the pains of childbirth. Why this apparent contradiction?

The image of the ideal midwife

The local woman would think that to be efficient, the midwife must have no other commitments; she was expected to be skilful, but also 'very punctilious in her affairs', and come without delay when she was called. They therefore preferred the midwife to be free from confinements on her own account; not to have children, or at least not to have any still with her, especially children of tender years, who would reduce her availability. In 1775, in Rioz (Franche-Comté), the women turned down a person who wished to become the midwife, because 'being liable herself to bear children, she could not give aid to those who would need it during that time'.[25]

The image of the midwife as the mother of a large family who had become a poor woman living on public charity is quite close to reality, an impression confirmed by the statistical survey on midwives conducted throughout the realm in 1786. Only one in five was under sixty, and two out of five were older. True, one can perceive regional variations, which depend on the conditions of entry upon this function. In Lorraine, for instance, where the midwife was elected by all the local women, they took very good care that she should be free of other commitments. Therefore an old woman was deliberately selected, as was also the case in the Soissons area, though there she was not elected. In the Lyon area and in Provence they were not so particular, and it was not uncommon for midwives to take up their duties at between twenty-five and thirty-five years of age. Were people there less interested in the proof of fertility which northern regions demanded of their midwives? Or did they think that a young midwife, even cluttered with children, was preferable – if she was capable – to a midwife who might be too old to get about easily? While regional variations are perceptible, it is none the less true that within a single province there were still wide-ranging differences, for a very simple reason: a community accustomed to being able to call on a midwife sometimes counted itself lucky to get the services of any woman who offered, whatever her age and circumstances: needs must . . ..[26]

In fact, women would accept a young midwife, a married woman with children, so long as she was resolute and self-assured, basing her assurance on experience, 'so that she would not be taken aback by the various kinds of labour'. The confidence inspired by the midwife was vital, the foundation of her legitimacy, the key word which was constantly heard on women's lips. And if it happened that the priest tried to stop the old midwife doing her job so as to bring in a new one, more devoted to himself, it was because of that 'confidence' that the women would refuse to change – for 'confidence cannot be imposed'.

A good midwife was reassuring and put people at their ease. She knew how to make the right gestures; she said words of comfort and encouragement which the woman found helpful. Though she might not always succeed, she had a sense of proportion; and the fact that she herself had borne many children no doubt helped her to take the meaning of a look or a moan. She kept company and delivered: it is not by coincidence that one of the French words for midwife is *sage-femme*, 'wise woman'.

The midwife was expected to have the physical build necessary for the work: she had to be strong, 'sturdy', 'nimble', 'graceful, with no bodily defects, with long supple hands'. But 'the spiritual side' was no less important. She should be 'virtuous, discreet, prudent, of good conduct and regular habits', 'zealous, mild and charitable'. Such was the ideal midwife – but the reality was sometimes far different.

The midwife's was a thankless task. In rural society, money was scarce and used almost exclusively for paying taxes and for indispensable purchases at the local market; it was not customary, until the eighteenth century, to give that 'small coin' which would recompense her for the sleepless nights and the exhaustion caused by her difficult work.

Charitable assistance

Everyone saw this as help given through charity, a function quite untouched by monetary transactions. This did not in the least mean that no-one ever showed the 'good mother' any gratitude – on the contrary. But this gratitude was shown only within a framework of symbolical interchanges. The remuneration – if any – would be in kind. A midwife who had spent hours saving mother and baby would enjoy the hospitality of the house during the three or four critical days of the confinement. She ate with the family, and if she was far from home, she was offered a bed for the night. She would also get a present, a 'gift in return': a capon, some eggs, some bread or a cake, or perhaps, in wooded regions like Lorraine, some firewood or faggots.

Of course, a lot depended on the prosperity of the household: in principle the midwife would get more from a rich farmer than a poor workman, especially in the lean period just before harvest. Thus it was often only 'the most comfortably off' who gave anything. In some very poor households it might even be the midwife who gave or lent the small bundle of linen which was indispensable for the new baby![27] Taking the good with the bad, these gifts would just about allow the midwife to make a living: 'they have a good deal of hard work for little reward', as the priest of Pancré (Lorraine) wrote in 1786. But what did that matter? For many of them, all that mattered was to help women in their travail. A charitable soul looks for no reward.

In the eighteenth century there were some notable changes of attitude, here and there, amongst village midwives. The development of courses in midwifery organized by intendants or bishops in the latter half of the century probably had something to do with it: since trained midwives expected to be paid in money and 'make a living from their profession', why should not some of their village counterparts have been tempted to follow suit? The diversity of attitudes is scarcely surprising in the circumstances. In the 1780s, in the subdelegation of Uzès (Languedoc), most of the midwives kept their traditional attitudes: the parish of Castelnaud, for example, had three midwives who 'are proud to say how disinterested they are, demanding no kind of reward for their services', while, at the same time, not far away in Saint-Dézéry, the three midwives 'flatly refused to help women who have not the means to pay the salary which they require for their work'.[28] These indications of a real change in attitude are perceptible above all near the towns, whence a stream of medical professionalism was flowing forth into the countryside. It was a whole attitude of mind which was changing; the village midwives would hold out for a long time yet against competition from the obstetrician or the professional midwife, but they themselves would begin to show a mercenary spirit which had for long been absent from their activities.

A miserable and downgraded task

The attitude of village women to their midwife was contradictory: they wanted her to be punctual and resolute, but at the same time, for reasons already explained, they often chose a quite elderly woman for the task. And her job was by no means always an easy one! She had to be available at any hour of the day and night, in all weathers, willingly facing bitter cold or intense heat, bad roads and dangerous encounters – with animals or men – to succour a woman in need. And quickly, always quickly – even if she risked breaking her neck! Elisabeth Tarche, from Ménil-en-Xaintois near Mirecourt, could tell a tale about that: a workman's widow of over seventy, she fell victim to her own devotion, 'having had the misfortune to fall over a slippery bridge in the dark, during a period of freezing winter cold, and break her arm in pursuit of her duties, having been called out in haste to help a woman in labour'.[29]

In such circumstances it was hardly surprising if people were reluctant to become midwives, and the job was greatly despised in country districts. It was such a thankless task that even the most avowedly competent ones often gave it up. One had to live; times were always hard; childbirth always monopolized the attention of women who had 'their own families to look after' and also had to give some solid help in the fields.

But, on a deeper level, what forced people out was the bad reputation of the job. From time immemorial it had been viewed with distaste. Astonishingly, even at the end of the eighteenth century there were members of the medical profession who were infected with such an attitude, such as a certain practitioner of Limoges who saw birth as 'the most filthy and lowly part of surgery'. Expressions which occur again and again in writings of priests and administrators, and which also express the feeling of people as a whole, bear witness to this dislike. It was a 'job which brings nothing but poverty and opprobrium in its train' (Castres); a 'discredited profession, the vilest of trades' (Craponne); 'the last of all the professions' (Ginal, Montauban election); and since 'all feel aversion for this task' (Branne, Bordeaux region), it was left to paupers at the bottom of the social ladder ('the higher sort find it demeaning'), to those who had nothing to lose and hoped they might have something to gain! Everyone agreed on the importance of the midwife's job, but nobody wanted to do it – for the sake of their reputation.

Should we perhaps connect this repugnance with regard to childbirth to the 'bad blood' which issued forth at such times and which, as everyone knew, was 'impure and corrosive', like menstrual blood? Did not everyone know that dogs who drank it died? Was it not the very symbol of the newly delivered woman? The idea was reinforced by the attitude of the Church, which kept up the purifying ceremony of churching until the nineteenth century. The absolute need for help in childbirth and the reprobation attached to the job put midwives in a permanently ambiguous situation. A midwife was not always treated with consideration just because she was a poor widow. And indeed, in the eighteenth century, the prosperous farmer and the squire called on her less and less for their own wives' confinements; whenever possible they turned to a professional midwife or a surgeon–obstetrician. But these were exceptions, for the village midwife continued to enjoy the confidence of most of the local women, who were not insensible to her devotion.

Midwives of town and country

(1)   In June 1666, the surgeon–obstetrician Paul Portal was called to the Rue Montorgueil to assist a woman, herself a midwife, who was afraid she was having a miscarriage. 'She had examined herself and her fingers had found only a rough surface'; indeed, the baby was dead and the obstetrician had to remove it piece by piece; 'the stench was so great', he adds, 'that I thought I should choke'. A long, taxing labour, in which the woman co-operated, and which, against all expectations, turned out well.

Like most midwives in the capital at this time, the woman had probably got some training by 'following an instructing professional midwife for two years,' but perhaps she had had the good fortune to attend a clinical course at the maternity hospital of the Hôtel-Dieu. A rare privilege if so! Once approved, she started to work in the district where she lived. In March 1666, when she was about thirty and had already built up a good practice, her husband died suddenly; this 'great misfortune' had a bad effect on her pregnancy and caused the death of her baby. She was left a widow with five young children to bring up. And she had only her profession.

Portal, fearing gangrene in the womb, told her as he was leaving to 'listen to her conscience'; but she had no time to listen to it, for

a lady in the palace of the Louvre sent for her to help her in childbirth. She went without taking any thought for what she had just suffered, about three hours before. She left her bed as if there was nothing wrong with her, and went on foot to help the lady for whom she had been called. She spent the night there and only came home the next day.

Twenty-four hours after the delivery, Portal called to see her: 'I found her in bed', he says, 'dining with the whole family on a calf's head.' When he heard about the previous day's escapade he scolded her, but she replied that 'what God had in His keeping was well kept and that hunger often brought the wolf from the wood'. 'I understood from that,' Portal adds, 'that it was necessity which had pushed her to this step.'[30]

(2)   In 1786, Marie Milliard, widow of Jean-Dominique Chapot, village midwife in Dombasle-en-Xaintois near Mirecourt, was fifty-two years of age. Her training had been exclusively practical: 'She was shown things only by the midwife (a village one like herself) who had preceded her.' The latter, having reached an advanced age, had asked to give up, and the local woman had agreed that Marie should take over. This was in 1776; two years later, the priest of Dombasle told her that a professional midwife from Paris was going to teach a course for country midwives at Neufchâteau. Marie Milliard would have been more than willing to go, but, alas, she had 'seven little children to bring up'!

She had a good reputation in the parish; she was said to work with a good deal of prudence, gentleness, vigilance and cleanliness. Marie thought she was very lucky: 'up till now, no labour has ended badly in my hands'; but it must be acknowledged that she did not hesitate to 'call in a surgeon–obstetrician when she thought the case demanded it'.

At present she was fairly satisfied with her job; she enjoyed a certain amount of authority among the women. Her trade brought her a few recompenses in kind, wood for the cold season, some soup, fruit, a bit of lard; a few wealthy families would give her 24 sous for a confinement and a few more when the child was christened. After fifteen days, as was the custom in Lorraine, she would accompany the mother when she went to be churched and would then receive a little present. These few incomings from her trade just allowed her to live from year to year. It was such a hard life! 'Sometimes she has to pass several days and nights with a woman approaching her confinement, sometimes without being offered as much as a piece of bread. Besides, she has to go for three consecutive days to look after mother and baby, and often for longer if the mother is not well.' If she had not much to live on, it was also because her man had died five years ago. Her 'five daughters, lace-makers, quite young', lived under her roof.

Marie Milliard had certainly thought of 'going somewhere else to learn a little' – for example, to Mirecourt, where a surgeon–obstetrician was giving lessons – but 'it is impossible for her to leave her house and leave her daughters without any guidance'. Nevertheless she would 'continue to do her best, as long as her legs will carry her.'[31]

A power in the community

Thus it was not surprising if people were infinitely grateful to the midwife and attached to her, and did not want to change. Some midwives carried on although they were blind; others, bent double with rheumatism or even paralysed, had themselves carried to the labouring woman's house to give advice and reassure the assembly by their presence.

Everyone in the community revered and feared the midwife. Everybody knew her and she knew everybody.

In Paris they do not realize that the good mother receives as much consideration in our remoter villages, where the best standards of behaviour are still maintained, as the Vestals did in Rome. She is not called "Madame" – seldom, at any rate – but neither is she ever called by her name or her husband's: she is the 'good mother', and this title is enough to attract an affectionate veneration.[32]

Despite its somewhat grandiloquent style, this text by Rétif de La Bretonne (end of the eighteenth century) clearly shows the consideration which the old midwife still received in the countryside. 'Good mother', 'wise woman', 'wise mother' or 'mother midwife', the name by which she was known, and which varied from place to place, conveys the respect in which she was held.

Even the men had some respect for her empirical knowledge: they expected her to deliver their wives from their perilous situation and to present them with well-formed and viable offspring. Moreover, they would not hesitate to complain bitterly about a midwife whose knowledge was all empty boasting; or, especially, of one who injured their wives by ill-considered interference, lacerated their private parts, were incapable of protecting the 'secret part' and returned them to their husbands as something less than true women.[33]

It could happen that a midwife profited from her good position in the community, or even abused it. A few years before the French Revolution there was at Cazejourdes, near La Couvertoirade on the Larzac, a midwife who, according to the local priest, behaved in a scandalous manner: 'capriciousness and vengefulness influence her conduct. She is quite capable of leaving women without any help'. Probably an extreme case – but revealing.

The midwife's role did not always stop short at the birth: where local custom did not include the use of nurses it was she (and her assistant) who would care for mother and baby in the days following the birth. She would come once or twice a day to make sure that the new baby was suckling well and that the mother's lochia were coming away satisfactorily. She could cure milk fever and take care of yellow-gum disease in the infant. She also went in for gynaecology: she could take care of a prolapsed uterus; she was sometimes called out for 'women's diseases'. Françoise Bonnard, of Tavers near Beaugency, did the job for ten years to the satisfaction of all; she was still bright and alert at sixty: 'people come for her from neighbouring parishes because she knows what to do about breast troubles and others'.[34] The midwife at Neuville-les-Raon, near Saint-Dié, 'can cure ruptures and hernias in children'.[35]

This habit of giving medical attention meant that midwives were called upon for all sorts of maladies which had nothing to do with their profession: even men consulted them. They then came into competition with medical practitioners and were denounced by some as 'folk healers' or 'peddlers of false secrets'.

This very varied activity could not but give the midwife an important social role. She brought to birth and nursed a number of the inhabitants; she also attended to the laying out of the dead. This was an old ritual, but as the task was found repugnant by most people, it was often (as at Minot in the nineteenth century) 'the helping woman' who took it on.[36] By presiding at births and preparing people for their last journey, the midwife held both ends of the thread of life. Most certainly such a role made her position unique.

But the real source of the midwife's strength was her domination over the women as a group: as we have seen, her influence over them was considerable. Bereft of self-expression, with little say in community decisions (which were the men's prerogative), women became themselves at a birth, grouped round the midwife. Her quasi-magical powers were all the greater in that locally the art of bringing to birth, with all its symbolic implications of oral wisdom and almost proverbial manual dexterity, was transmitted from mother to daughter within a single family.

Women closed ranks round the midwife, who, from the seventeenth century onward, after the Council of Trent, became the symbol of resistance to a kind of morality, a regulation of life, which people were attempting to impose on them from the outside. Since the sixteenth century, in the first great wave of witch-hunts, midwives had been one of the favourite targets of the inquisitors: quite a number of midwives-cum-witches, or midwives-cum-fortune-tellers or spellworkers, had gone to the stake. From the second half of the sixteenth century, the Church kept a close and incessant check on their behaviour at a birth, pressuring them into learning the formula for baptism *in extremis* and swearing oaths of loyalty, trying to discredit those 'sayers of spells', those 'sorceresses' who belonged to the 'dregs of society'. The need to extirpate practices whose symbolic character all too often had an aftertaste of paganism was becoming an obsession. What a priest might learn, often by chance, about the process of birth only too often confirmed him in that opinion.

8

Hastening the Hour of Deliverance

I have never brought any woman to birth in her bed, unless I was absolutely forced to do so by some urgent need.

Mauquest de La Motte, eighteenth-century obstetrician

In times past, preparations for a confinement were minimal: little or nothing was made ready, improvization was the rule. But if the material preparations were lacking, a profusion of symbolic protective rites made up for it – sometimes the same rites as in pregnancy. The woman put all her trust in these topical remedies, which helped her to overcome anxiety, discouragement and pain. For fear would seize her along with the first contractions: the fear of never bringing the child to birth. Also she was allowed to choose her position: she should have full freedom of body and mind so that the hour of deliverance might come – and, always, the sooner the better.

Preparing for the Confinement

This differed according to the area and the milieu. The pauper, stripped of everything, giving birth in a miserable hovel in the country, had nothing whatever in common with the 'lady of quality' comfortably installed in a nice room with a fire, who had sent for a box from Paris well supplied with 'compresses, bandages, draw sheets, hot cloths and other waxed cloths for the stomach and the breasts'.

The slight increase in prosperity which slowly spread into northern France in the second half of the eighteenth century, and especially in the nineteenth, did bring about an improvement, sometimes a very noticeable improvement, in the material conditions of birth which had prevailed since time immemorial in the rural areas. Until then the means at their disposal were very limited. There were a few everyday objects, better known to us from funeral inventories and obstetricians' notes than from the excessively stereotyped iconography of the 'Nativity': the household cauldron to 'take the chill off' the water needed to wash mother and child; a few old cloths, some rags to wipe the woman's thighs and clean the floor afterwards; a mattress before the fire, a 'square' – a cushion – which would be slipped under the woman's loins or thighs to make her more comfortable; a sheet to protect her from cold and prying eyes; linen, not new and therefore softer, for the delicate skin of the new baby. Add a chair for the

112

woman in labour to lean on during the contraction and expulsion phases, and the conjugal bed where the woman would be laid – *after* the birth; one or two bales of hay from the shed to strew the floor. Unhappily, all too often the finishing touch would often be given by the hook used to hang up a cooking-pot, a fire-iron or a set of scales: metal was scarce and expensive and if something was needed to drag out a baby which was dead or stuck, then – people used what lay to hand!

The equipment brought by the midwife was also very scanty: a pair of scissors or a sharp knife for cutting the cord, a linen thread to make the ligature.

But was that not enough, provided the labour went well? At the end of the eighteenth century, Madame du Coudray was advising nothing more for the midwife than to have ready 'two strings made of three or four-ply thread; these strings will be required to tie the cord . . .. To cut it, only blunt-ended or rounded scissors should be used, since pointed scissors can cause injury.'[1] Some midwives added to this necessary minimum a little vinegar, in which they would soak a 'bung' to put 'at the mouth of the womb' in case of haemorrhage. Very few had a probe in case of urine retention, because to acquire such a thing they would have had to go to a town. A midwife would probably add a phial of holy water for emergency baptism and some unguent whose secret was known only to her, and which she would use if there were complications.

The professional midwife's kit, if it conformed to the recommendations of surgeon–demonstrators on obstetrics courses in the later eighteenth century, was somewhat more substantial. It would contain a small amount of equipment for internal interventions, but not usually any kind of 'drug'. Probably for fear that the midwife might use it wrongly. However, even local midwives could get hold of drugs if necessary; and through the eighteenth century the quite frequent use of rye ergot to hasten labour was often criticized by doctors.

Instruments which a trained midwife must have
Cambrai district, 1788

syringe for enemas

smaller syringe for injections in the womb, if necessary

a few skeins of thread for ligatures[2]

Portable midwife's kit
Castres region, 1786

syringe for enemas and spare canula for injections

algalia – a hollow silver tube for emptying the bladder

a small syringe for the baptism

a canula tube for blowing air into the chest

two small bottles, one containing a few pinches of ipecacuanha, the other some kermes mineral[3]

All these instruments, which would be lent to the professional midwife for the duration of her activities, would mean nothing to the village midwife. What could she have done with them? This aura of medical professionalism was alien to her. But while the material helps used in labour were scanty indeed, the products of animal or vegetable origin were correspondingly varied and abundant.

A rich pharmacopoeia

Nature furnished all these products, in any quantity, and everyone in the village was more or less acquainted with the virtues of simples. As an infusion or a poultice, to hasten the contractions or ensure a rapid expulsion of the afterbirth, to stop a haemorrhage or cure after-pains, local-growing plants, oils and greases from animals, were in common use. The food, drink and condiments which would be administered to the woman in labour were constantly to hand.

From province to province, different 'specialities' were known: for instance, various fats, used to lubricate the woman's private parts and the midwife's hands. Regional variations in culinary customs meant that 'melted unsalted butter' was used in the Ile de France, Normandy and Lorraine, walnut oil in Aquitaine, olive oil in Provence and Languedoc, animal fats and lard in northern and central France (Berry, Auvergne and Limousin).

Very popular everywhere were honey, to sweeten drinks and restore energy, garlic and onion to 'revive the spirits and encourage dilatation'. Wine was also frequently used: in regions where no wine was produced (such as Picardy and Normandy), or was scarcer and more expensive, it was kept for great occasions, of which a birth was one. Was there some urgent need for a condiment which was not available? Someone would quickly fulfil it: generosity was easily prompted at those difficult moments and every woman considered it her duty, and a matter of pride, to offer what she had to hasten the labour and for the relief of her neighbour.

The eighteenth century saw important changes in the obstetric pharmacopoeia. They came first to the towns; but, carried by country surgeons and other quacks, certain 'drugs' were not long in appearing in country districts. The products of dubious dispensaries entered into competition with herbal medicines. Borax, laudanum and other narcotics, spirit of hartshorn, liquorice water, Carmelite water or Queen-of-Hungary's water, had travelled a long way into the countryside of north-west France by the beginning of the eighteenth century. La Motte could not find language strong enough to condemn abuse of them: he shows, with examples, the ravages of these 'degrading drugs' amongst newly delivered mothers.[4]

The great upsurge in colonial trade in the latter half of the century favoured the spread of new products known as 'pick-me-ups' or febrifuges, which were supposed to help in difficult labours. Coming through Marseilles, Bordeaux, Nantes or Le Havre, coffee, cocoa, ipecacuanha and cinnamon spread through cities, towns and finally villages. Pointe, a doctor of medicine from Lyon, states in the *Gazette de Santé* of 1780 that coffee was commonly used in several cantons of Languedoc and Provence.[5] This is confirmed by the inquiry into midwives of 1786. The Lyon region, in its turn, was beginning to be affected by this 'new fashion'. The consumption, even on a small scale, of these luxury items in the countryside raises a good many questions; in particular, how could villagers living in such poverty get hold of such costly products? Why this change of attitude towards the herbs which their native soil had been providing hitherto? Were not the wife, in her wish to 'save herself in her labour', and the husband, in his desire to save his helpmeet, committing themselves henceforward to an outlay which would have been unthinkable fifty years earlier?

Amulets, 'reassuring things'

As the first pains made themselves felt, the mother-to-be liked to know that those dear to her were by her side – especially the midwife, who would do her best to relieve her anxiety the moment she arrived. But the woman would not be wholly reassured until the amulets had been set up according to custom.

There were, indeed, numerous topical objects which were supposed to ease labour, and they were used as much as possible – more than was reasonable, according to the doctors. Sometimes the woman would already have made use of these magical objects during her pregnancy, fearing lest the fruit fall before it was ripe. They were sovereign against miscarriage, but were also – if well used – effective when the pregnancy came to term. Some were of local origin; others were brought from afar, and there was a whole collection of legends about their mysterious origins. All had been in use since time immemorial: their antiquity also contributed to their effectiveness.

These amulets belonged to the 'three kingdoms': animal, vegetable and mineral.

The 'eagle-stone' was certainly the best known, the most popular and the most sought-after of the mineral amulets, especially as it had a double value: as we have seen, it was a protection in pregnancy, but it also helped in labour. It had a great reputation and was widely used in every urban social milieu in the seventeenth and eighteenth centuries. Hence there are many authors who mention it in their works.

According to legend, the 'eagle-stone' should be sought just by the hole where the eagles had made their nest, or in the nest itself. The eagles would fetch it from far away, 'even to the great Indies, to save their young from lightning and from the ravages of time', says Pierre Pomet, author of a famous *Treatise on Herbal Drugs* published at the end of the seventeenth century.

The 'eagle-stone' or *lapis aetites*, or *lapis praegnans*, or, again, 'birthing stone', was usually the size of a pigeon's egg; it had the peculiarity of 'containing another stone within itself, which rolls about in it like a withered almond in its shell';[6] in fact, inside the stone one or two bits had become detached, usually bits of ferrous oxide, flint and aluminium, and when shaken they made a noise rather like a little bell.

Back in Antiquity the 'eagle-stone' already had the reputation of easing labour. Theophrastus and Dioscorides, Pliny and Galen, and later Matthiolus, acknowledged this virtue in it.[7] In seventeenth and eighteenth-century Paris it was sold by apothecaries, who laid in a stock from pilgrims returning from Saint James of Compostella. Frequent use was still being made of the 'eagle-stone' in all European countries in the nineteenth century. In fact these stones could differ in appearance: the most valued were 'flat, blackish in colour, with a frosted surface and a loud ring'. Some, mounted in silver, were like real jewels.

Other stone amulets, such as haematite and cornaline, also had the reputation, in past centuries, of being helpful in childbirth.[8] Certain agates were also favoured: according to Sébillot, at the end of the nineteenth century this custom was still alive in Lozère, where 'a horny and veined agate, carefully mounted in silver' was worn by women in labour. The 'women's stone' was another variety of mineral amulet used in the eighteenth and nineteenth centuries. Again in Lozère, at Vals in 1874, a stone of this type hastened the delivery. 'Greenish in colour, with black and white stripes, it was put on the belly of the woman in labour'.[9]

In the nineteenth century, in Aunis and Saintonge, it was also thought that birth could be eased if the labouring woman wore a drop of rock crystal found in a prehistoric burial place; this custom seems also to have existed in Brittany, though there coloured stones were used.[10] Thunder-stones found near megaliths could have the same virtues.

Most of these mineral amulets, which folklorists have shown to have been common in many regions through the nineteenth century, had probably been used consistently since the Middle Ages, or even since Antiquity. Even magnets, which were certainly in vogue in the eighteenth century, had already been cited by Pliny in his *Natural History* and by Renaissance authors.

Fossil shark's teeth, found near a dolmen, constituted a rather exceptional kind of amulet: they were of animal origin but had become part of the mineral kingdom. In nineteenth-century Saintonge there was an enormous shark's tooth which had come from Limbourg and bore the arms of the La Rochefoucauld family; it was considered to be exceedingly useful in a difficult labour.[11]

Amulets of animal origin were much prized, in the same way as mineral ones, but they were perhaps less common. In the seventeenth century, the surgeon–obstetrician Philippe Peu wrote that an eland's foot and 'the skin of an animal called Ruts' were believed to be helpful to women in childbirth. But without doubt, in the Middle Ages and up to the seventeenth century, it was bezoars which were most in vogue. They were called 'animal stones' or 'egagropiles', and were supposed to come from the stomachs of gazelles or goats living in the realm of Golconda, in the Indies; these 'oriental bezoars' were the rarest, the most sought-after and the most effective.[12] 'Occidental bezoars', coming from chamois in the Alps or deer in New Spain, were more common; there were also 'Germanic bezoars', 'monkey bezoars', 'ox bezoars' . . ..[13] These were concretions, spherical in form, made in animals' stomachs. Some were supposed to have a very pleasant smell and taste. Various properties were attributed to them; in particular, they were said to be 'of sovereign efficacity for women in the pain of childbirth'.[14]

Vegetable amulets, though less numerous, were none the less highly prized. In the first rank was the mandragora. The sixteenth-century author Matthiolus believed that the virtues of this fabulous root were not confined to making childless women fertile: 'Its juice taken in wine and honey' was acknowledged to have oxytocic properties: 'Applied by itself, in the form of a pessary, to the weight of half an obol, it attracts the menstrual blood and brings forth the child from its mother's womb.'[15]

But the most frequently referred to of all the vegetable amulets is incontestably the rose of Jericho. When its source plant, *Anastatica hierochuntica*, has fruited, its leaves drop off and the twigs curl into a ball so as to protect the ripe fruits; if this dried-up 'rose' is exposed to humidity, the twigs open out from their ball shape. Whence came the tradition of putting the rose of Jericho into water just as the woman was going into labour. According to one version of the belief, if the rose opens the pregnant woman will have no trouble with her labour; if it stays closed, the labour will be difficult.[16] A variant reported by Van Gennep from the Dauphinoise is certainly closer to what one might expect: 'Put a rose of Jericho near the bed of the woman in labour, and the pains will last no longer than this plant takes to open out.'[17]

The name of these 'roses' comes from the habit of bringing some variety of *Anastatica* back from a pilgrimage to the Holy Land, and it goes back to at least the sixteenth century, perhaps further. But others came from the African deserts. Their cheapness and their spectacular mutation made them very popular. They were highly prized in France, and in the whole of Europe, from the sixteenth century to the nineteenth.

Loan of magical objects

The mysteriousness of most of these amulets and the secret places where they were found contributed to their magical powers. They were an antidote to unnatural labour; they reimposed order on a disorder which threatened two lives. It is easy to imagine the deep-seated response to the mythical origin of the 'eagle-stone', with its reference to the greatest and strongest of birds and to the 'Great Indies'.

These amulets, animal, vegetable or mineral, were all more or less difficult to get hold of; thus, only aristocratic or bourgeois families possessed them. They were passed on from generation to generation as precious possessions; they were part of the family inheritance. In 1604, for example, Jean de Charmolue bequeathed to his cousin an 'eagle-stone garnished with silver, the fairest and best ever seen'. Some of these amulets had been procured in the Middle Ages, sometimes on the Crusades; but most of them were from the fifteenth and sixteenth centuries.

Naturally, the use of such precious stones was not confined to the family which had the great good fortune to possess them: they were loaned to any woman in childbirth, in the same way as the 'birth-bag' in the Auvergne, of which more later. If a community could not rely on the generosity of some furtunate amulet-owner, it would simply fall back on certain no less mythical objects which had been in use for generations.

The old snakeskin, which had been said by the seventeenth-century author Moyse Charas in his *Royal Pharmacopoeia* to be 'proper for the confinement of young women, if it is tied round the right thigh', remained in honor in many provinces, despite the Church's efforts to suppress it; it was sometimes superseded by a scarlet belt, or sometimes by a simple blue or yellow ribbon.[18]

Time and place of application

All these objects had to be handled with care. They were part of a ritual which had to be carried out scrupulously, for the sake of the labouring woman. The point of application of an amulet was vitally important. Except for the rose of Jericho, which was put to open up in a vase beside the woman in labour, amulets were placed directly on the woman's body, either on the abdomen (the snakeskin, the 'woman's stone') – because that was the seat of the trouble, the cause of the pain, and one had to act on the baby – or, more often, on the left thigh. It was tied on with a woollen thread, a lace or a strip of material.

No less important in seeking a good effect was the time of the application. The amulet had to be put on just as the first pains were being felt, but it was thought that the mother's life could be endangered if it was left, through forgetfulness or ignorance of the rules, longer than necessary. As soon as the baby was born the amulet must quickly be removed, or it might provoke a violent haemorrhage of the post-partum. The previously positive properties of the object were reversed and it could cause irreparable damage.

Amulets which could be applied on the body were not always available, and as the source of any kind of complication was to be sought in the baby, that is within the body, action could be taken via the mouth. The woman would be made to swallow an infusion of snakeskin, or a scrap of scarlet cloth or perhaps some magical formulae written on a piece of paper. All these different ideas were kept up in Provence, Lorraine, Berry and probably elsewhere as well, up to the nineteenth century, despite the prohibitions of priests, and especially of doctors.

Change in the attitude of doctors

Up to the latter half of the seventeenth century, doctors did nothing to call into question the general recourse to amulets. In his *Treatise on the Diseases of Women*, published in 1615, Jean Varanda advised wearing an eagle-stone round one's neck as a safeguard against miscarriage;[19] others expressly recommended it for childbirth. This shows that 'learned medicine' was still very close to 'popular medicine': it was still profoundly under the influence of the Ancients and of the doctrine of 'signatures'; in its concept of the body and in its practices it was still not fundamentally different from the traditional ways of working cures and helping women in labour. But from the 1670s onwards, some practitioners began to distance themselves from the amulet idea. Like the obstetrician Philippe Peu, they derided a custom which they were beginning to consider as childish:

One day a woman assured me very seriously that a stone which she had put in her hand brought her child to birth immediately: that it was called the Amazon stone, because the Amazons used it to the same effect when their time came. I duly thanked her for such a curious piece of information, and so as not to let so rare an ambiguity pass into forgetfulness, I immediately promised myself to find a place for it in this part of my book.'[20]

Peu's contemporary La Motte, who was more interested in psychology, under-stood how these objects gave reassurance. Why forbid their use, since they were not dangerous to the woman and gave her confidence at a time when she badly needed it?

However, at the end of the seventeenth century it was Peu's attitude which best reflected the opinion of the average doctor. They became more and more vehement in their denunciations of 'old wives' tales'; amulets were no more than 'trinkets', 'outdated trifles', 'baubles'. Here we touch on the profound change which was at work in the medical profession at the turn of the seventeenth century, especially in obstetrics. Doctors were all the more violent in their sweeping away of 'superstitious maxims' because they had been accepted, or even encouraged, by their predecessors up to that time. But the battle was far from being won! And even Peu acknowledged that some diplomacy was needed *vis-à-vis* obstinate midwives and gossips:

It must be admitted that if the obstetrician has some terrible moments in the exercise of his profession ... it is when the old-fashioned gossips bring out their nonsense with a prejudice and obstinacy which make it very difficult not to laugh to oneself, although one is often obliged (when it is of no great consequence) to let them carry on, and chatter on, without opposition, unless one wants to pass for an incompetent and have the whole pack of them at one's heels.'[21]

Even at the end of the seventeenth century, the obstetrician still had to reckon with the regiment of women.

The Woman in Labour: Differences in Behaviour

Women in labour followed a certain number of customs which are mentioned purely incidentally, and whose meaning it is not always easy to discern. They concern, first of all, clothing and ornament.

The mother's clothing

All knots, laces, fastenings and buckles were undone as soon as the pains came on. This was an elementary precaution: the woman in labour and her midwife must have no hindrances. It is a very old tradition: in the *Metamorphoses*, Ovid makes the goddesses do the same, and it is known to have been the rule in Greek and Roman society.

But loosening one's clothes did not mean undressing: semi-nakedness and complete nakedness were indecent, even if there were only women present; it went against the labouring woman's modesty and this might hold up the labour. There are, however, some cases in which the woman was stripped naked, as in the region of Dun-le-Roy, in Berry, in the eighteenth century; perhaps the idea was for nothing to get in the way of the midwife, and for the linen not to be spoiled. But such arrangements were rare: generally the woman was decently clad and the midwife worked away under her petticoats.

Other customs have a bearing on ornament. Did the woman feel her pains coming on? She had to do her hair; she took off her hair-band or head-covering. But what was the 'hairstyle for confinement' mentioned by obstetricians?[22] Nowhere is it explained. However, the ritual value of the act was undeniable: hair has a heavy sexual significance, symbolizing strength and fecundity. And it was really believed that the way it was styled could influence the outcome, good or bad, of the labour. This would explain its importance for the woman and the ripple of anxiety which ran through the gathering when the pains came on so quickly and sharply that there was no time to arrange her hair. Was there not once a saint who punished peoples for their bad behaviour by wishing 'tousled hair' on their womenfolk?[23]

Anxieties

By now the 'good mother' had arrived and the amulets had been ceremoniously disposed. The woman had nothing more to fear; and yet many and many accounts show her suddenly seized with anxiety, sometimes even unable to control herself. These sudden panics were more frequent if it was the first time the woman had given birth. Fear made them cry out and struggle as soon as they felt the first pains, as La Motte points out: 'The slowness and difficulty of first labours is ordinarily caused by the fact that most women are convinced, as soon as they begin to feel the pains, that they are suffering enough to give birth at once; the result is that they infallibly and immediately start to complain, cry out and struggle very hard.'[24]

It cannot really be said that screams are characteristic of this type of behaviour, for most women screamed during labour. They screamed, held their breath and screamed again, sometimes for hours on end, so that at the end of the labour they might even have lost their voices altogether, as the obstetrician François Mauriceau, among many others, observed: 'The throat is heated and made hoarse by the continual lamentations, by the screams and the great efforts to hold her breath that the woman has made during her travail.'[25]

The whole neighbourhood would be alerted and disturbed. But was that not just what was wanted? At Minot, three-quarters of a century ago, exactly the same thing happened. 'At that time they used to scream! Oh yes, they screamed! I don't know why, but women don't scream any more. . . . The old women used to say: "You had to cry loud enough for the whole village to hear!" '[26] Apparently, before the obstetricians took over the screams constituted a public affirmation that the confinement was really under way. It was a kind of cultural behaviour rather than an expression of pain; and this behaviour was common to all women, whatever their social milieu. At the beginning of the seventeenth century, the Queen of France, Marie de Medici, was encouraged not to neglect the ritual and to give free rein to her fears: 'The queen was about to give birth,' reports Louise Bourgeois, 'and I could see that she was trying not to cry out. I begged her not to hold back for fear that her throat would swell. The King said to her: "My dear, do as your midwife tells you, cry out for fear lest your throat should swell." '[27]

The seventeenth-century obstetrician was shocked by the screams and wails which dinned incessantly in his ears; when they were encouraged by the assembly, he would immediately demand silence and ask for 'superfluous persons' to be removed. All this row, he would say, got in the way of his work and tired the woman unnecessarily. Obviously he did not understand the dual purpose of these 'useless cries': relieving oneself by giving voice to one's anxieties and receiving the support and comfort of one's friends.

It is true that with experience in childbirth came a certain serenity; almost all reports emphasize the increased confidence of women from their second confinement onwards. In that case 'they let all these slight pains go by without complaint and ask for help only in the direst need, which make this second confinement prompt and fortunate, which would have been of the same kind as the first, and perhaps even longer, if the woman had not armed herself with greater resolution.'[28]

Thus the woman's personal behaviour pattern interacted with cultural tradition, making all kinds of nuances possible. It is worth insisting on this variation in attitudes, insofar as descriptions, especially by obstetricians, almost always pay most attention to exceptional cases and extreme behaviour, to the point of making these seem like the norm.

Positions[29]

During the contractions, many women could not stand any kind of restraint. They were therefore left a certain reassuring freedom of movement: they listened to their own bodies and chose the position or positions which best suited them, so as to give birth quickly and without too much pain.

The descent of the head below the pelvic girdle and the progressive dilatation of the neck of the cervix announced the final phase of labour; the woman then took up position for the birth itself.

Today, lying on the back (dorsal decubitus) has become so general that we forget that it is a comparatively recent practice, acquired only in the last two centuries, in France and in Western civilization as a whole. It was common in olden days to bear one's child sitting, crouching, kneeling, even 'on all fours'. Louise Bourgeois (beginning of the seventeenth century) talks a great deal about the great variety of positions women adopted; and as late as 1743, the obstetrician Pierre Dionis observed that some women were 'in the habit of giving birth standing, their elbows on a table; others in a chair, others on their knees, others on a mattress by the fire and others in bed.'[30]

Thus no study of obstetric positions can be confined to a simple list of cases, however 'quaint'. The position taken up by a woman in labour has not only physiological causes, but socio-cultural ones as well. It is indeed only to be expected that certain everyday habits, like squatting or kneeling, should be adopted straight way by women in childbirth. In this way every human group tends to prefer one or two positions which the women pass on from generation to generation. Therefore, childbirth draws on ancient thoughts and feelings about the body.

But it would be dangerous to schematize, first and foremost because the systematic study of birth positions comes up against the difficulty of documentation. Descriptions are often isolated and vaguely localized. Are we dealing with individual behaviour or regional customs? Added to that, in the eighteenth century the distinctions between town and country, and among social classes, were not always drawn. Finally, it is well known that a woman will not always spontaneously adopt the same position in each of her confinements, and that the same woman can take up different positions in the course of a single labour: a change of positions can reduce fatigue, and the movement can stimulate the contraction of the abdominal muscles and the progress of the baby through the pelvis.[31] However, some sources of precise information do exist, and these, patiently gathered and put together, make it possible to make out some regional characteristics and to follow long-term developments which may have taken place.

The positions for delivery may be brought down to two overall categories: vertical, the axis of the body being upright, and horizontal. The horizontal position will be examined alongside the study of the growing medical dominion over childbirth, for it was only at that time that it became general.

Four positions can be considered as vertical: crouching, kneeling, sitting and standing.

Crouching

Even today, after a century or more of medical domination, the first impulse of a woman having her first child, whose cervix is completely dilated, is to ask for a bedpan or want to go to the toilet. And up to the beginning of this century, the annals of maternity hospitals and textbooks of forensic medicine gave numerous examples of unassisted women whose labour finished involuntarily in a lavatory. Study of tribal societies tends to confirm the idea that the crouching position – as if going to stool – is certainly the most instinctive one; thus it is not surprising that it should have been in use in French rural society in past ages.

The crouching position ensures an easier expulsion because it allows the mother to make maximum use of her pains; besides, if the child appears suddenly, it is at no risk of falling from a height and being injured, the cord is rarely broken and, with rare exceptions, there is no fear of a prolapsed uterus. Besides, it was apparently thought essential that a child should arrive in the world by immediate contact with the Earth Mother. It is, indeed, well known that since Antiquity, and in very different cultures, the ritual of laying the child on the ground, and its symbolic 'taking up', has been considered very important, constituting the acceptance of the offspring by the father and the lineage.

Finally, this is the position in which the woman seems to have the least need of help, in which she can herself best watch her perineum and disengage the head of her own baby, if necessary. The crouching position is the one adopted by a woman alone, in her house or taken short in the fields. In normal circumstances, this position does nothing to make things easier for the assistant, who has difficulty in guiding the progress of the baby and watching the perineum of the mother. Thus when help was available, the woman would abandon this position, especially as it obliged her to be half naked – any kind of restriction was hard to endure, any button was a nuisance – and exposed her to chills, with all their awful consequences.

Also against the crouching position is the fact that it is hard to maintain for more than a few minutes: the circulation to the limbs is cut off and they go numb. But perhaps women in earlier times were more accustomed to it and could keep it up for longer by leaning the top part of their bodies on a stick or a chair-back.[32]

Kneeling

The kneeling position also seems to be an instinctive one, and for that very reason it was frequent in many provinces up to the nineteenth century. La Motte noted it in the Cotentin at the beginning of the eighteenth century, with the women kneeling on cushions to give birth. In the middle of that century the custom still persisted round La Ferté-Macé: the Marquise of La Chaux, in her *Memoirs*, condemns it as being particularly dangerous for country people: 'They must,' she writes, 'enjoy the most robust health in order to endure the violent shocks to their whole body in a labour sometimes lasting several days, almost always on their knees, which is the posture most likely to produce exhaustion, prolapse or heavy loss of blood, not to mention the cold they feel in this position.'[33]

At the end of that century, in Berry, women would kneel on a straw mattress and cling to the back of a chair, for in the kneeling position there must be a support for the upper limbs and some relief for the knees. This method was still in use at the end of the nineteenth century among the peasant women of the Creuse and Morvan, who 'often give birth alone, kneeling between two chairs, on which they support themselves, one arm over each chair.'[34] At the same period, in the Gâtinais, the woman, aided by a midwife, would kneel before the seat of a chair on hot ashes from the hearth; thus she gave birth to her child, whom the midwife or 'gathering woman' would take up; the practice lasted in this region until 1925, by which time a bale of cotton or straw had replaced the ashes, so that the baby would not fall on something uncomfortably hard.[35] Exactly the same technique was being used in 1906 in the Sarthe, at Mayet, where 'from time immemorial' women had been giving birth on their knees; the woman's legs were spread wide apart and a basket lined with straw was put between them to receive the child.[36]

If the woman was suffering from backache or cramps, she would abandon the kneeling position and support herself on both hands, or elbows, and knees. In some cases of malpresentation, or when the woman had a very protruding

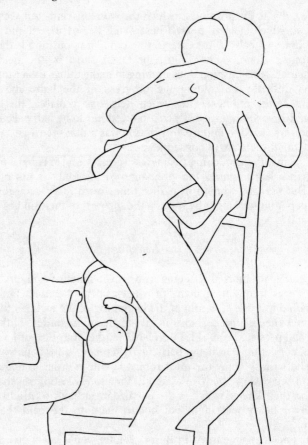

Sketch 1   Giving birth in kneeling position, against a chair-back. Berry, near Dun-le-Roy, 1786.

womb, she would instinctively go 'on all fours' to help the labour. This method was still in use in the eighteenth and nineteenth centuries. And obstetricians like Deventer, Sue le Jeune and Lefebvre de Saint-Ildefont recommended it strongly for some difficult births or when the woman was small, hunchbacked, ill-made.

Doctors of the 'Enlightenment' usually condemned the kneeling position if the birth, though normal, happened 'in posterior position', the child being received behind the woman. They were even more disapproving of the 'all fours' position. Such postures seemed to them wholly 'indecent'; they were 'repellent to humanity', they were too animal.

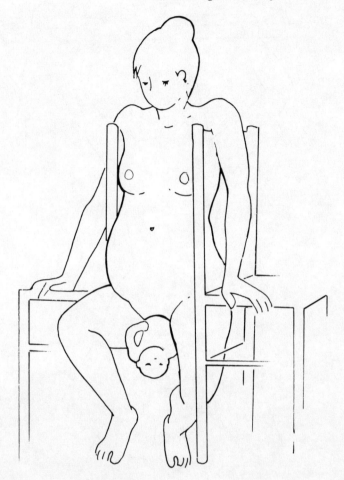

Sketch 2   Between two chairs. Morvan, end of the nineteenth century.

Standing

A standing birth can be accidental or deliberate. In the case of an accident, the woman is taken by surprise by the rapidity of the labour; the contractions are brief and cause the expulsion before she can take up any particular position. To this kind of accident we may add the case of a girl who has hidden her pregnancy and who, surprised by the pains and knowing nothing of birth, remains standing, hanging on to a table or a chair, or leaning against a wall, and finally lets the baby fall on the ground.

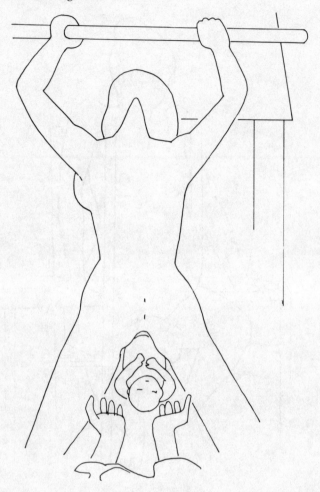

Sketch 3   Standing, with raised grip for the hands. Berry, near Dun-le-Roy, 1786.

Indeed, an accidental birth in the standing position is very often dangerous to the child, which may suffer injuries to the skull or loss of blood; it is no less to be feared for the mother, for a too sudden detachment of the placenta when the child falls may well cause a violent haemorrhage or even a prolapsed uterus. When it was traditional in some region or community, a standing birth was closely watched; the woman in labour was never left alone[37] and precautions were taken to avoid complications.

From the end of the seventeenth century to the end of the eighteenth, various textbooks of obstetrics show the persistence of the standing position, in Lower Normandy (La Motte), Lorraine (Didelot) and Flanders (Raulin). Other practitioners reported that it was also frequent in the Massif Central, especially in the

Cantal and the Upper Loire, where the custom was to endure until the beginning of the twentieth century.[38] It was, in fact, more particularly the mountainous regions, remote and isolated places where old customs clung, which longest remained faithful to this method of birth. This does not, however, mean that the practice did not persist to some extent in rural areas more open to medical influence, and even in towns. Thus in Limoges up to the middle of the nineteenth century, midwives were assisting women who were giving birth standing. A woman in the town who had borne five children in this way between 1850 and 1860 was astonished when in 1880 she saw one of her daughters stay in bed for the moment of birth.[39] This was an important changeover: the position passed on by tradition through centuries had given way in a single generation to the position favoured by the medical profession. The mother had no doubt kept up some rural connections, while the daughter, born in a town, accepted the lying position recommended by the obstetrician and the professional midwife. Some time earlier, at the beginning of the seventeenth century, Louise Bourgeois had perceived the new phenomenon of women who joined the new urban outlook by accepting a new position in childbirth: she noted that a woman from Anjou, who had come to live in Paris, went on 'giving birth on her knees, as they did in her own country', and thus emphasized both the endurance of older practices amongst recent urban immigrants and the fading out of rural attitudes in the second generation.

A goodly number of Breton women in the Ile-et-Vilaine region were still giving birth standing as late as 1914. But they were aware of the danger of this position for the baby and themselves, and so they 'placed a pillow between their legs to receive the child, and while pushing they leaned their elbows on a piece of furniture, or hung round the neck of one of the people assembled'.[40] Sometimes they gave birth leaning on the four-poster bed, 'with on the one side a neighbour, and on the other generally the husband, with her arms round their necks. Sitting before them was the midwife.[41]

The standing position, like the crouching or kneeling one, required some support for the body. This support differed from place to place. In Lorraine, around 1780, as the surgeon Didelot reports, women 'give birth standing, leaning on the end of the bed'; and at much the same time the surgeon Lecomte of Dun-le-Roy, in Berry, reported that the midwife would make the woman cling 'to a wooden bar fixed to the chimneypiece or some other place, arms raised, legs apart, body unsupported'.[42] Until 1925, in the Charente, it was again to a bar of wood fixed across the chimney that the labouring woman clung, with her back to the hearth where some vine-branches were burning. The woman was held up by assistants while the midwife, sitting on a low chair, took care of the delivery.[43]

Sitting

The sitting position has certainly been the commonest in Western Europe in the last three or four centuries.

A crouching position frequently turns into a sitting one. Fatigue makes the woman bend forward, fall on her knees, then backward and finished in a sitting

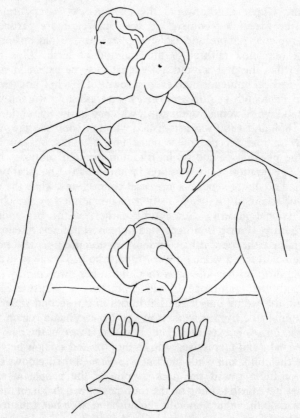

Sketch 4   Sitting on the edge of a chair or bed, supported by an assistant. After La Motte, beginning of the eighteenth century.

position on the ground. The birth will then be distinctly 'lateralized', the woman resting her weight on one buttock and one arm to raise her seat and let the child be born. This type of delivery in a sitting position is still common in certain African and Oceanic societies.[44]

In seventeenth- and eighteenth-century France, the woman most commonly sat on the lap of another woman who held her arms or the upper part of her body. In remoter places and isolated farms, it would often be the husband who held his wife still. When the birth was delayed, the task of the supporter was not always easy, in which case people might take it in turns; in any case, strong people were needed who could restrain the disordered struggles of a suffering and frightened woman. Obstetricians, if called out, did exactly the same. The midwife's place did not change: seated on a chair or a little bench which put her 'at the right height', she supervised the progress of the labour.

Sometimes the woman in labour sat on the side of a bed or chair; here again, the midwife would be in front of her, with their knees together. In the Antibes region, in 1786, 'she makes her spread her thighs as wide as she can, legs slightly bent, feet on the crossbar of a chair, and to keep up this position, she [the midwife] puts her knees against those of the patient'.[45] At the right moment the midwife held her 'pinafore' between the woman's legs to receive the child. This is what was called 'being born in an apron'. The custom used to be very widespread; it still endured around Bourgneuf, in Limousin, around 1860.[46]

The sitting position had several disadvantages: the midwife and the assistant were often drenched in the waters and blood; it could be difficult to supervise the emergence of the head, because the perineum jerked further backward with each contraction; the midwife, two thigh-lengths away from the woman, found it difficult to reach the vulva, so that the perineum was in a terrible state by the end of the labour. At the end of the nineteenth century a doctor in the Auvergne, where sitting births were common, pointed out quite seriously that 'perineums are not worn in this district'. Finally, it is known that the sitting position does not assist the contractions and does not allow the woman to make the best use of them; the push is not so strong, the mobility of the pelvis is reduced and the birth is therefore delayed.

To make up for certain disadvantages of the sitting position on the lap of an assistant, the beginning of the sixteenth century saw recourse to the birthing stool – later, chair. It was not, in fact, really a novelty: the Renaissance simply restored to favour the 'birthing machines' already known to the Greeks and Romans. Thus Ambroise Paré's *sella perforata* was very little different from the obstetric chair of Antiquity: it was a sort of three-legged stool, with a piece cut out of the front, and without a back; thus an assistant was still needed to support the back. The birth chair shown in Eucharius Rosselin's *Rosengarten* already included two important improvements: a low sloping back and arms to which the woman could cling during a contraction.[47] Paré had no doubts about the usefulness of this rudimentary chair and he justified its employment with the following arguments:

The pregnant woman is put in it, reclining on her back, so that she has freedom to breathe in and out; the *os sacrum* and the *os caudae* are in the air, under no kind of pressure, [which] means that the said bones can be disjoined and separated more easily. Similarly the *os pubis*, because the thighs are apart from one another; add to that that the midwife can do her work more easily, being seated in front of the pregnant woman. A pillow will be placed on the back of the chair, and some linen where the thighs will go, to make the pregnant woman more comfortable.[48]

There is a lot of difference between this still simple model and the birthing beds or 'lucinary beds' of the eighteenth century, with their reclining backs, stirrups for the feet, movable arms and separable 'fore-seat'! But the link, from improvement to improvement, is unbroken.[49] This piece of equipment, coming from the Germanic countries where the stool and chair first appeared, probably entered France via Strasbourg and Alsace.[50] It wrought a distinct change in the conditions for childbirth.

Chairs were supposed to diminish the fatigue both of the woman and of the person holding her up;[51] in actual use, however, it was realized that they had disadvantages of their own. They were heavy and difficult to move; the woman could not make the most of her pains, whatever Ambroise Paré had to say; she might even catch a chill. This last drawback was remedied by hanging the chair with draperies which prevented 'air having access to the buttocks, the external sexual organs, and especially the vagina and the womb, a thing to which the Ancients attributed a great number of distressing results'.[52] This obsession with cold even meant that heaters were supplied on some models (Heister's chair, for example).

The appearance of birth chairs had decisive results for the evolution of birthing positions. Because of its high cost, the chair spread especially among the wealthier classes, where it became a veritable family heirloom passed from generation to generation; in certain princely houses it was even decorated and covered in costly material.[53] It was in frequent use in the towns of northern France,[54] rarer in the countryside,[55] except in Alsace and eastern Lorraine, where the local midwife had a rudimentary folding chair, a lighter model, which she carried about with her.[56]

The introduction of the chair tended progressively to eliminate the father from the labour room, since his physical strength was no longer necessary. For the woman who was compelled to use it, the chair was not wholly a good thing: it became the very symbol of the physical pain attending on the woman in labour. It was a cold thing, alien to her familiar surroundings; it was frightening.

But the main consequences of the use of the chair was to restrict the woman's freedom of movement, reducing her to immobility from the first pain. The doctors and administrators who encouraged its spread in the seventeenth and eighteenth centuries made it an instrument of the extension of their control over childbirth. From the beginning of the nineteenth century, when its weight had increased because of the refinements it had undergone, some obstetricians toyed with the idea of restricting its use to hospitals. More than a century in advance, they were preparing the ground for a concentration of all care in the hospital environment. The delivery table of modern maternity hospitals is a direct descendant of the chair–bed of earlier days. The technique, introduced – so it was said – in the interests of the woman in labour, caused a radical modification in the conditions of childbirth.

Lying down

Observations by practitioners of the seventeenth, eighteenth and nineteenth centuries and evidence from anthropologists leave it in no doubt that the four 'vertical' positions were certainly those naturally adopted in earlier times by most women in labour. Opinions differ only as to which of the positions, crouching or standing, predominated.

There was no way that women's preference could go to the lying-on-the-back position. Firstly, because they instinctively felt that it did not supply the best conditions for the progress of labour. We now know that this position is the worst possible, because it causes compression of the big abdominal veins (aorta and lower vena cava) by the pregnant uterus, which increases foetal distress and is a factor in hypotension and haemorrhage in the mother.[57]

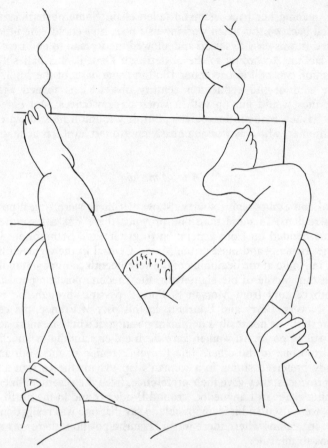

Sketch 5 Lying on the back: a plank fixed to the bedpost supports the feet. After Raulin,
Instructions succinctes *(1770). All sketches are by Daniel Gélis.*

The horizontal position, while not exceptional, principally affected women
who had some difficulty in bringing to birth, especially if they had been
suffering for many hours, and went exhausted to lie down on a straw mattress or
on the bed ... The bed! One had to be desperate to be reduced to that
extremity – fouling a set of bedclothes. Also, refusing as long as possible to lie
down on one's back was surely also a way of showing one's difference from the
animals, who always gave birth lying down – from that world of beasts which
was so close. This makes it easier to understand the long resistance of
countryfolk to the medical way of birth, which demanded a retirement to bed
the moment the first pains were felt.

A position midway between sitting and lying was in use in the countryside,
especially in the winter when one had to beware of cold. The birth would then
take place before the fire; the woman was seated on an old mattress or a straw

paillasse, leaning her back against a fallen chair. Some obstetricians, like La Motte, fell back on this when working in a poor household: 'the little bed', as they called it, was easy to set up and allowed the woman to endure a long and difficult labour. According to the obstetrician Depaul, this half-sitting, half-lying position was still in use about 1860 in some parts of the Midi.[58]

At the end of the eighteenth century obstetricians turned against this position; they would put up with it when circumstances, and especially the woman's wishes, made it unavoidable, but they found it most disagreeable for the practitioner, who was working nearly on ground level, crouching or on his knees.

'A local method'

Historical and ethnographic sources show that there were typical postures for different regions. In more than one province there was a favourite position which was handed on from generation to generation. Standing in Aunis and Saintonge, Brittany and most of the Massif Central in the eighteenth century; kneeling in Anjou at the beginning of the seventeenth century and in the Upper Maine in the middle of the eighteenth; the kneeling position persisted in the nineteenth century from Morvan to Poitou, passing through the regions of Puisaye, Nevers, Berry and Bourbon. In this part of France, the centre and central west, it was not really a dominant position; it would be more accurate to call it a pair of positions: women gave birth either standing or kneeling, often passing from one to the other. The Provence region of the Midi and Lower Normandy preferred sitting in a woman's lap. As for the eastern and north-eastern provinces, they gave their preference, from the seventeenth century, to the birthing chair. In Languedoc, around Bordeaux and in the north, different positions were used and it is impossible to say that one was really dominant. In any case, in regions where there was a favourite position, there was no lack of exceptions to the rule.

Nor were these preferences immutable: women were subject to certain influences which could sometimes change their behaviour: thus the progress of the chair in the north-eastern provinces caused a diminution in standing and kneeling births. However, there was lively resistance to change throughout the nineteenth century. By trying to keep up the 'local method', women hoped to preserve a certain 'way of being' at the time of their confinement.

Culture and physiology

If women in labour preferred the vertical positions it was because of the idea that they helped the birth of the child. They were bringing into the light a fruit which nature had brought to ripeness, giving a launch to the baby which had been made ready in the first phase of labour. However, unlike what happens in nature, when it is enough to shake the trunk and the ripe fruit will come loose and fall to the ground, the baby 'fruit' is, as it were, locked in the trunk itself, held in by the mucus and the dampness of the womb. Hence the search for a position which would give maximum play to the forces of gravity and let the child be born quickly. We now know that intra-abdominal pressure depends largely on the woman's position in the final phase of labour, and that the various vertical positions do most to help the expulsion. Thus our knowledge of physiological mechanisms assures us that the physical techniques of labour used in past times were effective.

The freedom of movement left to the woman helped the descent of the baby. Since the progressive shaping of the genital passage in human beings is asymmetrical, the change of position brought about a positive acceleration of the labour, thanks to an improved rotation of the head in the pelvis.[59] La Motte had a perfect understanding of this mechanism: by allowing the woman to adopt the position she preferred, and to change it, he was making the labour easier.

Until the middle of the eighteenth century, obstetricians succeeded in imposing the supine position only on a relatively small circle of their clients in the towns. In the countryside, where they rarely had a chance to intervene, they were often unable to change women's habits. They recognized that they were unlikely to succeed, except in 'remonstrating', and even then they could not 'lean too hard' (as Pierre Dionis acknowledged in 1743), if they did not want an abrupt refusal.

Behaviour changed only slowly in the countryside; even at the end of the last century, doctor–obstetricians were showing their irritation at this stubbornness as they reported that in Ile-et-Vilaine 'women *will only give birth standing up*', and that in the Upper Loire 'they make it *a point of honour to give birth standing up*'. Such conduct seemed to them all the more of an aberration in that the countryfolk no longer (they said) had the excuse of poverty, for 'modern interiors, more comfortable than earlier ones, are usually provided with a small bedroom with a movable bed'.[60] They explained the adherence to vertical positions simply by women's stubborn respect for tradition; they did not realize that the positions were reflections of a culture which was refusing to die out.

To bear a child in a crouching position, or standing before the hearth, implied a certain kind of awareness of one's own body and of life; it was one's own way of welcoming the new baby. Here we have a coherent ensemble of references and feelings which, after a long resistance to medicine and progress, finally sank in the great shipwreck of rural culture from 1914 onwards.

Get It Over Quickly

The midwife and women assisting a woman in labour knew from experience that childbirth always had an unknown factor: even if it seemed to be going well, it could become difficult, even critical, at any moment and for no obvious reason. Thus the midwife could be strongly tempted to take a hand early on: the ever-present fear of an accident urged her to hasten the labour, especially as, if the woman became exhausted and could not expel the baby, if she finally perished after four or five days in labour, it might be the midwife who got the blame. So the midwife's intervention, which ought to have been an exception, tended to become the rule, for fear lest she be accused of not having 'worked' enough, and soon enough. Good and successful labours were rapid ones.

Do not miss the time

All this haste had its disadvantages. There is considerable evidence to show that there could sometimes be confusion between real childbirth pains and mere colics when the woman had not yet come to term. Moreover, physical manipulation of the womb and sexual organs could have grave consequences for the health of mother and baby.

In her *Diverse Observations*, Louise Bourgeois has a chapter on this subject, entitled: 'How to judge if, the woman feeling unwell, it is really labour'. One must, she says, be careful not to 'make the woman labour' before the real signs have been recognized, for 'women often suffer pains which press on them as if they wanted to give birth, and yet it is not the labour; in some it is some small movement of the womb which wants to shift, in others it is colic.'[61] Now, she adds, there is an infallible way to find if the labour is real: hot cloths over the abdomen 'usually make the pain pass off; but if they are labour pains, the pain will increase with the heat'.[62] La Motte confirms that it is easy to tell the difference. If it is simple stomach pains, anodyne enemas will give relief; if it is really the labour, the woman should be left in peace, the labour will be the better for it. But to weary her and interfere with her unnecessarily will only complicate matters: 'If I could persuade midwives to use this method of not interfering,' he wrote, 'some women who spend three days in a difficult labour would be in it for only a few hours.'

We ought not to tax all midwives with incompetence: some of them had an excellent approach, as obstetricians were ready to admit; they were cautious and knew if a woman who was screaming with pain and holding her stomach was or was not about to go into labour. But behind the differing attitudes of midwives and practitioners, especially from the eighteenth century onwards, there was in fact a different understanding of the mechanisms of labour. The actual time of labour was different for the obstetrician and the midwife. The latter saw it as being short; she would speed it up so as to prevent accidents. The former, by contrast, counselled patience, letting 'nature' act without hurrying anything. The midwife would reply that nature does not wait, that there is a time for harvest and the gathering of fruit, and that by waiting too long one might lose mother and child and all. One must not let the hour pass! Thus the midwife's attitude reflected both the fear of complications and the physical perception of the rhythms to which mankind is subject and which must be respected.

'Using eyes and fingers'

Many midwives had a very false idea of the sexual organs and of the length of gestation. Let us pass by the extreme case in which the descent of the neck of the womb was mistaken for a tumour. Few indeed were the midwives who could do a vaginal touch and draw conclusions from it (or so the obstetricians said); and then, they did too much touching! Because there was touching and touching: the verbal similarities should not deceive us, for the word did not have the same meaning for everybody.

For obstetricians the vaginal touch was the only way to be sure that the labour had really begun; it informed them of the degree of dilatation of the cervix and the presentation of the child; it was the 'obstetrician's compass'. Now midwives, even if they could recognize dilatation 'using eyes and fingers', could not make the best use of the information thus gained. Whatever results they obtained from the vaginal examination did not in the least moderate their enthusiasm for 'working'.

Their ways of talking about dilatation and evaluating it show the differing approach to the woman in labour by the obstetricians and the midwives. More profoundly, it reflects two cultures, two approaches to the body. When evaluating the degree of dilatation, the midwives almost always refer to parts of the body. The yardstick was the hand, or part of it: finger, thumb, palm. 'I found the orifice of the womb . . . dilated by the length of the palm of one's hand,' says Louise Bourgeois, who, though she was midwife to the queen, still remained deeply influenced, in the dawning seventeenth century, by the old rural culture.[63] And if it was not the body which supplied the image, it was something from everyday life: 'I found the orifice of the womb as big as the string which village women use to lace themselves in.'[64]

From the end of the seventeenth century, the mental universe to which the obstetricians belonged was quite different: townsmen for the most part, they already had a different view of reality. It was coins which, in their eyes, best evoked the degree of dilatation of the cervix. The change in vocabulary comes in with Parisian obstetricians in the 1670s–1680s; some, like Paul Portal, still used two series of references. They might gauge the dilatation as 'the size of a halfpenny loaf', but already they were much more likely to refer to money: 'The child's head at the top appeared to be of the roundness of a silver crown, a little oval-shaped', or 'of the size of a thirty-sou piece'. In the eighteenth century references to parts of the body or to everyday objects disappear: coins or 'lines' become the only units of measurement.

The midwife 'at work'

When she arrived, the midwife wasted no time. She would sit down and begin to touch the woman, who would be opposite her, on the edge of a chair or the bed; sometimes she would make the woman lie down near the fire, on the paillasse or bed of straw which had been prepared: there, on her knees, she would begin her intervention.

She would take no particular sanitary precautions: until the end of the eighteenth century, indeed, it was exceptional for midwives, or obstetricians, to wash their hands before getting to work. About 1780, practitioners who were starting to realize the importance of hygiene were beginning to speak harshly about the midwives' black fingernails and dirty hands.

To the midwife's mind, the 'work' had to facilitate the opening of the private parts, stretch them and allow the baby to come out easily. To this end she pulled, patted and generally tormented the vulva. Her fingers, hands and even forearm, and the private parts, were smeared with a 'lubricant' which was supposed to stretch the ligaments, soften the tissues, help the child glide out of its mother's womb. This lubrication at the beginning of labour was a general practice employed also by obstetricians. Paul Portal used to smear his hands with fresh butter; La Motte sometimes used oil, but he preferred melted unsalted butter.

In fact, they did not wait for the onset of the pains before doing this anointing with grease. In the previous few days, the midwife would often have made repeated applications to the abdomen and private parts. Eighteenth-century obstetricians believed that such a preparation for labour was well advised; Didelot, from Lorraine, wrote:

The woman will be advised, seven or eight days before the birth, to rub her private parts with fresh butter, which will make the passage easier and more slippery; young women who have had no previous child will benefit from this method. These rubbings are even more necessary in women of an advanced age who are in their first pregnancy.[65]

To widen and stretch the passage, midwives also prepared fumigations, or, as in Languedoc as reported by Laurent Joubert in the sixteenth century, they sat the woman over a hot cauldron: 'The village midwives around Montpelier have discovered that if a woman in labour sits on the edge of a cauldron which has just been removed from the fire, she bears her child more easily. We know,' Joubert adds, 'that such a cauldron, which has recently held boiling water, has a warm rim, which could be called cold in comparison with something which is burning hot. Now, this warmth softens the rump and makes it more yielding; as do the softening fomentations which we use to that effect.'[66] In very rare cases, in well-off households, baths were also recommended to facilitate labour.

Between two contractions, before returning to the midwife, the woman would walk about the room; she would walk round the table, leaning on it or on two friends; to hasten the delivery, she was advised to move about, to go up and down a staircase. The body had to be shaken to detach the foetus, just as we shake a tree to dislodge the ripe fruit. And there again, the preparation often began several days before the birth: manuals of obstetrics from the sixteenth and seventeenth centuries emphasize the beneficial effects of horse-riding or travelling on carts on rough roads![67]

To bring out the child, the midwife also pressed on the mother's stomach: repeated massage, energetic rubbing and thumps on the back would surely bring on the birth! To the midwive's mind, delay could only be due to the weakness of the baby, which therefore had to be helped. The membranes, swollen 'almost to the size of a child's head' were like 'a pig's bladder full of water'; although they had come 'out of the orifice of the womb', they were too resistant to open of their own accord. Normally the midwife tore them with her fingernail, or with a pin or pair of scissors, but to make a good incision nothing was better than a grain of salt! Early piercing of the membranes, condemned by nineteenth-century obstetricians, was common practice to their predecessors. There was, however, a great risk of complicating the future course of the labour if the child did not come out soon after the waters.

Purging and vomiting

The constipation which so afflicted the pregnant woman was also a major obstacle to an easy birth: when the pains came on, a lazy bowel could prevent the normal development of labour, making the woman uncomfortable so that she hesitated to push. An enema just before the labour, when the 'large bowel' was obstructed, was found unendurable by some women because of its unclean consequences. And moreover, in the countryside neither the midwife nor the other women knew how to give an enema, nor did they have the necessary clysters. Thus, purgatives were often used. Rhubarb mixed with manna and white magnesium, and, in the Midi, cinnamon water, were the most common purgatives in the seventeenth and eighteenth centuries;[68] local herblore furnished a goodly number of others, which happily made it unnecessary to call on the quack in the next town.

Sometimes, to give the woman relief and speed up a long drawn-out labour, cupping was used.[69] Another reputedly helpful medicine was a cataplasm, of linseed and milk applied to the abdomen. The idea was to rouse and stimulate the child and encourage it to enter the world. In several regions – including the Lyonnais, where this usage was frequent in the eighteenth century – midwives readily made use of rye ergot, which they administered in broth, tisane, water or wine. After half an hour 'Normally the contractions of the womb are so active that the women give birth as it were in spite of themselves'.[70] In the absence of rye ergot, nothing was more effective in hastening the delivery than an increase in the contractions of the sternum. Midwives had often noticed that vomiting was a sign of the child's imminent arrival, and from there to the idea of provoking such vomiting was but a short step. Vomitives were in abundant use everywhere. A child 'placed too high' must be brought down by making the labouring mother's 'gorge rise'. To this end they sometimes irritated the throat artificially by making her swallow little feathers and bits of thread. Clearly they also tried to provoke nausea by suggesting disgusting things to eat, made of animal intestines and foul substances, the very sight and smell of which 'made the stomach heave'. Certain *Books of Secrets* of the seventeenth century, of which Madame de Rosemberg's was one, contain recipes for these revolting concoctions.

Obstetricians, and later, historians of medicine, used this sort of evidence to discredit midwives of earlier times. In fact, such preparations did not always need to be consumed: the smell and sight was enough to make one sick! But was not that exactly the desired result?

The midwives' 'little secrets' sometimes had spectacular results which left the medical men flabbergasted. Rigal, an obstetrician from Gaillac near Albi, reports that a midwife succeeded in a short time in delivering a poor woman who had been in labour for two days. 'Consternation was general in the village. However, a group of women assembled and held a council of war.' Some of them decided to call on 'a woman in the district who was supposed to have a remedy which caused a prompt delivery'. On arriving, this woman 'asked for a glass of broth, in which she put a greyish powder, and without any further examination she administered it to the sufferer. A few moments later, she vomited copiously, and almost immediately gave birth to a lively boy.'[71]

The high cost of outside medicines was one reason why some sixteenth and seventeenth-century *Pharmacopoeias*, like those of Fernel or Symphorien Champier, recommended local or regional products. And Constantin's *Treatise on Provincial Pharmacy* even suggested that animals, plants and all ingredients of medicines answered better to the temperament and complexion of the women taking them if they were gathered locally. Everywhere in the eighteenth century, as we have seen, exotic drugs were beginning to score, first in the towns, then, thanks to the peddlars, in the countryside. Many of them were expensive: ipecacuanha, or the recipes suggested by the much-reprinted *Charitable Remedies* of Madame Fouquet, were intended only for the wealthy. In the second half of the eighteenth century there was an upsurge in the use of chemical drugs. The memoirs of many an obstetrician show that these novelties were often tried out in the countryside: tartar emetic, for example, which when dissolved in water and drunk caused vomiting. But in the absence of such drugs, which were neither affordable nor available – and whose very existence was often unknown to midwives – there was still the well-tried remedy of warm vinegar: this inexpensive and commonplace product had no after-effects, unlike certain emmenagogues, 'revolting drinks' based on borax and hartshorn, which could cause grave disorders of the post-partum, convulsions and sometimes the death of the mother.

PART IV

Between Mother and Child

9

Birth: A Double Liberation

This Leonard delivers all those who are in chains.
Jacopo de Voragine, The Golden Legend

Nine months of close dependency culminate in a brief but intense physical encounter, the labour and birth. Two partners suddenly become rivals in a 'war' of which the outcome is doubtful. Birth is an experience of 'unequalled combat'.

The mother, at the culmination of her ordeal, must deliver herself of her burden at any cost. As for the offspring, its growth now ended, it must break through the siege of its body so as to be 'born into the world'; nature offers it only one way: it must force the passage, or remain a prisoner.

Birth is an ambiguous thing. Who is prisoner of whom? Who is responsible for the delay? The child, for failing to end a reclusion which was initially protective, but has become dangerous? Or the mother, for failing to deliver herself of a fruit which she has sheltered and nourished and which is now threatening to put an end to her? The signs can suddenly be reversed and become ominous: happy co-existence can suddenly give way to unforeseen crisis. The end must come quickly. Two bodies separate, one from within the other.

Since Antiquity, medical orthodoxy, under the influence of Hippocrates and Galen, had insisted that it was the child who played the active role, at least in the first stages of labour. It was the child which came 'knocking at the door' asking 'Dame Nature to open to him'. The midwife was the 'porteress', helping the door to open from the outside of the mother's womb, if necessary.

Louise Bourgeois explains the onset of labour as being the movements of the child wanting to leave the womb, because there is no more room for it and because it is no longer getting all the food it needs. It comes out to seek what it can no longer find within the membranes which sheltered its growth. This image of the mechanism of birth, passed on by the medical textbooks, reappears in popular belief: thus the well-known 'kicking' in the seventh month is a preparatory phase for the exit from the womb: the child is turning into a suitable position for birth. In a second stage, the mother's efforts – that is those of the mother and of the womb – supplement those of the baby. The mother must make the best possible use of her pains, because it is these pains, caused by the

141

disordered movements of the baby, which announce the imminence of the birth.

Thus, a good coordination of the efforts of mother and baby is essential for a successful and rapid labour. Contents and container act in concert to bring about their separation. Misunderstandings or contradictory struggles on one side of the partnership will endanger the successful outcome, or at least, delay it.

This is indeed an odd situation! But the behaviour of the womb is always surprising: is it happy to be freeing itself of the baby, or does it do all it can to hold on to it? As for the baby, it wants to leave its protecting 'womb-home', pushing the door as the father had done at its conception, but in the other direction. The 'lodger' takes leave of its host. But let any difficulty arise and the 'womb-home' becomes a 'fortified mansion', a 'fortress' which holds on to its prisoner at the risk of losing the mother and turning itself at the last into a 'womb-tomb'.

To the attendants it was never the mother, suffering and exhausted, who was the accused. The baby was the guilty one, the 'parasite' from which the mother must at all costs be liberated. This was the midwife's image for a difficult birth, and it allows a better understanding of the extreme measures which she sometimes resorted to. For her, the great debate of the Church and the doctors over the right choice between the lives of mother and baby simply did not arise when she saw that the mother was in danger of death. The cherished fruit had become the source of evil; responsible for a critical situation, it and it alone had to be the victim, if victim there was.

Deliverance, 'Bringing to Bed'

The word for 'to give birth' used in French textbooks of the sixteenth and seventeenth centuries is *s'accoucher*, a reflexive verb which indicates that the woman played an active part. In the eighteenth century the growing tendency of the obstetrician to intervene deprived her of all initiative (or so it has been suggested): from then on the word is *accoucher*, or the passive *être accouchée*.[1] Indeed, to give birth – *s'accoucher* – was first and foremost a self-liberation, disencumbering, delivering oneself of a burden, setting free the fruit at the end of the gestation; and the captivity image was so strong that it imposed itself on the symbolic level. An image of monastic seclusion: sometimes 'the woman is so enclosed and shut in that her child is as if bound and made captive; though making great efforts, it struggles in vain to get free from that dark cloister.'[2] The image of a gaol holding someone against his will: thus the woman goes on a pilgrimage to some Virgin of Deliverance or some saint known for his ability to intercede for the liberation of prisoners. Some of these shrines bear witness even today to the real importance of those ancient customs: at Notre-Dame d'Orcival, chains from captives freed in the eighteenth and nineteenth centuries still hang from the façade, and at Avioth, near Montmédy, the remains of fetters hung on the statue of the Our Lady the Receiver are still to be seen. The behaviour of women in labour also witnesses to the depth of this feeling of captivity. When the pains were at their worst, some would undertake 'to have a novena said, others send to ask for masses to be said; others have the girdle of Saint Margaret brought to them, others vow to put their children in holy orders .... As for those in a position to do so, they promise to deliver a prisoner.' Thus writes the eighteenth-century obstetrician Pierre Dionis.[3]

But this captive body was also subject to evil forces. Birth was one of those vital moments when contrary forces were in contention. There was always the fear that some ill-intentioned hag might harm the woman in her labour through magic words or gestures. By crossing one's arms or legs in a certain way or tying a symbolic knot in a piece of string one could interrupt the natural course of things and block the labour. Here we can make out a whole domain of correct postures for the limbs, correct positions for hand and fingers, a complete code which must have developed in dim antiquity, for it is found in some mythological stories. Ovid's *Metamorphoses* tell the story of Alcmena, whose labour was deliberately held up by Juno-Lucina, who sat on the threshold with her fingers interlaced and her right leg crossed over her left knee. Fortunately, Galanthis, the maidservant, was on the watch; she saw through the trick and announced to Juno that Hercules was born. Lucina, taken aback, leapt up and unlaced her fingers; the spell was broken, and Hercules was born the same instant.[4] In the Roman world, and in the beliefs of many peoples down to the beginning of the twentieth century, we find this idea that the obstacle of two linked hands, a symbolic knot, created an obstacle to birth in the woman's body.[5] Giving birth, being delivered, was to break a bond, a fetter.

To counter evil spells, or simply to bring the baby down out of the womb, amulets were applied to the lower part of the body as soon as the first pains came. Between pregnancy and birth these magical objects migrated down the body. For nine months the thing to avoid was the interruption of the pregnancy, so the baby must be kept high up by wearing objects round the neck or arm. At term, in contrast, the baby was attracted towards its natural exit, towards the ground. The analogical virtue of the amulet allowed the mother to 'bring her child to ground' without difficulty. The 'eagle-stone' was the image of the mother's womb containing the baby, and the stone which shook about inside it 'are considered to be daughters of the mother-stone which contains them in its womb'.[6] Its convincing exterior reinforced the sense of power attributed to it: some 'pregnant stones' were pear-shaped, like a uterus, with the veins standing out in relief. The symbolism of the bezoar came from its origin: this amulet had power to attract, essentially, because in the animal's belly or bladder it attracted hairs and concretions which were parasitic on them. Indeed these amulets, many of them of animal origin, were considered to work equally well on animals. Pomet's *General Treatise on Drugs* concludes that if eagles brought aetites to their nests it must be to 'help their young to hatch';[7] and even in the nineteenth century amulets were still being used to help the breeding of domestic animals. A 'thunder-stone', a prehistoric axe, was still being put in hens' nests 'to ensure a good hatching' in some regions of France in about 1850,[8] perpetuating a tradition according to which fertility and birth in animals were fundamentally identical, in their mechanism, to fertility and birth in man.

In the absence of 'topics' people sometimes took to more spectacular, or even brutal, methods equally intended to speed up the labour and 'help the woman free herself from her fruit'. In nineteenth-century Saintonge and Poitou, when the labour was slow, a 'sack-man' was called in to shake the woman violently, as he would if he were filling a sack of grain.[9] What was done very often had symbolic implications. One well-known custom is the 'hammering of the spleen' described and illustrated by G. Vuillier in Corrèze at the end of the last century.[10] The same therapeutic method was, in fact, often also used for women in labour: the heavy hammer brandished by the blacksmith, stopping a few inches away from the womb, must have convinced the onlookers that a rapid expulsion would ensue. The woman, reacting with very understandable and instinctive fright, stiffened and thus restored vigour to her contractions.[11]

In the eighteenth century the practitioners began to distance themselves more and more from the 'medicine of signatures', and declared that amulets were a reflection of superstitions that would be swept away by the progress of science. None the less, a good number of them were still influenced by the theory of the humours and were convinced that there was a specific 'topography' of the pregnant and labouring body which had to be acted upon. Thus, up to about 1750, bleeding was commonly used when the woman had convulsions: in the arm during pregnancy, in the leg during labour, depending on whether one wanted to restrain or encourage the action of gravity.

'Captivating the Womb'

At the onset of labour the womb always feels exceptionally sensitive. Sometimes it 'rolls about in the belly like a ball', sometimes it rises towards the stomach as if to suffocate the labouring woman. The midwife's task was therefore to curb its harmful inclinations, taming the itinerant, 'wandering' womb, that 'stirrer of civil wars' which governed the fate of two living beings. When it migrated to the upper part of the body, Louise Bourgeois advised 'pounding some rue on a heated scoop, then putting a fresh egg-yolk on it and sprinkling with a little brandy: place on the navel'.[12] Clearly the object was to bring the womb back to the mid-point of the body, which it should never have left. In case of delay, if the womb still refused to 'surrender the baby' the midwife acted on the lower part of the body and more energetically, 'by rubbing the insides of the thighs, from top to bottom, by cups applied to the inside of the thighs, repeated as necessary'. But often the medicine had to be applied via the nose or mouth, or by the lower route, to the private parts. From above, the womb was sent down by making the woman breathe in nauseating smells; from below, it was attracted by moisture, by squirting the most delightful and subtle perfumes which would 'captivate' it and make it let go. Thus Jacques Duval, at the dawn of the seventeenth century: 'Perfumes of labdanum, bdellium, alypta, moschatel, ambergris, musk and civet are required for the lower parts; but to the nostrils bring asafoetida, partridges' feathers or old burned shoe-leather'.[13] Mention of civet – the oil produced by sweat on human testicles – among the perfumes supposed to delight the 'mother' and bring the child to birth, introduces a very significant sexual connotation.

Birth and Sexual Symbolism

Birth was inconceivable without reference to the father. Already, some time before term, he would have gone in to his wife, their embraces being no longer forbidden: on the contrary, since the fruit was ripe it must be put to the test, prepared for the shock which would separate it from its mother. Intercourse also opened a way for the child, 'greasing the passage' and widening it. The idea that the coating of sticky slime which covers the child's body at birth was simply the diluted sperm of the husband was still very strong in the seventeenth century. This rather unexpected participation of the husband at the birth was recommended by the 'great Ancients': Guillemeau (early seventeenth century) recalled that Aristotle 'does not recommend making love to one's wife all through the pregnancy, but only just before the birth, to shake up the child and bring it out more easily, because coming into the world after such an act, it is ordinarily as it were covered and surrounded by glair and mucus, which makes its passage easier.'[14] The husband's urine was also supposed to have oxytocic properties: a woman in a difficult labour would drink it and it would help shorten the travail.

Certain items of the man's clothing were in frequent use, especially in southern and central France. His everyday hat, or, more often, the night-cap he had worn at the moment of conception, was put on the woman's abdomen or vulva in the hope that the womb would recognize the odour of the progenitor and promptly expel the baby; for the same reason the woman would sometimes wear her husband's trousers. Bonnets, berets, hats or trousers were often turned inside-out with the idea of assisting the ripened seed, which the husband had planted in the womb nine months earlier, to emerge.

In the sixteenth century, Laurent Joubert had seen the reason for this odd employment of the male clothing: the husband, reluctant to remain in the room where his wife was giving birth, had his bonnet confiscated 'as if to say that from the man came this swelling of the belly, as if he had a venomous sting; he or his bonnet applied thereon works like an antidote and brings down the swelling'.[15] Sometimes the husband's responsibility was enunciated more clearly: an attempt was made to facilitate the delivery by punishing him symbolically through his sexual attributes. Round Ruffec and in Poitou, in the nineteenth century, they would hope to relieve the woman's pain and hasten her deliverance by throwing a pine-cone, representing the male organ, into the fire.[16]

This reference to the husband's sexual organ is not the only one of its kind: the 'private parts of the wife' also form part of the analogical arsenal. The rose of Jericho, whose role as amulet we have already examined, is a good example. The change undergone by this vegetable hygrometer, however spectacular, is not alone sufficient to explain its popularity. The Seigneur de Bussy, of Picardy, gives us the key to it in his 'book of reasons': in 1713 his wife was seized with labour pains, and to prevent complications an anastatic was hastily thrown into some water. 'This rose,' he writes, 'though very dried up, immediately opens out and blossoms into the same shape as the woman's nature.'[17] The dilatation of this vegetable vagina is a piece of sympathetic magic supposed to ensure the dilatation of the cervix and the free exit of the baby.

Normally, as we have seen, virgins did not attend a confinement. But if the birth was too long delayed, their presence became desirable; once again the signs are reversed and opposites attract. This custom, which lingered in places until the nineteenth century, shows the importance attached to the symbolic link of virginity with fertility; virginity carried the potential for life and could facilitate a birth when all the experience of married woman and the midwife was insufficient to deliver the woman of her child. About 1850, at Nozeroy in the Jura, 'when a woman feels the first pains of childbirth, a young virgin is immediately called in, sits by the mother's bed and holds her hand until the moment of delivery'. In that case the presence of the virgin was not even connected with a difficult birth, it was automatic. Could it be a trace of the ancient cult of Lucina, goddess of childbirth and herself a virgin?[18] This image of delivery helped by the presence of, and contact with, a virgin is a powerful one. But then, had not the Church since the Middle Ages made the Virgin Mary the greatest intercessor for women in childbirth?

Christian Practices, Traditional Practices: A Case of Osmosis

Most of these practices were taken over by the Church. For centuries it tolerated or even encouraged the wearing of amulets to ensure a swift and successful labour. But it tried to eliminate beliefs whose sexual symbolism was too obvious. No more allusions to the womb as an organ apart, alive with its own imperative desires. If the labour was difficult one should look to the morality of the parents. And no more symbolic allusions to the sexual organs; the merits of the rose of Jericho may have been acknowledged, but it was not for the same fundamental reasons: it became 'the rose of Our Lady' which a pilgrim brought back from the Holy Land; a rose without a thorn pure as the Virgin, a rose which was reborn and brought deliverance. No mention of the couple's sexuality, especially the husband's: the Virgin's 'attracting power' replaced the 'fluid' coming from articles of male clothing. The function of the father as progenitor disappeared from the symbolism of birth.

In hagiography, that episode in the life of a saint which made him or her into a favourite with women in labour was always given prominence. Saint Leonard saved a queen in danger of death during a difficult labour; Saint Margaret became the patron saint of childbirth because, just before her final martyrdom, she asked permission to pray for herself and her persecutors, 'adding that any woman in labour who called on her would give birth without peril'. But there is more to it than that, because these saints of childbirth had often, characteristically, been themselves liberated in life from an unjust imprisonment. The life of Saint Margaret is perhaps the best example, for, thanks to the Cross – that is, to faith and prayer – she escaped from the dragon, symbol of paganism and evil, which had swallowed her up.[19]

The Church was no more consistent in this domain that in any other: it went through periods of rigour and of relaxation. There has been much justified stress on the periods of increased severity in Church teaching and on the Catholic Reformation of the seventeenth century, after the Council of Trent.[20] The rituals surrounding the childbed at that time had a strong whiff of magic about them: at a time when the cult of the Virgin was being strongly promoted, even the use of certain relics of the saints had been forbidden because they gave rise to practices judged to be superstitious. In 1698 the Bishop of Rouen, making a pastoral visit to Sainte-Marguérite-de-Caprimont in Normandy, ordered that it be 'forbidden to use relics for pregnant women and that they be kept in the sacristy and not in the tabernacle'.[21] A few years earlier the Abbé Thiers' *Treatise on Superstitions* had proscribed the use of amulets, phylacteries, protectives, letters or notes. They were, he wrote, 'superstitious remedies which are tied round the neck, arm, hands, feet, legs or other parts of the bodies of men and animals'.[22]

Prayers for use in childbirth in the seventeenth century also show this hardening of attitudes in the Church towards women in labour, who were frequently reminded of the 'humility fitting their station'. But we may well ask ourselves how representative these texts, often the issue of rigoristic morality, really were and what impact they had. Did they really make the mass of the population, living mainly in the country, change its ways at all? Examining the situation in the eighteenth century we are brought to an ambiguous answer. Could we blame a degree of Enlightenment 'laxity' which perhaps undid what the seventeenth century had begun to do? What is certain is that in the countryside there was resistance to change. In the nineteenth century a slow osmosis took place between the old rural beliefs and the teachings of the Church. Ritual objects, and the ritual itself at the time, bear witness to this interpenetration.

The birthing bag went on being used for centuries in central and southern France; it was still much believed in at the end of the nineteenth century. Protected by one or two coverings of canvas, texts of prayers and invocations rubbed shoulders with little miniatures on parchment or paper illustrating the life of some saint helpful in childbirth, most commonly Saint Margaret. Thus, in a birthing bag from the Aurillac region examined by A. Aymar in 1924 there were, besides some beads from a rosary, ribbons, medals and medallions, fragments of wax, and a bundle of manuscripts, some illustrated.[23] It was the whole range of possible aids in case of a difficult birth. These objects were from different ages: evidently an attempt had been made to reinforce the virtues of the talisman by successive additions from the thirteenth century to the eighteenth. This anxiety not to neglect any propitiatory object resulted in an exceptionally rich collection which witnesses to the syncretism of popular belief. The thirteenth-century text is made up of extracts from the Old Testament; the medallions are consecrated to Saint Margaret, the Virgin and the Infant Jesus; a 'most precious oration found upon the Sepulchre' rubs shoulders with a magical phylactery from the fourteenth century and a veterinary recipe from the sixteenth. Which gives the idea that the bag was also used for calvings and so on. Thus Christian and secular references intermingle; and sexual symbolism is not forgotten, for there is also, attached probably in the eighteenth century, 'a long double chain, of metallic thread, rolled up like a coiled spring, and surprisingly elastic', to which are fixed 'several tassels in the shape of pine cones'.[24]

In the nineteenth century, around Angoulême, they still relied greatly on dried snakeskin placed on the abdomen of the labouring woman: but as the serpent was also the symbol of evil, and it was known that the clergy disapproved of the practice, there was a compromise: the snakeskin was removed as soon as the child appeared 'so that it should not belong to the devil'.[25]

Is this, then, an incomplete Christianization of pre-Christian, pagan practices? That is one of the essential aspects of the debate on 'popular religion'.[26] It seems that such an osmosis of beliefs and practices around the woman in childbirth could only be established and endure because of the existence of common systems of thought: in particular, the same system of references by analogy, the same value placed on virginity alongside fertility, an often identical way of viewing the ritual – as is shown by use of the birthing girdle.

Hagiographic texts always attach great importance to anything which binds, knots or, conversely, unfastens and sets free. The symbolism of girdles which so often comes in incantations is also very much present in the Christian tradition. Saint Margaret's girdle is a good example. Saint Margaret as an overseer of childbirth had been very popular since the Middle Ages.[27] In the eighteenth century, women approaching their confinement would have a candle burned in her chapel in the cathedral at Amiens and would send for the girdle which was kept at Saint-Acheul.[28] As for the girdle owned by the abbey of Saint-Germain-des-Prés, whose reputation among pregnant women has already been mentioned, it was only brought out for the confinement of queens and dauphines of France.[29]

Popular as it was, the cult of Saint Margaret could not hope to equal that of the Virgin. Since the beginning of the seventeenth century the girdle of Notre Dame de Quentin, in Brittany, had enjoyed considerable prestige; according to a record of evidence from 1620, 'it daily performs many miracles, restoring sick people to health; but often women in travail are greatly relieved by it'.[30]

Church ceremonial was not much different from the rite of application of amulets as already described; contact with the body remained vital; the girdle was placed on the abdomen, just as the snakeskin had been earlier. The frequent calls on the girdle very soon raised the problem of its preservation. A deposition made at Quentin in 1611 indicated that the girdle was carried 'beyond Guingamp, to Guingamp itself, to Saint-Brieux, Moncontour, Lantréguier and other places'.[31] Now, women in their pains incessantly put their fingers on it; their sweat was helping to wear out the material . . .. Thus, here as in all other cases, there was recourse to substitutes. In 1614 Louis XIII forbade taking the girdle out of the sanctuary; from then on they made do with bringing to women in childbirth a ribbon sanctified by contact with the relic. This custom lasted up to our own time.[32] Another Virgin's girdle, actually more ancient than that of Quentin, was particularly venerated in Anjou, at Puy-Notre-Dame. In southern regions there was perhaps less call on the Virgin's girdle; with one exception, but an important one: Notre Dame de la Dourade, at Toulouse.

Contact with the relic was not always considered sufficient. Words must be spoken and prayers said.[33] The weight of words was essential; and, as for any magical invocation, they had to be in the right order. A pious prayer written on a piece of paper had exactly the same virtue; the text was often only one of the talismans that the woman in labour would place between her skin and her petticoat. That is, if it were not intended for internal use . . .. The habit of administering 'pieces of scarlet' (scraps of cloth swallowed by the woman) or slips of paper on which were written formulae against evil spells and pain was in fact very widespread, so firm was the conviction that the womb could be effectively acted on from the inside: the power of writing! The Church could only get the better of these magical practices by Christianizing them. At the beginning of the twentieth century, Alsatian pilgrims returning from the great Swiss Abbey of Our Lady of the Hermits at Einsiedeln brought back small images of the Virgin succouring women in childbirth; these squares of paper were swallowed when labour began.[34]

10

Suffering to Give Life

The throat is heated and made hoarse by ... continual lamentations, by screams.

François Mauricean, 1668

Until the end of the eighteenth century it is rare for our sources to face up to the pain of childbirth. The doctors were less interested in the woman's feelings than in ways of bringing a successful end to the most difficult of confinements: thus obstetric expertise took precedence over all other considerations. Inquiries into eighteenth-century midwives, in which popular practices are often mentioned, are equally disappointing: it is only exceptionally that the sufferings of mother and child are mentioned at all.

While pain *per se* was little studied in treatises on obstetrics, doctors' memoirs or official documents, it does sometimes make an appearance – in the most violent and unendurable forms. Denouncing the sufferings caused by the behaviour of which midwives were guilty became, for eighteenth-century obstetricians, a weighty argument to discredit the former in the public eye.

'Suffering in Childbed'

Evidently not all women experienced the same intensity of pain; numerous examples show, in fact, that a single woman may endure very variable amounts of pain in her successive confinements.

The obsession with life-threatening complications meant that the ideal confinement was considered to be a rapid, and *ipso facto* less painful, one. Be quick: that, as we have seen, was a midwife's only way of sparing the labouring women intolerable pain. And Mauquest de La Motte defines a good confinement as one in which

the child follows immediately after the waters when the membranes rupture ... as it happens [he adds], 'to four or five persons in this town [Valognes] whom I customarily attend. These women are so fortunate in their confinements, that feeling a slight pain when they awake, or rather on being awakened by this pain, they send for me at once; if I delay even a little, I find that they have already given birth. What I have just advanced is so true, that one of these women, being surprised by childbirth pains one day, and being alone in her room, wanted to call to one of her neighbours through the window; there she gave birth and the child dropped to the floor; to this accident she added a second,

150

which was to return from the window to her bed, dragging that unfortunate child right across the room by the cord, without either mother or child suffering the slightest inconvenience.[1]

On the other hand, some confinements were a sort of martyrdom for the woman, who emerged exhausted by pain. Such as the woman who was eventually relieved after 'she had been sick for two days and her waters had come away twenty-four hours previously, her lips and tongue as dry as if they had been roasted, her teeth all black through the violence of the continual and intense pains which she was suffering, without a moment's respite, since her labour began.'[2] Two, three or four days of labour was nothing exceptional; an 'unnatural' presentation would baffle the village midwives – and some surgeons turned *ad hoc* obstetricians.

However, even a quick birth, so much approved of, was not always free from intolerable pain. In 1697 La Motte was called to a woman whom he found in 'urgent and redoubled pain'; the child was head down, but the head was at a distance, and it was ... the face which appeared in the passage; hence the violence of the labour:

The violent pains, which increased without respite, were endured because of the vigour of the sufferer, and were of such great assistance, together with that which I was able to offer, that she gave birth safely an hour and a half or so after my arrival. I delivered her and let her rest without doing anything more to her, that is, of what was necessary to get her to bed. So exhausted was she by the violence of the labour, although it had not lasted long, that she could not even speak . . .. The mother's pains were so violent that I had to exhort her incessantly not to give voice to them save to the extent that nature compelled her to do so, in my fear that she would burst her chest or stomach, or at least burst open some vein which would cause her death.[3]

As we have seen, pain, or the fear of pain, was expressed by screams and writhing on the part of the woman in labour. By screaming she could free herself from apprehension, but she could also give voice to her pain in order to lessen it. In that sense it was also a cry for help and comfort: the woman, alone with her sufferings, wanted reassurance. Sometimes a friend could help her over this difficult time: at Merry-Sec, near Auxerre, at the end of the seventeenth century, 'it is believed that when a woman cries out and screams while another is in labour, these cries and screams make the labour easier and diminish the pain she feels'.[4]

Pain often made the woman struggle so violently that she had to be held down firmly by several strapping female friends. Sometimes she accidentally bit and mutilated her tongue, so badly that it needed careful attention; in the days following on the confinement, some women were unable to move, so crippled were they by excessive 'moving about'.

The Causes of Pain

Women did not all suffer the same intensity of pain; neither did they all suffer for the same reasons. A prolonged absence of help in a difficult or unnatural labour was the most usual cause of intense pain; but partial or total urine retention caused by a malpresentation was no less to be feared: 'The bladder, being full and compressed by the baby's head, causes cruel pain to the sufferer';[5] only use of a probe could relieve and calm the woman. That is, if the midwife actually possessed one and knew how to use it. In 1699, an obstetrician called in haste to the side of a labourer's wife could scarcely believe his eyes when 'I found a woman so prodigiously swollen up that her belly was close to her chin, being almost without a pulse and quite cold, and who had not passed a drop of urine for three days.'[6] Rachitis of the pelvis, which was not uncommon, was certainly one predisposition towards a long labour, highly risky and painful. In such cases the baby's head, even if of average size, could not pass properly through the pelvic girdle. It is well known that inadequate nutrition in early childhood has a direct effect on the structure of the pelvis in adulthood.

Not all the causes of pain were of physiological origin. Popular opinion, at least, held that the body had to 'make ready', 'lend itself' – adapt. According to a belief which was very widespread up to the nineteenth century, the first labour was the most painful because it was 'making the way': the eldest child was, as it were, boring out and polishing up the parts of that strange mechanism, the female body, and thus preparing the way for its brothers and sisters. 'The common man,' adds Laurent Joubert, 'cannot comprehend how so large a body (that of the baby) can emerge from the normal passage without violence, and that this is the cause of the intense pains which are felt by the woman in labour, especially with her first children. For after that part has often been opened, it does not hurt so much.'[7] This idea of a progressive shaping of the mother's body by her labours was still held by surgeons as reputable as Mauriceau and Portal at the end of the seventeenth century, but it began to be opposed at the beginning of the eighteenth, when La Motte considered that it was erroneous and that 'the woman suffers just as much' and 'is in just as great a danger with the tenth, twelfth, and fifteenth child as she could have been with the first'.[8]

'Lessening the Pain'

In their textbooks, obstetricians and professional midwives advised a charitable attitude towards the suffering woman. Madame du Coudray recommended reassuring her by telling her the labour was progressing well; Gilles de La Tourette, an obstetrician of Loudun at the end of the eighteenth century, emphasized that the most essential thing was to distract her from her pains: 'When a woman is suffering in childbirth,' he wrote, 'one must make efforts to distract her by agreeable conversation which will amuse her and make her forget her discomfort.'[9] Reassurance, distraction, must surely be the best way to ease the labour and so put an end to the pains under which the woman writhed. But she had to be made to feel at ease, both physically and psychologically, because the labour could be speeded or retarded by her attitude of mind: 'It is the nature of joy to open up and dilate; that of fear, on the contrary, is to compress and close up.'[10] But could that really cancel the pain? Louise

Bourgeois was honest enough to admit that one could make use of 'remedies to lessen the pain, but not for removing it altogether'.[11]

Traditional pharmacopoeias put certain analgesic drugs at the disposal of midwives. They would know of fungi, herbs or roots which would help to lessen and even eliminate the pain. Soporific sponges, known since the Middle Ages from the medical schools of Bologna and Salerno, were sometimes used by surgeons for difficult labours which caused horrible pain to the woman. Their composition varied, but the drugs most commonly used to render the woman somnolent or insensible were henbane, hemlock, mandragora and ground ivy. The sponge would be dipped in a decoction of the drug and put before the woman's nose and mouth; return to consciousness was contrived by rubbing the face with another sponge soaked in vinegar.[12]

Did women in earlier times have a higher resistance to pain than their modern counterparts? Was their pain threshold different? It is hard to be sure. One thing is certain, however: pain in former times was part of daily life; it was a harsh world for all, especially for women and very young children; the struggle for existence, especially in the country, took place in a general climate of violence,[13] and the ability to endure was certainly greater then than it is now. But for a woman in labour, mental images of the process rather tended to weaken this capacity for endurance. With the baby on the way, the woman was caught up in a 'whirlwind of images and fears': a feeling of insecurity, fear of the unknown, fear of death. Terrifying memories, perhaps buried since childhood, might come to the surface, upsetting her and thus making her more sensitive to pain.

Pain is a good example of 'the influence of cultural tradition on the development of organic phenomena'.[14] Language has an essential part to play in this: some words occur again and again in the sources, words such as tearing, hooks, forceps, blood, infection. They were loaded with significance for any woman, conjuring up violent aggression, cold, sometimes death, always pain.[15] For fear and anxiety act on the cortex to bring about a lowering of the pain threshold; in contrast, if those in attendance could restore the woman's confidence the threshold would rise again. The physiology of pain has recently been revolutionized by the discovery of endorphins (endogenous morphines): we now know that the brain can manufacture chemical compounds which can block the nerve cells, especially those which conduct sensation. Thus, to decrease pain there are two possible methods used today, which witness to two attitudes towards pain in childbirth: the contemporary psycho-prophylactic method called 'pain-free labour' (PFL), which suggests a 'cerebral brake' on the biochemical mechanism and maximizes the absolute control of the instinctive and emotional parts of the brain by the upper cortex;[16] and the 'Leboyer method' which is a 'rehabilitation of the emotional brain'.[17] Certainly it was this 'emotional brain' which was called on in former times during labour, with the reassuring presence of other women, a great freedom of movement and the woman's freedom to cry out in her pain as much as she felt inclined.

Reports by anthropologists and evidence from certain eighteenth-century practitioners allow a rather closer approach to the realities of pain in childbirth in the France of two hundred years ago. Observers in tribal societies have been impressed by the apparent indifference to pain of their women: they sometimes give birth all alone,[18] but more often with the assistance of a midwife or a few friends; they show themselves 'dumb and patient, and willing that the child should inflict any pain to accomplish the delivery'.[19] The women's phlegmatic attitude is usually imposed by strict rules: any audible complaint is reprehensible; to express one's pain by screaming would be dishonourable. In reality attitudes are not always so simple: silence and calm can suddenly give way to a 'plaintive cry' and a convulsive movement of the body as a fresh pain comes on. The behaviour of women in provincial France in early modern times was rather different, since screams were permitted and even encouraged. However, this was not always entirely true, according to eighteenth-century doctors: apparently countrywomen and townswomen did not always feel pain in exactly the same way.

The contrast of town and country was a favourite theme in medical discourse during the Enlightenment: the idealization of rural living induced practitioners to portray women in the villages and hamlets as healthy, sturdy bringers of life, being close to nature and ignorant of pain (or very nearly), unlike their etiolated and sickly cousins of the city, for whom labour was always an ordeal. In fact, these moralizing remarks did not originate in the eighteenth century; already, in the second half of the previous century, Laurent Joubert had noted that 'village women and other working women, who ordinarily do hard physical labour, and spend more time on their feet than sitting, have much easier deliveries than merchants' wives and townswomen who spend most of their time in repose and sitting down, not working at anything save sewing and embroidery'.[20] But it was certainly the eighteenth century that fixed the image of a 'civilization of manners' which enfeebled and softened up the human constitution and made it more sensitive to pain.

The desire to forestall the dangers of labour and preserve the mother's life became more and more definite among the better-off people in the towns in the latter half of the seventeenth century. It was then that a new way of 'government for pregnant and labouring women' began tentatively to emerge: women were kept immobile for months on end and bled at the slightest provocation; there was an obsessive fear of chills, and in consequence, the 'heating method' was developed. The result was doubtless a passage from insufficient precautions to an ill-considered protectiveness, with no benefit to the woman, left at the mercy of the slightest false step or the most trivial cold. Dulled reflexes, faintings at the slightest provocation, reduced resistance to pain: this heralds the 'age of the vapours', convulsions and panic in childbirth.

Alongside this change in feelings and behaviour were two other elements which contributed to curtailing women's freedom still further. Firstly, the Church's fulminations, which inclined more and more to consider women in labour as guilty: their pain was the proof and the punishment of original sin. Obstetricians also became more severe in their attitudes: noisy exclamations of pain were suppressed. Thus the trap closed round the suffering woman: she suffered because she had to, but she must learn to suffer in silence.

Pain as a Symbol of Motherhood

In that most Christian country, seventeenth- and eighteenth-century France, the image of woman in childbirth was indeed that of a creature in pain. Woman was the very symbol of sin; she was guilty of the fall of man, and if she suffered, it was because she, as a 'daughter of Eve', had to redeem that original fault. It is not surprising that in some seventeenth and eighteenth-century texts, written under Jansenist influence, the 'Prayer of the pregnant woman awaiting her confinement' amounts to a willing acceptance of pain:

In my confinement, strengthen my heart to endure the pains that come therewith, and let me accept them as the consequence of your judgement upon our sex, for the sin of the first woman. In view of that curse, and of my own offences in marriage, may I suffer the cruellest pangs with joy, and may I join them with the sufferings of your Son upon the cross, in the midst of which He engendered me into eternal life. Never can they be as harsh as I deserve, for although holy matrimony has made my conception legitimate, I confess that concupiscence mingled its venom therewith and that it has urged me to commit faults which displease you. If it be your will that I die in my confinement, may I adore it, bless it and submit to it.'[21]

The woman in labour had her place in a world where only suffering and penitence could confer grace. Christianity fostered and encouraged the re-demptive aspect of pain in childbirth. This attitude was not, in fact, confined to Judaeo-Christian civilization: the theme of expiatory suffering by women in labour runs through other cultures; but first the Bible and then the Church's teachings did strongly favour the emphasis on pain in their image of childbirth. 'They that sow in tears shall reap in joy', as the psalm says; and even today, when an apprentice, clumsy with his tools, hits his thumb, a popular French saying conveys in its own way that same reference to work accomplished through physical pain: 'That'll drive the lesson home!'

The image of motherhood is inseparable from that of pain. Anyone wishing to simulate the act of giving birth will imitate suffering and writhing. This was indeed the most spectacular manifestation of the couvade, the 'man-childbed' endured by some husbands: the man would writhe in agony like a woman in labour. Since the birth of a child is conveyed through the sufferings of the mother, it was only natural that it should be shown forth through symbolic pain on the part of the man claiming to be the father. The cultural dimension of pain could not be more clearly manifested.

And the Baby Suffers Too

Up to the eighteenth century, if the texts speak of pain they are always referring to the mother's pain; they do not even consider the hypothesis that the child could suffer at birth; the first cry was never interpreted as a sign of pain; after a long and difficult labour the attendants were so surprised at having managed to bring forth the child alive that there was no room for any other emotion than joy: the cry meant life. When it went on longer than normal those present might be surprised, but no-one, not even the hastily summoned obstetrician, blamed the anomaly on pain felt by the new baby:

The child, which I many times believed to be dead towards the end of the labour, came into the world with a wail which lasted a good two hours, and thrived from then on. It turned out to be dumb. I do not know if the labour had perhaps done some damage to its organs, or caused some obstruction to the nerve, which made it lose the use of it . . . for this child, now a growing boy, is not deaf and in fact is highly intelligent.[22]

If the child's sufferings went unrecognized, it was, of course, mainly because it could not express itself using ordinary language: hence the common idea that a baby is an incomplete being without feelings or sensitivities. But it is probably also because the image of the baby as a parasite causing pain to its mother was no encouragement to pity its own fate. Significantly, obstetricians, when describing cases, sometimes omit to tell us what happened to the baby. In a remarkable description of a face presentation in 1671, Paul Portal emphasizes the mother's sufferings: 'She begged me incessantly,' he reports, 'to give her some relief, or to open up her abdomen, because of the great weight which she said she felt in her womb and in the surrounding parts, such as the bladder.' Young and brave, she had complete confidence in her practitioner, and, Portal adds, 'she suffered with constancy all the pain the child and I could inflict on her.' This determination saved her life, and Portal spares us nothing of the circumstances of her restoration to health or of the treatment she was given. Only in the last few words does he speak of the child, and they are eloquent in their very brevity: 'I have heard that the child died' is Portal's conclusion.[23]

In the eighteenth century, more precautions were taken during the labour and attempts at reanimation might be made, showing a renewed interest in the baby: the stress was on preventing physical damage and keeping the child alive, and this marks an important advance on previous practices. Nevertheless, the question of the baby's sufferings was never clearly enunciated.

11

Stages in the Delivery

The Midwife's Way of Doing Things

An experienced midwife was capable of recognizing immediately if a woman's 'time had come'. On arrival she would ask how the woman was feeling, whether she had pains and what they were like, where they started and ended; if they were little, strong or frequent, if they began in the loins, running through the belly without stopping at the navel, and even if they ran along the armpits and finished inside, in the lower part of the abdomen'.[1] But the midwife knew by experience that pains could be deceptive, and so she based her diagnosis on other indications.

Spasms and vomiting were considered by the midwife to be sure indications of the onset of labour.[2] Late seventeenth-century obstetricians like Mauriceau, Portal and La Motte also regarded vomiting as the main symptom of the commencement of labour; thus sickness marked both the beginning and the end of pregnancy. In some women it was accompanied by convulsive shivers.[3]

The midwife also inspected the woman's abdomen: 'She palpates it and looks carefully at it' so as to assure herself that 'its higher parts are as it were empty and collapsed inwards, the lower ones exceedingly full and heavy' – which, according to Guillemeau, the obstetrician who gave his approval to this method, 'will show that the baby has descended.'[4] Finally, 'to make even more certain', and in particular so as to find out whether dilatation had begun, the midwife proceeded to palpate the private parts of the woman, after smearing her hands with fresh butter or lard. 'If she notes that the cervix is dilating, both on the exterior and on the interior, it is a sign that labour is beginning.'[5]

As we know, the midwife was not always as cautious as that, because she was usually incapable of doing the palpating which was the only way of discovering the nature of the presentation. At this early stage of labour she would be content to act on the external parts, attempting to stretch them to speed up the dilatation. At that time the womb was seen as a sanctuary whose internal arrangements must not be disturbed. It was only when the bag of waters

157

Breakdown of the midwife's work plan

1 Help mother	put in suitable position	head
		chest
		buttocks
		knees, feet
	moral support	
	material assistance	dilatation of opening of the womb
		piercing of the membranes
2 Help child	head	
	shoulders	
	put near the 'mother's parts' immediately after birth, then take away a few moments later and lay on its side until first cries	
	tie cord in two places; compress and bandage	
	pass baby to an assistant for wrapping in warm linen	
3 Help mother	detach and extract placenta and appendages	
	protect private parts from cold	
	allow a short rest	
4 Help child	wash in warm wine and fresh water	
	put on swaddling clothes	
	lay on its side	
5 Help mother	toilette	
	prepare bed for a longer rest	

After Madame du Coudray, *Abrégé de l'Art des Accouchements*, (Paris, 1785), pp. 61–90.

appeared at the vulva that the midwife would make any pronouncement on the presentation: in popular belief, 'the membranes take on the form and nature of the part which is presented first',[6] a belief which inevitably caused errors of judgement and ill-judged interventions.

Pressed to declare the sex of the child-to-be, the midwife would play the game, even if only to accentuate her own importance. She would claim to be able to tell from the colour of the waters as they came away. If they were 'pallid', 'they usually denote that it is a girl. If they are reddish, that it is a boy'.[7] In fact the midwife was not the only one to 'divine from the waters' in this way: most of the surgeon–obstetricians of the earlier seventeenth century did exactly the same.

Bread in the oven

Here again we find the metaphor of the bread in the oven, the 'mother as the cook of the baby': it allows us to understand certain practices preparatory to the confinement. Van Gennep, in his *Folklore of the Dauphiné*, reports that towards the end of the nineteenth century midwives in the Diois region used to put 'a hot loaf on the abdomen of the woman in labour' and make her drink 'an infusion of wood ashes': these methods, intended to ease the labour, must be understood as traces of sympathetic magic.[8] There are other, similar practices justified by the image of the womb as a warm place comparable to an oven, and not all of them concern preparations for the confinement: for post-partum haemorrhage Louise Bourgeois recommends taking 'clean earth, such as is used for the floor of an oven, mixing it with strong vinegar, spreading it on a cloth and putting on the loins: this moderates the warmth of the blood and stops the flow'.

If the baby is a loaf of bread, then it must have help to come out of the oven. The midwive 'settles herself near the woman', sitting on a low chair, 'in such a way that she can easily insert her hand or grasp the woman's private parts when necessary'.[9] She gave advice to the woman, 'asking her to hold her breath and keep her mouth closed, and to bear down as if going to stool'.[10]

Until the bag of waters burst, the midwife kept a close eye on the woman's abdomen and the neck of the womb. From time to time she pressed 'gently on the upper part of the abdomen with the flat of her hand, bringing the baby down little by little'.

This 'expression of the baby' was approved of by obstetricians in the sixteenth century (Roderic Castro, Rueff, Rhodion, Paré) and in the seventeenth (Guillemeau), but strongly disapproved of in the eighteenth. Thus, in 1770, Raulin denounced the consequences of such methods: 'The abdomen must not be pressed on, as some midwives do,' he says; 'it would be a foolish and imprudent thing to do and would endanger the child, which would be damaged by it; it might even die'. And although 'uterine expression' (also called the 'French push') was still recommended by some obstetricians even in the nineteenth century, it was only in cases where the baby was distressed or the mother's health gave cause for anxiety – heart trouble or emphysema.[11].

When dilatation was slow the midwife would make use of 'a cordial compounded of liquorice water, cinnamon water and extract of hyacinth'. She might make the woman swallow an egg, thinking that it would bring down the baby by sympathetic magic, since (as the obstetrician Paul Portal remarked) 'the child in the womb bathes in the waters like an egg-yolk in the egg-white'.[12]

The fish in the pond

At this point another image took over from that of the womb as oven: that of the womb as a watery environment. The rupturing of the membranes and the coming away of the waters mark an acceleration in the process of labour: inside, warmth and dilatation give way to dampness and movement; 'the waters in which the child bathes' gush forth from the womb; like a stick of wood carried away by the current, the baby 'fish' is about to leave its 'pond' to be born. Unfortunately the child did not always follow the waters which had nourished it; it might get stuck; the mother's private parts, dried out like a sandy beach in the sunshine, made the birth ever more difficult as the hours passed. 'The waves break on the beach, recede again and leave it almost dry.'[13] At that point the midwife had to 'urge the woman to a special effort', seize the child and drag it – which was not always easy, because 'the feet slip out of her hands like an eel'. Then she had to get a cloth, wrap it round the part of the child's body which was presented, and pull. At last the child would emerge from its unhealthy lair. Sometimes, alas, too late: its body was covered in a 'greenish scum such as is found in summer on stagnant marshes'. It was dead.

However, in the great majority of cases the labour was natural and the outcome good for both mother and baby. As soon as the waters had come away, the midwife's work was confined to waiting for the 'fruit to fall of its own accord, being in a perfect stage of ripeness' – to receive the baby, then the placenta. But, while Nature could be a good mother, she still needed some help! The midwife would set about disengaging the advancing head; if it was temporarily held up by 'the rigidity of the cervix, the resistance of the coccyx and the folds of the vagina' she would move it very carefully, laying her hands on either side of the face; she would pass her hands under the chin, and out would come the head. 'Ordinarily the body follows the head,' as midwives were fond of repeating so as to reassure themselves; she would move the baby from right to left, then left to right, very gently so as to avoid dislocating the limbs or neck. An experienced midwife knew how delicate the baby was and she took good care. Finally, one last contraction would expel the child.

The newborn baby was laid between its mother's legs, on its side, back to the vulva so as not to get the post-partum emissions in the face. The cord was put round its body to avoid compression, which might still be dangerous. Not until the first cry was the cord cut and removed.

'Preparing the Navel-string'

First, the midwife made a double ligature with linen thread, the first 'about four to six fingers' length from the child's abdomen', the second near the placenta. Then she cut the cord with a knife or pair of scissors, then carefully 'brought the cord up to the chld's abdomen'; she wrapped it with 'a piece of well-worn white linen' – less harsh than new cloth on that delicate skin – on which she had put 'a little unsalted butter, or oil or grease'.[14] Ambroise Paré recommeded a piece of folded linen 'soaked in rose or sweet almond oil to soothe the pain'.[15] Rose oil was still often used in the countryside, where asepsis was still unknown, in the early twentieth century.

Ways of tying the cord varied, as did the time when this was done. Some midwives cut the cord before tying it on the baby's side; others were accused of tying it too soon, before it had bled sufficiently, effectively killing the newborn baby.[16] Sometimes they might cut it too short, or worse still, forget the ligature altogether, causing umbilical hernias.[17] Doctors and priests reporting such incidents often tend to paint a gloomy picture of the midwife's conduct, but the large number of actual cases shows beyond doubt that there was often real negligence – or was it always negligence?

Cutting and tying the cord was not just a skilled job: there were numerous superstitions attaching to this vital stage in the process of labour and birth, and it was surrounded by a complex ritual. Cutting the cord meant a definitive separation of mother and offspring, giving autonomy to the child. This was no simple act in a society which saw symbolic significance in everything. And the task must fall to the midwife, since it was she who had held the two lives in her hands since the onset of labour.

This cord, symbol of months of close relationship between mother and baby, had to be treated with care. Before cutting and tying, the midwife began by pushing the blood from the placenta – that is, coming from the mother – on towards the baby's body, as if to give it a last benefit from that source of life. After the cutting, however, the blood escaping from the part of the cord hanging from the child's body had lost its capacity to nourish; it was now just 'bad blood', corrupted moreover by the air, and if no care was taken it might poison the baby; the midwife would express it by pressing outwards, before making the cut. Probably some midwives thought that these 'superfluities' ought to be left to drain away for as long as possible, so did not tie the cord at all. And their behaviour was but a reflection of precepts by ancient authors who advised not tying too soon, or even thought that tying was not really necessary. Even in the eighteenth century this 'draining of the poison' was seen as a means of protecting the child subsequently from smallpox.

In conformity with an ancient practice, the ligature was made nearer or further from the abdomen according as the child was girl or boy. Laurent Joubert reports that the 'village midwives' preferred to leave a 'good length of navel-string' in the case of a boy, 'because they think that the male member will take its pattern from it, and will become bigger if what still hangs from the navel has remained a good length'; for a girl, on the other hand, 'it is fitting ... that it should be stretched and tied very close, so that the womb which comes from it should have a narrower neck the more it is stretched'.[18] But a concern for sexual conformity was not always the reason for such practices. In the Landes early in the present century, the cord was always cut twenty centimetres away from the navel, the reason being that its length had an influence on the larynx: 'The longer it is left, the better the chance of the child having a beautiful voice.'[19]

The umbilical cord was also considered to be a good indicator of the couple's future fertility: the knots in it were counted carefully, for they were believed to represent the number of children which the woman had still to bear. 'And if there is no knot, she will have no more. And if there is a great distance between the said knots, the woman also will put a good interval between one pregnancy and the next; and if the distance is small, she will put scarcely any interval.' Finally, if the knots in the cord were black or red, 'she would have as many boys; and if they are white, as many girls'.[20] This belief was already known to the medieval Arab doctors Avicenna and Razes. It probably arose from the inevitable comparison between the 'strings of eggs' found in the bodies of laying hens and the 'knots in the cords of the afterbirth'.

Finally, great importance was attached to the shrivelled end of the cord which fell off, with the ligature, after a few days. When the child reached the age of three or four, it would be set to untie the ligature, and its skill in doing this would be a measure of its intelligence and cunning. In the nineteenth century, the mother would keep the cord very carefully so that it would bring her boy good luck when he became a man: sewn secretly into the lining of a garment, it would ensure that he drew the 'lucky number' which would exempt him from military service.

When the cord had been cut, the child was usually taken to the hearth: it was important to protect it carefully from cold, always dangerous to a newborn baby, especially in the winter season. A bandage was put over its eyes so that the brightness of the flames would not hurt them; coming from the darkness of the womb, it might be blinded if this precaution was not taken. Then the midwife would turn back to the mother.

Bringing Out the Afterbirth

Until the placenta had emerged, 'nothing was finished yet': the mother still had 'one foot in the grave'. Even the usual term for the placenta in the French of the time, the 'delivery' or 'deliverance', clearly shows that it was only after its expulsion that the woman could really be considered out of danger. The gravest complications could ensue if it adhered; sometimes it stuck so closely to the womb that it appeared to be wedded to it, like a glove clinging to a hand or a piece of dough clinging to a table top. Portal met such a case in 1672: 'I slipped my fingers into the back part of the womb and the inferior, that is the lower, part of the afterbirth', he writes. 'I separated them gently, slipping my fingers up to the end, as bakers do when they are trying to lift a mass of dough which has been put on a table without sprinkling it with flour first.'[21]

When the placenta came away piece by piece, it was always necessary to ensure that nothing was left at the end. The mother's recovery, and sometimes her very life, depended on this precaution. After delivering another woman, Portal reconstituted the placenta: 'I noticed,' he reports, 'that four fingers' width was missing, which I removed, and at once this woman returned, as it were, from death and told us she felt quite well.'[22]

There were three possible ways to deal with a recalcitrant placenta, 'gnarled as bacon rind' and adhering firmly to the bottom of the womb. Portal would put his hand methodically into the womb and detach it gently. Some midwives would extract the 'deliverance' by pulling on the cord; they were incapable of waiting until nature should rid herself of this now alien body of her own accord, and, eager to be finished quickly, they took the risk of breaking the cord, or worse, of causing a prolapse of the uterus. Their haste came from fear that the neck of the womb would contract too quickly after the birth of the child, a fear shared by many practitioners until the eighteenth century. However, the commonest method was to attach the cord to the woman's thigh, and wait. This way of doing it is explained by the midwife's fear that the afterbirth would go back up the womb, to the 'top of the abdomen', and choke the woman.[23] This was in fact the method recommended by Louise Bourgeois, who declared that during the two thousand deliveries which she had performed, she had not had her hand in the womb more than twice.

To facilitate the expulsion of the placenta, the midwives had perfected some simple empirical techniques. These were to press on the woman's abdomen, massaging it with the hand; or to make her blow as hard as she could into her hands or an empty bottle. This custom persisted everywhere up to the nineteenth century, and up to 1920 in Burgundy, the Landes and the mountains near Nice.[24] The respiratory effort tended to stimulate the muscles of the abdominal wall and uterus, and so facilitate the expulsion of the placenta.

Sternutatories had also been in use, since the fifteenth century: powdered hellebore, pepper and spurge were supposed to be particularly effective in childbirth and the delivery of the placenta, and they were recommended by doctors. At the beginning of the seventeenth century, Jacques Duval advised giving the woman 'sneezing powder so that, when sneezing, and at the same instant pressing on and squeezing both the nose and the mouth, the violence of the sternutation affects the lower parts more than the upper ones' – and thus helped the emergence of the placenta.[25] This method was still being recommended by Cosme Viardel in the mid-seventeenth century, but it was severely criticized, as being harmful, by Paul Portal a few years later.

One final procedure was used by midwives: the provocation of nausea in the newly delivered woman. The method was exactly the same as that used in cases of difficult labour. They would put threads or hairs into the mother's throat, or make her swallow, willy nilly, a vomitive potion compounded of 'cyclamen root or common sowbread', ground to a powder, added to half a glass of wine. 'This drink caused two or three fits of vomiting, which were soon followed by the expulsion of the afterbirth.' It seems that this remedy was efficacious; but it had the grave disadvantage of causing loss of blood later on.[26] Matthiolus says that a decoction of medlars and birthwort was equally excellent in cases of retained placenta.

But all in all, there was nothing better than a potion based on powdered umbilical cord, or animal afterbirth! This was frequently used in the countryside of Normandy, as Jacques Duval points out: 'Those who, deprived of the comforts of the town, are obliged to make use of what they can find in the fields, make a fumigation with cat's or lamb's droppings and horse's hoof, or even apply a cow's afterbirth to the abdomen; or they administer some potion of it which they have kept, ground down and mixed with white wine.'[27] Up to the end of the seventeenth century people were not content with animal afterbirths: powdered human afterbirth in a glass of water was also swallowed by a mother who took a little too long to reject the placenta and its appendages. Even in towns, all apothecaries had some at the bottom of some pot or other, as is shown by their inventories at the time. So great were the virtues of placental opotherapy that it was in frequent use; indeed, it is possible that extract of placenta really worked. However, as the eighteenth century went by obstetricians started to object to a type of sympathetic medicine which they held to be singularly repellent. La Motte, at Valognes, at the beginning of that century, and later on Fried, in Strasbourg, firmly rejected its use, maintaining that with a little patience the placenta would be expelled naturally.

Through the nineteenth century, while the ingestion of powdered placenta to help the expulsion progressively disappeared, some symbolic customs remained. In the Landes, the husband's beret – because it obviously looks like a placenta – was put inside out on the woman's head, and was supposed to ensure the delivery of the afterbirth.[28]

12

The Placenta: Double of the Child

The placenta, breast to the embryo
William Harvey, De generat. animal.

The rituals surrounding a birth were not unlike those surrounding a death. A dead man left his bodily remains and his clothes behind him; just so, a newborn baby appeared along with the placenta and its appendages, which were carefully attended to because they were part of the mystery of birth.

The child came into the world along with its 'scrip', the placenta, the intermediary which had given him warmth and nourishment and protected his growth in the womb. It used to be believed that this nourishing capacity could continue after the expulsion of the placenta at the birth, until the cord was cut. The cutting of the cord marked the final physical separation of mother and child, and of child and placenta.

Instinctive Repugnance?

Nowadays the merest allusion to that mass of flabby tissue provokes a feeling of disgust. Produced by the body, and from its depths, the placenta is in the twilight zone of childbirth, as a sort of counterpart to the child, and it is almost never spoken of. If one asks most women who gave birth at home in the 1920s and 1930s, they often do not know what became of the placenta; they are even visibly surprised at being asked about it.[1] It is not talked about because it 'does not exist'.[2] While in some human societies the placenta is always treated with respect[3] and handled with ritual care, in Western societies it 'no longer exists': veneration on one side, total neglect on the other.

In France, however, this denial of the placenta is of recent date. Up to the nineteenth century, it was seen as the child's 'other self', his double. It was also the rootstock, symbolizing the transmission of fertility; it was respected, it 'existed'.

The sudden feeling of repulsion for the human placenta led to the suppression of the instinctive behaviour seen in domestic animals with their own placenta. Everyday observation shows that all female animals eat these residues after the birth; sometimes even the males participate in this feast at the expense of the afterbirth. Both oviparous and viviparous creatures, both wild animals and tame, practice this ingestion of the former surrounding of the embryo.[4] This 'devouring' of the placenta by animals did not escape the notice of the authors of obstetric textbooks. As early as Mauriceau they were noting that 'in animals . . . each of the young has in its cell a kind of personal placenta, which the mother eats as soon as she has voided it, having gnawed and severed with her teeth the umbilical vessels adhering to it.'[5]

Countryfolk were always opposed to this habit. A farmer's wife would take away eggshells as the chicks hatched so that the broody hen could not eat them; the alleged reason was that the chicks might hurt themselves on them! And even nowadays a stocksman will remove the placenta which a cow or mare has just expelled, 'for no other reason than a feeling of disgust'. This popular taboo was reinforced in the nineteenth century by the teachings of veterinary surgeons who advised removing the placenta after a calf was born: 'It is repugnant,' says a textbook on veterinary obstetrics, 'and for that reason, it must certainly be prevented.'[6] This insistence on repugnance and disgust is not gratuitous: it is a tone calculated to arouse distrust. It was thought that letting a female eat the eggshells or the placenta would encourage her to devour her own young. The farmer's wife did not want to 'get the hens into the habit of eating eggs'; and the sacs and the bloodstained straw must be removed when the sow had finished pigging, because they 'encouraged her and pushed her to the act' of devouring her own progeny.[7] Thus farmers were advised to keep a close eye on the sow so as to save the piglets from her ferocious appetite and put them to the teats immediately, since 'once they have sucked, she leaves them alone'. As a matter of fact, if a sow, or a cat or bitch, does happen to devour its young, it is apparently by mistake, 'such females being under the impression that they are eating the afterbirth which has been taken away'.[8]

But what was being monitored, besides the behaviour of the animals, was that of women. There was a suspicious awareness of ancient customs which had to be concealed and suppressed. The lurking image of the mother eating her placenta perhaps concealed another lurking image: the mother devouring her own children. In the eighteenth century it was in fact known that there were cultures in some parts of the world where this actually happened. In his *Varieties of the Human Race* Buffon reports that in North America mothers and fathers sometimes ate their babies immediately after the birth.[9] The same custom is attested in the last century in Australia, where a mother would love her offspring, 'but this did not prevent her, in times of famine, and especially if she had borne twins, from taking one of them for food'.[10]

No-one could be indifferent to such things: they raise questions about our own past. Did our ancestors follow suchlike 'barbarous practices'? And how can we fail to be repelled by the idea? In which case the best thing is to exclude the placenta, to deny its existence, as if to deny antecedents which cast doubt on our very humanity.

The Placenta Does Exist

The placenta is what comes *after*, the last thing to be expelled from the womb. Language itself gives it its place in the process of birth: 'afterbirth', *arrière-faix* in French, *Nachgeburt* in German. It is the product of a second expulsion; hence the word 'secundine' (*secundinae mulierum*), in use up to the beginning of the nineteenth century. But, as experience showed that only the arrival of the placenta could put an end to the mother's danger, it was also known in French as the *délivre* or *délivrance*, the end of the perils of childbirth.

The physiological role of the placenta during gestation used to be closely associated with its symbolic function. For nine months it was first and foremost the 'child's nurse', a sort of fellow-prisoner on which the foetus relied absolutely, an intermediary which took food so as to give it to another. No less important was its role as protector; while its function as a biological filter was not fully understood,[11] it was known to provide the foetus with material comforts. It helped to make the prison endurable. According to the Hippocratic tradition, which persisted until the eighteenth century, the child rested upon it in a sitting or crouching position: it was 'the seat of the child'. The popular image was rather different from the learned one: the child resting in its mother's womb must surely be lying down, thus the placenta was 'the child's bed'.

The placenta brings us into contact, once again, with the image of the womb as an oven. Along with its appendages it constituted the 'residue' after cooking was completed; however, this description had no pejorative overtones – on the contrary. During pregnancy the placenta had acted like a raising agent, allowing the 'dough' to take shape. After the expulsion it retained its identity as a 'rootstock' or 'thallus', a little piece of fertility. In comparison with the 'bread' – the baby, which, being mortal, was perishable – the placenta guaranteed the continuance of the cycle of life. Its form, and its function in preserving the human 'plantation', earned it the designation of 'cake'[12] which it retained up to the dawn of the present century: it was as nourishing as bread, but of a higher quality, the best part of the 'cooking'. In various parts of France it was known as a 'loaf', 'tart' or 'biscuit'.

After birth, when the placenta acquired autonomy, it was never, symbolically speaking, considered to be separate from the child: a very strong and close link always remained.[13]

What is to be Done with the Placenta?

The placenta simply could not be neglected: the child's future career depended on it, because the child inevitably suffered from the repercussions of any misadventure on the part of its double. Thus it would be unseemly and imprudent to consider the afterbirth as a useless encumbrance. As a bodily product, like nails and hair, it has 'an ambiguous function, healing or harmful, according to the intentions of the use'.[14] At all costs, animals and other people must be prevented from getting hold of it: the subsequent fertility of the parents and the phratry depended on it. For these reasons the fate of the placenta was never left to chance.

In most cases it was buried by the father immediately after the birth, under the floor of either the house or one of the outbuildings, so that the household would benefit from its power to encourage fertility, whether in the garden or in the fields nearby. After that it was important to leave it alone, to dissolve slowly into the life-giving soil. In the Landes, early this century, 'it was most often buried in a corner of the garden where the soil was not due to be disturbed for a long time'.[15] In most regions it used to be put at the foot of a young fruit tree, which probably implies a sort of symbolic return to the 'mother', the tree.[16] In any case, there was nothing more similar to the structure of the placenta than the underground part of the tree: the endless ramifications of the rootlets were like the veins and arteries in the placenta. In Germany a choice was made according to the sex of the child (since trees also have sexes): a pear-tree for a boy, an apple-tree for a girl.[17] In nineteenth-century Anjou the placenta was buried near a flower, which then became a sort of 'breast-brother' to the baby.[18]

The placenta could also be hung up to dry in a secret place in the house, often in the chimney corner: this custom persists to this day in northern Portugal.[19] In Germany it was tied to the branch of a tree and left to dry in the open air.[20] In all parts of France, up to the beginning of the nineteenth century, it was partially reduced to powder and used in folk medicines.

Sometimes the placenta would be thrown into water. It should be said that this was infrequent, at least in France.[21] This might be seen as a simple desire to get rid of it, to hide something shameful; thus, when a midwife had been unable to remove the afterbirth in one piece, she might throw it away into a river so that the obstetrician would not be able to inspect it later. It might also be thrown into the 'privy', for the same reasons or simply to get rid of it, especially from the nineteenth century onwards, when its long-remembered symbolic function was at last beginning to recede.

Cremation of the placenta was certainly another late practice which aimed to conceal a mistake. Seventeenth and eighteenth-century obstetrical textbooks note cases of placentas thrown 'behind the fire' or 'under the coals' by midwives before the practitioner's arrival. The surgeon Philippe Peu tells how he was called one day to attend the wife of a valet, and 'having asked to see the afterbirth', he was told that it had been 'thrown among the ashes'.[22] Peu is quick to criticize the midwives' habit of 'being in such a hurry to throw away the afterbirth, to put it on the fire, or on the ashes', because he saw it as an obvious wish to get rid of incriminating evidence. Such practices were, naturally, confined to the towns, where the midwives might think such an inspection likely. They may indicate a change of attitude towards the placenta; but they remained very marginal,[23] for one very important reason: throwing the placenta on the fire was supposed to bring a risk of inflammation in the mother. A perfect example of the vigour of tradition influenced by the doctrine of 'signatures'.

But, going beyond its supposed symbolic function, the placenta was also rich in healing virtues, which certainly were not going to be neglected.

Placental Opotherapy

The idea of using the placenta in medicine goes back a long way. Placental opotherapy was practised in Antiquity, and Hippocratic texts speak of the human afterbirth as an element in the pharmacopoeia; the doctors of Salerno went on prescribing it, as did the practitioners of the seventeenth century; but in the eighteenth century the medical profession showed signs of rejecting it: the placenta became something repugnant which must be got rid of. And it was not until the end of the nineteenth century, under the influence of Brown-Séquard and his school, that there was a renewal of interest in the human placenta, whose immunizing and galactogenic properties were then being discovered, or rather, rediscovered.

Old apothecaries' notebooks and lists of drugs always considered the human placenta to be particularly effective in treating freckles, various naevi on the body, and erectile tumours. A choice must be made in advance, for not all placentas had the same virtues, as Nicolas Leméry commented towards the end of the seventeenth century: 'Those coming from the birth of a boy,' he wrote, 'are preferable to those from that of a girl. It must be selected when freshly emerged from a strong, healthy, unblemished and good-looking woman; it is applied to the face, still hot from the womb, to remove freckles.'[24] Some apothecaries judged that the afterbirth from a first child was richer and therefore more effective. The placenta's capacity to help skin regeneration had certainly been proved experimentally.

It was also held to be of sovereign effectiveness in the treatment of epilepsy and apoplexy. In the mid-eighteenth century David Planis Campy advised using the product of an evaporated distillation of the secundine, and as late as 1739, Frederick Hoffman was maintaining that there was no better remedy than powdered human placenta.

In many parts of France, it was part of the ritual of birth to place the placenta on the baby's face and body and on the mother's breast. Doctors found this prospect revolting, and unfailingly protested against this return to primitivism whenever they happened to witness it! If they had taken the trouble to inquire, they would soon have discovered the reason: in the Landes, where the custom was practised until the beginning of this century, rubbing with the placenta was supposed to protect against chapping, and in particular cracking of the nipple.[25] It was a simple, and (apparently) effective means of preventing prospective problems with the suckling of the child.

Indeed, it was often thought that the placenta could help the mother's milk. According to early medical theory, menstrual blood turned into milk after the birth and so made it possible to feed the newborn baby. This change, it was believed, needed to be stimulated and encouraged if the milk was slow to come or remained insufficient. It was known from experience that the baby's energetic sucking of the nipple was the principal factor in encouraging the production of milk;[26] but it must also have been proven that eating the placenta helped the milk to come.

It is hard to be sure if eating the placenta for therapeutic reasons went on in France up to the nineteenth century; our sources are unusually discreet about this subject. But it does seem probable, on the evidence of other European societies up to the middle of the last century. Even at the beginning of the twentieth century, eating the placenta to stimulate the milk was commonplace among the poor people of the Abbruzzi: to stop the flow from drying up the mother was made to drink 'a broth made with chicken meat with a fragment of the actual placenta of the recently delivered woman'.[27]

But therapeutic reasons, profound and justifiable as they might be, are insufficient in themselves to justify the prevalence of the custom of eating the placenta in Western societies up to recent times.

'The Fertile Cake'

The power of conferring fertility which was attributed to the placenta was certainly more important than any therapeutic action. It has, in fact, always been thought capable of assisting in procreation. Old drug lists never failed to point out the aphrodisiac properties of human and animal afterbirths;[28] the 'hippomanes', or fleshy membrane made up of the placenta and appendages with which a foal is covered at birth, was the base and foundation of the 'love philtre' of Antiquity.[29]

The placenta was also long believed to be the specific for infertility. J. Constant de Rebecque's *The Charitable French Doctor* (1683) still advises childless couples to take powdered human afterbirth. Placentophagy, the custom of eating the newly expelled placenta, has existed at various times amongst peoples of very different cultures. From the sixteenth century onwards, European travellers to the new world were much struck by this custom, which they unfailingly reported. After a voyage to Brazil in 1556, Jean de Léry wrote that Indians, like animals, ate the afterbirth immediately after expulsion;[30] at the beginning of the eighteenth century, Gemelli Carreri reported that among the Yakonde of Siberia the father would take the afterbirth as soon as it appeared, cook it and eat it with his friends and relatives.[31] There can be no doubt that the habit of eating the placenta was extremely widespread at one time.

In Europe, however, doctors and churchmen were more and more repelled, from the end of the seventeenth century onwards, by this custom of placentophagy, so 'repugnant to humanity'. In the course of the eighteenth century, powdered afterbirth disappeared from the pharmacopoeia, and in medical discourse a certain embarrassment begins to appear whenever the placenta is mentioned.

One question in particular caused much dispute among obstetricians – and theologians – in the mid-eighteenth century: what did Adam and Eve do about the cord and placenta of Cain? The importance of this debate at the time may seem grotesque to us; in reality it indicates the uneasiness caused in 'enlightened' milieux by the obvious truth that men and women had been, and perhaps still were, guilty of the bestial act of eating the placenta! Thus in Jean Astruc's manual of obstetrics, published in 1768, no less than thirteen pages are devoted to the problem. Among the five solutions he offers, the most striking is the second, which shows the difficulty he felt himself to be in: 'He [Adam] thus knew, having seen it many a time, that the young of all quadrupeds are born with a shapeless mass attached to their navel by the umbilical cord. He also knew that the females of such animals, even those which did not live on flesh, would eat this mass, or placenta, after dropping their young.'

At this point in his deliberations, Astruc hastily dismisses the idea that Adam might have imitated the animals of the earthly Paradise when his own children were born: 'I do not mean to say,' he writes, 'that Adam ate their afterbirths.' Unfortunately Astruc's remark rather invites the contrary interpretation, and some of his contemporaries did not fail to see it. Sue le Jeune, reporting in 1779 on what Astruc had written, was indignant: 'This idea is *now* repellent to our minds.'[32] By thus energetically repelling the idea that the practice had truly existed in ancient times, it was made to look all the more unlikely that it might still exist.

Thus the fertility rite which placentophagy entailed was condemned; but this did not mean that the symbolism of the placenta as giver of fertility disappeared. From the end of the seventeenth century, or even earlier, the authority of the Church produced a modification in meaning. As in other cases, this was encouraged by the persistence of the image, and the word itself.

In all social levels in France, the word 'cake' was always the one preferred to designate the afterbirth; 'placenta' was more learned, more 'medical' and thus less common. In the ceremony of churching, which the Church fostered energetically, especially from the seventeenth century, the woman coming solemnly to her purification would bring 'two rolls', 'two pieces of bread' or 'two cakes' to be blessed.[33] One would then be offered to the sanctuary or to the priest; the other was taken back home and shared among the members of the family, or more often (in the eighteenth century) among the village women of childbearing age, especially those who were still childless. At the end of the nineteenth century, the following advice was still being given to such women in Lower Poitou: 'Eat part of the churching cake and you are bound to conceive.'[34] And in the Vosges Highlands, at about the same time, if a pregnant woman was at a wedding feast she would offer the bride, as the feasting commenced, 'a piece of bread which she sanctifies with the sign of the cross and gives to her saying "May it do you as much good as to me." '[35] The final stage, in Alsace, was to make the cake in the shape of a child, as is shown by the cake-tins in the Alsatian Museum at Strasbourg: by then the image of the child had completely ousted that of its 'double', the placenta.

The provenance, shape and date of making the cake might vary from place to place, but the offering and the sharing out were always part of a fertility ritual. The cake of dough simply replaced the 'cake' of the afterbirth. As it became Christianized, the symbolism retained something of its original value for a time; but as the nineteenth century went by it was gradually forgotten, and the practice became part of folklore before disappearing altogether.

Placenta

Doctors	*Midwives and common belief*
1 It provides nourishment	
'pancreas of the womb'	'nurse to the child'
'uterine hearth'	'nursing mother'
'embryo's nipple'	
2 Child's resting place	
'seat'	'couch'
'cushion'	
'cloaca'	
3 That which comes 'after'	
'afterbirth'	'afterbirth'
secundinae mulieris	'delivery'
	'secundine'
4 Coming from the oven	
'cake'	'cake'
	'loaf'
	'tart'
	'biscuit'
	(Christianized practices)
	'rolls' for the churching
	'pieces of bread' for the churching

Outer Membranes

'chorion'	'tunics'
chorema	
1 *loculus*	
'outer membrane'	
'amnion'	
2 *amnios*	'lamb's tunic'
'lamb's tunic'	'Saint Francis' tunic'
'outer membrane'	'coif' or 'robe'
	for a boy: *for a girl*:
	'cover', 'armour' 'alb', 'robe'

Sources: Louise Bourgeois, Madame du Coudray, Jacques Duval, Harvey, Laurent Joubert, Paul Portal.

13

The Governance of Mother and Child

At the expulsion of the placenta, the midwife would check carefully 'to make sure it was all there'; satisfied, she would set it aside, and make sure that the mother was well and that the lochia were flowing normally. Then she would turn back to the child.

Care of the Child

Taking up the child, the midwife would first check that her hasty ligature held firm; then she would see about cleaning out its stomach and purging it, washing it and clothing it.

'Clean the interior'

The midwife would prepare a spoonful or two of warm wine, into which she would pour a little honey or sugar; this liquid she would pour gently into the baby's mouth. She might mix in a little Venice treacle 'to comfort the stomach and cleanse it of some filth which might otherwise injure it'. Some midwives even went so far as to give neat wine, 'saying that wine thus administered prevents the child from getting drunk easily when it begins to grow up':[1] the first wine the child drank would make it resistant to intoxication later. The wine – preferably red wine – was supposed to 'make up the stomach' and 'make the child strong'. In nineteenth-century Berry it was said that 'the redder the wine, the healthier-looking the child will be when it grows up, that is to say, the ruddier complexion it will have'.[2] This use of wine, neat or diluted, was common down to the beginning of the twentieth century; it was thought that a small spoonful of neat wine, espeically after a rather long labour, 'helped the child recover its spirits' and 'cuts through the phlegm' it usually had in its throat; finally, 'the vapour of the wine, mounting to the brain, strengthens it' and ensured that it was never subject to epilepsy, 'which disease proceeds from no other cause than the weakness of the brain'.[3]

After doing what she could for the stomach, the midwife took thought for the intestines. The child must bring up the meconium, the blackish plug which obstructed the larger intestine at birth. Ambroise Paré advised purging it with 'sweet almond oil, syrup of roses, Venice treacle or a drop of honey as big as a chick-pea'. Midwives were more likely to use a piece of cooked apple, whose laxative virtues had been recognized for many a year. Their next task was to cleanse the baby of the blood and 'as it were, pommade' which covered its body.

Washing the new baby

The midwives took great care in removing the sebaceous coating which was then seen as a sort of residue of sexual relations during pregnancy. They knew that it was necessary to 'wash and cleanse the child, not only its face, but also its body and the corners of the armpits, groin or buttocks, and joints'. Some of them used melted butter, some rose oil, others walnut oil. All would try to 'make its skin stronger, and block the pores so that the outside air could not damage it, and altogether to strengthen it all over'.[4] In removing this 'soft, white substance, greasy to the touch' they were imitating other viviparous animals who, by instinct, lick their young as soon as they are born.[5] These ablutions could be performed by rubbing with scented water, or in a bath of lukewarm water with a little wine in it. But it was vital not to put the child in water that was too hot, for that might give it a 'swarthy skin'![6] On the other hand, 'to plunge the child into cold water as soon as it was born' seemed contrary to the law of nature. What it needed was 'a bath at the same temperature as the womb'.

On this point, Rousseau himself counselled prudence; he advised starting with a warm bath and lowering the temperature little by little until one gradually got to a cold one. In olden times, among the northern peoples – Scandinavian and German – who practised immersion in cold water, the idea was to test the toughness of the newborn child; and even in the nineteenth century, Russian babies went straight from a warm bath to a cold one, as if to temper their bodies – which caused the death of a goodly number of them.[7] Needless to say, such practices have nothing more to do with the washing of the baby. Cultural attitudes took priority over the concern for cleanliness.

In France in the seventeenth and eighteenth centuries, the washing was often rounded off by the cleaning of ears, eyes and 'all the child's orifices', using 'little tents' – twists of fine linen. This was also recommended by late eighteenth-century practitioners' manuals, which aimed at giving advice to mothers, midwives and nurses.[8]

As she washed it, the midwife would check that the new baby was not afflicted with some malformation – perforated anus or urethra – which might cause its early death; unhappily, there was nothing anyone could do about such a handicap in country districts.

When the baby had been a long time in the birth-canal, it was necessary to 'treat the injuries and bruises it has received in emerging from its mother's womb';[9] sometimes it was in such a sorry state that its very humanity was in doubt. In 1709, Mauquest de La Motte delivered the wife of a tanner in Valognes of a boy 'which was certainly the most hideous thing imaginable, with the face rather of a monster than of a child, because of the awful colouring and swelling of its face, and the disproportionate thickness of its lips, which caused all those present to look at it in consternation'.[10] In such cases a cloth soaked in warm wine or brandy and applied to the contusions of the face would bring the child back 'to its natural state' in less than twenty-four hours.

Resuscitating a Baby

After a long and difficult birth there was always some justifiable fear for the life of the baby. Had the cord been compressed in the canal, or was it twisted round the baby's neck? Then the baby would be choking, its body bluish red, or perhaps livid; it would seem unable to take its first breath, and would be motionless, as if dead: apnoea. At that point only prompt and skilled action by the midwife could save it; she would be careful not to cut the cord, for, to her mind, a return to life could only be achieved by keeping the link between child and placenta.

The midwives' resuscitation techniques were, to say the least, rudimentary, and many had been arrived at experimentally; they showed a certain amount of common sense, and quite often proved efficacious.

To bring 'apparently dead' babies back to life, 'to revive the vital spirits' in them, the midwife would do her best to keep the baby's body warm, or warm it up if necessary. For she knew by experience that a drop in body temperature, especially in winter, would bring about an early death; this child, just come lifeless from the warmth of its mother, must be preserved. So it was wrapped in cloths which had been warmed before the fire, and set down near the hearth.

Starting the breathing

But warmth was not enough; the breathing must be restarted. So the midwife would make haste to insert a finger and remove the mucus which obstructed its throat and nasal passages. If necessary, she would try resuscitation by insufflation: she would take a mouthful of wine or brandy and blow sharply, releasing a fine spray into the mouth or onto the face of the baby. In 1786, the Priest at Boyne, in the Millau region, reported that the local midwife, Françoise Lavabre, aged sixty, had told him that 'when children appear to be dead, she would quickly take a mouthful of brandy and blow into the baby's mouth'.[11]

Exactly the same method was used at the beginning of the seventeenth century to resuscitate a newborn dauphin in a very sad case – it was in fact the future Louis XIII – or so we are told by Louise Bourgeois, who brought him to birth:

I looked the child in the face, and saw it was very weak from the pains it had endured. I asked Monsieur de Lozeray, one of the king's chief *valets de chambre*, for some wine. He brought a bottle; I asked him for a spoon. The king took the bottle he was holding. I said to him: 'Sire, if it were any other child, I would put some wine in my mouth, and would give him some of it, for fear lest the weakness last too long.' The king put the bottle up to my mouth and said to me 'Do as you would for any other child.' I filled my mouth with wine and blew some into him; at that very hour, he came to himself and tasted the wine that I had given him.[12]

'Seasoning' substances were, as is well known, important in old-style medicines. The midwives unfailingly made use of them; they would chew up some onion or garlic, or some grains of mustard, and blow them 'into the mouth, the nostrils, the ears and even the fundament'; in Provence they would 'chew up some cloves and breathe into the child's mouth'.[13]

Insufflation through the mouth or nostrils was a frequent practice: the midwife would blow air into the chest, not too hard so as not to inflate the stomach too much, but hard enough to 'detach the mucous material filling the bronchial tubes'. Some of them would jib at such an unattractive task, if the child was covered with blood and filth even to the face; in that case they would make use of a 'feather-stalk' or 'straw', pinch the child's nostrils together, and blow; to clear the tubes so that the child could take its first breath, some midwives even made use of the household bellows.

Some midwives also recommended damp linen and baths. Cloths would be soaked in lukewarm water, wine or brandy and placed on the child's body – on the head, chest, stomach, or even on the cord; this would be done several times if necessary.[14] A warm bath with some admixture of wine or spirits might receive child and placenta together.

Acting on the placenta

Everywhere, the placenta was supposed to be essential in resuscitating a newborn baby. In his *Manual for Attending to the Sick* (1786), Carrère declared that in Languedoc 'in this connection there is a fairly general custom: the placenta is laid on the stomach of the child, or the afterbirth is dipped in warm wine before the cord is cut'. This method was not new, for medical authority had been recommending it since the sixteenth century. Ambroise Paré himself was in favour of it: 'The said child can attract and receive heat and some remains of spirits still contained in the said afterbirth', he writes, 'for which reason you should place it on the stomach of the child and leave it until it has exhaled all its warmth; for in this way it will help to augment its strength and in consequence to prolong its life.'[15]

Since the placenta did not retain its heat for very long, efforts were made to preserve it. In late eighteenth-century Provence, for example, village midwives 'try to warm [the child] before tying the cord, by placing the placenta on burning coals or by frying it . . . in a pan with some wine'.[16] A perfectly logical step, if not an effective one: the afterbirth, engorged with blood, was warmed so that the vital fluid would begin to move again, pass to the newborn baby and bring it out of its torpor.

To start the heart beating

The midwife would often make use of simple methods of mechanical stimulation. The commonest was rubbing with wine, cider, vinegar or brandy – over the whole body, but in particular the chest, stomach and temples. In some cases the soles of the feet, stomach and heart region would be rubbed instead, without applying liquid. In cases of cardiac arrest the midwife might even suck on the child's left breast; this method, which was to be taken up by some obstetricians in the eighteenth century, was already known in the Germanic countries and in Eastern Europe in the second half of the seventeenth.

This succour proved successful in Kilia on 24 June in the year 1681. In vain we had laboured at pricking the child with horsehair, blowing in its mouth and lower abdomen; it still would not give any sign of life. Finally the midwife began to suck the child's left breast; scarcely had she begun than the child gave proof that it was alive . . ..[17]

In truth, none of these procedures was new: they belonged to an old stock known since Antiquity. And a midwife who pushed the blood back along the cord in an attempt to resuscitate the child was unknowingly following a precept laid down by Aristotle.

Resuscitate or let be?

For many years things were done which we now find quite astounding. Madame du Coudray, writing her textbook at the end of the eighteenth century, was indignant at the careless attitude of midwives and onlookers towards the apparently dead newborn baby:

They make haste to wrap it in a rag and expose it on the ground in one of the furthest corners of the room so as to spare the mother so sad a sight; there can be no doubt that some are buried which are certainly alive . . ... I found one of these children which had already had one of its toes eaten by a dog, without anybody noticing; surely such negligence is most painful to our humanity.[18]

Making every possible allowance for dramatic exaggeration in such a description, we must still ask: why in such cases was the newborn child not better treated? Was it because help to the mother took priority? Or was it because they knew by experience that even if it was revived, a baby which had suffered from prolonged apnoea would never be more than a weakly creature and a drag on the family? Must we see this 'negligence' and reluctance to help as a disguised form of infanticide? Perhaps we should see this attitude as no more than resignation in the face of death, which used to be so omnipresent in everyday life.

Neither did obstetricians give any sort of priority to the resuscitation of newborn babies, up to the mid-seventeenth century. If they did intervene, it would only be with the most rudimentary resuscitation techniques, scarcely different from those used by some midwives. Textbooks of obstetrics, too, have little to say about resuscitation, and François Mauriceau was the first to devote a whole chapter to the question. He rejects the custom of placing a clove of garlic or a piece of onion in the child's mouth, and the placing of the placenta on the baby's stomach, because its weight works against 'the most important thing', the establishment of breathing; he is opposed to attempts at warming the afterbirth on a fire or in warm wine.

Around 1660–70, the desire to save a child born apparently dead appears a little more clearly in the towns. Mauriceau is thus a witness to a change in public attitudes. He notes that an apparently dead child can be saved by prompt action and suitable techniques; but it was not really until after 1740 that the movement broadened and began to bear fruit.

Post-partum Care

After washing, the child was entrusted to a nurse to be dressed. The midwife turned back to the mother, to take further care of her before putting her to bed. She would check once again that the cleansings were in order.

Ejecting the lochia and 'clearing the bowels'

Usually the midwife arranged the woman so that she was 'neither lying, nor sitting . . . with her head and body a little more upright than if she were lying, so that the cleansings can flow more easily.' To make this position easier to assume she 'puts under her calves a rolled-up pillow, so as to keep her knees up and so that the thighs and legs are nowhere lower than horizontal'.[19]

The lochia would be more or less abundant according to physical type: some woman 'emptied too much', others 'too little'; those who had 'too much blood' or 'a superfluity of thick black blood' risked a rapid deterioration in health. To encourage purgation and overcome discomfort among women whose blood was 'too thick', Louise Bourgeois advised administering, first thing in the morning, 'a lotion of maidenhair fern, with honey and water, or of hyssop, or syrup of absinth with white wine'; any broth must be of 'roots and aperient herbs'. She also recommended bleeding from the foot, preferably in the morning. Finally, it was a good idea to administer, two or three times a day, a fumigation which would draw off the 'bad blood' and cleanse the womb – but not before the eighth day, or 'there is a fear of drawing it too low'! To encourage the blood to flow, a final touch was rubbing with violet oil 'in the pit of the stomach and on the groin',[20] for there was 'nothing more harmful than retained lochia'.[21] On the other hand, those who had too little blood had to follow a diet suitable to their constitution: little and often was the golden rule.

Constipation could once again be a threat to the woman's health. The custom of staying for several days in bed – longer in the town than in the country, in well-off households than in poor ones – had a lot to do with it: 'New mothers, because of being in bed, lose the benefit of regularity,' And so, to avoid the complications caused by lazy bowels, midwives would make sure to 'give purgation by mouth' immediately after the birth. 'They make them take two spoonfuls of olive oil with sugar, to make their bowels move: this is the customary remedy of the poor.'[22] Louise Bourgeois disapproved, since purging seemed to her to be too risky: 'One should take care only of the intestine.' In years of experience she had all too often seen careless nurses who took it upon themselves to 'give senna to new mothers from the first few days after the birth, whereby several became dangerously ill, and others died.'[23]

Avoiding chills

The midwife's next task was the toilette of the mother. She would clean vulva, buttocks and thighs, stained with blood and lochia, with warm water, alone or mixed with wine. This toilette was normally performed quickly, especially in winter, for fear of chills to the stomach or the 'mouth of the womb'. Thus much more importance was attached to the protection of the private parts than to the toilette as such. The midwife would put 'a cloth, or a good clean sponge, washed in warm water and wrung out, between the [woman's] thighs and near her nature, fearing that being thus open, cold air might find its way inside'.[24] Popular opinion held that if the lochia did not flow satisfactorily, and above all if a cold draught got into the womb, this might cause 'an abundant harvest of after-pains', the colics which so painfully affected many new mothers. With the first child they were supposed to be less frequent than with later ones; God, it was said, wanted not to frighten them 'from the beginning of their bringing children into the world'.[25] Many were the concoctions which were tried to attenuate and even prevent these stomach troubles after subsequent confinements. Louise Bourgeois boasts of the virtues of 'Queen's powder' containing comfrey root, peach stones, nutmeg, yellow amber and ambergris which was crushed and mixed with white wine or broth. But it was simpler for the midwife just to take the placenta and put it on the mother's stomach, just as she had done to warm the child; apparently this proved a great comfort to the mother.

To maintain a good protection during the next few days, a piece of good dry cloth, folded in two or in four and warmed up, was put at the opening of the womb. The midwife 'usually calls it a blocker, because it blocks off the private parts of the new mother and stops air and cold from getting in, which might prevent the evacuation of the cleansings, and cause swelling of the womb and other undesirable symptoms'.[26] However, this 'blocker' or 'warmer' must not be too tight, or it might stop the flow of the cleansings and cause fainting due to the vapours which would then be unable to escape.

Bandaging the abdomen

Once the 'woman's nature' was protected, the midwife would busy herself with the bandaging of the abdomen. 'A triangular compress', one corner of which descended between the thighs and covered the warmer, was applied to the abdomen; the two other points were 'raised over the sides as far as the chest. This compress was often made of a 'large towel folded in three or four . . . a foot wide, hugging her abdomen tightly enough for her to feel no pain, but so that the whole lower abdomen is well and completely pressed.'. The 'corner between the thighs' could be raised at regular intervals for changing the warmer.[27]

This bandage had a dual purpose. Firstly it was intended to keep in place a womb which might be floating about in a 'garment' now too large for it. Fear of a slackening and dropping of the womb is evident in the way the bandage was applied: under the bandaging, 'over the navel', the midwife would put a poultice of tow, 'moistened with two eggwhites' with cloves and pepper. This constituted a spicy bait for the womb, which would thus be attracted upwards; and it would be kept there by a bandage tight enough to 'let it firm up as desired, without swimming about here and there'.[28] But from the later sixteenth century onwards, in the easier circumstances of the towns, the new mother also hoped in this way to avoid those stigmata of maternity, the stretch marks, and regain her 'girlish contours'. It is rather doubtful if the bandage was any help in removing stretch marks on the abdomen. Mauriceau and Peu in the seventeenth century, La Motte in the eighteenth, thought it was more likely to aggravate them, since the skin on the abdomen only became more 'wrinkled and loose'. They also believed that by bandaging the new mother too tightly, the midwife made her more likely to suffer a slackening of the womb – the contrary effect, in fact, to the one they sought.

Diet for the New Mother

In the country, a woman was given something to eat immediately after the delivery. Midwife and nurse, fearing that she might turn faint, would give her plenty to eat and drink; what was given varied from place to place. Some items occurred everywhere, however, being part of the ritual meal after a birth. Such were broth made from a capon, preferably a white one, often earmarked months ago for this service; squabs or partridges did the same office for people of quality. Stewed meat was preferred, as being more digestible; fruit was avoided as being 'too windy'. To drink, white wine or claret was recommended, but also walnut liqueur and sometimes brandy.

Giving a thick soup of bread, vegetables and fat, or roast meat with wine, shows an eagerness to restore the woman's strength, to 'repair the languishing faculties, both vital, animal and natural' of a woman who often emerged exhausted from her ordeal. Doctors protested at what to them was untimely overfeeding: they were not against giving food to new mothers, but they rejected the idea of overdoing it, and giving strong drink and the whole in too much of a hurry: why could the midwives not learn to wait? Paul Portal recommended some sweet almond oil and maidenhair syrup, and giving no nourishment for two hours, 'for fear of vomiting, which could cause a slackening in the ligaments of the womb'.[29]

A desire to see the new mother on her feet as soon as possible is not in itself sufficient to explain the abundant food, and the sweet and alcoholic drinks, which were pressed upon her. The main thing was to 'repair the blood' and nourish the womb. The women who helped at confinements were so convinced of this that, 'according to Laurent Joubert, they seemed determined to stuff and fill them up like shopping baskets rather than to feed and nourish them'.[30] It was the emptiness of the womb which made them fear the worst: best to fill the void left by the baby as quickly as possible, with a generous amount of 'food which would stick to the ribs'.

From the seventeenth century onwards, doctors advised taking into account the temperament and habitual diet of the new mother. 'A woman of quality' must not be 'treated like a rustic', nor must a 'rustic be given the same food as a lady of quality' – or one might kill both of them. Louise Bourgeois said that 'ladies of the first rank' must eat lightly, while 'robust and hard-working women' needed substantial feeding. 'The stomach of the one is delicate, that of the other is strong and cannot be satisfied with light meals; for if these strong stomachs do not receive, soon after the delivery, a hearty soup with onion or egg, or a big helping of milk broth, their stomach acts like a mill which has no grist and catches fire'.[31]

Should a New Mother be Allowed to Sleep?

The woman, bandaged and fed, would be put to bed, but so great was the fear of haemorrhage that she would not be allowed to sleep in the hours immediately following the birth: there was a horrid fascination with the idea of death stealing up on a sleeping victim. The bystanders would do all they could to keep the new mother awake, and doctors were always complaining about the 'chattering mob' which surrounded her bed. What they were really criticizing was the amount of noise made by relatives and neighbours, for, until the beginning of the eighteenth century, midwives and obstetricians also preferred the woman to be kept awake for three or four hours, in case of some sudden complication. Louise Bourgeois was of that opinion: 'Care must be taken,' she says, 'that during the loss of blood [the cleansings] the woman is not allowed to sleep, however much she desires it, for a weakness may carry them off when you think they are only resting'.

From the 1720s onward, there was a radical alteration in the obstetricians' attitude. Up till then they had advised letting the woman rest but not go to sleep; thereafter they advised both rest *and* sleep, believing that there was no real fear of haemorrhage if the placenta had been correctly removed. In 1724, in his *General Treatise on Childbirth*, Pierre Dionis bore witness to this change:

In former times it was not allowed for women to go to sleep immediately after their delivery. I was made to stay at the queen's bedside for three hours after she had given birth, so as to talk to her and prevent her from sleeping; but nowadays that custom is rejected; they are allowed to sleep as soon as they have taken some broth, because it is said that repose and sleep make up for all the fatigues of labour.

Silence, stillness and isolation: these were the precepts which the obstetricians were to attempt to impose in the course of the eighteenth century.

A Part of Oneself

This child which the mother had nourished with her blood for months on end was like a little part of herself. Maternal instinct made itself felt long before the birth. Obstetricians report cases of pregnant women with a too narrow pelvis or a haemorrhage before term, who must have known they were in danger but who still refused a premature labour, in the hope of saving their babies. Such an attitude might have something to do with religious scruples, but it is much more likely to be due to the mother's desire to bear a living and viable child, even at the risk of her own life. It seems, in fact, that refusal of induced premature labour, especially in cases of persistent haemorrhage, was commoner in the seventeenth and early eighteenth centuries than it was after 1750. Medical domination of labour certainly has something to do with this change.

But the maternal instinct emerged most strongly when the birth had been particularly difficult or even critical. La Motte tells how he came to the help of a poor woman in Cotentin at the end of the seventeenth century: it was an arm-first presentation, and before his arrival the midwife had several times tugged on the limb, but in vain; the surgeon had completed the delivery by torsion of the uterus, but the child had been born without a sign of life. The swooning mother, though she had suffered for hours, had but a single thought: her lost child! Although she already had several children, and the new arrival had already been baptized, she was 'in floods of tears', says La Motte, 'because of the supposed loss she had just suffered.' And indeed, half an hour later the child had been revived.

A mother's attachment to her newborn child could also show in more tragic circumstances: if the woman knew that she was doomed to die. One day in 1681, the Parisian obstetrician Paul Portal was called to a woman who had been basely abandoned by a surgeon anxious not to strain his reputation in a labour that he could not conclude successfully. The surgeon had told her with brutal frankness that she was doomed:

He told the woman that she must confess herself. The patient having asked him when she should do this, he replied that she should do it immediately, because he found her like to die. I cannot think [Portal goes on] that a woman who had been through fearful sufferings, feeling herself enfeebled and hearing such a doom spoken so bluntly, could be much astonished . . .. She asked to see her child, feeling no other pain than a certain nausea. However, scarcely had she made her confession than she died.[32]

This was doubtless an extreme case, but it reflects a real truth: a woman strives to transcend her own death by leaving issue on this earth: at least the child will survive her! 'All men love to see their line continue.'

While evidence of maternal love is scarce in the sources before the middle of the eighteenth century, it would be rash to infer from this that mothers in former times did not love their children.[33] Perhaps we are too inclined – naturally enough – to look for the signs of love which we expect, those we use ourselves. But is that not to confuse maternal love, a constant, with its expression, which has varied as the centuries have passed? Besides, is it not an oversimplification to speak of mother-love in general terms? For we must take into account the important differences between women in the town and in the country, and between different social levels. We are, in fact, comparatively better informed about townswomen in better-off households than about coun-trywomen. Thus our opinion is distorted by the nature of the sources, which concern only a minority of mothers. What is more, our information about the attitudes and feelings of mothers is usually supplied by men. What do they have to say?

In the sixteenth and seventeenth centuries, moralists, educators and doctors, far from declaring that mothers did not love their babies and children, actually opined that their indulgence was limitless and that their bringing up of their children was quite pernicious: they ought to have been far stricter! These authors, often fathers themselves, show that in ordinary households, in both town and country, mothers and babies were very close. The doctor Jacques Duval, talking of the immediate aftermath of confinements and in particular about 'retained lochia', emphasizes the state of impurity in which women find themselves at this stage, and is highly critical of their behaviour. To what lengths will they not go? Indisposed as they are, they dare to cradle their babies! Therefore he enjoins them to 'refrain from this excessive zeal for kissing and embracing their children'. Do they not know that they risk contaminating the baby and giving him 'herpes, scabies, and other skin infections'? Such outbreaks of emotion were suspicious, unworthy of true women and true mothers: 'It can be seen that in their rashness they love like monkeys, who, it is said, hug their young so tightly, in their ardent love, that they suffocate them'.[34] Love like monkeys . . .!

For townspeople very conscious of their 'humanity', an overdemonstrative attitude of mothers towards their babies became a mark of 'animal' behaviour. It might be all right for mere peasant women to behave like that: they lived surrounded by animals and naturally ended up living like them! But ladies of quality in the towns must refrain from such excesses. Such opinions, which appear in the course of the sixteenth century, must be seen as one manifestation of the change in attitudes towards children in aristocractic and higher bourgeois milieux.

PART V

The Socialization of the Child

At last the long-awaited child had arrived. In the humblest cottage, in a château or in the royal court, the birth must be celebrated: everyone fêted the coming of the new human being as well as he could afford to. But the newborn child must be born again, in baptism. This sacrament was also a rite of passage, marking the new baby's official entrance into the secular community, its socialization. The child then turned 'from an object into a human being'. It had begun as nothing or almost nothing; it became somebody, because now it had a name.

14

Welcoming the New Baby

Universal Rejoicing

Since there is nothing worse than to die leaving no progeny, any newborn child
was to be welcomed; and since, unfortunately, so many died, it was better to
have a goodly number, to safeguard the continuity of the family. Children were
a blessing from God, an honour He conferred on good Christian couples and
for which He must be thanked.

As for the mother, she was never tired of gazing at her offspring, which she
had just brought into the world: her joy was a pleasure to see:

The woman, delivered from the pains of childbirth, rejoices to have given her spouse a
pledge of her love, and to all those around her she expresses feelings and marks of
gratitude for any services they may have done her. She laughs and jokes; she asks to see
the child which has caused her such pains for nine months. The great pleasure and joy
which she takes in seeing him stretch his arms and legs chase away the memory of the
cruel pains she has suffered in her travail. The child's first cries so move her that her
heart, filled with joy, shows excess of it by the tears she lets fall in spite of herself. The
mother's tenderness, most marked at this moment, is so great that she is not repelled as
she freely caresses this child covered in mucus, blood and pommade; her sensibility and
careful thought prompt her to make excuses to any she thinks she may have offended in
the violence of her pains. This scene is in every way a most affecting one.[1]

We may be surprised by the modernity of this sensitive and touching account,
written during the Enlightenment: it shows that a mother's outpouring of love
for her baby belongs to all time.

Visiting the new mother

The birth was surrounded by collective rejoicing. Relatives, friends and neighbours came to tell the father and mother of their joy at seeing them blessed with
an heir. The birth was a convivial affair, welding the family and the community
together round the child.

188

The women in the village, or surrounding streets, were quick to hear the news, in the few days following the confinement. One by one they would come to admire the pretty baby and wish it welcome and good health: *Lou boun Dio vous guardo*, 'The good God keep you!', they would say in Languedoc,[2] while in Limousin the cry was *Oh! lou piti mignar!* [or '*lo pito mignardo*'] *Que lou boun Di li froje!* ('Oh, the pretty little thing, God bless him!')[3] Everybody laughing, joking freely, interrupting one another.

The search would be on for a likeness to the mother, the father, any near relation. Alsace, like all provinces, had a choice of proverbs designed to reassure the family that the child was on their model: *Wie der Acker, so dir Reuewe* ('As the field, so the turnips') or again *De Apfel fallt nit wid vom Baum* ('The apple doesn't fall very far from the tree').

Sometimes the little thing was so unprepossessing that the mother had to be consoled: *A wieschdes Wiegelkind, a schenes Gassekind* ('Ugly child in the cradle, pretty child in the street').[4] The father was called *godard*, a nickname still in use in several towns in Lorraine up to the mid-nineteenth century: 'This nickname, which will stick to him until another child is born in the locality, is not always taken in good part, nor with very much pleasure, because of the bad jokes and silly remarks attached to it by ill-intentioned people'. However, in the opinion of the contemporary observer who reported this custom, there was no need to get annoyed, because the name, derived from the Latin *guadere*, 'rejoice', expressed the joy 'which must be inspired by the birth of a new heir'.[5]

In aristocratic and high bourgeois circles, where the appearance of the baby was a social occasion, the 'visit to the new mother' in the 'lying-in chamber', was a real ceremony. After the birth the young mother was transported from her 'childbed' to a 'great bed with rich hangings', around which stools and cushions were set ready for the friends. New mothers, 'with ribbons in their hair' and 'dressed to the nines' received visitors in a decor eloquent of luxury:

As for their gowns, they are of crimson, straw-coloured or white satin, velvet or cloth of gold or silver, the women being very wise in their choices. They have necklaces round their necks, gold bracelets, and are more covered in jewels than an idol or the queen of hearts; their beds are clad in Holland lawn or the finest cotton, and so well arranged that no fold is deeper than any other.[6]

This fashion probably came from Italy at the end of the fifteenth century: the theme of 'visiting the new mother' was frequent at the time in Italian iconography. The custom caught on quite quickly in France, for at a period of rapid extension of commerce and wealth it answered to a strong taste for ostentation and self-dramatization. Pamphleteers and chroniclers were scandalized by this ostentatious luxury, which they saw as an outcome of the excessive vanity of womankind, just when women were actually being imprisoned by this passive role of representation. From the *Fifteen Joys of Married Life* to the *Chitchat of the New Mother* via the *Dark Terrors of Marriage*, the lying-in was a rich feeding-ground for antifeminism. The 'cacklings' of this womanish assembly put one in mind of the farmyard . . . .

Gossipy, 'precious' or 'learned' as in later Molièresque comedy, the assembled women were ever afterwards to be considered 'ridiculous' and their talk empty. Even at the beginning of the fifteenth century, Christine de Pisan had been weighing up the danger posed by this expensive luxury and this encouragement of vanity to the reputation of women; but her alarm call seems to have found no echoes, for the custom of 'visiting the new mother' endured, in all its ostentation, up to the eighteenth century.[7]

Whether in town or country, the visit always meant bringing a present. Women coming to visit the new mother always brought some concrete token of their joy at seeing her happily delivered and the child born at last. In wealthy town society the present had become an expensive item, if it were not a real work of art. In the fifteenth century a new custom, again of Italian origin, was introduced: the 'new mother's plate', most often made of china (as in Urbino) and richly decorated with allegorical motifs, the most frequent being the childbed of Myrrha.[8]

While the presents offered by village women also changed through the centuries, they retained their symbolic value for far longer. Until the beginning of this century they were most often presents in kind; and in some villages in the Charente apples were being given to the new mother as late as 1947.[9] Cakes, small round loaves and eggs were the most usual gifts: as tokens of fertility, they always figured in the innumerable depictions of the birth of the Virgin by Italian painters of the quattrocento.[10] In Provence, the 'first neighbour' to come visiting must be sure to remember the customary good wishes for the child:

She brought him as a gift a piece of bread, an egg, some salt, a match, saying:

> *Siegue hon coume lou pan, plen comme un iou,*
> *Savi coume la sau e dre coume uno brouqueto*

('May he be as good as the bread, full as an egg,
Wise as the salt and straight as a match.')[11]

Good, full (of health), wise, straight: was not that the perfect picture of a fine child?

The mother was included in these good wishes: in the last century, in Limousin and Haute Provence, the visitors would never leave the new mother's house without leaving her a small coin, one or two sous, 'or, for the very poor, a nappy-pin'.[12] This ritual had a dual significance. It protected the mother – and, indirectly, the child – against the machinations of some bad neighbour who might try to 'take her milk away;'[13] and at the end of the lying-in period the little hoard thus gathered would pay for the 'churching ceremony' of the new mother.[14]

Through the nineteenth and early twentieth centuries, a gradual increase in prosperity in the countryside and the influence of urban models helped to distort the significance of these gifts to the new mother. The market value of the gift, or its 'utilitarian' character, became more important than its symbolic value. They would give a rattle, a broach, or, more and more commonly, an item for the layette, as a help in meeting the expenses.

Libation and agape

One could not celebrate a birth without eating and drinking. But before the beginning of the libation and agape, deference must be paid to certain immemorial customs. Even in the seventeenth century a frugal meal was still offered to 'the guardian fairies' who would not fail to come and shower gifts on newborn babies: a little table would be set up before the hearth on which would be laid out 'three cups, a jar of wine, three loaves of best wheat flour; and one or two torches which must burn throughout the night'.[15]

In the country, it was generally the guests who brought the food and drink. There was no better way to show their joy than in this collective meal. The custom existed in some provincial towns in the sixteenth century. Some books of manners from Limousin give a particularly appetizing picture of these plentiful *coumeradis* attended by men and women from the family and the neighbourhood. One would bring some chicken or hare pâté, another a goose, a third a sucking pig or four roast chickens, yet another a pint of wine. And so to table. Tongues wagged; it was a warm, noisy occasion with good company. Everybody sang and wished long life to the baby. The new mother in the midst of all this junketing did not always feel too comfortable: eighteenth and nineteenth-century doctors protested against the overeating which might bring on milk fever and be injurious to her health. In any case the *coumeradis* gave rise to 'such abuses, that the consuls had to forbid them'; but the tradition endured until the beginning of this century, with one alteration: the feast took place on the day of the christening.[16]

Children of lords and princes

The birth of a child to the local lord or prince could hardly be a matter of indifference to their vassals or subjects. Especially the birth of a boy, because it safeguarded the lineage or consolidated the throne. Villages, streets and town squares saw the rejoicing; everyone took part as best he could. The common people had their dancing and feasting, while the social élite strutted through civil and religious ceremonies. Everything was ordered in accordance with a ritual which might have taken centuries to evolve, with currents of sympathy and gratitude mounting towards the lord and his lady, or the prince and his consort, and their offspring: mounting, but not mingling. It was a collective gesture in which everyone had their own place and their own part to play.

The birth of a child in the local château helped to strengthen allegiance to the lord. The announcement of the news, and the homage to lord and lady, followed age-old customs. In some parts of Poitou, as soon as the lady felt the first pains of childbirth 'one of the vassals would stand before the main gate of the château, armed with a shotgun, to give warning to the vassals of the lordship as soon as her child was born.'[17] On such an occasion the locals had to pay certain feudal dues, the nature of which was determined by mutual agreement.

Thus, an agreement made in 1483 between the Marquis of Causans, Lord of Brantes in Provence, and the local peasants, obliged the latter to bring to the château, at each confinement of its mistress, 'Two torches weighing five pounds, marchpane, a pound of sugared almonds, a pound of fine spices, a pound of pepper, a quarter of Ducis powder, a half-load of good wine for making hippocras, a three-pound sugarloaf, ten pounds of honey and a load of wood.' In return, the lord undertook to 'provide the head of every family, at the time of his wife's churching [*in resurrectione dominae*] a meal suited to his condition'.[18]

The greatest moment, however, was a royal birth. The whole country transcended diversities of place and condition to unite in thanking God for deigning to safeguard the future of the kingdom. The first third of the seventeenth century marked a turning point in the customs surrounding a royal childbed. All the children of Marie de Medici and Henry IV were greeted amidst a cheerful disorder, vividly reported by Louise Bourgeois; joy was unconfined, and there is no doubt that the joviality of the monarch had a lot to do with this. After the birth of the dauphin,

The king brought the princes and several lords to see him. The king let every member of the king's and queen's household see, and then sent them away to make room for others. Everyone was so joyful that he could scarcely speak; everyone embraced everyone else, without regard to their higher or lower rank. I have heard that there were ladies who met their own servants and embraced them, being so beside themselves with joy that they did not know what they were doing.[19]

Some two hundred people were there, trampling over one another and exchanging congratulations. What with the crowds, and the news that it was a boy – the queen fainted. Louise was 'annoyed' to see her thus. She too began to shout: 'It was "most improper to bring all these people in before the queen was safely in bed!" The king heard me, and came and tapped me on the shoulder and said, "Be quiet, midwife! Don't be angry: this child belongs to everybody, and everybody must be allowed to rejoice at it." '[20]

In subsequent reigns the etiquette became stricter and the ceremonial more complex. When the first pains were felt – acknowledged not by a midwife but by the court obstetrician – the superintendent of the queen's household would send to warn the monarch, the princes and princesses of the blood, ministers and ambassadors. They dropped everything and rushed to the queen's bedside. 'The chancellor of the keeper of the Seal would kneel beside the bed of pain, and an enormous screen was placed behind the lofty audience'.[21] When the child was born, if it was a dauphin, he was placed on a silver tray and conducted solemnly to his apartments, escorted by officers and bodyguards. The royal infant was laid in his cradle and the Grand Master of ceremonies conferred on him the insignia of the order of Saint Louis.[22]

News of the birth did not take long to travel beyond the palace gates. After the birth of the future Louis XIII at Fontainebleau in 1601, 'the whole night was given up to fireworks, drumming and trumpeting; barrels of wine were broached to drink to the health of the king, the queen and the new dauphin.

Everywhere were people riding post-haste to take the news to various countries and through all the provinces and good towns of France.'[23]

In Paris, a cannon was fired; then all the bells of the Hôtel de Ville, the Palace and the Samaritaine began to ring and went on all day, sometimes all night as well. It was the signal for public rejoicings and commemorations. In October 1781, a young Breton doctor, Louis-Marie Lavergne, wrote to a friend describing the spectacle he had just witnessed in the capital at the long-awaited birth of a dauphin:

There are public rejoicings every day, consisting of a general illumination, fireworks, dancing, free performances in the public squares and at crossroads. That is to say that money is thrown right and left to the people, with bread, sausage and cervelat. A quantity of barrels of wine have been broached . . . .. The Place de Grève, where the Hôtel de Ville is, has seen the most brilliant spectacles. The Hôtel has been magnificently illuminated for three nights on end. The governor of Paris, M. le duc de Cossé, goes there every evening in a carriage . . . with a sizeable entourage. He drove around a great bonfire, accompanied by the provosts of the merchants and the aldermen, who all threw money right and left amongst the people, and then gave the signal for the celebrations to begin.[24]

In Paris and all the other important towns, the apogee of the official celebrations was a solemn Te Deum, preceded or followed by a procession with the greatest pomp. The corporations in their best robes, local and provincial dignitaries, all took this opportunity to express their satisfaction at this perpetuation of the royal line; 'addresses', congratulations by the score, and good wishes were publicly announced for the royal couple and their heir. The whole kingdom gathered round the dauphin's cradle to renew its allegiance to crown and king.

Younger children were by no means fêted in the same way as a dauphin. The birth of a daughter, in particular, did not cause any great excitement. At best, a princess was no more than a pawn on the chessboard of European politics, a useful cog in the machinery of alliances maintained by the royal power.[25] The same feeling permeated every level of society: a daughter had less value; she would have to be found a husband and a dowry; she would be a burden, in fact.

The mother was indeed symbolically 'penalized' if she gave birth to a daughter: she had not done her work well! In La Marche in the nineteenth century she would be comforted, after the delivery, with a slice of bread dipped in warm, heavily sweetened wine, as a reward for bearing a boy; but for a girl 'she would have to be content with some salted milk broth'.[26] There was a similar custom in Poitou in the eighteenth century: when the lady of the château bore a son, the vassal with the shotgun received a white loaf and a bottle of wine; but if it was a daughter, he was given only black bread and a glass of water.[27] Often the entire ritual of the announcement varied according to the sex of the baby. Around Bressuire in the 1730s, the vassal would appear before the door of the chamber and cry: 'Long live her ladyship and the newborn child!' Then he 'was expected to drink a bottle of wine at one draught, and to eat a pound of white bread with a partridge strongly seasoned with salt and pepper;

the whole supplied by the Lord. If the lady had borne a daughter, the vassal was given nothing but a bottle of water, a piece of black bread and a cheese.'[28]

This muted welcome to women coming into the world was general in Western Europe; in the last century it could take unexpected forms. 'In Schaffhouse, in Switzerland,' Michelet reports, 'a maidservant announcing a birth must bear two bunches of flowers, in her bosom and in her hands, if it is a boy; one bunch only if it is a girl.' At Neftenbach, the new father of a boy received two cartloads of wood, but only one if it was a girl.[29] Doubtless these differing reactions, dependent on the sex of the child, answered to men's desire to re-establish a kind of masculine continuity: the father claimed to be the incarnation of the family line, and believed that he could not be 'renewed' except by another male.[30]

Protecting the Child from Harmful Spells

The birth of the child was a reassuring thing, but it began a period of uncertainty which would end only with the christening. It was always the first hours of life which decided the child's future. The forces of evil, lurking in the shadows, were on the look-out for this easy prey, a human offspring not yet properly recognized, accepted and socialized – because it had not yet a name.

At first sight, there seems to be an infinite variety of protective rituals, each region sounding its own original note; but in fact the differences are minor and the same essential attitudes are found everywhere.

Metal and rosary

To protect the child it must first be isolated. Until the christening, it was kept away from outside influences, shut up in the enclosed world of the house, the one room. To take the newborn baby out would be to risk its life. 'The child must not go from under the roof', as they used to say in some Alsatian villages, meaning that all outside the domestic space was dangerous territory. What infinite precautions would be taken on the day of the christening, to prevent the forces of evil from reaching the infant on its way to the church! So great was the spite of sorcerers and evil spirits that the child was not safe from their machinations even within the house; it therefore had to be defended against those who sought to interrupt its growth, carry it off, change it or kill it. In the Sarrebourg district people lived in fear of the spirit of earth, the *Erdmännchen*, which landed on the child's breast in the night hours and sucked its blood: the next morning, the little chest, sore and swollen, would give proof that the vampire had been. Throughout Alsace people also feared the *Doggele* or *Letzekäppel* – the creature with its bonnet back to front – or the *Schratzmännel*, who sat on top of children and suffocated them.[31]

The best protection against this string of elves, devils and evil spirits, all adept at forcing a way through doors and windows, was the pentagram which the midwife would have taken care to draw on the threshold, and whose symbolic outline was known to her alone. Beings seeking to harm the child always found some cunning way of getting into the house; for example, they might hide in some object which had been loaned out, just as it was being returned. Therefore, before the christening the parents never gave up any utensil, garment or piece of furniture. It was not even sufficient to prevent objects from travelling between inside and outside, between private and public space: certain metallic items were actually brought into the chamber, items which were supposed to act as deterrents. In Aunis and Saintonge, for example, a piece of iron was set down next to the child.[32] In Lorraine and Alsace (Sundgau), 'a knife, point forwards, was fixed to the cradle or bed'.[33] It was not only metal, however, that could deny passage to evil influences. The father's breeches, hung on the wall as in Thuringia or placed near the bed as in Saintonge, could also keep evil spirits away;[34] around Altkirch the same virtue was attributed to a pair of shoes, so long as the toes were turned towards the points of access to the room; but they could also be arranged in a cross.[35]

These protective rituals did, in fact, become Christianized in the course of the nineteenth century: consecrated rosaries, garlands from Corpus Christi, leaves from a prayer book, or amulets were placed in the cradle or on the child's body, as if to constitute a last line of defence against black magic. In Alsace they would make three knots (symbolizing the Trinity) in the *Wagelseil*, the cord by which the parents could rock the cradle from their marriage bed. In any case the mother would never fail to 'cross' her child after swaddling it, just as she 'crossed' her loaf of bread with the point of a knife before cutting the first piece.

The salt and the candle

Still, ancient taboos continued to exist alongside such Christianized practices: the mirror, for instance, which must never be shown to a new baby for fear of stopping it from growing and causing illness or premature death. Or weighing the child, an idea energetically opposed by the mother: 'If you weigh a child you bring it bad luck!' as a peasant woman of Labruguière, near Castres, said in 1909 to a doctor who had suggested weighing her baby; and she added, 'If I weigh him, the poor child will never grow!'[36]

Salt, which is, of course, used in all rituals of exorcism, was a sure and frequently used recourse. Salt prevented spell-casting. Sometimes it was given to the mother after the birth: she had to put a few grains in her hand, lick them with the tip of her tongue, then throw the salt over her head. Hence the Alsatian expression *im Salz sitzen*, to sit in the salt, which described the situation of the woman after performance of the ritual.[37] In Limousin and Périgord mothers used to wear a little bag of salt round their necks to keep their milk coming, for one of the most dreaded forms of black magic was a sorcerer causing the mother's milk to dry up. A little salt would also be thrown into the hearth to protect the household, and the newborn child would be rubbed with it. Around Charente and in Provence, at the end of the nineteenth century, a packet of salt was laid on the child to keep off the evil eye;[38] a century earlier, at Coudray-Saint-Germer near Beauvais, a pinch of salt would be slipped into the swaddling bands of unbaptized babies being left to their fate.[39]

All in all, the best protection for the child was to watch over it and leave a candle burning constantly by its side. This apparently universal custom was of very ancient origin, as is the funeral wake at the other end of life. Often the tiny flame which chased away the frightening powers of darkness was that of the 'Candlemass candle', bought to celebrate the Purification of the Virgin on 2 February.

Between birth and baptism, then, for one or two nights, members of the family and neighbours took it in turns to watch over the child. During this time the parents must be careful not to 'call the new baby by the forename or forenames chosen for him, or even to speak them in the hearing of anyone whatever';[40] if they neglected this precaution they would give sorcerers or demoniacs a means of doing grave harm to the child, and might even cause its death.

Foreseeing the Future

A newborn baby was an unknown quantity. It bore no real indications of what it would become. However, its body provided some information about its immediate fate: if strong, there was good hope that it would live; if weakly, unfortunately one must take that to mean . . .. But could one ever tell the potential of that nameless body, that mind which would take months or even years to develop? Luckily, there were signs to speak to the child's destiny. The moment of its arrival into the world had in a way decided its destiny; but its place in the family and the character of the presentation could also reveal something of its future life.

Lunar 'prognostications'

Answers to the inevitable questions could perhaps be found by questioning the stars, studying the phases of the moon, consulting old books of magical lore or evoking oral tradition. Untangling the threads of destiny by recourse to astrology was a universal practice: even the Church sometimes yielded to this thirst for knowledge – completely unorthodox as it was, since God alone was master of human destiny, and it was in a way sacrilegious to try to discover its course and its ending.[41]

True, the example was set from above. Horoscopes were more the rage than ever at court in the sixteenth and seventeenth centuries; it is well known that magicians and diviners figured prominently in the retinue of Catherine de Medici. It was to her that Auger Ferrier, a doctor and native of Toulouse, dedicated his *Astronomical Judgements on Nativities* in 1549. In this work he examined the most serious question of all: 'if the child will live or not', and his would-be solution is couched in the following (to put it mildly, hermetic) terms: 'When the dominator of the ascendant is misfortuned by the lord of the eighth house, the child cannot live, and even less if the lords of the triplicity of the temporal luminary be misfortuned.'[42]

But no matter! The style found favour and the book was a success, as the numerous contemporary editions and translations show. Ferrier became the queen's principal doctor, but continued to enjoy a great reputation at court for his horoscopes.

When the future Louis XIV was born, at 11.15 in the morning of Sunday, 5 September 1638, under the sign of Mars, his horoscope was of course established. This dauphin had been so long in making his appearance that it was important to know as soon as possible what kind of future he could expect. The task was given to a brilliant mathematician, a professor at the College de France. And there was nothing surprising in that. Like many others at the time, Jean-Baptiste Morin was both a scientist and an astrologer: he had the horoscopes of innumerable celebrities, not excluding Jesus, to his credit – and he was recognized astrologer to the royal court.[43]

The moon used to be seen as the great and universal regulator. We have seen her supposed role in conception; her influence was no less when it came to births. She 'removed the swelling' from bellies which she had previously made to 'swell'. It was an old belief – thousands of years old. Had not Aristotle stated that animals were born on the rising tide and died on the outgoing tide? And Pascal himself declared that 'People are not naturally born, nor do they die, in the three hours following the moon's passage to the meridian.'

Even today it is thought that the moon has a great influence on the moment of birth. The staff of maternity hospitals always await the full moon with trepidation, for it is supposed to bring a larger than average influx of babies, even though modern babies appear to a very different pattern from their predecessors. Chronobiological studies have increased greatly in the last thirty or so years.[44] Some researchers, such as Menaker, Buhler and Gauquelin, think that there is indeed a connection between the full moon and a significant rise in the number of births; others, like Reiter, Hoseman and Meyer, think that there is no obvious connection between the number of births and the phases of the moon.[45] Lunar influence may be probable, but it is hard to prove, for other elements play a part, particularly the combined attraction of the sun and moon, and above all, the effects of atmospheric pressure.[46]

In earlier centuries, authors of 'books of reasons' sometimes recorded very carefully the phase of the moon in which their children were born. A new baby, like all living things, was 'under the moon' – for better or worse! Astrologers had drawn up a calendar of lucky and unlucky days, which was eagerly consulted as soon as a child had embarked upon life. Zoë Guinot de Channes, in Champagne, had thus drawn up a table of correspondences. According to her calculations, a child born

On days 1, 6, 9, 13, 16 of the moon …	would have long life
On days 3, 5, 7 …	would cease to live
On day 2 …	would grow very tall
On day 4 …	would be treacherous and perfidious
On day 8 …	would be good-looking
On day 10 …	would travel a lot
On day 11 …	would be witty and very clever[47]

By integrating the birth of the child into the lunar cycle, it was hoped to 'weave its web', leave less to chance, and so reduce the need to worry.

Hour, day, month

But, while the moon had an important influence on the birth, it was important not to neglect the cycle of the sun. To be born with the dawn was singularly lucky: the conjunction of a child's birth with that of day guaranteed the former a long and happy life. The reverse, being born between eleven o'clock and midnight, the preferred hour of the infernal powers, was very unlucky. At Rochechouart in Limousin it was even a sign of great misfortunes, and at Ambierle in the Forez, it foretold the child's premature death.[48] The folklorist L. F. Sauve reported about 1880, from the Vosges Highlands, that 'this belief is so deep-rooted that if some women are seized with the pains of childbirth under the menace of these fearful hours, the tearful family will beg the midwife on their knees to do all she can to advance or delay the birth.'[49] Now, it has been scientifically established that, while most babies are born in the early hours of the morning, labour often begins in the middle of the night[50] – a fact which must have led to a good deal of extraordinary behaviour in past ages.

In northern and eastern France midday was also believed to be an unfortunate time: in Alsace it was held that a child arriving in the world at that particular moment 'would go hungry all its life'.[51] In Quercy the opposite was true: 'The best time to be born was midday, because that hour was considered to be the best of all.'[52] It all depended where you were.

Everywhere, Sunday was a lucky day to be born, because it was the day of Resurrection of Our Lord, but also because it was the sun's day. The German *Sonntag* means just that (as does the English 'Sunday'), and in Alsace, where old peasant traditions were slow to die out, there was a kind of proverb which said *A Sonntag's Kind, a Glickskind* (Sunday's child is a lucky child).

Friday, the day of Christ's death, was of course the opposite of Sunday: it was a day of mourning, no marriages ever took place on it, and it was not a good day to be born on. As for the poor child who was born on Good Friday! It would have nothing but poverty and ill-luck as its lot in life, which was likely to be short in any case.[53] Lucky days for a birth often corresponded to 'joyous Christian festivals' and unlucky days to Christian ceremonies 'marked by sorrow and penitence'.[54]

The calendar of the months was likewise characterized by an alternation of favourable and unfavourable times. Some months were particularly to be feared. November, of course, because it was the month of the dead; August, because fortune (it was believed) never smiled on children born in that month: 'Month of August, desired by none', it was said.[55] May was no better: 'Nothing born in May is worth a thing', people said; May children were even supposed to be idiots. A saying in the Confolens region preserved the memory of the rather unpleasant welcome reserved for those who came into the world in May. What are we to make of this?

Ko que naï an mëï dé maï
Prin yo per la paôto, fou yo laï.
(What is born in the month of May,
take it by the foot, and throw it away.)[56]

The length of the days in the month also influenced the height of human beings: in Limousin it was firmly believed that children born in December and January, whose days were the shortest in the year, would always be short; in Saintonge those born in March were supposed to have big heads.[57]

But the worst off of all were those born in the fasting time of the Ember Days, especially Advent and Lent. They were naughty, always into mischief, and, in Alsace, detested by their parents; they were accused of being in league with evil spirits, and an early death was often wished on them ....[58] As for children born in the 'black nights' from 20 to 24 March, it was hardly worth taking care of them, so sure was everyone that they would soon die.[59]

Dark days were not always fatal, however. On the contrary: in the south-west, children born on 2 November were sure of a happy future and were treated with the greatest respect. When they were grown up they were called *armiers* or *armaciers* (in Quercy and Albigeois), from the Occitan *armo*, 'soul'. Because they had been born on the day of the dead, they were thought able to get in contact with ancestral spirits; and, since any injury to the domestic economy, any illness among beasts or men, was usually attributed to discontent on the part of a deceased relative who considered himself neglected by his descendants, the *armier* or 'soul-man' was a useful intermediary, who could help to settle disputes between this world and the next.[60]

Place in the family

The time of birth was not the sole criterion for elucidating the life the new baby could expect: attention was also paid to its place in the family. First children were always more welcome than younger ones. Procreation being the purpose of marriage, the first child was proof of the fertility – that is, the success – of the couple. Subsequent births were not such great events; in fact they were no more than a continuing biological process. Only the lack of a male heir, if there were already several girls, could maintain interest in the impending offspring – until a boy was finally born!

The last-born in a family often received special attention: in Lorraine it was called the *niau*, like the nestling or chick which remained longest in the nest because it was weaker than the rest of the brood. In Anjou it was the *caillaud*, *cailleraud* or *chopiot*; around Nevers the *culard*, in Champagne the *charculot* and in Franche-Comté the *culot*, weakly and shivery like an 'autumn lamb', [61] as if it had been conceived too late, by parents of lesser 'vigour', its brothers and sisters having already exhausted the best of the seed. It was always supposed to be small, but clever, like Tom Thumb in the story.

Tom Thumb was not only the last child, he was also the seventh in an uninterrupted sequence of boys. The theme of the seventh son, or daughter, recurs frequently in European folklore and popular tale. Because of the magic number 7, these children were credited with supernatural powers. In France and the British Isles they were capable of working cures by rubbing or by touch; they could inherit the secrets of a sorcerer from another family, and they could be sure of 'making their way' in life. The seventh son of a seventh son had the remarkable power – shared only with the kings of France – of touching for scrofula.[62]

In Spain, the fifth and sixth consecutive sons automatically became *saluda-dores* – healers. In France, the third child might also have certain powers, if medieval texts are to be believed. In the *Romance of the Rose* the poet says that third-born children accompany 'Lady Abundance' in her nocturnal sallies three times a week; the spirits of these children leave their bodies to follow the 'mysterious divinity' into the village houses. Nothing can stop this assembly, which brings prosperity and abundance so long as it receives offerings. There is a significant resemblance between this account and stories of the *Benandanti* of Friuli in the sixteenth century, as studied by Carlo Ginzburg. They, too, were connected with a propitiatory agrarian ritual; they, too, owed their powers to their birth: not to their place in the family, but to the 'caul' they bore when they came into the world.[63]

'Born with a Caul'

The caul, a part of the amniotic membrane which covers the head of some newborn babies, sometimes as far down as the shoulders, was once supposed to have beneficent powers. A baby's body emerging thus 'clad' from the maternal womb was considered to have some special protection, and the expression 'born with a caul' became a proverbial description for someone who always enjoyed good luck.

The idea that children 'born with a caul' would have everything they wanted in life was very widespread, as many ethnographic reports testify. It was also very ancient, for there is a Chaldean text which states that 'if a woman bears a child with a caul on its head, good fortune will come to the house'.[64] In Europe, the literary tradition is usually traced back to Aelius Lampridus, who wrote a history of the Augustans in the fourth century: he reported that Roman midwives used to steal the caul and sell it for a large sum to lawyers, who greatly prized it because they were convinced that 'if they had it on them when they were pleading in court, it was a great help in winning the case'.[65] Stealing the caul in this way could be very harmful to the child, because its good fortune and physical well-being were guaranteed only on condition that it was never parted from that 'little piece of skin it brings from its mother's womb', in the quaint words of the fifteenth-century 'Distaff Gospel'. On that condition, it would be spared illness and injury; the 'lambkin membrane', worn as a talisman, would protect it in battle and preserve it from drowning.[66]

The Church fought against such superstitions, all the more so as it knew that priests connived at practices ill suited to their ministry. Thus women anxious to reinforce the magic virtues of the caul could persuade priests to say blessings and masses of consecration, as is proved by a deposition made in 1580 by a peasant of Friuli before ecclesiastical authorities who suspected him of sorcery: 'My mother,' he told them, 'gave me the caul in which I had been born, saying that she had had it baptized with me, and had nine masses said over it, and had it blessed with certain prayers and scriptural readings.'[67]

In the last century, bishops forced priests to refuse to bless cauls, but women found a means of having masses said over them by hiding them under the altar![68] The belief in their virtues was indeed firmly rooted. However, as far back as the sixteenth century some people, especially in the towns, thought it no more than 'an allegory of those who are born of rich and prosperous parents,' as Laurent Joubert put it, 'so that they need do nothing but please themselves and increase their own honour with no constraint of necessity. It is commonly said of such people that they are fortunate and were born fully clad, meaning with many possessions acquired from their parents. Others, who are poor from birth, do indeed come naked into the world.'[69]

The social dimension here was more important than the myth, the 'wellborn' child than the favourite of fortune. It was indeed a sad falling-off, for the child born with a caul was not the only one to profit from that fortunate accident of birth: the caul invested him with certain powers which were a boon to the community at large.

In the sixteenth century, the *Benandanti* who roamed the countryside of Friuli, defending the fruits of the earth and battling in the Ember Days against sorcerers out to devastate the crops, constituted a sort of brotherhood, all of whose members were distinguished by having been born with a caul. Owing to this singular birth, all of them had the amazing gift of being able to escape from their own bodies to gain the ritual 'battlefield'; there, armed with a fennel-stalk, they strove to frustrate the vile machinations of the sorcerers, who fought with sorghum branches. By this symbolic defence of the herds and harvests 'against the enemies of people's property and the fertility of the earth' they contributed to the survival of the community from which they came.

The *Benandanti* were also supposed to be able to detect sorcerers and deliver the victims of evil spells; above all, they were said to 'see the dead'. They were, in fact, associated with a mysterious nocturnal procession which took place during the Ember Days and was attended by all those who had died an early death. This 'wild hunt' was headed by a female divinity who symbolized both wealth and abundance; from place to place she became Abundia, Diana, Perchta, Holda. Thus the *Benandanti*, as protectors of the most precious possession of the community – the harvest – and as intermediaries between those who had died 'before their time' and the society of this world, spent their time in good deeds.

In many European popular traditions, the caul was the seat of the 'external soul'; it symbolized the passage between the world of lost souls – of stillborn children, murdered adults and soldiers slain in battle – and the land of the living. It was because of the caul that a *Benandante* was able to go 'in spirit' wherever duty called, for the caul 'bound him to a destiny from which there was no escape'.[70]

The myth of the *Benandanti* was certainly not confined to the countryside of north-eastern Italy; as Carlo Ginzburg believes, it was probably connected with 'a complex of traditions which was widely scattered for almost three centuries in an area stretching from Alsace to the eastern Alps'.[71]

Like the caul, certain abnormal presentations of the baby at birth could bring good luck. Because the child normally 'came into the world like a swimmer, belly down',[72] it was thought that one born 'looking at the sky' would have an unusual destiny to match its unusual entry into life. Thus was born, in 1608, the Duke of Anjou, fifth child of Marie de Medici and Henry IV. Louise Bourgeois saw this altogether exceptional presentation as a token of predestination:

Of a hundred children, sometimes not a single one is born [in this way]; although it is said that is how girls come, it is not true. Of all the children I have delivered, I do not think that I have delivered thirty like this. Coming in this way, I believed that it was such a good augury for him and for all of France, that I was delighted at it; and indeed, all persons of judgement who heard of it, thought it would bring so many blessings, gains, obedience and contentment to the king and queen; that more could not said, for those things which look to heaven are beyond terrestrial nature.[73]

Born Feet First

Since Antiquity it had been bad luck to be born feet first: it was as ill-omened to be born this way as it was fortunate to be born with a caul. 'It is not natural,' Pliny comments, 'for a child to come into the world feet first. That is why those so born are called 'Agrippa' – *aegre partos*, born in pain.'[74]

It is true that birth feet first is risky: the baby only has to raise its arm in the passage and it is stuck in the womb, and in peril of its life; but it was not merely a synonym for a difficult birth. It was the omen which mattered, and it was a bad omen. No Latin author could fail to think of the birth of the monster – the birth of Nero, who indeed had been born feet first. Of the murderous impulses of that son who had had his mother murdered and the Eternal City burnt to the ground, whose tragic fate had been sealed the moment he arrived in this world.[75]

Being born feet first has always been associated with the idea of death. European funerary rites, which died out only recently, show that death was interpreted as 'a passage made feet first', and that was how the deceased crossed the threshold of his house. In contrast, it was inadvisable to put a newborn baby with its feet facing the door, or it would die.[76] If a child born feet first did survive, it might be credited with outstanding gifts: in Brittany it could cure sprains; in Scotland, it could soothe rheumatism and pains by 'trampling on the affected part'. It could relieve pain in the feet – or by the feet.[77]

As Nicole Belmont has shown, in traditional societies bodies were supposed to be disposed differently at birth and at death. People were born 'head first', and this disposition should be maintained in life. In death it was reversed: people died 'feet first'. A child arriving feet first at birth overthrew the natural order of things, in an untimely anticipation of the reversal of the body in death. Logically, the fate of this child could not but be a sad one.[78]

Birthmarks

Stains imprinted on the body of a new baby were always considered a bad thing: it was imagined that a child 'marked' by a naevus would be dogged by ill-luck throughout its life. Inevitably, the temptation was to efface it.

Around Cambrai, during the last century, young mothers were advised to lick the mark while fasting every morning, for the nine days following the baby's birth. If she found the task unappetizing she could delegate it to young dogs.[79] Treatment by saliva, a survival of ancient magical healing practices, was a sovereign method of getting rid of marks and warts which came from the world of the dead – and smelt of death.[80]

Of all 'bad signs', the worst was surely the conspicuous 'blue vein' which some babies bore on their temple, or on their forehead between the eyebrows. Everywhere it was believed to foretell premature death; in Alsace it was the 'graveyard sign' (*Kirchhofzeichen*) or the 'artery of death' (*Todesader*).[81] It could indeed be an outer sign of a venous stasis which would rapidly kill the child. The only recourse for the parents, if a fatal outcome were to be avoided, was to go on pilgrimage. In Brittany, the baby afflicted with 'Saint Divy's evil' was taken to Saint Nonne's stone at Dirinon; in the nearby Leon district its head was ducked in a holy well to get rid of 'Saint Vizia's vein'.[82]

The child's body 'spoke for it', revealing the dangers which threatened it, by its superfluities (birthmarks, excrescences) and by its insufficiencies. Thus, if a child was born without nails it was 'a token that it would have a long life', according to the obstetrician Jacques Guillemeau.[83] Even the smile of a sleeping child was seen as a bad omen: 'smiling at the angels' meant that it would very soon 'accept their invitation to go and join them in heaven'.[84]

Preparing for the Future

Two rituals, performed at the birth of a child, were intended to give it a better future: the planting of a commemorative tree and the offering of a coin.

The custom of planting a tree to commemorate the perpetuation of the family tree is an ancient one, which has survived in places down to the twentieth century. In Alsace, it was the father or grandfather, who supported the family line, who had the honour of putting the sapling in the ground: most often a fruit tree, sometimes a fir, oak or chestnut. In highland Alsace the daughter's tree was 'in a family field somewhere on the communal territory', while the son's was 'in the orchard behind the house' which he would later inherit.[85]

This 'birth tree' would go with the child, and then the adult, through their whole life: it was the 'tree of life'. Indeed, a strange 'sympathy' of mysterious correspondences would be established between an individual and his woody alter ego. The tree was 'the visible symbol of birth, growth, the prime of life and its ending'. If the man left home, the tree remained in his birthplace, as the mirror of his destiny. If he died far from home, then in Haute Bretagne,

Normandy or Wallonia his rosebush would wither, in Lorraine the roses would fall, in Poitou they would fade.[86] Everywhere, tales and legends have preserved the story of unfortunates who were murdered, or fell under an evil spell, and whose misfortune could be learned of from their birth-trees. According to a tale from Berry, Saint Honoré of Buzançais, who had gone to sell some farm animals in Poitou, had told his mother that she need have no fear for his safety so long as his laurel tree remained green. One day, all of a sudden, without apparent reason, the leaves of his birth-tree withered up. And it was thus that the poor woman discovered that her son had met with misfortune: he had been murdered.[87]

Returning to a more prosaic level, preparing the child's future meant wishing him material prosperity in this hard world. The ritual of the coin, a very widespread one, goes back at least to the sixteenth century. In Languedoc it was slipped into the swaddling bands; in Charente it went into the cradle.[88] At Saint-Dizier-Leyrenne, in the Marche, at the beginning of this century, it was a gold piece which was put in the baby's hand 'so that it would become rich'; nearby, at Saint-Vaury, the child was put on a table and 'rolled about on top of some gold pieces'.[89] The gold piece was certainly a late development, for it assumed a certain prosperity; as for the ritual itself, it had some connection with the 'rolling' of the baby on the altar stone after the ceremony of baptism.

Most probably it was the more prosperous classes of the towns who launched the fashion of the gold piece: it was given by the grandmother to the midwife, who rubbed the baby's lips with it for aesthetic reasons. But by the end of the seventeenth century the custom had already changed considerably: 'Several of our midwives ... rub the [babies'] lips with a gold piece as soon as they enter the world,' as the Paris obstetrician Philippe Peu reported at the time:

It is, they say, to bring out the colour and make them a bright red which they will then preserve all their lives. Seeing their determined adherence to this gilded ceremony, it is easy to believe that they have inherited it from earlier times, from those happy days when a pistole [a gold coin] meant less to a bourgeois than it now does to a person of quality. The aged grandfather, delighted to see himself reborn in his grandsons, would bring out the gold piece from his pocket, trusting the midwife, who would drop it in her purse. Today it is not so simple: people are more thrifty. You can rub the child's lips as much as you like but the coin will go back to him who gave it. The day is coming when it will be quite forgotten.[90]

15

Socializing the Child: Giving a Name

The choice of available forenames changed considerably between the Middle Ages and the nineteenth century. There used to be strict rules about the transmission of forenames, which were indeed family heirlooms. They were not so much a means of individualization as an identification of the child (and later the adult) with a family line. The forename was not chosen at random, for it implied more than was apparent at first sight: it was linked with beliefs about the cycle of life.

As the modern period came in, the child of the family line, inseparable from it and dependent on it, gave way to the child as an individual, singular entity. And indeed, the changes in the bestowal of forenames bear witness to this change in structures and behaviour.

Giving the Name

Naming the newborn child was an essential ritual. The name was a mark of recognition and belonging, an attachment. A child born dead, or which died before it could reach the font, remained nameless – a being whom people had failed to retain and to recognize. Certainly it would suffer for that, and see that others suffered too.

The name that the child received at its baptism was not the result of an arbitrary decision, much less of fashion, for giving a name was a commitment on the part of both child and family. But, while a forename designated one individual and placed him in the series of his family and line of descent,[1] it could not differentiate him or identify him. Several people in the village, perhaps a few dozen, would have the same forename: it 'signified, assimilated, but did not singularize'.[2]

The bestowal of forenames has aroused a fresh interest in recent years amongst historians, sociologists, ethnologists and anthropologists.[3] While it would still be premature to attempt a global approach to the problem, studies based on parish registers, certain 'books of reasons' and ecclesiastical documents have made it possible to discern some essential elements.

Nowadays, forenames are chosen and known long before the child is born. The choice is up to the parents, and they would resent any attempt to deprive them of a freedom of choice which they look upon as their right. People today look for an unusual name for their child, or one which they think sounds distinguished; but in fact, the attempt only leads them back into utter conformism, since they do nothing but echo the fashion of the moment. In past centuries things were entirely different, for 'the desire to individualize the child by an original forename was subsumed in the imperatives of affiliation',[4] the need to transmit the real and symbolical possessions of the family from generation to generation; and the forename was an essential part of this moveable patrimony.

It seems to have been towards the end of the thirteenth century that a change began to appear in the world of Western forenames.[5] Until that time people had had a single forename, and often a nickname, indicating their origin, profession, place of residence, distinguishing mark or trait of character, which would eventually become the family surname. The overall organization of this world always remained approximately the same: a small group of leading names favoured by the majority alongside a collection of little-used ones. In the fourteenth century, these less popular names became more numerous, giving a theoretically wider choice. But the principal change at this period had to do with the 'head group'. In Avignon, the 'feudal forenames' of Guillaume and Raymond, Alasacie and Douce, began to fade out; 'Catherine' became more popular and 'Jeanne' made its appearance; in particular, new masculine names like Christophe, Sébastien and Antoine suddenly became very popular, and the Church, which was fostering new forms of devotion, encouraged these new selections.[6]

In succeeding centuries the pool of forenames became shallower, with the progressive disappearance, quicker in some regions than in others, of outdated feudal names, which were replaced by a smaller number of names belonging to the patron saints of the Catholic Reformation. In the seventeenth century, three or four leading names for each sex sufficed for half the population. In Saint-André-des-Alpes, four names – Jean, Antoine, Honoré and Pierre – designated two-thirds of men born between 1650, though seven names – Marguerite, Catherine, Jeanne, Honorade, Marie and Isabeau – were required to cover the same proportion of the women.[7] This wider dispersal of feminine names did not occur everywhere. At the same period in the Vexin, the situation was reversed: four names sufficed for half the girls, while seven were needed for the same number of boys; and by the end of the century, with the narrowing of choice, three names were enough for half the women, but five were still needed for the men.[8]

At this stage, the names favoured by the Catholic Church, in its crusade to reconquer the popular mind, became firmly established. 'Marie', still third after 'Marguerite' and 'Anne' a century earlier, was now to outclass all the others. At the end of the sixteenth century, it was already in first place in Normandy, but almost unknown in French Catalonia; but by the end of the next century it was borne by 60 per cent of girls at Perpignan. The same tendency is found everywhere. The fashion for double-barrelled forenames did not weaken it, but, on the contrary, reinforced its primacy. The only names which could possibly stand up to it were those of saints whose cult was fostered by a religious order, such as Colette (of Corbie) or Rose (of Lima). On the male side, the post-Tridentine Church encouraged the spread of François, favoured by vivid memories of the *poverello* of Assisi and 'recharged' by the example of that great bishop, François de Sales. The Church also had a weakness for 'Joseph', and its vogue grew steadily through the eighteenth century. Joseph was the perfect model of the good husband and father in the imagery of the Holy Family then being developed by the Church, but, in that century haunted by thoughts of the Latter End, he was also the symbol of the good death, peaceful and well-prepared, which was such a consolation to the Christian mind.[9] However, this did not allow him to trump the faithful apostle, John, who since the fourteenth century had held his first place without any real anxiety. In Anjou 'Pierre' and 'René' were preferred to 'Jean';[10] in the Franche-Comté, 'François' and 'Claude',[11] but in general the Catholic Reformation if anything increased its popularity. 'Jean' was for boys what 'Marie' was for girls. Indeed, had not the two been associated ever since they met at the foot of the Saviour's cross?

Control over forenames became an important source of influence for the Church in the seventeenth century; it was facilitated by the spread of the cult of patron saints. Apostles, evangelizing bishops, founders of monasteries, saints of the Catholic Reformation, were held up as models of virtue and piety. Ecclesiastical statutes and manuals of popular piety emphasized the need to inculcate into children a positive image of the saint whose name they bore so that they would model their behaviour on him (or her). The catechism of the Council of Trent set the tone by laying down that the child should be christened with

a name which must be that of someone who, by the excellence of his piety and his faithfulness to God, has deserved to be numbered among his saints, so that, by the resemblance of the name he bears, he should be further urged to imitate his virtues and holiness; he should strive to imitate him and pray to him, and hope that he will be his Protector and Advocate with God for the salvation of his soul and body.[12]

Giving 'pagan' names to children now looked like an error which must be firmly opposed; for the forename would *ipso facto* be spoken incessantly, and so would constitute a living echo of unacceptable beliefs. An insult to the true faith, a permanent challenge to the authority of the Church: 'Those who give or affect to give the names of Pagans, and in particular of those who have been among the most impious, to those being baptized, are much to be blamed,' emphasizes the catechism of the Council of Trent. 'For they show thereby the small esteem in which they hold Christian piety, since they take pleasure in perpetuating the memory of impious men, and want the ears of the Faithful to be continually battered by these profane names.'[13]

The logic of this 'pedagogy of the forename' brought the Church to make pronouncements on the orthodoxy of names; there were good ones which must be promoted and bad ones which must at all costs be eliminated. With the same vigour it pursued the battle against the feminine forms of male saints' names and vice versa: to the Church, every name must correspond to one saint whose authenticity had been recognized. Bishops intervened to make sure that priests turned down any name which did not fit the criteria.

The attitude of the post-Tridentine Church to forenames reveals a grim determination to eliminate old patterns of solidarity; by giving primacy to the personal relationship between a man and his patron saint, it was encouraging the emergence of the individual the better to control him. Further, the Church was not content merely to persecute pagan names; in France, after the Revocation of the Edict of Nantes, it felt that its crusade for the purgation of forenames was an ideal weapon to bar the further progress of Protestant heresy. Thus forenames became one of the bones of religious contention.

When the Protestant synod of 1562 advised choosing names from the Old Testament, however, it does not seem to have wrought such a profound change in habits as might have been thought. It seems to have been respected more in the sixteenth century than in the seventeenth, and more in the north of France than in the Midi.[14] In eighteenth-century Provence the tendency was reversed to the point where boys' names were chosen more and more from the New Testament, as girls' names had always been. However, in certain inward-turning communities in Brie, such as Nogentel, two-thirds of girls' names were still being chosen from the Old Testament.

As a general rule, non-Old Testament forenames seem to have remained more popular, bearing witness to the force of habit and to the limited influence of the protestant priesthood.[15] For both Protestants and Catholics, habits of naming could not be changed without some profound reason: the forename was an inheritance which was passed from generation to generation and to which people were strongly attached.

The Forename, a Family Heirloom

The speed with which yesterday's fashionable names disappear today has now created a situation utterly different from that which prevailed for centuries. In a single family, the range of forenames was limited, and the periodic return of three or four of them was like an illustration of the cycle of life, one generation following another. All structures made for permanence, and if there were changes, they always came 'from outside', because a novelty had been brought in by a godparent, or because the father, as a temporary migrant, had brought back new customs from the town.

The rules for the transmission of forenames explain their stability over the centuries. In a more or less closed society like the rural society of former times, the need for individualization was limited, and certainly did not come out in the choice of original forenames. A man was known by the quality of his senses, for his 'keen eye' or 'good ear'; or by his strength, his skill, his ability to invent remedies or potions, to trap wild animals, to find a good place for picking mushrooms.

The family group was still more important than the individual, the desire to individualize the child was subsumed in the need to pass on the family inheritance; to every generation 'the real and symbolical inheritance of the family must be passed on according to the rules, and the forename was one element in it'. In most regions, custom demanded that the baby's name should be chosen from those his ancestors had borne before him. For a boy the preference went to the paternal grandfather's name; for a girl, to the maternal grandmother. In Limousin and Périgord, all the grandchildren, not just the godson, would call their grandparents 'godmother' and 'godfather'.[16] By jumping a generation, the forename helped to reinforce the image of the cycle of life as conceived by country people. The great wheel of the family could go on turning now that the transmissions of the forename had given it the necessary fresh impetus.

In places where there was a patrilinear system of inheritances, as in the Sault region of the Pyrenees, there was a corresponding bilateral system of spiritual affiliation.[17] Godparents were chosen from the two family lines, the paternal and the maternal; once designated, it was hard for them not to accept the task. But the spiritual relationship thus established gave the godparents certain rights: they alone could give the child a name, and in theory the parents could not oppose their choice. In fact, this right was subordinated to custom, especially in the case of an eldest son on whom rested the future of the family line. In any case, while the godparents were entitled to give the child their own name, it could happen that they were chosen precisely with an eye to the name they would then confer.

In Alsace, where the customary system was different, the bestowal of the forename followed other rules. The first child normally bore the name of one of its parents, the father's for a boy, the mother's for a girl. The transmission of the *Hof*, the inalienable part of the family inheritance including the house and most of the land, favoured the eldest son: as inheritor of the patrimony he also inherited the name, the *Hofname*, and 'the individuality of the heir [was submerged] in the permanence of the family line'.[18]

Names and Resonances

Every name had its own little music, its power of evocation by sound, echoing its models, its history: it contained an emotional charge which it is often difficult to feel fully today. 'Louis' was a 'reminder' of the saintly King Louis IX, and symbolized balance, justice, magnanimity: it undoubtedly contributed to the image of the king as father of his people which was fostered by the French sovereigns of the seventeenth and eighteenth centuries. René – re-né, reborn – was one who had overcome death and come to life a second time. Marguerite originally meant 'pearl', later 'daisy'; the flower Rose later designated a model of holiness, Rose of Lima. Every family descent was aware of the resonance and the appeal to the imagination of the forename which recurred in it like an heraldic blason. No-one would know who had originally chosen it; the little music had its element of the unknown, its mysterious origin.

Forenames took account of the bearers' place in the family, setting the eldest apart from the younger ones. In some regions, a nickname would range the younger ones in order of their place in the phratry. At Cunfin, in Champagne,

the sons received local nicknames: the second was *bisso*, the third *lami*, the
fourth *dondon*.[19]

The family forename was not just a token of affiliation, it also showed a link
with the land, the ancestral possessions: it was one of the symbols of auto-
chthony. This link with the land, with the place, could go beyond the strict
confines of the 'household'. According to a tradition inspired by the Church,
some part of the Christianization of the locality might have been performed by
the eponymous ancestor, the more or less mythical saint or bishop who had
evangelized the country round: Claude in the Franche-Comté, Ours in Upper
Provence and the Val d'Aosta, Leonard in Limousin. People identified themselves with him, not with the patron saint of the parish, who never had any great
influence on forenames. In regions where it was adopted, the name would
spread out from the centre and die away on the margins, where it was in
competition with another. There was a kind of solidarity among those who bore
the same name: 'shared identity encouraged the idea of a common destiny'.

But if it was the deep roots of the name which gave it its strength, they could
also cause it to weaken when the territorial identification began to fade: this
certainly seems to have been the case in the nineteenth century as rural
structures began to break down. Every day the town set the tone a little more
clearly, and anything which recalled the attachment to the mythic and ancestral
ground was 'old-fashioned', out of date, devalued. It is significant that from
1880 to 1900, in Limousin, the name 'Leonard' was considered as 'uncouth'
and ceased to be used.[20]

The forename seemed to be an 'essential element of the person', as is proven
by the care that was taken not to divulge the name of a child before baptism, for
fear of black magic; or by country people's habit of giving a new name to mark
the great 'passages' in life, confirmation, marriage, maturity.[21]

The system for conferring forenames, normally rigid, did not lend itself to
much variation: up to the last century, permanence vanquished change. And
because forenames always reveal something of their owners' way of life, any
change in them is indicative of a profound change. This is indeed what is
revealed by the two great disjunctions of the sixteenth, and later of the
seventeenth and eighteenth, centuries.

Forenames Are Not What They Were

The changes in the choice of names in fourteenth-century Avignon are
significant: 'the emotional explosion' which was the result of the misfortunes of
the time expressed itself in the appearance of a galaxy of new names. The
apostles Peter (Pierre), James (Jacques) and John (Jean) still enjoyed the favour
of the faithful, and they kept their attachment to the old local saints like Veran,
Agricol, Castor and Siffrein; 'Marthe' was still popular, as one might expect;
but 'new intercessors' had made their appearance: Antoine and Sébastien, who
protected against plague and epidemics; Catherine and Cécile, whose virtues
and virginity were held up as examples now that a 'new European model of
marriage' was taking hold.[22]

In fact, the crisis of the fourteenth century was bringing about a growth in the number of unmarried women, an advance in the age of marriage which implies a growth in asceticism.[23] The 'courts of heaven' looked quite different when people were having fewer children – a result of late marriages – and the abyss between this world and that of their ancestors was becoming ever deeper. The 'orphaned' men of the towns were seeking, in the society of the world beyond, in these reassuring and protecting saints, substitutes for the ancestors, who would help them to forget their irrevocable severance from their family predecessors. The severance was definitive, and all the more interesting in that it seems to have come about before the Black Death: a structural mutation, more than a consequence of that cataclysmic epidemic.

The seventeenth-century mutation fits into a context which in some ways recalls that of the fourteenth century. The period of upheaval, war and plague which had begun in the latter half of the sixteenth century had wrought a profound change in social relationships, bringing once again late marriages, an increase in lifelong celibacy, and difficulty in launching boys in life, in 'placing' girls and endowing them with dowries.

There is evidence to show that contemporaries perceived the changes which were then transforming people's outlook and behaviour. In the 1622 *Chitchat of the New Mother*, a mother bitterly remarks that her daughter had already given birth to seven children:

'If I had thought that my daughter would be getting down to work so soon', she said, 'I would have let her tickle herself up till she reached the age of twenty-four without getting married . . . now that it is so much trouble to marry off the girls and provide for the boys; in the long run, willy nilly they will have to become monks and nuns, for offices and marriages are just too expensive.'[24]

The remark was apt at a time when new forms of devotion were flourishing and religious orders springing up everywhere! In these favourable circumstances, the powerful Reformed Catholic Church could not, however, prevent a noticeable modification in naming patterns in the seventeenth, and especially the eighteenth, century. It was then that the custom developed of giving a baby several forenames. According to Abbé Thiers, it appeared in Italy in the second half of the sixteenth century before passing into Spain, then Germany, and finally France. In reality it was certainly earlier than this, as is proved by the example of Florence, where the twofold forename was widespread by the end of the fourteenth century. But Thiers' overall schema was correct, except that the new system of naming spread according to the stage of evolution of social structures in the different regions. Everywhere it was the urban élite which introduced the innovation, which then spread to other levels of society. Abbé Thiers emphasized this, blaming the nobility for an innovation of which he disapproved. 'Gentlemen were the first to begin to have several names,' he insists. 'Later this abuse was introduced into the Third Estate, where, in their foolish vanity, they presumed to impose two names upon their children.'[25]

Twofold, and later manifold, forenames were indeed considered as a mark of social superiority. Thus, in the world of the judiciary of the Franche-Comté in the seventeenth and eighteenth centuries, the number of forenames grew as

212 Socialization of the Child

one rose up the hierarchy: the usher in the lower court usually had only one, while the magistrate of the *Parlement* had two, three, four or sometimes even six![26] San Ildefonso de Liguri, born near Naples at the end of the seventeenth century, received ten forenames, and there was a Colonna in Rome who was equipped with twenty-four of them! Twenty-four protectors!

In a strongly hierarchical and compartmentalized society like that of the estates of the *ancien régime*, where everyone knew his place, and people were torn between the desire to conform and the desire to rise in the social scale, multiple forenames were a compromise between those contradictory tendencies.[27] They made it possible to attain to some sort of distinction while preserving the essential; to reconcile a reference to one's relationships and symbolic inheritance with the individual's ever more emphatic desire to assert himself; to respect the demands of the past – the first forename was always the 'family name' – and the aspirations of the present; and the other forenames, by which the child was never actually called, referred to the protective saints charged with watching over his destiny.

Let us not exaggerate the implications of this change, however. Until the nineteenth century the family line still took precedence over the individual in rural society, as is shown by the very frequent custom of reattributing the names of deceased elder children to younger ones and giving them the same godparents: to blot out death, to 'remake' the dead child, so that in the end the name, and thus the line, would not perish.

Another sign of the change in outlook was the introduction of new ways of choosing godparents which corresponded to new ways of choosing forenames. Once again it was the towns which took to the change most readily. Towards the end of the seventeenth century, in the society of the *Parlements* and among the lawyers of the Franche-Comté, godparents were beginning to be sought who were no longer members of the family, but belonged to the professional and social milieu.[28] Such a choice showed 'an apparent indifference to the hereditary character of the forename'; on the contrary, it showed a preference for a widening of the family circle, a strengthening of alliances which gave priority to the social, horizontal dimension of godparent–godchild relationships. People were severing themselves from the ancestral, vertical world, from a past which it was becoming more and more difficult to make a part of themselves.

PART VI

The Divagations of Nature

Nature can act idiotically at times.

Louise Bourgeois

Nature is not always 'pure as the driven snow'. Country people knew it well, for in some years they had to endure fearful deviations on her part: harvests laid waste by storm or frost, herds devastated by epidemics.

Similarly, a confinement which began auspiciously could suddenly turn to catastrophe, without apparent reason. Even today, one confinement in ten is likely to develop complications. It is quite likely that in former times there were more 'risky' confinements. One thing is certain, however: it was that 'one in ten' which would leave the strongest impression on people's minds. Uneventful births had no history; they almost never held the attention of witnesses – doctors, priests, administrators. It was the divagations of nature, extraordinary, striking, which were recorded. Thus the sources at our disposal constantly give priority to the bizarre, the dramatic, so much so that the proportion of normal births to difficult ones, with complications, is reversed.

Disturbances of the natural order were not shown only by difficult confinements: the quality of the 'fruit' was sometimes compromised as well. A weakly, even monstrous baby, or a stillborn one, was profoundly disturbing.

16

The Falling of the Flower

Those who lose their children by chance, as for example through injury, unintentionally ...

Louise Bourgeois

Nothing was ever certain until the day the corn was harvested or the fruit was picked: a frost in spring, an equinoctial gale, a heavy rainstorm, could always 'make the flowers fall' and put an end to the ripening. A foetus was as fragile as a flower, and like a flower, was never entirely safe from accidents. It did not take much to put an end to the fondest hopes.

The Silence and the Fear

The mischances of pregnancy were always referred to by metaphors alluding to perturbations in the natural cycle. If a baby was born before term it was because it 'couldn't hold on' or 'wasn't firmly hooked'; the mother had 'exerted herself', she had had 'a rupture' and the child 'had got unhooked'. Up to the beginning of this century, a miscarriage was referred to as a 'sprain'; the woman 'sprained herself', 'did herself an injury', 'hurt herself'. In popular speech, she 'broke her egg'.[1]

Doctors in the seventeenth and eighteenth centuries preferred to speak of 'abortion'. What always amazed them was the littleness of the aborted foetus. Metaphors borrowed from the animal or vegetable worlds are used to express their astonishment and their desire to give a name to this little, unfinished human being, and define it by comparison.

An embryo a few weeks old was

As big as a large haricot bean (Portal)
An embryo the size of a clove (Portal)
A child no bigger than a grain of wheat (Mauriceau)

A three- or four-month-old foetus and its appendages was

A membrane the size of a good ostrich egg, and the child the size of a newly hatched chick (Portal)
A little bladder full of water, the size of a hen's egg, in which was a living child as big as a cockchafer (La Motte)
A three-month foetus as big as a skinned mouse (La Motte)

216

Let us not be deceived by the colourful way the medical profession described the aborted offspring. Normally a miscarriage was shrouded in the greatest discretion; the accident was concealed; even the husband was not always told, especially if the loss occurred at a very early stage. In the aristocracy, abortion was felt as a disgrace: the woman would not even tell her closest friend. At court, the end of the queen's hopes was a real tragedy: she would scarcely know how to confess it to her husband.[2]

Normally there was no call on any medical skills: 'In this sort of delivery there is no room for the surgeon or professional midwife.'[3] Thus, abortion was only brought to the attention of doctors if there were complications. A strong feeling of guilt induced the woman to keep her loss a secret: she would be convinced that she had had something to do with the unhappy outcome. Fear of barrenness visibly shadowed women who had lost their first baby: such a miscarriage was a bad sign, believed to presage others to come. This was confirmed by Didelot, an obstetrician from Lorraine, in 1770:

A miscarriage is infinitely more harmful than a birth at full term, and women who have had one run a great risk of having a second, quite apart from several inconveniences which they cause. I consider such an accident to be the most terrible and unfortunate one which can happen to a pregnant woman, both because the death of the child is assured and because the mother is in danger of the same fate; also it is one cause of barrenness.[4]

We now know that repeated miscarriages are often due to an hormonal insufficiency which can only be overcome by specific treatment and a long period of rest.

Besides permanent sterility, with no possibility of descendants, women also feared that the aborted foetus might be denied baptism and buried in unconsecrated ground. Pregnancy was a fearful ordeal for those unable to carry their babies to full term. But women faced with miscarriage were not always prisoners of silence and fear. From the middle of the seventeenth century, better-off women in the big towns began to ask the obstetrician to intervene and help them escape the consequences of an interrupted pregnancy. Practitioners were able to gain more experience, and tried to learn more about the causes of miscarriage.

Causes of miscarriage, according to a Parisian obstetrician (1694)

General causes

Bad constitution in male or female

Vitiated seed, or seed sown at a wrong and unhealthy time

Womb not in the right condition for a good germination

Particular causes

Regarding the mother:

The mother must be asked about

the progress of the pregnancy: repulsions, nausea, blood loss, agues, etc. place where she was brought up

climate of the place where she lives: has she moved house recently?

her parents: has she some hereditary disease, 'and especially if her mother was subject to abortion, either by accident or by the defects of her constitution'

what she has been doing since reaching the age of reason. At what age was she given in marriage? 'Whence one may judge if she has been placed in the married state too young, or too old.'

her temperament: dry or replete, robust or delicate

her bodily build: tall or short, well-formed or ill-made, 'especially as regards the organs of generation'

humours and passions

work and behaviour: does she raise her arms when yawning or drawing water? Overexertion; excessive frequency of, and 'indiscretion' in, marital relations; chills or sunstroke

dress: clothes which fit too tightly

fatiguing journeys in carriage or on horseback

Regarding the child:

stage in the pregnancy: is the child at term or not? For it is less strong at three, five or six months than at seven, less strong again from seven to nine months; but according to the best Hippocratic tradition, the child's vigour is greater at seven months than at eight

a bad or unnatural position in the womb can cause premature birth

the state of the child: living or dead? And if dead, for how long? Is it 'vitiated in the face, navel, situation of the private parts'?

Regarding the afterbirth.

It becomes wholly or partially detached if the cord is:
too long or too thin, and is around the child
too long, too thick, liable to break
too short, threatening to cause detachment of the placenta

Regarding foreign bodies:

presence of molae or false seeds[5]

'So Small, So Human'

After the accident, the aborted foetus was often treated with astonishing offhandedness. It could get lost: La Motte speaks of a 'little cockchafer of a foetus' which, having been baptized, 'was so entangled in the linen that it could not be found. I believed,' he adds, 'that it had been trampled underfoot, having fallen to the ground with some clots of blood which had accompanied it.'[6] Sometimes it was even treated as a piece of rubbish and dumped accordingly.

However, from the sixteenth century onwards the medical world and the educated public began to take a certain interest in the aborted foetus. We should probably construe this as a curiosity about the origins of mankind, at a time when the study of embryology was just beginning. In their desire for further knowledge, surgeons seized every opportunity to perform autopsies on the corpses of aborted babies. To complete their education and that of their pupils, some kept glass flasks at home with complete foetuses in them; if such were unavailable, they procured their skeletons. The aim was clear: to reconstruct the chain from the first days and weeks of life to full term. At the end of the eighteenth century, the great anatomical collections like that of the Veterinary School at Alfort, and some private collections of lesser importance, bore witness to this scientific interest. According to his *Catalogue of Anatomical Specimens* (compiled about 1800), Pierre Robin, an obstetrician from Rheims, had in his cabinet ten foetal skeletons whose size varied from a little over five centimetres to fifty centimetres (from two to twenty inches);[7] but this practitioner also possessed 'embryos, foetuses and products of miscarriages . . . which he uses in his lectures' (to trainee midwives).[8] The contemporary fascination with humans in miniature is undeniable: 'so small, so human!' Curiosity about 'these wonderful little objects' sometimes overcame whole communities, which queued up to view an embryo on display in a saucer! At last, a chance to discover what was normally concealed in the maternal womb – the first uncertain stirrings of a new life . . ..

The Time of Miscarriage

It was summertime which was the most dangerous period for pregnant women. In the country, the hot months coincided with haymaking and harvest, in which they often took part: long days of toil, particularly taxing for those expecting a child. It was then that the frailest of them would lose their fruit. Years of famine were also years of miscarriage. To the customary dangers of the summer months were added the threat from insufficient, and deficient, food during the difficult period between spring and the summer harvest.

Summer was likewise critical for pregnant women in the towns. At Rheims, in the later eighteenth century, abortions generally occurred between July and October.[9] It was at the beginning of the pregnancy, at the moment when hormonal secretion gave way to the nourishing of the foetus via the placenta, when the placenta became 'breast to the child', that accidents happened. They afflicted all women, without regard to social milieu. A weak constitution would predispose them to an interrupted pregnancy, and rashness or an unhappy chance would do the rest. Good company and late nights for aristocratic or bourgeois women; overwork in the lower classes.

Successive pregnancies were not all alike. Through a woman's life, some seemed to be more dangerous than others. First pregnancies, the doctors said, often ended in miscarriage because the woman did not realize that she was pregnant; she took no precautions, indulged too much in sexual pleasure, and so stupidly lost her child.

It might be worth seeking statistical confirmation of these hints by the reconstitution of families and a study of the normal interval between pregnancies. Mireille Laget's survey of the people of Languedoc in the eighteenth century shows that the critical period was rather that of the second pregnancy, when the woman had not yet recovered from her first confinement and was actively engaged in caring for her first child.[10] The end of the fertile years was no less dangerous: the mother's constitution would have been enfeebled by successive pregnancies and she would lose the fruit of her womb when she was about forty, in her fifth or sixth pregnancy.

It is very hard to determine the rate of miscarriages. Because the woman would conceal such an accident, abortion leaves few clues; very often we have nothing but case studies reported by the doctors. Only those practitioners' notebooks which were regularly updated can give a certain evaluation of the frequency of the phenomenon; and such notebooks are few. Those left by Pierre Robin of Rheims cover a practice lasting over a quarter of a century (1770–97). There are clear notes on miscarriages for only thirteen of those years. They represent a little over 4 per cent of total attendances, but there are perceptible fluctuations from year to year: in 1781, on average, one miscarriage in every eleven attendances; in 1787, only one out of thirty-seven.[11]

Prevention and Cure

Miscarriages had their repercussions on women's health. The loss of blood which often accompanied them was particularly to be feared, because its effects were lasting. 'Some women,' says La Motte, 'are left with a long and troublesome headache, and their faces never regain a healthy colour.'[12] But some women were even more deeply marked with the feelings of failure and guilt which went with involuntary abortion. There are many accounts which bear witness to their frustration. This makes it quite comprehensible that doctors should have been concerned to prevent the accident, or to give some help after it.

In his *Advice to the People on their Health*, Tissot advises women anxious to avoid the worst to go to bed immediately if they injure themselves: 'They should go to bed at once,' he writes, 'and lie on a straw palliasse if they have no mattress; feathers are very bad in such cases; they should remain thus for several days, without moving and almost without speaking.' He also recommends a diet made up exclusively of farinaceous soups, and bleeding, observing

that 'there are robust and sanguine women who are at risk of hurting themselves at a certain time; they guard against this accident [he adds] by having
themselves bled a few days before this period.'[13] Louise Bourgeois also
believed that in case of accidents 'the first remedy is bed', and she advises
against 'any labour of body or mind'. She mentions the case of a pregnant
woman who fell through a trapdoor and who had lost at least 'a small panful of
blood; and who was put to bed two days later'. Louise treated her with
homeopathic methods; the colour red, warmth, and the symbolism of eggs
played the leading role in the treatment of this blood loss:

I made her take the germs of seven or eight eggs in a fresh egg, with red cramoisie silk,
cut up small, about sixty grains, then I had a poultice made for her of white cypress,
marjoram and rosemary, as much of one as of the other, pounded on a hot scoop,
sprinkled with warm wine, put between two linen cloths on the abdomen above the
navel, and had it reheated two or three times a day. I can assure you that she bore her
child two months later, this being the full nine months. I can see nothing better to do
than this, as soon as a woman thinks she has done herself an injury. And [she concludes]
I think that I have helped to save more than two hundred.[14]

17

The Unripe Fruit

Women must regard the child they bear in their womb like a fruit hanging from a tree: if this fruit is detached before it is perfectly ripe, it will never be so good, and will spoil; the same with the child.

Didelot, Instructions for midwives, *1770*

Nowadays a premature baby receives intensive medical treatment: it is isolated and fed artificially, its breathing and heartbeat are monitored twenty-four hours a day; the incubator completes the maturing process which the mother's womb was unable to bring to fruition. In the early modern period, by contrast, there does not seem to have been much concern about its survival. Is this unconcern only apparent, or did people really think that nothing could be done about it and that this 'unripe' child was only enjoying a short reprieve from death?[1]

Born Before Term

The premature child was the very symbol of human frailty. Its slight weight, its small size, made it, like the aborted foetus, a subject of astonishment. Folktales preserve this interest in mankind in miniature. How strange, even fascinating, are the Hop o' my Thumb, the Tom Thumb, the French *Petit Poucet*, of popular tales! Especially as small size often went with unusual intelligence and great practical cunning: 'Poucet' 'was the most cunning and wise of all his brothers, and though he talked little, he listened a great deal'.[2] This taste for the marvellous often caused confusion between actual observations and pure invention.

Furthermore, doctors' reports themselves helped greatly to give credit to the idea that in some cases children could be born well before term and yet survive. Montanus says that he knew of a child born at five months who reached adulthood. Cardano reports that a wine merchant's wife once showed him her daughter, born at five and a half months. Spigelius speaks of a man of forty who had come into the world at the beginning of the sixth month: 'He showed good evidence of this, which he always carried on him,' he continues; 'his mother had been obliged to put him in cottonwool until his bones had grown strong enough for him to be put in swaddling clothes.'[3] And Brouzet reports the story of the child from Marseillan who was born in 1748, in the fifth month of his mother's pregnancy:

He lived as foetuses do for the first four months after his birth, that is to say without crying, without suckling, without making any apparent excretions and without any other movement than that of swallowing a few drops of warm milk. After these four months, or nine months after his conception, he suddenly emerged from this kind of lethargy, cried, suckled, moved his limbs, and grew so much that at sixteen months he was bigger than children usually are at that age.[4]

The halo of legend surrounding such tales springs, once again, from the uncertainty about dates of conception.

Premature Birth, Honour and Inheritance

If some births were considered to be very premature, it was because women did not know for certain when they had conceived. The fact that some women continue to show a menstrual loss in the first month of pregnancy may explain the error. Conception just before the period is a frequent cause of confusion, according to Mauriceau:

If [the woman] has intercourse with her husband on the point of her monthly flow, and becomes pregnant, then she will make her reckoning of her state from the time when it disappears, which will be about right; but if she conceives immediately after her period, which most often happens, and indulges in coitus every day for a whole month, at the end of that time, if her menstruation does not come, she will certainly consider herself to be pregnant; however, she will not know by this sign which blow has gone home, and within three weeks, or a month more or less, when she entered this state.[5]

But certainly less attention would have been paid to premature or tardy births if there were no question of succession depending on them.

'Jurisconsults,' says Nicolas Venette, 'like to be certain of a fixed time for the birth of children, so as to share out the inheritance fairly and not give a share of it to a child which was not legitimate.'[6] The interests of the family could be compromised by a doubtful birth. And the mother's honour did not always emerge unscathed from such a test. As for the husband, he could not be immune to disappointment, even if he thought he had assurances:

A lady ... gave birth seven months to the day after she had been married, although her worthy husband had married her on the steps of the convent; none the less her spouse's mind suffered thereby; but having hidden his suspicions, he did not neglect to make advances to her as soon as she had arisen from her childbed. She became pregnant immediately, and gave birth a second time after seven months. Thinking her husband to be displeased at her fertility, she was surprised to be congratulated on this second premature confinement, and to be told that he had never committed the folly of condemning her for the first one, but that he had not had the strength to absolve her, for which he most humbly begged her pardon: these two children were brought up so well, that one was killed at Ramhilles, and the other at the battle of Malplaquet.[7]

How Many Premature Children? How Many Survived?

How many of these premature babies managed to hang on to life? The study of prematurity, like that of miscarriage, is bedevilled by an insufficiency of source material. Practitioners sometimes report particular cases, rarely a series of statistics. These make the three tables given by François Mauriceau in his *Treatise on the Maladies of Pregnant and Newly Delivered Women* all the more valuable.[8] The 181 observations recorded by this obstetrician in his third table are particularly interesting. Let us recall that at the time children were considered to be viable at seven months. Now, in this table children born in the seventh month of pregnancy constitute 1.65 per cent of the total (3 cases), and those born in the eighth month 17.7 per cent (32 cases). Thus almost one child in five was born before term; this proportion is certainly slightly higher than the average insofar as the obstetrician was called out mainly in difficult cases, in particular in cases of premature delivery followed by complications. Material conditions, inadequate food and nutritional insufficiency were often behind premature births in the seventeenth and eighteenth centuries. A proportion of 15 per cent thus seems normal;[9] a bad harvest, epidemic or war would cause a significant rise in this proportion, when one child in every four or five would be born before full term.

Premature babies were the first victims of the high mortality rates afflicting children in the first week after birth; often they could not feed, while the mother had no idea of any other way of feeding' than by the breast. Some pathetic attempt might be made to feed them with scraps of bread or cottonwool soaked in milk . . . and they would die of hunger two or three days after their arrival in the world. A premature child which survived was an exception, almost a miracle. The reflex to suckle was vital: if the child could take the breast after birth, it could then 'be brought up'. In 1703, La Motte delivered a seven-months pregnant woman of a child which was 'small but quite strong. As soon as the mother was delivered and put to bed,' La Motte recounts, 'I had presented to the child the nipple of a wetnurse who happened to be present; it took it and suckled wonderfully well, and fed very well thereafter.'[10] The baby would very often be a little enfeebled during the first two months, but thereafter it could 'catch up' very quickly. After which it was considered that it could survive.

After birth, the nurses would also take care that the baby did not lose any heat: like all newborn children, premature babies would be laid near the hearth, wrapped in scraps of cloth. They were so small that 'the linen and swaddling bands which usually served for other children' would be considered 'useless' in their case. Then they would be put in a little basket lined with tufts of wool, or cottonwool if it was of good family. Thus Henry, Duke of Longueville, who died at sixty-eight, 'came into the world before term in 1595; he was put in a little box full of cottonwool, which was carried about in a pocket.'[11]

Despite a rather fraught entry into the world, some children born before term later became famous: Galileo, Newton, Pascal, Voltaire and, nearer our own time, Victor Hugo, Darwin and Einstein. It is possible that premature birth compels the child to a kind of precocious adaptability by subjecting it to 'exceptionally rich and varied sensorial stimulation'; however, it would also have to have 'a particularly vigilant, exceptionally loving, that is to say again, exceptionally stimulating, mother'. Michel Odent believes that in such circumstances it is not unlikely that there might once have been 'an infinitely greater diversity than in the ordinary population, and (why not?) a significantly higher proportion of "geniuses" '.[12]

18

Unnatural Delivery

The child presented only one of its legs, the first; which is a bad first step in this dance.

Jacques Duval

Birth could be a long and taxing process for both mother and child. If both had been through a bad time, they sometimes remained marked for life, in body and mind, by their ordeal: tears and prolapses could make the woman an invalid for the rest of her life, and as for the child, weakly and handicapped, it remained forever a burden on its parents, brothers, and sisters.

The Unforeseen Drama

Textbooks were never tired of repeating that every birth was an individual case and that the greatest care was needed. Act without haste, proceed methodically, keep a close eye on the woman without ever rushing her: such must be the code of conduct of the perfect obstetrician and the good midwife. For in this field, more than in any other, it was impossible ever to be sure of anything. No room for presumption!

All those who assisted women in their confinements knew that one day they would be confronted with a situation for which they were unprepared. They were haunted by the idea of malpresentations and difficult labours which went on and on and risked 'ending badly'. Why did women whose pregnancies had been uneventful suddenly find themselves on the point of death during their confinements? Why did mothers of several children, whose deliveries had all been uneventful before, fail to give birth, after two or three days of agony, to a child which was even then dying in their womb? 'Nature has secrets and ways which are unknown to us.'

As soon as we open one of those obstetrical textbooks written in the seventeenth or eighteenth century, in which obstetricians like Mauriceau, Peu, Portal, La Motte or Dionis reveal the way they overcame often tragic situations, we are tempted to make – consciously or unconsciously – a comparison with modern circumstances and to say that mothers giving birth today are fortunate indeed! Blood, sweat, screams, the agony of broken bodies, horror even, breathe through those pages. These series of cases are like collections of newspaper stories, each more pitiful than the one before. Our idea of birth in

226

former days is inevitably marked by such dramatizations, since the textbooks, along with reports sent by practitioners to the Royal Academy of Surgeons, are our most valuable sources for the past history of childbirth. Obstetricians were not necessarily overfond of morbid detail; it must be remembered that the essence of their practice consisted of interventions in serious cases, so that they naturally have a good deal to say about them. And it was also a chance for them – or some of them – to show how indispensable they were, how they alone could save mothers and children. Reading them, we sometimes wonder if there was such a thing as a normal birth, without serious consequences. For other reasons, the selective memory of ordinary people contributes to this same dramatization of childbirth. The memory of a woman who had suffered horribly and died without bringing her child to birth would long remain etched on the memory of the villagers or local townspeople. Heartrending scenes, screams, despairing relatives, would not easily be forgotten. Later on two hundred, three hundred women might give birth, but the story of the one which ended badly would always come back, like a leitmotiv. So true is it that the abnormal, if tinged with horror, is better remembered.

The image of a good delivery was, as we have seen, a short one, when the woman was delivered 'in the time it takes to say a *miserere*'. Thus the labour which midwives and audience would find most alarming was that which began under the best auspices and then developed complications without apparent reason. It was then that the experience and character of the midwife or obstetrician were put to a severe test. The fight for a life turned to a fight against the death which was threatening two living people.

In the night of Monday 16 to Tuesday 17 May 1698, La Motte was called to the wife of a shoemaker of Valognes, pregnant with her first child:

I found her with quite strong, but infrequent pains, the child well positioned and the waters beginning to form. As I was her near neighbour, I returned home, not yet seeing anything to make me stay with her any longer. The [next] morning, I found her in the same state as I had left her. I continued to see her from time to time during that day, and until Friday evening.

The pains increased, the baby's head advanced, the waters appeared well formed to the point where the membranes were emerging; the obstetrician decided to rupture them to hasten the delivery. No result. The woman finally gave birth on the Sunday night, after six days of agony. 'The woman was suffering all this time, almost without respite and without sleeping for a single hour. But fortunately,' adds La Motte, 'she did not lack courage; on the contrary, she repeatedly took something to keep up her strength, which saved her, for without it she would have succumbed in this long labour.'

Such an ordeal was an event in a little town like Valognes; the whole population was stirred by it: 'This unhappy woman was surely going to succumb!' Great was the surprise of all 'to see the child in the church, and even more to see its mother in the street ten days later, in perfect health'.[1]

But there were some even more dramatic cases, in which the woman was saved *in extremis*, due solely to the skill of the midwife. In 1610, in Paris, Louise Bourgeois accompanied a doctor to a woman who was said to have been in labour for nine or ten days and who had been given up for lost. The midwife wrote:

We found a woman who seemed doomed to death, a pale face with staring eyes, pinched nose, breath which stank of death, into whose stomach nothing would go which she did not immediately vomit up again; she had drunk two good pints of water in an hour; they were no longer able to boil water for her, so they gave it her as it was, and often an eggyolk which she immediately brought up again; she had no childbirth pains, but finding the womb open and the waters beginning to form, soft and ready, I easily realized that she had been in labour, but that, nature being exhausted and without aid, the child had gone back up, and was suffocating her and causing the vomiting.

This idea of the child 'going back up' and causing suffocation or convulsions in the mother recurs quite regularly in reports. Louise Bourgeois administered a remedy of her own:

I made her drink rhubarb water, which was ready made at our house, which she did not vomit up . . . and every hour I made her take an eggyolk, which stayed down; then nature began to gain strength, and the pains of childbirth began to return . . . at the end of the operation she gave birth to a very large, well-grown boy, which was extremely feeble and lived for two days.[2]

The pain could be contained, accepted or violently expressed, there could be an attitude of resignation or of panic: every woman reacted in her own way against the adversity and death which lay in wait for her. One April Sunday in 1666, Paul Portal was called to help a hydropic woman in the Rue Saint-Germain-l'Auxerrois:

This woman was prodigiously fat, swollen by the affliction of her body; and besides this swelling, she had under the navel a tumour larger than a three-pound loaf, which seemed flatulent and caused the sufferer great anxiety, because she had seen several surgeons and midwives who had all alarmed her, having told her that she was in danger of death; which had frightened her so much that she confessed so as to be ready to die well. Although we did all we could to reassure her against the fear they had put in her mind, she never stopped telling us that she was as good as dead, and would never rise from her bed; which was the belief of all those who had seen her.[3]

Other women showed extraordinary courage and dignified resignation to the fate they thought would be theirs. At Coutances, in 1721, one who was at term saw her waters break when she went to stool; she was worried, 'having heard that if such an accident happened, the labour usually proved more difficult'. Three days passed before the pains took her; but the presentation was very bad and the child would not come:

Without showing any surprise [reports the obstetrician who was called in] I warned the sufferer by general remarks about the need to deliver a woman artificially on many occasions, and that such a delivery was often more prompt and went better than one in which nature is expected to act alone . . . . The lady, who understood what I was trying to say, told me that she was not surprised; but since it was necessary to die, she asked me for time to set her affairs, and her conscience, in order, and that after I was to do what I thought best. She asked me if she would have to suffer long and if an hour would be enough; I assured her that the delivery would be over in half a quarter of an hour.

All went well; the mother was delivered and the child saved, 'and I can tell you,' adds the obstetrician, 'that of all her preceding deliveries, though they were natural, she did not feel as well as after this one'.[4]

Into the room – invariably overheated – in which the woman lay in labour, any complication would throw confusion: soon the air would be unbreathable. The anxiety of all was aggravated by a feeling of helplessness. By the light of a few candles the uncertainty began, soon to turn to drama. Everything was impregnated with the 'stinking and deathly' odours of mortifying flesh, sweat and urine. Add to that at times vomitings of blackish bile accompanied by 'gobbets of what looked like cooked pig's blood, with the same colour and a most unpleasant smell'.[5]

Certainly the principal cause of difficult labours used to be the narrowness of the pelvis. Malnutrition in early childhood caused malformations and narrowing of the pelvis in women; the child could not pass through the narrow gap, the labour might last for days . . .. Days of agony for the mother, and for the child, which might be born with a swollen head, 'pulled out as if it were made of squeezed butter'. But the outcome of such a combat could never be certain. The fate of such unfortunates was more or less sealed in advance: rickets was an unfortunate inheritance and a bringer of further misfortune. At Bellevaux, the hospital of Besançon, on 15 March 1777, the surgeon Nédey, in front of an obstetrics class, attended to a girl of fifteen, 'lame and with atrophy of the right arm and the left thigh, with obliquity of the womb'. The forehead and occiput of the child occupied the whole of the right iliac cavity and its face was turned towards the left cavity. The practitioner had great difficulty in bringing round first one foot, then the other; finally he was able to turn the child round, but he then found the obstacle of the head, too big for a pelvis whose circumference was 'everywhere more than an inch narrower than normal, well-formed pelvises'. The child was brought forth, still with a quiver of life; as for the mother, she died five days later of gangrene of the vagina and womb. Unhappy humanity![6]

The failure of deliveries at term on women whose pelvises were either badly placed or narrowed by rickets could encourage practitioners to intervene some weeks before term, or as soon as the first pains appeared. The husband and family were not always very enthusiastic about sucn precautionary interventions. The idea that the woman would be barren afterwards was deeply rooted in people's minds. But a midwife or surgeon would be equally reluctant to intervene, for fear of being blamed for the death of mother or child; so the husband had to be asked in advance to waive the responsibility of the operator, 'because on such occasions, he or she who operates, the woman chancing to die, are always the cause of it, according to evil serpents' tongues'.[7]

Who is Responsible?

When the labour did not proceed normally, the entourage was indeed tempted to seek a cause for this: there was a desire to know and understand. The ready-made culprit was the child: it was accused of having made a bad job of its 'dive', or of being lazy and making no effort to set its mother free. But the midwife too would receive a part of the blame; and not always without reason. Her imprudence or misjudgement often was at the back of accidents which had the gravest consequences for mother and child.

Still on the subject of imprudence: midwives in eastern France had the habit of seating labouring women on a kind of improvised *chaise percée*. The discomfort of the position that this made women adopt for hours on end, the extreme tension that was inflicted on the perineum, could have fearsome consequences.

On 5 May 1778, Marie-Joseph Gavard, aged 29, expecting her first child, quickly gave birth in this position to a healthy baby. The midwife came back to see the new mother the next day and asked her if she felt at all unwell; she examined her briefly and found the genital organs in the most natural state; she gave her a slap on the thigh, saying, 'You're very lucky; your body is like that of a girl of fifteen! After my first confinement my two holes had come together and I couldn't sit down for six weeks.' However, she noticed a tumefaction of the perineum, which, like the thighs, was bloodstained; she had an emollient lotion brought, which she had had made as an enema, with the intention of using it for washing the private parts. And it was then that she discovered a wound which seemed to her 'so enormous, that her arms fell to her sides and [she] retired without saying another word to the patient.' Much upset, she hurried to see the obstetrician, who was often 'her help and comfort in her misfortunes', and told him the whole story. The latter has left us his account:

When I arrived, I introducd my finger into the anus to check that the sphincter was undamaged; I did the same with the vulva, and my hooked finger emerged through the perineum after raising the fourchette; I applied to these parts compresses soaked in an emollient lotion . . .. After five or six days' visiting, the swelling had diminished and I had the idea of measuring those parts with a measure attached to a folding rule; the width of the vulva was only one inch three lines (about 3 cm) and the wound in the perineum two inches four lines (about 5.5 cm); the wound stretched right along the raphe, which was torn in several places, but the most extensive tear was made of a strip of skin as wide as a thumbnail and which left the fatty bodies exposed on the opposite side, which had been torn away; and the tear stretched on each side of the folds in the skin of the anus, embracing it in the branches of an inverted Greek λ and ending at the level of its centre.

For ten days, the wound was greased with Samaritan balsam, and the obstetrician administered emollient injections to bring down the lochia which were stagnating in the curve of the vagina; then a bandage was applied, and the wound, which was threatening to remain as a fistula, closed after seven weeks.[8]

Sometimes unexpected difficulties and the disagreeable remarks of husband and entourage could bring a midwife to the brink of despair. It was then that, to overcome the difficulty, she might resort to desperate measures, using a hook on the back of the fire-shovel or a stirring spoon to extract a child which might not be dead, at the risk of seriously injuring the mother on the way . . .. Some inexperienced midwives even confused the different organs! Like this one, who was luckily helped by Paul Portal in Paris in July 1666: 'Hunting for the afterbirth in the womb, which had at that point descended, instead of grasping the afterbirth, she got hold of the internal orifice of the womb, thinking she was pulling on the placenta.'⁹ Fear of the woman dying on her hands often incited the midwife to manipulate the sexual organs to as to widen the passage; the result was often a tumefaction of the vulva and a more difficult and painful delivery thereafter. Thus the wife of a 'merchant stocking-maker' was maltreated by an impatient midwife; Philippe Peu, who was at length sent for, tells the story:

The poor woman was giving voice to continual fearful screams. Her belly, raised nearly as far as her chin, was hard, tense and very painful. Putting my fingers in the vagina, I found the internal orifice half open and tattered on the whole of its external circumference; between it and the bladder I recognized a tear about four finger-spans wide or thereabouts, which seemed to have been made by her fingernails with a view to passing her hands over the head of the child to pull on it by force, which on the contrary must merely have made it go up higher. Indeed, the patient maintained to the midwife, in my presence, that being in a hurry to be done with it, she had made every effort to drag forth her child from her, that she had suffered much from this, and from that moment she could no longer live or endure.

This woman was saved, but 'she has had no further children.'¹⁰

Incompetence, panic, ill-judged intervention, lack of skill, were not confined to midwives. Obstetrics were 'in fashion', and for the surgeon they were a way of raising himself at last to a position of social respectability, of emerging from the lowly estate in which he had been kept for so long by the doctors who despised him. So he would set himself up as an obstetrician for better or worse, after going to some cutler in the town for the instruments which symbolized this new art: forceps and head-puller, separators and perforators. These cold, shining metal instruments terrified women as much as did the infamous hooks, so redolent were they of wounds, blood, incisions and rummagings in the belly, a pierced and broken infant.

There was no need, alas, for the perforator or the 'iron hands' to maltreat a poor woman crying for mercy; the mere hand of an overbold and undertrained practitioner was often enough, as is shown by this story reported by Mauquest de La Motte. It happened in Caen in 1713:

As I entered the court and mounted the stairs, I heard some fearful screams; having been introduced into the chamber, I found (what I had not expected) a surgeon of the town already at work, in his coat and jerkin, his sleeves not rolled up, who was beside the patient, one knee on the ground and the other foot apart, using only one of his hands, with which he was doing her outrageous violence, to draw out a child which had emerged as far as the armpits, and his other hand gripping the edge of the bed, which was nearby, near the truckle bed on which the patient lay. I remained there about a quarter of an hour, until he was done, during which time my hair stood on end, and I shuddered with horror to see the exercise of such cruelty. Three times I offered my help, but he refused to accept it.

Such scandalous behaviour could not but lead to a crisis:

The child breathed a few more sighs, as I was told, for I did not have the resolve to stay any longer to see how he would set about delivering her. I thought, having seen her suffer such violence, that this lady would not live out the night, and even more so when I found out that he had started an hour and a half before I arrived; and nevertheless she lived for three days. Will not the ghost of this lady cry for vengeance on one as unworthy of the name of obstetrician as is this man of whom I speak?[11]

The woman and her innocent child were already in enough danger, without those to whom they looked for help adding to the torment of their bodies and causing irreparable harm. Every day the saying proved itself true: indeed the woman in labour did have one foot in the grave!

Marked for Life

Even when they escaped from such dangerous situations, mother and child often kept on their bodies the stigmata of their ordeal. Mental and physical handicaps afflicted children to an extent which it is hard to gauge. No doubt doctors, administrators and priests in the second half of the eighteenth century tended to exaggerate the unfortunate consequences of the midwives' incompetence. Their reports were not unbiased: they were part of a publicity campaign intended to discredit midwives in favour of obstetricians. But it remains true that the amount of precise evidence, offered in good faith, puts the seriousness of the evil beyond doubt.

In the villages, many a cripple and imbecile owed his infirmity to an incompetent midwife. The very survival of posterity seemed threatened to contemporaries, who demanded intervention from above to stop the damage. In 1775 a doctor, Augier du Fot, sounded a real call of alarm:

How many feeble [children], helpless, crippled? As we come out from mass in the parish church we groan to see those children who must replace those to whom they owe their existence. What hope for the next generation? How many useless creatures? How many children atrophied, hunchbacked, deaf, blind, one-eyed, bloodshot . . . with twisted legs, lame, contorted, hare-lipped – deformed, ill-shaped children, almost useless to society. The health of the greatest number of them is nothing but a convalescence, soon to end in premature death.[12]

A slightly lurid picture of a real problem in the countryside, which finds tragic confirmation in nineteenth-century registers of conscription.

Women who had managed to survive a difficult birth often had much difficulty in resuming a normal life: afflicted in body, they said that they felt as if they had 'returned from another world'; they were sometimes doomed to be in need of assistance all their lives long; even when the household was prosperous enough for them to be able to look after themselves well, eat well and 'recover their health', they were bitterly aware that they were no longer as hearty as they had once been.

Weakness, prolapsed organs, generalized malfunction, incontinence, itchings, bothered them all the time and almost made them regret they had become mothers . . .. These broken women were the living symbol of ill-fated childbirth, of what they had had to endure to ensure the perpetuation of the family line.

Take the bourgeoise who was delivered in July 1668 by three Parisian celebrities, a doctor and two surgeons, one of whom was the obstetrician Paul Portal: did she feel that she had escaped the worst, after a labour lasting eighteen days? And yet the child had presented well, head first; but 'the mother's external parts, thick and hardened, prevented dilatation, and therefore the emergence'. Enemas, bleedings, cordials, were administered with the greatest liberality, but in vain: 'The child would not quit its position.' Thus they came to the sixteenth day, giving the woman no other nourishment than eggs:

On the seventeenth, and the following night, the patient suffered cruel pains and vomited quantities of water. On the eighteenth, at eight o'clock in the morning, we recognized [Portal writes] that our patient was worsening and that her strength was ebbing . . .. We were all three of the opinion that the child was dead . . . and we decided to operate, after the patient had received the sacrament and put her conscience in order, which she did.

Then one of the surgeons 'set to work' with a hook, which he tried to lodge in the child's head so as to withdraw the body; but his efforts were in vain. Portal took over, using only his hand:

With my fingers I separated all the parts of the child's head, as gently as I possibly could, for fear lest they injure the patient, who was suffering horribly all this time. I withdrew them one after the other, and all the substance of the child's brain oozed out. I then repelled the child's trunk or body, which was still in the womb, where it was held by the shoulders, which had not been able to emerge from the internal orifice. I had great difficulty in repelling it, so as to be able to bring the feet together, so as to have a better grip when pulling; and having finally found them, I guided them out and brought out the rest of the corpse in one piece, except for the head, and I then withdrew the afterbirth.

The woman was given a potion supposed to strengthen her and stimulate the flow of the cleansings, then some broth. In the evening she was given an enema, which was renewed in next morning. The private parts being 'black, mortified and almost without feeling', they were rubbed 'quite briskly, twice or three times a day' with a sponge dipped in warm salt water. She was bled unsparingly, both from the arm and from the feet. She was also made to take cardiac stimulants made of scorzonera water and holy thistle, with the addition of alkermes and lemon. Which, according to Portal, worked very well; but the period of recovery was excessively long:

She was three months in bed and every day she said that she still felt as if she was in labour. She has had no other children since that time, although she has always been in good health, excepting that she is subject to pruritus or itching, which troubles her, and is caused by a white discharge which incommodes her greatly; and she can find no relief from it except when she douches herself with spirits of wine, according to the report made to me.[13]

We can have no difficulty in believing that women who had been through such ordeals were marked for life. Hernias and prolapses were common and made every effort painful. Trusses, of cork or elastic rubber, were expensive, hard to obtain in the countryside, and, especially, unpopular.[14] These ill-starred confinements, which wrought such havoc on the bodies of women in childbirth, left their mark no less on people's minds. The very idea of motherhood became unbearable to some exceptionally sensitive girls, who refused marriage to avoid the traumas of childbirth. An attitude of refusal which it would be rash to generalize, but which tells us a good deal about the mental image of childbirth which many people had.

Delivery Without the Mother

The most astounding deliveries, for the entourage, were certainly those from which the woman was 'absent': when her body – living or dead – was the passive theatre of a birth, she having lost consciousness. Such abnormality always troubled people's minds.

The delivery took place 'without the mother' in three cases: when convulsions had thrown her into a prolonged coma; in case of sudden death at the term of pregnancy, or shortly before; finally, when, after her death her 'side was opened up' by a Caesarean operation.

'My burden is gone'

On 8 September 1745, at Douai, a surgeon named Rigaudeaux was called out at five in the morning to deliver a woman in a nearby village. He could not get there until half-past eight, and when he arrived he was told that the woman had died nearly two hours ago, carried off by convulsions which had lasted since the day before. Rigaudeaux asked to see the dead woman; she was already in her shroud, so he had it removed so as to examine her. He could discover no flutter of the heart or the pulse:

He held the mirror to her mouth, and the glass was not dimmed. There was much foam on her mouth, and the belly was prodigiously swollen. Driven by he knows not what presentiment, he thought of putting his hand into the womb, and found its orifice much dilated, and inside he felt that the waters had formed. He tore the membranes and felt the child's head, which was well presented. Having repelled it so as to have the freedom to introduce his whole hand, he put his finger into the mouth of the child, which gave no sign of life. Having noted that the orifice of the womb was sufficiently open, he rotated the child, pulled it out by the feet quite easily, and put it in the hands of the women present. Though it seemed dead to him, he nevertheless exhorted them to take care of it.

After three hours of effort, the women succeeded in bringing the baby round and ran to warn the surgeon, who had gone to dine with the priest. Encouraged by this result, the surgeon asked to see the mother a second time. She had been put back in her shroud, and 'even shut up' in her coffin; 'He had all the funereal apparel removed' and examined her, but decided she was dead, as after the former examination. 'He was, however, surprised that, although she had been dead for nearly seven hours, her arms and legs had remained flexible'; but having been unable to bring her round, he set off back to Douai, 'after having advised the women present not to bury the dead woman until her arms had lost their flexibility'. So they continued to tap on her hands, and rub her limbs and face with essences and vinegar. After two hours, the woman recovered the vital spark. She was still alive in 1748, as was her child, 'and,' a commentator adds, 'one would even say that both are very well, if the woman had not remained paralytic, deaf and almost dumb; nonetheless, we can still say that she got off lightly'.[15]

This very detailed and surprisingly dramatic text is not unique; a quite similar case was reported by Chaptal at Montpellier around 1785. The woman had been struck with apoplexy and, 'showing no sign of sentience', gave birth to twins. Despite the mother's apparent death, the surgeon, like his colleague of Douai, doubted if this was so ('I suspected that she was not dead'). Thanks to a potion of his own contriving and to the application of leeches, he succeeded in bringing the new mother slowly back to consciousness: 'When she came to herself, she found that her burden was gone, and cried out that she was pregnant!'[16]

The outcome was not always so fortunate: it could even happen that death struck the mother just before her confinement and carried off both her and her child; but nature sometimes offered strange surprises.

The delivering of a dead woman

Nobody could be indifferent to the sight of an obviously dead woman giving birth to a child. Life emerging from a dead body was a grave perturbation in the natural order.

In his *Anatomical Histories*, Thomas Bartholin records the story of a woman who died six weeks before term. As the child in her womb was believed to be dead, she was prepared for burial:

They washed the body, wrapped it in a shroud sewn close to the body, as is customary, and, these preparations made, they waited calmly for the day of the burial. Forty-eight hours after death, the woman's lower abdomen and breast swelled, the shroud tore asunder, and it was noticed that the cleansings were flowing in abundance. The woman present, busy with quite other things, approached in astonishment, and, parting the thighs of the corpse, they found a little male child, perfectly formed, which had just emerged and whose afterbirth had remained in the passage. The child was buried with its mother in the cemetery.[17]

Before such astonishing cases the doctors could only bow their heads: decidedly 'nature can sometimes do things which surpass human knowledge'. The idea that a woman could give birth after death was widely accepted at the time, and 'experience alone, if Bartholin is to be believed, could have given rise to this conviction in uneducated minds'. Furthermore, uncertainty about the tokens of death and fear of mistakes made people take precautions: 'Women preparing the burial of those who die when with child shut a needle, scissors and thread into the coffin, as if the ghost might need these instruments to tie and cut the umbilical cord of the child which is to be born'.[18] To doctors and churchmen such behaviour savoured of superstition. It was better to intervene while there was still time, using, if need be, a 'salutary violence'.

The 'non-born' child

A Caesarean could be seen as a 'birth without the mother', because in most known cases the woman was already dead when the operation took place, which makes it clear that this was a final effort to save the child's life, or at least to confer the sacrament of baptism as the Church desired. If the woman was still alive things would not be much different. It was in any case unusual for her to remain conscious throughout the operation. Obstetricians at that time very rarely used anaesthetics and found it enough to have the woman held down by several people. Thus it needed uncommon resistance to pain and force of character to endure such an ordeal: the incision of the abdomen was very painful and often caused a 'weakness', a loss of consciousness on the woman's part during the rest of the operation, which generally did not last more than a few minutes.

Often, the family opposed the opening up of a woman who had died before giving birth. The idea of attacking a dead body with cold steel was repellent and seemed to many like an act of sacrilege: to mutilate a dead person was to kill her a second time. In vain might the practitioner or priest speak of the life of the child: their reply would be that 'if the child wanted to be born, it had had plenty of time for it', or 'it must certainly be dead by now', or again that 'this poor woman has suffered enough already; now she must be left in peace'. While the family might well accept a Caesarean on a living woman, because it meant a last chance of saving her life, they considered it pointless and indecent to torment a lifeless body. For exactly the same reasons they were opposed to dissections and autopsies.[19] Knowing that she must die, the mother herself sometimes refused to have her corpse tormented. But what if the child *did* want to be born?

At the beginning of this century, in one of the principal towns of Sicily, a noblewoman, mother of seven boys and pregnant when she died, called her children to her and begged them earnestly to grant her two things: the first, not to allow them to perform a Caesarean operation on her after her death; the second, to bury her in her best clothes. She died, and the children obeyed her only too well. The archpriest of that place presented himself with a surgeon for the operation; their prayers, their arguments carried no weight with the children, who, sword in hand, violently repulsed the surgeon and the priest. A few days after the mother's funeral, the rumour went around that the clergy of the church where her body was buried had stripped it of all its rich garments. The sons loudly demanded that the tomb should be opened to see what had really happened. A fearful and deplorable sight! They found the mother with all her garments and near her two twins which had come from her womb and died. God's hand fell heavily on that illustrious and wealthy family: all those children died in poverty, and crushed by the most humiliating misfortunes. The facts are undisputed, but I will be pardoned for giving no name either to the family or to the town where this unhappy event took place.[20]

   This orotund and highly moral tale is too contrived to be entirely convincing to us, but it is not impossible that it made some impression on public opinion by playing on the horror of burial alive which swept through the whole of European society from about 1720. Nobody relished the idea of finding themselves alive but six feet under, through an error on the part of their entourage! So who would not shudder to imagine the fate of a little child, symbol of innocence and frailty, born of a mother dead and buried too soon? Since there were proofs that a child could be born after its mother's death, one might as well help its arrival through the 'emergency exit' of the Caesarean operation. Even if such an intervention was opposed to the last wish of the mother, and to those of the family, the life and spiritual destiny of a child were well worth going against the opinion of its parents!

   A child which survived after the operation on its dead mother could not be considered like any other child. Not only because it had escaped a fearful death, but also because of the very nature of its birth: such a birth was unnatural, it defied common sense, overthrew categorizations and visibly upset all those present.

   A child born by Caesarean was considered as 'non-born'; it had not 'come into the world', but been dragged from the place where it had matured. In fact, the Caesarean birth of a man of the church was part of the repertoire of miracles: by stressing this peculiarity the saint's *Vita* would go back to the myth of the birth of a god or hero and give it a Christian colouring. The holy man had not emerged from the head or thigh of some god, but, more prosaically, from a woman's womb. Such was the case in 1058 with the Count of Lingsow, later to become Bishop of Saint-Gall and nicknamed *ingenitus*, that is 'uncreated'. In 1200, at Lérida, a living child was taken from a woman who had died in childbirth two days previously – so the legend said. The hand of God was seen in this unusual birth and the child became a churchman, which seemed only fair in the circumstances. The future San Ramón was then endowed with the nickname *Nonnato* ('non-born') and remained in Spain, up to the twentieth century, the great intercessor for women in childbirth. One who had come so hardly into the world was well placed to help other children to be born.[21]

19

Death, the Greatest Aberration

At the age of four hundred fourscore and forty-four years, Gargantua begat his son Pantagruel upon his wife named Badebec, daughter to the king of the dimly-seen Amaurotes in Utopia. She died in the throes of childbirth. Alas! Pantagruel was so extraordinary large and heavy that he could not possibly come to light without suffocating his mother.

Rabelais, Pantagruel II

The close combat of mother and child was a redoubtable duel: the mother's womb could become the baby's tomb, and the mother gave the child life at the risk of her own. Flesh was born of flesh in wounds, violence, pain, sometimes death. And death was so closely associated with the image of childbirth that its fearful prognostication was never absent: it was part of the order of nature, and it was not within the power of humankind to do anything about it. Only God, in his infinite mercy, might put off the hour . . ..

Death Took Her Suddenly

A long and difficult birth prepared the entourage for the idea that the woman might die. But after an uneventful labour, a sudden death, which could not possibly have been foreseen, would throw them into utter confusion.

In March 1707, a marquise of thirty-eight, asthmatic, bore her first child without complications; there was only a little trouble in removing the afterbirth, because the cord had broken. At last it was done and the woman could rest. La Motte, who attended her, tells the story thus:

She was put to bed, and spent the day and night in great tranquillity. In the morning I took leave to return home; I was surprised to find, very early next morning, an urgent message telling me to return to see that lady, but I was quite convinced that milk fever must be the reason for my return. When I arrived I found her very uneasy, having had no rest all night because of a pain in the exterior surfaces of the iliac bones and the right groin, with some sort of difficulty in urination.

La Motte made a cataplasm of camomile, flax and melilot, which was applied to the afflicted part. The woman urinated and the pain abated; the cleansings became normal once again. As a precautionary measure, the obstetrician asked the help of a doctor, who found nothing wrong in particular and confined himself to giving her a mild enema. The next day

this lady felt some vapours; but as this was normal for her when she was menstruating, there seemed nothing surprising about it to us, and the fever was very low; nevertheless, with these slight symptoms, at about ten o'clock in the evening, at a time when we were in no anxiety whatever, the breathing became quick and difficult, the chest became congested, and the patient died within two hours, without any further suffering; this was the cause of great astonishment to the doctor and myself, though we had no reason to reproach ourselves for having omitted to do anything which might have prevented that catastrophe.

The practitioners formed the hypothesis that her bad chest, along with milk fever, had something to do with her sudden death: 'This in truth was what we judged to be the true and sole cause of her death, not having been able to ascribe it to any other, nor find any remedy to prevent it.'[1]

The culpable hastiness of midwives was another cause of fatal accidents. Their fear that the orifice of the womb would tighten too quickly and retain the placenta urged them to pull on the cord as soon as the child was born; too violent traction at that stage might cause inversion of the viscera or massive haemorrhage. But the pregnant woman herself, in her imprudence, sometimes contributed to a suchlike terrible end, as is shown by the case of the wife of a Parisian 'instrument maker', a woman of sound temperament, already the mother of nine children, who despite some stomach pains felt in the morning when she was at term, 'had nevertheless gone into town on business of hers':

She dined with the family, and after dinner she asked her husband to fetch the midwife. But scarcely had he departed when she felt such a great pain that she was obliged to lie on a convenient bed. In that moment the child presented its feet and slid suddenly into the pelvis as far as the neck, the head remaining in the cervix . . .. The midwife, arriving and finding this state of affairs, withdrew the child without foreseeing what would become of the mother, who lost a very great quantity of blood, which made her so weak that she died.[2]

Such floods of blood over the floor, as much as screams of pain or the unbearable stench of putrefaction, would terrify the bystanders; the woman would fall into syncope, her life flowing away with her blood. The fate of the child was no more to be envied; its body was even worse treated than that of the mother, especially when the horrible hooks came into play. But it was not always necessary to go to such lengths, for unhappily nature sometimes undertook to endanger the life of the child before humankind could take a hand.

The Child Did Not Live

A bad malpresentation could, in some circumstances, cause the sudden end of one who was just entering on life. A prolapse of the cord, or shoulders jammed after the emergence of the head, would threaten it with asphyxia if the midwife was at all slow to intervene. But while her lack of haste sometimes had catastrophic results, haste and rough treatment could also be fatal. She pulled too hard on an arm and it came off; she broke the ribs, they projected and caused the mother fearful agony.[3] Bound together in the giving and receiving of life, mother and child were bound together also in death after their tragic duel. The wisest of obstetricians was not immune from error, or an unhappy chance which he could not cope with. One day in May 1691, La Motte was called to a village near Valognes to help a woman who had been in labour for two days. The cord had just emerged, with one arm, and the child was face up. The obstetrician seized the feet within the womb to perform a rotation; the body pivoted, the arm and cord went in again and the child was brought out, feet first, as far as the thighs:

I baptized it, and then turned its body over to put it face down, and went on pulling as far as the shoulders and neck. After I had disengaged the arms, I shook it gently once or twice, and even pulled quite hard, several times, to finish this delivery, which obliged me, following my usual procedure, to put my finger in its mouth; I found instead the back of the neck, and that the neck not having followed the movement of the body, it had been twisted.

The chin got hooked on to the *os pubis* and La Mote needed both hands to turn the head round:

I gave the little body to the patient's husband to hold, while I repelled the back of the head with one hand and freed the chin with the other, trying to turn the head round as far as I could. At the same time I told the husband to pull gently, but he pulled so hard, in the hope of relieving his wife, that he fell six paces away from the bed, with the body of the child, the head remaining behind. This spectacle took me aback . . . I could scarcely condemn the hastiness of the patient's husband; his intentions were good, and my lack of warning having been the sole cause, I was obliged to keep quiet about his part in it, while heartily promising myself that I would never again accept such help, which I had taken in preference to that of the midwife, of whom the husband had nothing good to say.

Using a scalpel, La Motte then proceeded, without much difficulty, to remove the head.[4]

Fetid oozings from the woman's private parts were no good omen. The mother's groans urged people to wish her a speedy deliverance, but as they did not know the signs of a child that was certainly dead, they awaited a chimerical deliverance. And yet to wait was to risk infection for the mother, contaminated by the child decomposing within her.

One evening in November 1699, a woman at term felt some slight pains; the night passed and in the morning the waters burst; the child's head came into the passage, but did not engage. For four days there was no change; fever appeared, then, on the fifth day, delirium.

The face seemed puffy, the eyes sunken and dying, the lips violet, the breath stank intolerably, the abdomen was tense and raised up to the chin, and the head of the child jammed the passage so tightly that it had let nothing escape, on one side or the other, since the waters had burst . . . which made it impossible to give her enemas, or use a probe, and also made her womb so tight, hard and tense, with colics, more or less severe, going on all the time, and some reddish serum emerging from the private parts, rather like water from washing a wound, of so foul an odour that no-one could remain with me in the room . . ..

Seeing that the child had given no sign of life since the day before and that 'nothing more was to be expected of nature', the obstetrician, fearing for the mother's life, decided to intervene. He was encouraged to do so by a collegue whose advice he sought. Helped by a few women, he had the mother put in position, after which, he continues,

I opened up the child's skull with my scalpel . . .. I partly emptied out the brain, and with my hand, which I introduced into the skull, I hooked the head with my fingers, and pulled it out without the help of any other instrument, together with the rest of the body; I held out the child, which was still moving, behind me, and did so for long enough to allow my collegue to baptize it.

He then undertook to deliver the woman, but the cord was so rotten that it came away in his hand; the placenta was also decaying and he had great difficulty in detaching it:

As soon as the passage was free, everything which had been retained for so long came out in quantity and with a noise like someone upsetting a five or six-pint jug full of water, the anus raised high, as I have never seen it before or since. No-one could endure the horrible stench which came out after the child, which meant that I alone was left to put the patient to bed, and I did the best I could until the air cleared a little, after which she was given all the necessary attention.[5]

A dead baby in the mother's womb did not always begin to decompose. In certain extra-uterine pregnancies, it might not ever be expelled at all; it remained in the mother's abdomen for years, as if petrified. Such was the famous foetus of Sens of which Ambroise Paré speaks in his chapter on 'Monsters', and which was found in 1582 at the autopsy of a woman of sixty-eight who had 'borne it in her belly for the space of twenty-eight years'.[6] Such things seemed quite prodigious at the time, and practitioners were particularly fond of collecting such 'curious' specimens, which ornamented their showcases and the shelves of their anatomical cabinets.

But it could also happen that the foetus was ejected 'piece by piece' by the womb which had engendered it and then retained it for longer than it ought to have. In the *Journal of Medicine* for 1783, a surgeon from Montbrison reported the case of a woman married in 1775, who had had three perfectly normal deliveries in the first five years of her marriage. She then became certain that she was pregnant again; at four and a half months she felt the child move and after nine months she felt the pains of childbirth; the midwife was called. The pains lasted for three days, and on the fourth the woman lost a lot of blood; her abdomen subsided and the pains ceased; the child ceased to move. The woman, like the midwife, believed that she had had a 'false pregnancy'; and six days later, she went back to work. Her abdomen, however, remained harder and more swollen on the left side; a doctor was consulted and said something about obstructions. As she felt no inconvenience, she thought no more about it.

Fifteen months went by; then she had a swelling at the navel, which burst after application of emollient cataplasms and discharged foul-smelling pus:

The suppuration continued for some time in the heat of the summer; worms and gangrene appeared, which caused a very considerable destruction of substance and formed a positive ulcer. In the month of December 1782, several bones appeared at the bottom of this ulcer; the patient's husband withdrew four of them, of which the largest was the femur. Every day he removed more of them, which emerged on their own account, or which the patient withdrew.

The ulcer around the navel was now ten centimetres across; this worried the woman, and she called in the surgeon:

At the bottom of this ulcer I noticed a number of bones which I recognized as those of a child at the full term of nine months; I disturbed several of them, but in fear of causing a haemorrhage, I confined myself to removing three of them, that is one parietal, one temporal, and a femur. I made several visits to this woman, during which I removed, with the forceps used for operations on polyps, all the bones which had sunk very deeply into the spongy tissue.

The mother had digested the child and was rejecting the bones one by one. The surgeon undertook to reassemble all the pieces with the greatest care; after a few months he was able to reconstitute, like a jigsaw puzzle, the skeleton of a fully developed baby. Three pieces were detached and sent to the Academy of Surgery in Paris, together with a descriptive memoir countersigned by the local priest and magistrate. And the report concluded on an optimistic note: 'The woman who is the subject of these observations never ceased to perform all her housework, and is currently enjoying the best of health.'[7]

Death at a Later Stage

Even when the labour had gone well, mother and child were never entirely immune from accidents. In such cases it was all the more difficult to accept the death of one or other of them, for they were thought to be safe once the ordeal of the confinement had gone by.

Infections, imprudence and annoyance

The causes of death at a later stage were numerous and varied; but probably the most frequent was infection due to the insanitary conditions of the confinement. The most elementary rules of hygiene were seldom respected, especially in the countryside; frequent touching with dirty hands encouraged the development of centres of infection. And then, sufficient attention was not always paid to the state of the placenta, which, as we have seen, was often extracted much too hastily; since its completeness was not checked, some fragments of it were sometimes left in the womb, and a crisis would occur suddenly three or four days after the birth; a powerful jet of blood would spurt out, drenching the woman who, if prompt assistance was not forthcoming, died in a few minutes.

Often it was not so much ignorance of the ill as inability to do anything about it which provoked the fatal issue. Rupture of the uterine wall, the 'crevice of the womb', was especially to be feared. In the month Messidor of Year VII of the French Revolution, Planchon, a surgeon, was called to a lady named Revaux, residing in the Rue Saint-Antoine in Paris, who was pregnant with her fourth child. She had been in great pain for several hours, but could not bring the child to birth; its arm, which had emerged as far as the shoulder, was already black and livid; the womb would no longer react. Exploring it, Planchon discovered an opening five centimeters wide, through which 'the peritoneum and the intestines were clearly perceptible to the touch'. The eight-month foetus was dead and was extracted by inversion; then the placenta was detached and extracted in its turn. The mother

felt quite well after the delivery. She felt all the bitterness of a loving mother who had lost the fruit of such sacrifices. To calm the sorrow of that noble soul, all the care of the entourage, all the eloquence of friendship, were required . . .. The night was bad and sleepless, the abdomen became tense, fever mounted, the mouth became dry, with a burning thirst. The cleansings flowed in abundance and without loss.

She had to be catheterized for retention of urine.

Despite all the care lavished on her, the second day was no better. 'The abdomen swelled up like a balloon; the fever, and dryness of the tongue and skin, the extreme thirst continued; on the third day the mouth turned black and there were crusts on the lips. All the signs of corruption appeared.' After blistering of the legs, she was relieved by a massive evacuation, and there was a respite until the seventh day. The fever continued, however, and the cleansings had an intolerable stench. From the ninth day to the seventeenth the abdomen swelled once again and the woman brought up 'several small pieces of the actual body of the womb, of the width of a fingernail, which exhaled a terrible odour . . .. It was then that the legs, thighs and buttocks began to be infected in spite of abundant suppuration from the blisters.'

On the eighteenth day there was a little abatement; a mild purgation was administered and the abdomen subsided slightly. On the twenty-eighth day the fever dropped and she was purged again: 'She took some pure broth for the first time; during the night she enjoyed a few hours of sound sleep.' They began to hope again . . .. But very quickly the fever reappeared. Soon the mouth was crusted all over, so that she could scarcely drink: 'No greasing could remove the encrustation. . . . Every time the patient turned over in bed, more than a chopine of greyish, stinking serous matter emerged from the vulva. Repeated injections, up to six times a day, brought no relief to the patient, and did nothing to reduce the stench of suppuration which came from the vagina.'

This state of affairs prevailed until the forty-second day, when

the fever gained in strength and was accompanied by delirium and twitching of the tendons; the mouth was in a fearful state, nothing had been able to cleanse it; legs, thighs and buttocks became shining and tense right under the skin, in spite of the enormous suppuration of the vagina and blisters; the abdomen, which had remained a little tense, became soft and flat again. It was only then that we were able to discover by touch a long

244   *Divagations of Nature*

tumour, whose base appeared to be adhering to the womb, in the left iliac cavity, whence it stretched almost as far as the short ribs, in the lumbar region.

On the fiftieth day, the poor woman suffered a terrible choking fit which nearly killed her; she brought out from her vagina

a soft body as big as a fist, yellowish white in colour and with an unbearable stench, which seemed to the surgeon to be a clot of decayed blood. From that moment the crises came thick and fast. The tumour grew; on pressing on the abdomen one saw a jet of suppuration, as thick as a little finger, emerge from the vagina, so that by repeting this pressure from time to time, as the patient often did herself, the tumour could be made to disappear entirely.

Skilled practitioners saw the woman, but agreed that her case 'was beyond their art'. Planchon had suggested an operation, but the woman and her family rejected the idea; then the patient made up her mind to have it, but just as the surgeons were going to begin, she refused. She died two days later. Thus ended the fearful agony of a woman whose body had been eaten away, in two months, by corruption.[8]

Women of the lower orders who went back to work too soon could find that their imprudence cost them their lives. They would have their hands and feet in the icy water of a stream and pond as they did their washing; they would be too quick to remove the 'blocker' and the linen which protected the vulva and lower abdomen from chills; they would have themselves churched too soon and were caught by the chill air on the way to the church, or by the cold and damp inside the building. Then the evacuations would abruptly cease, the abdomen engorge, an abscess would form in the groin, the fever reappear, and after a few days' delirium the woman was no more.

Fear of annoyance could also have grave consequences for particularly delicate new mothers. La Motte reports the case of a gentlewoman who had had an uneventful delivery and who, five days later, had a compote of apples made for her by her sister.

The husband chancing to enter the chamber, asked who had made the compote, and why his own sister had not made it; the lady, thinking that he was angry, was upset, and this upset was followed by a slight shivering, then fever, colics and finally the suppression of her cleansings with oppression; the abdomen became hard, tense and painful, and death ensued despite all the remedies which were attempted to save her.

Such cases involved psychological phenomena which could not be reduced to ordinary medical norms, and the practitioner could only give voice to his astonishment: 'The reason was so trifling,' he emphasizes, 'that no-one who had not seen it would have believed it.' The autopsy showed that the womb had returned to normal, 'which was all the more unexpected, to the doctors, in that they hoped to find there the seat of the ill and the cause of death.'[9]

In 1787 a doctor, Moussard, had a twenty-year-old woman in his care in the Aubagne region. Her cleansings had suddenly stopped flowing after the birth. Moussard was of the school which thought that all the usual medicines and remedies were powerless to overcome afflictions of the soul, and that only 'mental help' could cure a 'mental affliction'. He succeeded in finding the cause of the indisposition which was threatening the woman's life, and in proposing the 'remedy' that saved her:

She had been a mother for thirty-six hours; but her soul, locked in grief since the time of her marriage, which her family held accursed, had not been given up to joy at the sight of the little creature to which she had just given life; moreover, her grief and anxiety had grown from that moment . . . . It was then that the poison of sorrow infiltrated all her senses and disturbed the ordering of all her functions; the memory of her error, the indifference of her loved ones, the absence of a concerned mother, perhaps even the threat of poverty: all this absorbed her faculties, and sleeping, as it were, in total apathy, life and death had no attractions or terrors for her. A few questions, which she answered only with deep sighs and broken murmurs of 'father' and 'mother', told me what the problem was; I encouraged her greatly; I promised to think of her, and left her.

The new mother's health deteriorated rapidly. The cleansings ceased, the abdomen was bloated, cold sweats appeared, the woman's eyes were burning, she choked, and soon convulsions began; the extremities turned cold, the pulse was enfeebled . . . . The doctor, helped by the priest, brought the woman's father and told him that he alone could save his daughter by his forgiveness; the latter was told of her father's presence. The doctor reports:

She could scarcely hear me; seeing her father, I gave her the idea that a reconciliation was possible, and got her used to this idea. 'I will die happy,' she told me, 'if my father pardons me and if my son . . . by his caresses . . .' At these words the father flew into her arms: 'Live, my daughter, I forgive you, your love has blotted it all out and has restored mine to you.'

The scene was right in the sentimental and moralizing tradition of the eighteenth century, as illustrated by Greuze; but the reconciliation had such an effect on the new mother's mental state that she was restored to health. 'Give consolation before medicine; this area of medical practice is still little cultivated,' is Moussard's conclusion.[10]

But alas! moral support was of no avail against the viral epidemic, puerperal fever, which for centuries wrought havoc among new mothers.

The Black Death of Mothers

Of all the ills which used to afflict women after their confinement, none had a more terrible reputation than puerperal fever. The suddenness of the attack, the rapid progress of the disease, its often fatal outcome, made it a terrifying illness, one more exaction made on womankind by motherhood. The disease was all the more to be feared in that the medical profession had little idea of its aetiology and for centuries could offer only derisory treatment.

A disconcerting malady

Puerperal fever was disconcerting because it could not possibly be foreseen; it could strike any woman at any time, even after a perfectly normal birth. All might go well until the second or third day; then disturbances appeared which quickly spread alarm among the entourage. In 1783 Archier, a doctor working near Salon-de-Provence, reported in the *Medical Journal* on the case of a peasant woman he had examined:

The wife of a certain Férand, resident in the Maret, gave birth quite normally on 7 September 1783, and was calm until the ninth, when a mild fever developed, which was taken for milk fever, but instead of enlarging and swelling, the breasts shrank, becoming wrinkled and soft; the fever was not high; the pulse was small, concentrated and a little fast. This state did not alarm the patient's relations. On the tenth, the abdomen became painful; these symptoms continued until the eleventh, when they were complicated towards evening by a vomiting of greenish matter; I was then called, and saw the patient at 12 o'clock in the morning. Hearing what had preceded, and having made the necessary examination, I recognized puerperal fever . . ..

Though he had litle hope, the doctor prescribed some treatment; the woman spent quite a quiet night and the abdominal pains ceased; on the morning of the thirteenth 'her eyes were almost dimmed' and her 'face was discoloured'. She lost consciousness during the afternoon and died that same evening.[11]

Unlike the 'miliary' fever of newly delivered women, which generally appeared immediately after the birth and could last up to the fourteenth or fifteenth day, puerperal fever was a short, deferred fever which ended in the death of the woman between the fifth and seventh day. The table is taken from observations by Alexander Gordon, a doctor who had to combat an epidemic of puerperal fever in the Aberdeen region between December 1789 and March 1792: it shows the time between the first signs of the illness and death.[12]

Time since first symptoms (days)	Number of deaths
24 hours	2
36 hours	1
3	3
5	15
7	3
11	3
23	1

The violence of the malady and its tragic outcome left a deep impression on people's minds. Jean-Jacques Brieude, a doctor from the Auvergne, tells how around 1765 'a miliary lacteous epidemic [probably puerperal fever] carried off all the newly delivered women of the end of the Jordanne valley; . . . during the epidemic so many died that young girls recoiled from marriage. Since that time,' he adds, 'people are so frightened that as soon as it appears the family is flung into consternation.'[13]

The maternity hospital in Paris remained subject to sudden recurrences of death from puerperal fever until the middle of the nineteenth century. Foul air, bloated bodies under the bed linen, an unbearable spectacle productive of panic terror . . . . In their novel *Germinie Lacerteux*, the Goncourt brothers give a realistic picture of the epidemic:

In the Maternity Hospital at that moment there was one of those terrible epidemics of puerperal fever which bring death to human fecundity, one of those infections of the very air which can empty the beds of the confined one after the other . . . . It was as if a plague could be seen passing, a plague that turns faces black, sweeps all before it and carries off the strongest, the youngest; a plague coming from the cradles, the black death of mothers . . . . The sickness itself had a shape of horror and an outward monstrosity. In the bed, under the light of the lamps, the sheets could be seen rising horribly, in the middle, from the swellings of peritonitis.[14]

These unforeseeable and ravaging fevers did a lot to establish the sinister reputation of the public hospitals, where the disinherited came only to die. They probably also encouraged couples to limit the risks of childbirth, and therefore procreation, just when methods of limiting births were beginning to become available in country villages. Recourse to contraception meant rejection of the risk.

To seventeenth-century doctors, puerperal fever was something new: apparently the disease appeared in 1652 in Leipzig, where it astonished 'by its novelty', its malignity and the vast numbers which fell victim to it'. It then spread rapidly throughout Germany, and then into France; in 1664 it claimed hundreds of victims in Paris; in 1770, London and Dublin were affected in their turn, and there was not a country in Europe which seems to have escaped the disease in the seventeenth or eighteenth century. A first visitation conferred no immunity. After a few days the disease would reappear abruptly, and strike down once again dozens, if not hundreds of woman; at Frankfurt-am-Main in 1723, at Paris in 1746 and 1774, at Berlin in 1778 and 1780 . . . . Not a year went by in which it did not strike, somewhere or other.[15]

The overcrowded hospitals were a fruitful field for puerperal fever, and mortality in them was generally very high. Of the 17,876 women who gave birth in the Hôtel-Dieu in Paris from 1776 to 1786, 1,142 (or 6.4 per cent) died of the disease; the mortality was 3.8 per cent in 1776, but 9.6 per cent in 1778, when the epidemic flared up again. In reality death struck much more often than the statistics indicate, for some of the infected women were taken elsewhere to die and so did not figure in Tenon's statistics. Most importantly, we do not know the exact number of sufferers, though the relation of morbidity to mortality would have been instructive.[16] Where it can be established, we can see that an infected woman was often as good as dead. Welsh, a doctor who fought the Leipzig epidemic of 1652, managed to save 'scarcely one-tenth of the women lying in on whom it spent its rage'; and Jussieu's memoir on the 'poisoning' at Paris in 1746 reveals that none of the sufferers in the Hôtel-Dieu escaped death. In London, according to Hunter, the 1770 epidemic had the same effect, carrying off 31 women out of 32.[17]

248 Divagations of Nature

Symptoms and causes

Until the mid-nineteenth century, the aetiology of puerperal fever was little known, despite doctors' efforts to put a bit of order into the storm. In 1782 the *Medical Journal* suggested that two types of symptoms could be distinguished, as shown in the table.

Permanent symptoms	Intermittent symptoms
Sudden fever, perceptible but not yet very high	More or less violent shivering
Small, concentrated, slightly fast pulse	Vomiting of green or slightly yellowish matter
Breast shrink instead of increasing in volume	Nausea unaccompanied by vomiting
Abdomen becomes distended and acutely painful	'Milky' and foetid fluids in the wrong place
Loss of strength	Dull eyes, discoloured face
Lochia continue to flow	Tongue damp and covered with white slime, quite thick[18]

From the mid-seventeenth to the mid-nineteenth century, the medical profession wasted much time on conjectures on the nature of the malady, and proved powerless to combat it.[19] Some doctors believed that it was a putrid fever due to vitiated air; others saw it as the consequence of a chill rashly contracted by the mother: a window left open, a premature stroll in a nearby garden would thus be at the root of the trouble. Leake, an English doctor, was of the opinion that the mental anxiety, sorrows and troubles of poor women who gave birth in the hospitals created a fertile field for puerperal fever.[20] But what the doctors denounced most vigorously was mistaken diets, the 'heating' method and the overfeeding,[21] especially the cakes and milk broth which were lavished on new mothers! Thence came those 'spreadings of the milk', those 'lacteous engorgements': the woman in fact fell victim to a positive subversion-by-milk which progressively invaded her body and finally caused her death. The trouble was caused by 'the spilling of milk over into the cavity of the lower abdomen instead of mounting to the breast. This milk goes sour in a few hours. The intestines are swollen and covered with a red inflammation, and the spilled mark is found to turn into cheese, a quantity of two hatfuls at least.'[22] Indeed, at the autopsy all the internal organs seemed to be swimming in 'milky and serous fluids' similar to 'curdled milk' in a 'milky and foetid lymph'. The septicaemic form of the disease visibly induced observers to take the abundant pus for 'milk gone astray'! In the eighteenth century, this theory of lacteous metastasis found favour with most French doctors.

However, midwives and practitioners since the seventeenth century had been aware of the contagiousness of puerperal fever: Philippe Peu reported at that time that in one great Parisian hospital all the women lying in died without anyone knowing the reason; now, he added, it had been observed that in the room where the new mothers were there were many patients who had undergone surgery. 'These patients were removed from the room and the mortality ceased.'[23] Thus they had recognized the contagiousness of the disease and established a link between its spread and hospital overcrowding; unfortunately the lesson was not paid much attention.

From 1750, the English obstetricians John Burton, William Smellie, John Leake, Alexander Hamilton and Charles White also asserted the contagiousness of puerperal fever and cast doubt on the adequacy of the lacteous metastasis theory to explain this scourge. In advance of their continental colleagues they took measures to isolate sufferers and so limit the spread of the disease. Charles White compared puerperal infection to infection of wounds and stressed the importance of certain rules of hygiene. This struck a new note. Though ignorant of microbian infection and the conditions which encouraged it, these practitioners were beginning to determine empirically the aetiology of the disease. However, when in 1795 Gordon, in Scotland, methodically demonstrated the nature of the contagion, he was not listened to. It was because he left no doubt of the responsibility of obstetricians and midwives in this spread of the 'poison'.

'I had evident proofs,' he wrote, 'that every person who had been with a patient in the puerperal fever, became charged with an atmosphere of infection, which was communicated to every pregnant woman, who happened to come within its sphere.' And he proved that such or such a midwife who had delivered an infected woman had then been a carrier of the disease, transmitting it to all the women she delivered in the next few days.[24] Gordon was even honest enough to admit his own responsibility in spreading the epidemic which raged at Aberdeen at the end of the eighteenth century.[25] Puerperal fever spread most easily in the hospitals, but was also helped by the practitioner or midwife working in women's homes, since the most elementary hygiene, washing the hands, was neglected.[26] From the urban centres where it almost always originated, the disease could then reach the suburbs in the wake of the obstetrician or midwife.[27] Though Gordon's treatise on the epidemic was known on the continent, his conclusions were practically never followed. They had no more effect on the medical profession than Semmelweiss's recommendations a few decades later. As if doctors refused to see what was staring them in the face: quite unintentionally, they could themselves be the bringers of death.

Treatment

For centuries the doctors, being ignorant of the real causes of the disease, could only advise totally inadequte methods of combatting it. 'External' remedies like 'baths, bleeding from the arm and foot, blistering and cupping, leeches, cataplasms anodyne, tonic, vulnerary, antiseptic' were all used in their turn, without success. To prevent the 'spilling of milk' into the lower abdomen, some practitioners recommended 'suction on the nipples by young dogs, with a view to making the milk mount up again'.[28] Mauriceau, La Motte, Puzos and Levret advised treating the disease as an inflammation of the lower abdomen.

The great increase in cases of puerperal fever in Paris in the 1770s impelled the medical profession and the government to take serious notice of the scourge. In 1781, Doulcet, a doctor, thought that he had at last found a miracle cure – ipecacuanha – and, convinced that it was a sort of gastric fever, he prescribed 'the American elixir' to a woman in the Hôtel-Dieu who was feeling the first symptoms of the disease. Fifteen grains of ipeca in two doses provoked heavy vomiting, which saved her. The treatment was generalized and the results were extraordinary:

Nearly two hundred women, as is proved by the table of those who were infected with the disease, which could easily be put before the eyes of the government, have been restored to life. In fact, we lost none save those (five or six in number) who absolutely refused to take the remedy and whose obstinacy could not be overcome.[29]

This success aroused general enthusiasm, and Doulcet, encouraged by the government, wrote a brochure which was distributed through all the provinces in 1783 by the administration; puerperal fever had become part of the State's concern for public health.[30] Then the failures began, and Doulcet had to admit that there were two kinds of puerperal fever: a simple one which one could hope to cure with his remedy, and another one which he had to admit he was powerless to overcome .... The epidemic which Doulcet put a stop to was probably one of those 'lacteous miliary' fevers which were endemic in a few places; it had been confused with puerperal fever, which could only be overcome by effective preventative action. Which was exactly what Gordon was to prove at Aberdeen. Between December 1789 and October 1792, the Scottish doctor succeeded in obtaining a significant reduction in mortality rates, thanks to a few elementary precautions which prevented contagion: careful washing of hands, disinfection of clothes and instruments, burning of contaminated bed linen.[31] The results were spectacular! Out of 77 women who were infected, 49 survived, that is two out of three, though it was thought they were all doomed. That was the path to follow . . . but it was not followed. And three-quarters of a century was wasted in consequence.

Thus three generations of women in childbed remained vulnerable to the infection because great obstetricians like Depaul denied the microbian origin of the disease and refused to wash their hands in a solution of disinfectant before operating. It was the work of Pasteur and Lister which supplied the proof that the contagion was indeed of microbian origin, and made the necessity of asepsis finally convincing. From 1879 onwards, the use of carbolized dressings put an end to the scourge, and to the terror of the new mothers. It had taken more than two centuries to vanquish that terrible contagion.

A Flower Nipped in the Bud

Death stalked the newborn child even more closely than the mother. It was quite an achievement to come safely through the first month, so many and so fearsome were the threats. Often the trauma of delivery left the child gasping in shock. What could be done for it in the depths of the country, far from help? Furthermore, until the beginning of the eighteenth century, the town itself could not do much more to save the baby. Its only chance was to be capable of taking the breast; if it could not feed itself it was as good as dead, for there was no satisfactory technique of artificial feeding in those days.

The absence of rules of hygiene put the suckling child under a constant threat. In a universe which believed in magic, dominated by symbolic rules of medicine, everything depended on the child's constitution, and on chance.

More benign afflictions, like yellow gum, caused little alarm, because people knew by experience that within a few days the 'bad colour' would pass off and the child regain its vitality. The scabies and 'milk scabs' which were so common were tolerated, or even encouraged, for it was firmly believed that such imperfections had a protective role.[32]

Stomach troubles, the notorious 'suckling's colic', were more to be feared, because they could be fatal; they were fought with unguents and cataplasms made of pellitory and spinach, fresh butter and pork fats, beaten eggs with walnut oil, applied to the skin. Louise Bourgeois also recommended 'cutting a part of the navel [i.e. part of the umbilical cord], putting it to dry slowly in the oven, they drying it to a powder and putting a little on a finger-length of pap each evening.'[33]

In the country, diarrhoea and convulsive colic raged, particularly in summer. Mothers helped with the work in the fields, but according to doctors, the time of the hay and corn harvests could spoil or dry up their milk. Fully occupied in these exhausting tasks, women were often unable to continue feeding their babies, so they weaned them and put them, sometimes very abruptly, on to pap and bread-and-milk. Such ill-prepared food, quicky spoiled by the great heat, caused looseness of the bowels, enteritis and intestinal diarrhoea, which could put an end to the baby in a few days.

But those babies which were weaned were already quite well grown, for weaning took place later then than now: children remained 'at the breast' up to eighteen, twenty or twenty-four months. Alas! many babies never reached that age – especially those who were unlucky enough to 'come into the world' in midsummer or at the beginning of autumn. Like August kittens, they were thought to be difficult to bring up. And indeed, these unfortunate children had little time to blossom: the mists and damp of an early autumn, the sudden onset of cold at the beginning of winter, would seize on them before they had gained in strength, and a flux would carry them off one fine day . . ..

But what mothers feared most of all was an epidemic. More than smallpox, which seems to have affected children over a year old more than babies, they feared the 'purples' – measles and scarlet fever – and the miliary and putrid fevers which were often endemic in a district. Thrush, apparently more benign, could have consequences no less perilous. It was a buccal mycosis which showed up as white patches on the baby's mucous membranes; the mouth 'got hot', the child could no longer suck, and so was doomed. Louise Bourgeois described it as a 'cancer of the mouth in small children' and empasized how serious it was: 'A thick, white cancer had seized the child by the tongue and palate; [it] invaded all its gums and all its mouth and throat, so that it became feverish and was no longer able to suck.' This baby seemed doomed: none of the remedies recommended by learned doctors had any success, so Louise proposed a remedy of her own, a decoction of sage and honeysuckle, to which she added sour wine and rose honey. 'A little stick wound round with a scrap of wool' was dipped in the brew and touched to the affected places. 'The child was able to swallow that very day, and the next day it took the breast.'[34]

Acceptance of Death?

People were not indifferent to the ravages of death among women in childbirth and newborn babies, as we have seen. A wife's sudden death was a disaster for her husband and her little children. And to make out that a peasant was afflicted less by the death of his wife than by the death of one of his cows, as some eighteenth-century administrators did, was an insult to country people and showed a complete misunderstanding of their feelings. To cite the fact that men who had lost wives in childbirth soon remarried as evidence that their affection for them was shallow was to forget that the difficulties of daily life often obliged a widower to marry again, so as to give a mother to his little children.

It is true that the attitude to life typical of rural areas led to an apparent apathy in the face of death, to what we should nowadays call fatalism. Death, cruel as it was, was part of the cycle of life. The death of a mother or child was hard to live with, but at the same time it was accepted as being part of the natural order of things.[35] For peasants knew by experience that existence was made up of 'good times and bad'; that not every year was good for the fruits of the earth and of mankind, that there were good harvests and poor ones. Should they protest and complain about that? Who might be listening? God? Surely yes, and they never failed to call on his protection. But when ill-fortune struck, what else could they do than clench their fists, look for a new wife, hope for a new child?

Their grief at the loss of a child was hidden and suppressed, but sometimes it broke out in spite of them. A woman who acceptd pain and the risk of her life to carry on the family could hardly bear the death of a newborn baby. It was not only the body, under the violent onslaught of childbirth, that had to suffer then: the mind was saddened by the loss of the innocent child, and the woman found it all the harder to live with her loss in that she both accepted and rejected it at one and the same time.

Louise Bourgeois tells in her book the story of a childhood friend of hers who was also a neighbour in the Faubourg Saint-Germain at the end of the sixteenth century. This woman's first child was born dead, and worse still, she was ill-attended during her lying in, so that 'about five or six days after the birth, her mind gave way and she was so crazy for four years that nothing like it was ever seen, for in spite of her husband and guardians she went about stark naked, in the streets, without her shift, and got into houses, where she frightened all who saw her.'

After four years she recovered a little; pregnant again, she gave birth to a daughter, and 'nothing untoward happened either at her confinement or afterwards'. A few years later, she gave birth to two children, one dead, and the sight of that child was once again unbearable to her. She took advantage of a moment when she was left alone to throw herself into a cesspit:

God preserved her, for her clothes caught on some wood which had been used for scaffolding; her guardians, returning to her chamber and not finding her there, were alarmed, all the more so because in both her derangements she had always tried to throw herself into the privies; they went to see and found the privy seat outside, and in alarm called for help in pulling her out. She was found alive and not hurt in the least, and from that hour she moderated a little; however, she went for eighteen months without recovering at all.[36]

After a painful loss, nothing was sadder than suchlike 'reversals of the spirit'. A mother's death was never really accepted, all the less in that it also posed a grave threat to the child, for everyone knew that without its mother it had very little chance of life. Furthermore, in popular belief the destinies of mother and child were closely connected. If the baby did survive, the mother would not abandon it, but go on caring for it; when all was still, she would come to see it. Thus, in the legend of Mélusine, the serpent-woman returned every evening to see her children.[37] In Alsace it was even said that a woman who had died in childbirth would suckle her child for six weeks, that is during the time between the confinement and the churching ceremony. But this link could only be kept up if the woman was buried in her shoes: the roads of the next world are rough, and the mother could not travel them, to come and feed her child, without her shoes on.

A legend from Alsace tells of a woman who died in childbirth and was buried without the usual custom being observed.

On the very first night, she came back in her white shroud, knocked softly on the window and said, 'Why did you not put my shoes on? I have to walk on thistles and thorns and sharp stones.' Her husband put a pair of shoes ready for her outside the door, and for six weeks, the spirit returned every night to cradle the child.[38]

In most European countries, shoes were part of the symbolism of the next world; this tradition was very ancient, and still very much alive in the early modern period. It came up in the Ensisheim witch-trial of 1593. At Wasselonne in 1653, during a pastoral visitation, the behaviour of a midwife named Sarah was examined. She was said to make use of all kinds of superstitious and magical practices in the exercise of her profession; thus, when a woman died in childbirth, Sarah would put into the coffin a bobbin of sewing thread, scissors and a threaded needle, but also a new pair of slippers.[39]

The Church tried to turn such beliefs to the advantage of the Virgin, and according to legend Mary was a second mother to these little orphans. At Illzach it was said that she welcomed and nursed them at the *Milchbrunnen*, the famous 'spring of milk'.

20

Where Does the Beast End and Man Begin?

Nature has immutable laws from which she never departs. A woman gives children as a plum tree gives plums or an oak tree acorns. It would be as strange to see a woman bring forth an elephant, toad, serpent or pigeon as to see a pigeon, elephant, serpent or toad bring forth a human child.

J. B. Salgues, On Errors and Prejudices ... , *1847*

'Nature forgets herself sometimes': so much so that a monster sometimes emerged from a mother's womb. But between the child and the monster, there was a whole series of cases which passed by imperceptible degrees from the normal to the abnormal. Disease, fleshly excrescences, certain dispositions of the head or limbs, could throw a jarring note into the formation of a body. A supposed contamination of mankind by the animal or vegetable world, between the worlds of the living and the dead, a slip on the part of nature: monstrous births savoured of all this. But they also furnished mankind with a standard of comparison: as a perturbation of the established order they induced him to wonder about his own nature.

Hernias and Whooping Cough

All the evidence goes to show that hernias used to be very common, affecting adults as much as children. Peasants would often give themselves a 'rupture' by carrying loads that were too heavy, or doing work beyond their strength; but these ruptures or prolapses were often a legacy of early childhood and were the result of careless treatment of the baby. Mothers and nurses 'changed' the child very infrequently, so that for hours it had to lie in its own filth; it might cry, but as the crying was supposed to be a sign of vigour, it was left to cry . . .. It might also cry because it was being eaten alive by vermin: lice swarmed on its head, and its body, tied up in the swaddling clothes, was infested with fleas. And so it would cry at the top of its lungs, poor thing! Cry until it got the rupture, the simple or strangulated hernia which, if it survived it, would afflict it all its life long.[1]

255

No doubt some attempt was made to relieve a child whose 'bowels fell' or which had 'wind in the pouches'; and some midwives were very good at reducing hernias. But sometimes there was a great temptation to use radical treatments. Louise Bourgeois says that she had occasion to cure, very simply, hernias which 'they wanted to lance, thinking that they were swellings in the bowel'.[2] And we know that in the eighteenth century, administrators in the Laon district and in Picardy had to take severe measures against quacks who were ranging the countryside in search of baby boys with hernias, and castrating them by the dozen!

Hernias, like warts, could be combatted by magic. Such superfluous bloating of the flesh could only be removed by transference. In the middle of the last century, at Sandarville near Chartres, the ritual had been Christianized, but the old practices had not disappeared. To cure the little sufferer, people would go on a pilgrimage to Saint Jouvin; they would have a gospel and a novena said, 'then they would take an egg which they would bury in the grave of a baby boy; when the egg was addled, the child was cured.'[3] Passing through a tree was a frequent measure. Jean-Baptiste Thiers, priest of Champrond-en-Gâtine in the Perche, reports that in the second half of the seventeenth century it was customary to split a young oak down the middle; the father and mother would then stand on each side of it and pass the child with the hernia through it three times.[4] This custom seems to have been common throughout all of Western Europe, and still survived in Provence at the end of the last century. A folklorist reports:

After selecting a strong-looking tree, they would split it along its whole length, without uprooting it or extending the split down to the roots; then, separating the two parts, the little hernia-sufferer would be passed through it, three or seven times. The two parts of the stem were then brought very closely together and kept in contact with the help of a very tight ligature; if they grew together, and the stem of the tree had become whole again the next year, then the child was cured; if, on the other hand, the split had not healed, they could predict that the child would have the hernia all its life.[5]

No less worrying were babies with whooping cough. Known as the *quinte* in the Caux region and as 'Saint Vrain's evil' in the Perche, whooping cough or diphtheria cast doubt on the humanity of its victims. They were thought to 'yap like small dogs', 'bray like donkeys' or 'croak like crows'. Each fit seemed to put their lives in danger; the whole poor little body was shaken by the terrible coughs; it seemed that they were going to choke, whence the name of 'blue evil' often given to this scourge. So pious mothers turned to the healing saints for help: Saint Vrin who could soothe the 'blue evil', Saint Blaise who relieved sore throats, and Saint Corneille who soothed those who cried like birds.[6]

Hernias and whooping cough are hardly tokens of a monster, but they imply two essential elements of monstrosity. Besides birthmarks (naevi), the body at birth could carry fleshly excrescences (hernias and warts) which were like little fragments of the world beyond, coming from the world of the dead.[7] As for whooping cough, it raised the question of animal contamination. How could parents possibly not be alarmed by it?

Imperfect Beings

Some of 'nature's jokes' might affect the body only superficially, and bring about no more than a certain clumsiness in movement: one can live perfectly well with six fingers on each hand! Having six fingers on each hand, or six toes on each foot, or both, was considered more as a curiosity than a real monstrosity. It only caused raised eyebrows when it was hereditary: the genetic transmission of anomalies was a challenge to people as a whole. In the eighteenth century the example was reported of a Maltese, Gratio Kalleria, who had six fingers on each hand and six toes on each foot, and who had four children, Salvator, George, Andrew and Maria. The eldest had the same characteristic as his father, and of his four children three also had it. Of George's four children, two were affected by what was considered as a 'family trait', and another had the six fingers, but six toes on one foot only. Andrew, Gratio's third son, was free from the deformity, and so were his children; as for Maria's children, only one, out of four, had the six fingers.[8]

Comparable cases were observed in families of Lower Anjou in 1774,[9] and Maupertuis mentions a hereditary deformity which had come out in four successive generations.[10]

These excess fingers were considered as unseemly, especially in good society: if Anne Boleyn was considered a beautiful woman in both France and England, it was because she was good at carefully concealing that 'vice of confirmation' of which Henry VIII himself remained unaware for quite a time. 'What would they have said if they had known that besides six fingers on each hand, and perhaps as many toes on each foot, she also had three nipples?'[11] History does not tell us if this aberration of nature contributed to her fall from her husband's favour and to her unhappy end.

Luckily, not all women endowed with three nipples shared the tragic end of the English queen! Indeed, these women seem to have been particularly sought after, for tradition had it that they had 'an inclination to pleasure'. If one was not lucky enough to marry one, one could always go and ogle their generous endowments at some fairground stall. In his *Philosophical Dictionary*, under 'monster', Voltaire reports 'the surprising history of a woman who not only had four nipples, both large and small, but also bore on her rump a sort of excrescence covered with skin and hair, quite long and tasselled at the end, which looked like a cow's tail'. This 'extraordinary' and 'incredible' creature drew the whole of Paris to the fair at Saint-Germain, where they paid good money to take a look at her.[12]

If the best authorities are to be believed, women with many nipples were very common in Ancient Egypt, Greece and Italy. Did the Artemis of Ephesus, wearing her many breasts as some wear medals, perhaps work so much on the imagination of women who came to pray to her for an easy birth that it 'marked' their unborn babies?

In any case, in the seventeenth and eighteenth centuries, people were convinced that the number of young which certain female mammals could drop depended on the number of their teats; and nature had had the foresight to ensure that if necessary, women would be able to suckle twins. It followed that those who were more generously endowed could logically have multiple births, a prospect which sometimes made marriage seem rather less attractive . . . . In the eighteenth century a story was told of a rich heiress who had four breasts, and who had consulted a doctor in Basle 'to find out whether, if she married, she would be at risk of having four, or at least three, children at a time, a belief which old wives had communicated to her'. The doctor sagely replied that there was nothing to fear; but as two assurances are better than one, the family also consulted the Faculty at Tübingen before allowing the marriage . . . . 'The daughter's wedding was celebrated, and, so they say, she never had more than one child at a time.'[13]

Some of the imperfections which were revealed at birth could have grave consequences if nothing was done. Obstruction of the 'natural openings of the body' – eyes, mouth, urethra, vagina or anus – required attention from a doctor. The commonest, and the gravest, threat to the baby's survival was anal imperforation, which could take various forms. Sometimes the anus was blocked by an external membrane which stretched under pressure from the meconium, and it was sufficient to incise the membrane; sometimes the membrane was further up the intestine, and was more difficult to locate and pierce; and finally, sometimes there was no apparent anus at all: thick, hard skin made it impossible to discover the rectum, and the child was doomed.

Imperforation of the vagina was often not discovered until the time of the first menstruation, at about fourteen or fifteen years of age. Surgeons' observations show girls in their first period suffering in this way for days, until an operation – all in all, a benign one – saved them from this predicament.

Blockage of the mouth was rarer, but it is quite obvious that it had to be operated on immediately if the child were to be saved. 'Sometimes the lips are stuck together or merged,' wrote Deleurye, a surgeon, in 1770; 'they must be separated; if it is a simple membrane it can be slit; if it is a merging, an incision is made along the cleft which is always marked; the opening can be small, it will grow sufficiently with time.'[14]

A hare lip posed no immediate threat to the newborn baby, unless it prevented it from suckling; but it caused a lot of anxiety. This perpendicular cleft in the upper lip did indeed make the child look rather like a hare. Now if we think of the repulsion which people used to have for that animal, we will understand the anxiety of parents with a child afflicted with such a malformation. Surgery could compensate for this failure of nature. If the operation was not urgent, the experts considered that it was better to put it off: the operator then had an easier job of it and the child recovered more quickly. In the countryside, this operation, though technically feasible, was seldom performed: there was little information about it, there was not enough money, and the child would keep its deformity life long.

Like hare lips, bodily imperfections could stir nightmarish thoughts: they were not monstrous, but they did raise questions. But with a uterine mola there was no room for doubt: that 'insensible mass of flesh, usually flabby, of variable and indeterminable shape', could be no other than the fruit of a monstrous conception or of witchcraft. Its 'irregular shape' gave rise to the weirdest interpretations on behalf of the women who had witnessed the event. Some would have 'seen' the woman give birth to a dead animal, rat, mole or tortoise; others saw a living four-footed animal, armed with claws or hooked nails – a harpy. Midwives maintained that certain molas were capable of walking about the chamber when born, that there were flying molas which could hang from the ceiling, and that others tried to hide and even to re-enter the womb which they had just left . . .. Sixteenth and seventeenth-century doctors like Cornelius Gemma, Levinus Lemnius or Thomas Bartholin still gave some credence to these stories, which seemed to be out of some medieval bestiary.[15] It was Levret, a surgeon, who showed in the mid-eighteenth century that these fleshy masses were in fact the product of a pregnancy which had not been able to reach full term: after the death of the foetus, the placenta continued to grow in the womb until it was evacuated, sometimes along with the remains of the foetus which had survived the dissolution consequent on the abortion.[16]

Between the minor corporal imperfections of newborn babies and the shapeless mass of a mola, there was an inexhaustible breeding ground of monsters by excess (a more or less complete union of several foetuses), monsters by default (acephalic or cyclopic), monsters of uneven growth (nanism) or with wrongly situated or structured parts (displaced limbs or organs).[17] It was a vast field of teratological variation, first justified and scientifically classified by Geoffroy Saint-Hilaire. People in general were no doubt little interested in these problems of classification: it was nature's errors, in all their strangeness, which at once fascinated and terrified them.

Showing Off the Monster

There were very few people in the countryside who had never had the chance of seeing a two-headed chicken, or a calf or sheep with five feet. Such 'oddities' were brought out at fairs, and later at agricultural shows. With human monsters it was different: fear and shame rather encouraged parents to hide them.

In towns there was not so much caution: monsters were put on show and attracted the idly curious. The *Parisian Journal* cites the case of two Siamese twins who were born at Aubervilliers in 1429: 'They were christened and were kept above ground three days so that the people of Paris could see this remarkable phenomenon. Indeed, more than ten thousand people, men and woman, went from Paris to see them. By Our Lord's mercy, the mother was delivered safe and sound.'[18]

It was in the eighteenth century that this interest in unnatural birth reached its height. At Beauvais in 1701, Grenoble in 1704, Bagé-en-Bresse in 1773 and again at Rheims in 1789, people crowded into the parents' house to gape at the odd creature. For several days they talked of nothing but the monster; local gazettes duly gave much publicity to the event, and at Rheims an engraver made a print to show the prodigy. And then, there was always some surgeon or doctor alert enough to send a detailed memoir to the *Medical Journal* or the Academy. As for the father, he could do quite well out of showing off his monster. At

Rheims, 'there was at the door of his house a wooden platter, where everyone put something according to his generosity; he collected six hundred odd francs.' The father at Bagé was better inspired: he turned down the local doctor's suggestion of performing an autopsy on the foetus, pickled the body in a jar of brandy and showed it off from town to town for profit. This birth was a windfall for a man who hitherto had had great difficulty in earning a living. But the image of a monster must have gone through some singular changes to drive people to such extremes.[19]

Such monstrous foetuses were particularly sought after by those who kept a cabinet of curiosities. Medical men especially were eager to acquire them, and made them into prize exhibits in their collections of anatomical specimens. They would rub shoulders with their neighbours from the animal kingdom, in accordance with the contemporary zeal for comparison. Thus, the Dutch anatomist Pierre Camper kept a goodly number of monstrous calves, lambs, dogs, cats, pigs and ducks, which could be conveniently studied in relation to abnormalities in the human foetus.[20]

When giving birth to a monster meant profit, it was only to be expected that public credulity would be exploited some day. In the early days of November 1726, the news reached London that a woman in Surrey had just given birth to four rabbits, in the presence of a surgeon called John Howard, an obstetrician of thirty years' experience. A few days later, he announced that he had 'delivered Mary Tofts of three more rabbits, that the last of them had moved in her womb for eighteen hours before dying, and that at the moment when she was delivered of it, another, about to be born, was to be seen'. On 9 November three more half-formed rabbits were born. The surgeon then had Mary taken to nearby Guildford, where he lived, 'for,' he said 'he did not know how many rabbits she might still have in her womb'.

The king took an interest in the poor woman and sent his own surgeon–anatomist; when he arrived, Mary Tofts was just going into labour with the fifteenth rabbit. He relates:

We found her dress'd in her Stays, sitting on the Bedside with several women near her. I immediately examined her . . .. I waited for the coming on of fresh Pains, at which time I deliver'd her of the entire Trunk, stripp'd of its skin, of a Rabbet of about four Months growth, in which the Heart and Lungs were contained with the Diaphragm entire. I instantly cut off a piece of them, and tried them in Water; they seemed but just specifically lighter than it [this was a sign that the animal had breathed] . . .. Her pains were pretty smart, and lasted for some minutes; they went off the Moment she was delivered, and she seem'd chearful and easy; walked by herself from the Bedside to the fire, and sat on a Chair, where I examined her . . . as there was no Blood or Water that issued from the Vagina, after I had delivered her, I again examined that Part, and found it not in the least inflamed or lacerated. Upon examining her Breasts, I found Milk in one of them, but only a little yellowish *serum* in the other.[21]

The surgeon questioned the woman and learned that she had married a journeyman clothworker who had given her three children. She was strong, but of low intelligence and a gloomy cast of character. She told how the previous April,

as she was weeding in a field, she saw a Rabbet spring up near her ... this set her a
longing for rabbits, being then, as she thought, five Weeks gone with Child ... the same
Night she dreamed she was in a Field with ... two Rabbets in her Lap .... About
seventeen weeks after her longing, she was taken with a Flooding ... which made her to
miscarry of a substance that she said was like a large lump of Flesh .... Three weeks
after this, she was again taken with a flooding, and voided another substance like the
former .... Mr Howard ... some days afterwards came to her and deliver'd her of some
parts of the Animal first mentioned.[22]

After a fortnight, she was churched, and all seemed to be over until Mr
Howard once again delivered her of a whole series of rabbits.

The court took an interest in this multiple rabbit production; it was decided
to clear the matter up by sending two more surgeons in succession, one being
Richard Manningham, one of the greatest English obstetricians of the time. He,
scenting an imposture, decided to separate Mary Tofts from her entourage; he
had her brought to London, where, on 2 December, she had further pains.
That evening, a servant came to admit that on her request he had procured a
rabbit for Mary Tofts. She was imprisoned, and eventualy confessed the
deception. It was a woman, whose identity she refused to reveal, who had
advised her to simulate these extraordinary births, assuring her that she would
gain a handsome profit therefrom.

The Woman told her she must put up her Body so many pieces of Rabbets as would
make up the number of Rabbets which a Doe Rabbet usually kindles at one time ....
From that time Mary Tofts did often, by the Assistance of that Woman, convey parts of
Rabbets into her body, till at last she could do it by her self, as she had an Opportunity,
and that she did continue so to do.[23]

Mary Tofts spent a few weeks in prison, then returned to her Surrey village,
where she died in 1763. The most astonishing thing about the whole affair is
the naivety of the local surgeon, who was well and truly led by the nose. True,
belief in fortuitous conception was in vogue at the time, and it was thought that
pregnant women often fell victim to their own imagination. Could they not
actually conceive the misshapen creatures or animals which obsessed them
during their pregnancies? But Mary Toft's imposture proves to the hilt that the
time had passed in which monstrous births were considered as an ill omen for
the future.

Changes in the Image of the Monster

The monster has a long history. From Antiquity to modern times it has gone on
engendering a rich tradition; and today, when monstrous births are concealed,
the monster still lurks in our imagination. It arouses astonishment and anxiety,
because 'teratological tokens have the characteristic of being highly unusual,
that is to say, first and foremost, out of the ordinary in the broadest sense of the
word.'[24] Monsters are among the *mirabilia*, the 'facts of nature' at which men
gape and marvel; they are a manifestation of a hidden meaning which escapes
us; they are both 'wonderful' and 'terrifying'. And the belief in the existence of

races of monstrous men, from Antiquity to the end of the sixteenth century, comes from that dual and apparently contradictory feeling: astonishment and the prodigies of nature, and the fear conjured up by talk of headless men.

They were yellow and shining like gold and were about six feet tall, and they had no heads, but had their eyes, nose and mouth in the middle of their chests. And over their navel their beard grew so long that it covered their knees. And King Alexander seeing this sort of folk who seemed reasonable enough (for they did them no harm, but offered them the fruits of their earth in great abundance), had thirty taken for the marvel that it was to see them, and took them with him as long as they lived.[25]

This passage from Jehan Wauquelin's *Treatise on the Marvels of India Discovered by Alexander*, along with many other fabulous tales, helped maintain the myth of headless men and of the mysterious East. But what was the monster which could arrive so unexpectedly among ordinary people? What did its appearance signify? Why there, and then? Different times produced different answers. In the sixteenth century a vital break occurred, when the inherited teratology of Antiquity collapsed, and on its ruins was gradually built up the modern equivalent.

Token of the gods' anger

In ancient Greece, physical abnormality was felt as a punishment even more terrible than sterility. The birth of a monster child was a warning from the gods. Its 'heavy carnal reality' made the monster into an instrument of divination. In Sparta, children born club-footed, or with syndactylism or excess fingers or toes, were considered abnormal and exposed. They were a token of the anger of the gods and also the reason for it.[26] And so it was as a safeguard against what they foretold that monsters were got rid of.

The birth of a monster offspring involved not only the family, but also the group and the territory it occupied; the *teras* presaged barrenness in women and animals and failed harvests: 'May the earth bear no more fruits, the women no longer bear children like their parents, but monsters; may the young, even amongst the flocks and herds, no longer follow the nature of their kind.' So was couched a curse on the people of a city who had commited sacrilege.[27]

In Republican Rome, monstrous children were rejected with the same determination: they were not killed, but left to die, for killing them might expose one to trouble later from their unquiet souls. As in Greece, the monster aroused fears of a collective crisis, the return of war, invasion, calamity. According to Livy there was a particular fear of children who spoke in their mothers' womb, hermaphrodites, and animals which behaved in especially peculiar ways. Thus when in 50 BC a mule produced offspring, this prodigy immediately put 'the citizens into discord, good people in panic, the laws were overturned, midwives delivered abominations'.[28]

In Greece, it appears that children were exposed in some uninhabited place; in Rome, a place near water was preferred, and the monster might be put on the water in a box.[29] Certainly they were not buried, because putting a dead child under the earth was a symbolic reinsemination of the great mother, allowing it to be reborn in some more fortunate sibling, and it was important not to let that accursed seed germinate once again.[30] To avoid the body touching the earth, it was quickly carried to the river. The water was probably thought of as 'a vehicle capable of carrying away the pollution as far as possible'.[31]

In spite of the Church's reservations and denunciations, divination was not given up in the Middle Ages. Christian authors themselves were not immune to the temptation to interpret signs and so mark out the pathways of the future. Saint Augustine's hostility to divinatory practices did not deter Isidore of Seville from rehabilitating them: monsters were not, of course, a manifestation of the gods, but a sign from God, warnings just like those he sent out via dreams and prophecies.[32]

Monsters in the Divine Schema

Were monsters accidents of nature, or were they part of the divine schema? The question is a very old one.

The first hypothesis was Aristotle's. For that philosopher, monsters were facts of nature which should be studied through the sciences of nature. The Mother of All sometimes falls into error, carries out her undertakings imperfectly, and in a word, gives birth to untrue species, that is monsters. A child which does not look like its father is in itself a sort of monster, because the motion coming from the semen has been unable to dominate totally the matter supplied by the woman. But to Aristotle the monster is no more than evidence of a certain failure of nature; it never has any part to play in divination. That, in fact, is his only point in common with Augustine, who thought that monsters were part of the divine plan.

It was Augustine who, on this point as on many others, determined the position of the Church for centuries to come. Monstrous offspring are not errors, Creation's rejects, but 'marvels', willed by God and contributing to the beauty of the world. It is because they lack a global vision of Creation, and tend to isolate its component parts, that men feel repulsion for monsters. Seen as an integral part of God's work of God and necessary to it, monsters lose their ugliness in men's eyes: monstrousness in detail must not distract from the harmonious beauty of the whole. It appears that to Saint Augustine's mind this argument applied to whole races of monsters, for other writings by him tackle the monster question from a wholly different angle. Monsters – individual monsters this time – appear there as a reminder of our fallen humanity. Nature has been corrupted by original sin; corporeal defects 'have no other end than to manifest the penal nature of our moral condition'.[33]

It was in the Middle Ages, and by playing on people's habitual fear of monstrous offspring – animal or human – that this note in Augustine's thinking found the greatest resonance. A monster was the sign of immoral conduct in its parents. Unhallowed behaviour engendered an unnatural fruit. The couple was punished, through their child, for the transgression of some taboo.

What taboo? 'Any malformation of a child at birth was normally seen as an accusation of sin in its parents, and more in particular, of a sin against chastity, since the child is the physical fruit of its parents' sexual commerce'.[34] Monsters were conceived by those who had intercourse during the woman's 'monthlies', or by those who broke the taboo on sex on Sundays, which were 'a time for kissing'.[35] The late sixth-century author Gregory of Tours reports:

> There was in Berry a woman who, after having conceived, brought into the world a son whose knees were caught up against its stomach, the soles of the feet against the thighs, the hands stuck to the chest and the eyes closed. It was more like a monster than a member of the human race. And because many made it a figure of fun, and its mother was accused because she had borne such a son, she confessed in tears that it had been procreated on a Sunday night . . .. It is enough, the priest declared, to indulge in pleasure on other days; leave out that day, in the honour of our unsullied God. Because spouses who have intercourse on that day would have born to them children that were crippled, epileptic, or leprous.[36]

Parents were injured in that they held most dear, their child, whose deformed or monstrous body accused its parents of failing it. This justification of monsters by their parents' misconduct almost ceased to be invoked in the modern period, when it was rather the mother's depraved imagination that was blamed. But the idea that monstrous offspring were the parents' fault remained.

In the sixteenth century, extreme mental anxiety, the feeling that all had fallen into chaos and perversion, encouraged people to see monsters as a presage of the end of the world. The monstrous body of the newborn child was an image of the monstrous, dislocated, formless body of civil and religious society. It did no more than recall what was unnatural about that time of civil war: families torn apart, relatives killing each other, ravaged countryside. The allegory of the new monster appears repeatedly in writings of the time. 'Monsters never seen by our earliest ancestors . . .' sighs Ronsard.

The ever-growing numbers of books and broadsheets disseminated texts and images which strengthened fears of divine punishment. In 1495 and 1496, for example, in Germany there came, one after the other, announcements of the birth of twins joined at the head at Worms, of a sow with two bodies at Landser, and of a double goose at Gugenheim; engravings by Dürer and Sebastian Brandt enjoyed a wide circulation. The birth of monsters or stillborn children, a rain of stones or the passage of a comet, prophecies of all kinds, all helped to keep up panic fears.

But monsters also became one argument in the controversy between Roman Catholics and Protestants. In 1496, after a terrible flood, a monstrous foetus was found in Rome, beside the Tiber, where it had been left by the receding water: the 'Donkey-Pope'. An engraving spread news of the event throughout central Europe. Melanchthon drew on it for a pamphlet against the Church: 'It must be admitted,' he wrote, 'that God himself brought forth that abominable papacy in such a guise, so that men might reflect on it . . .. Just as it is wholly unsuitable that a human body should have an ass's head, so it is wholly unfitting that the Bishop of Rome should be head of the Church.'[37]

A monstrous animal born in 1552 at Freiburg in Saxony gave Luther occasion to publish his story of the 'Calf-Monk'. Without any doubt it was a sign from God, who wanted to draw attention to the abominableness of the monkish state! The monster's anatomy was a denunciation of monks: its big ears denounced the auricular confession to which the regular clergy were so much attached; its hanging tongue clearly showed that 'their doctrine [was] something other than a tongue, that is, simpering babble and frivolous words'. A calf's head on a body clad in cast-off clothes like a hooded mantle was 'just the right lid for the pot'.[38]

The Roman Catholics took up the challenge: they denounced heresies as moral monstrosities. But it was not until 1609 that they found an answer to Melanchthon's pamphlet, which had struck at the heart of the Church, at Rome. For in that year it was in the heart of the Reformation, in Geneva, that the prodigy appeared. A woman had been in travail for eleven days, and the doctors could see nothing to do other than 'cleave' her to bring the child from her womb. A neighbour came to visit her, along with her chambermaid, who was a catholic. The midwife asked the latter what catholics did in such situations. The chambermaid replied that they commended themselves to God and the Virgin and said a prayer to Saint Margaret.

The unhappy woman who was in travail, having heard these words, spoke thus: 'I would rather die or truly give birth to a calf than allow a prayer to be said to Saint Margaret on my behalf.' A very unworthy reply for which she was quickly requited: for instead of a body with a rational soul which she had in her womb, she had a brute [bestial] body, and on the instant was delivered of it, that is, of a calf, as she had wished, which was taken and shown by the midwife to the lords of the Great Council.

One magistrate declared that it was a result of the mother's imaginings, another stressed that 'this could happen naturally'; but the author of the account, a catholic, claimed that the hand of God must be discerned behind this miraculous punishment, for 'although Our Lord is all goodness and mercy, he does not neglect – when necessity and the importance of his honour and his saints require it – to make the effects of his great power felt'. The monster was flung into the Rhône, 'where marks of blood can still be seen on the water, not moving except when, being disturbed by the waves, they move now here and now there, crying "Vengeance, vengeance!" '[39]

When they sought to discover the causes of such abnormalities, people readily imagined some contamination, some guilty relations with an animal. Bestiality, real or imagined, has produced a copious literature and aroused the liveliest condemnations of the Church. There again the tradition was an ancient one. Aristotle had reported that such abominable couplings were common in the burning zones of Africa, which he set down to the 'incandescence of the blood' aroused by the extreme heat of the climate. And Plutarch, in his *Banquet of the Seven Sages*, declared that in Greece a herdsman had once brought back to his master's house, as a curiosity, a foetus 'which he said had been born of a mare, of which the upper part as far as the neck and hand had the shape of a man, and the rest that of a horse; crying, in fact, no more or less than little children do when they emerge from their mother's womb'. A friend who had seen the strange creature advised the master to stop employing young herdsmen – or to give them wives.[40]

Stories of couplings between women and apes who had carried them off are found in some tales of exotic voyages in modern times: the result was always a kind of hybrid. In the seventeenth century, it was still given out as

a well-established fact, [that] a brigand of a region in Germany lived with a cow, of which
he had a son, who was baptized and instructed in the Christian faith; this latter gave
himself entirely up to piety to make up for his father's crime; however, it was added, he
always had certain inclinations alien to men, such as living in the meadows and eating
grass.[41]

Where do beasts end and men begin? How could God endure such abominations?

Until the Enlightenment, people were never tired of describing the fruit of
such illicit unions. These extravagant tales expressed the anxiety and fear
provoked by creatures which they did not know how to handle. Were they
killed?[42] Were they still thrown into the water, as in Antiquity? The example of
the calf at Geneva would seem to prove it, but further evidence is needed. No
doubt they were often left to starve to death.

Their burial was a problem. The Church preferred to have them buried at a
distance; at Rheims, in January 1789, the parish priest of Saint-Symphorien
had quicklime and aqua fortis thrown on the corpse of some Siamese twins to
burn them up. Blot out every trace, to blot out the fear . . ... But the hesitations
of ecclesiastical authorities were more manifest when it came to the emergency
baptism which people were allowed to perform at home. For the baptism of a
monster immediately raised the essential questions: was it human or animal? In
the case of Siamese twins, was it one creature or two? The formula for this
baptism was adaptable and the sacrament was conferred 'conditionally'. A
manual of obstetrics from Champagne declared in 1778:

When it is a monster that comes into the world, it must be baptized conditionally, saying;
'If thou be man, I baptize thee in the name of the Father, Son and Holy Ghost.' If the
monster has two heads or two chests, they may be baptized separately as I have just said,
or together saying, 'If you be men, I baptize you in the name of the Father, Son and Holy
Ghost'.[43]

The choise between single and double baptism could cause a certain amount
of confusion. On 29 July 1770 a monster child was born at Troo in the
Vendôme region: there were in fact two male children, joined at the chest and
lower abdomen and with their heads facing each other. 'One of them died
coming into the world after having received baptism. The other was carried
living to the church. But the theologians of that country, seeing them as a single
individual, feared to be too prodigal of the sacrament which the first had
received, and refused to confer it on the second. Can we not believe,' added the
doctor who reported these facts, 'that having two heads, two bodies and no
doubt a double set of all viscera, they had, independently of each other, a right
to the grace of baptism?'[44] Where begins the Other?

Variety of Nature, Unity of Being

The image of the monster bequeathed by Antiquity could not emerge unscathed from the upheaval of the Renaissance. The discovery of a new world

revealed animal and vegetable species hitherto unknown, intermediary species to an extent. Such were the ostrich, a bird which runs and cannot fly; the sea-calf, which swims and cannot walk; the flying fish, which can both swim and fly; the coral, a kind of stone plant . . .. And all those species had their place in nature's reservoir, because nature had willed them.

It was in Ambroise Paré's *On Monsters and Prodigies* that monstrous offspring began to be distinguished from prodigies; from then on, divination by monsters was done more cautiously. This new approach to the monster was the result of the new definition of the idea of nature in the sixteenth century, and of man's relationship with this 'great mistress'. In that context, as Jean Céard has pointed out, Paré's work 'can be considered as the most sustained attempt to "natural-ize" monsters'. Each monster witnessed in its own way to the greatness of nature, the 'handmaiden of God'.

The time of the monster as sign or enigma had gone by. Monsters were now to be accounted for purely by the interplay of physical forces. From then on 'theologians and physicians were no longer pursuing the same goals'.[45] The monster became more and more a medical object, and should be spoken of 'properly, as a physician would'. The *teras* was no longer willed by the gods, or by God; it was man himself who was at the origin of maladies and monstrosities. Thus we see, behind this modification in the relationship of man and nature, the rise of a new awareness of the body and its treatment: monsters spring from man's lack of respect for his own body.[46]

This development also made it possible to cast off the teratology of monster races which so fascinated the Middle Ages. Thus Liceti, in his *Treatise on Monsters*, does not even bother about the question of whether they exist or not; he simply sets them aside, just as he sets aside beings which were only slightly malformed, 'those which are degenerate through some small superfluities of nature', like the hunchbacked or the lame. By this restating of the problem of monsters, doctors of the end of the sixteenth century and the dawn of the seventeenth – Liceti, Weinrich, Riolan – were refuting 'the reasoning which, by continuous gradations, fitted the most abnormal of monsters into the beauty of the world' – the work of God.

For the men of the Renaissance the monster had a twofold virtue. Firstly, it helped to open men's eyes on creation, being 'like a contrasting mark of the power of God'; it arouses us to an awareness of difference, and this reading of nature is a wonderful thing for him who engages in it, for it reveals the infinite variety of things, a theme dear to humanist thinking.

But monsters also drew attention to human beings and their delimitations. The problem was articulated by dual monsters. The monster born in Orleans in 1792 had 'a double trunk, a double head, double arms' and was still alive at six weeks; and 'although the intelligence is not well developed at six weeks, each head could easily be seen to have different affections and motions. One sometimes slept while the other was awake; hilarity was written on the right-hand face while indifference and calm dominated the left-hand one. The two heads were analogical, but not alike.'

The author of these observations, Jean-Baptiste Salgues, could not help asking himself what would have become of them if 'they' had survived:

Who knows what would have happened as a consequence of the variance of their affections, the collision of their ideas and desires! Let the metaphysicians, who explain everything, explain to me, if they can, these strange jests of nature, this mysterious complication of the faculties of feeling and intelligence; let their metaphysics explain this bizarre interplay of physical laws. This individual, which had only one sex, one pelvis, two feet, one belly: did it have two souls, or only one? If it had only one, how did it act on a double brain? How did it react to the two sets of organs which were sending it sensations? Was it both sad and gay, stupid and sharp-witted, good and evil? And in that case, what was the result of their operations?[47]

Alas, such monsters did not live long enough for their faculties to be tested. It was as if nature, having proved that such creatures could exist, then hesitated to let such beings, potentially uncommon, exceptional, monstrous, go on living. Monstrous? Salgues goes on:

In truth, I have never understood why the name of monsters should be given to individuals equipped with two heads; as for me, I would willingly submit to such a deformity. I would let one rest while the other was working; my ideas would be the calmer, more judicious, more lucid, for it . . .. The same individual could be both poet and mathematician, man of war and theologian, lawyer and doctor; he would be an encyclopaedia in himself.

Still more astonishing and complicated was the case of the baby 'with two brains'. Even more than Siamese twins, it posed the question of the double, of two beings fused into one. On 20 July 1684, a woman of Normandy gave birth to two male children. One was normal, but lived only six hours; the second

had an exceptionally big head [which] seemed to be made up of two other heads put together; it had four eyes, two hooked noses, two mouths, two tongues and two ears. The interior was also double: it contained two brain-pans, separated by a cartilaginous partition, and two little brains, quite complete. The interior of the chest also contained two lungs and three hearts; the other viscera were single. This little monster lived for an hour, and would perhaps have lived longer if the midwife had not dropped it. What would have happened if it had had a longer career, if it had reached the age of reason? How would it have coped with its two brains, its three hearts and its two lungs? Would it have had two minds? Would it have felt things three times as keenly as other creatures do?

What weird and wonderful discourse had been cut off by that stupid accident! The reporter adds:

I read in Diodorus Siculus that the ancient people of Taprobane had a double tongue cleft to the root, which made their conversation singularly animated and gave them the pleasure of speaking to two people at the same time. Would my little fellow have enjoyed the same faculty? Would he have been able to devote one of his tongues to the Norman patois and the other to French?

'All these mysteries are very difficult to elucidate,' our philosopher concludes; but there was no ban on giving free rein to one's imagination![48]

The androgyne was the ultimate example of the single being that was sexually double. Sexual anatomy has been a point of contention in all societies, and not all androgynes had an easy time of it! In many cases they were destroyed at birth, because they presented the worst kind of monstrosity. However, from Egypt to Babylon, from Greece to Germany, bisexual divinities abounded in the pantheon. 'The fertility goddesses were both virgin and mother, but in a primitive state of which traces survive into historical times, their very sex was far from clearly defined.'[49]

The Cosmos itself was androgynous. 'The sacred coupling of Sky and Earth is a fundamental myth, and its androgynous tenor is fundamental.'[50] Sometimes, alongside the original heirogamy, there was a myth of the original egg, also conceived of as androgynous; this was the case notably in the Orphic tradition, where carnal bisexuality was the dominant image.[51]

And then, one fine day, the circle broke clean in two: on the one side man, on the other, woman, and each doomed to seek the other ever more. 'Regrets for the time of unity, nostalgia for Eden, for a world without seams or differences'.[52] At the same time, mankind, made profoundly uneasy by shapelessness, vagueness, indifferentiation, must have needed pairs of opposites: good and evil, day and night, yesterday and tomorrow. In that case the androgyne appears as an attempt to surmount manicheism, the universal 'binary' schema. 'One-in-two' was at the same time 'scandalous, unthinkable and much to be desired'.

Conclusion

For the men of the past, who had the 'spectacle of nature' constantly before their eyes, putrefaction and germination were the two complementary states of living matter: their alternation created movement and was the vital source of energy for the world. The woman's womb, like the great womb of earth, was a crucible in which the seed sprouted to ensure a perpetual new beginning. The animal, the vegetable and the human all obeyed the great law of the universe. Everything perished, and was born again. Only the pace differed, according to the species.

In a world where nothing was lost for ever, but all things alternated in one vast circular movement, in which death was merely one stage in life, man alone was free from the seasonal determinism of conception, and differed from the rest of creation in his way of maintaining the cycle of life. He was none the less deeply marked by his environment and by the impressions he received from it, the signs that challenged him. But there was another side to this richness of analogical thought: thus, during pregnancy and childbirth, woman constantly had to be on the alert, respect taboos, make use of objects and gestures which had power against evil magic, protecting her fruit and herself.

Awareness of life, in this universe of magic, was indeed awareness of the body first and foremost: a body always in search of an illusory autonomy, a body which seemed to go through times of captivity and of freedom. Ways of speaking constantly recalled a nostalgia for banished freedom. A pregnant woman was 'taken', she awaited her 'delivery' just as the baby did; when the first pains came, all the exits from the birth-chamber were closed, symbolizing an enclosure to protect against baleful influences and encourage the child to be born. The captive queen in Shakespeare's *The Winter's Tale* gives birth in the castle in which she has been flung, a prisoner. Walled in by the stones of the fortress and the cell, walled in by the flesh of the mother's womb,

'This child was prisoner to the womb and is
by law and process of great nature thence
freed and enfranchized'!

Birth was an escape. Man was marked for life by that initial liberation. His

270

reverses of fortune made him a captive once again: prisoner of an adversary, of the elements – shipwreck, flood – of the dark forces stirred up by a sorcerer to make him impotent, of disease (always felt to be a taker away of liberty), of his passions. As for a rickery ('knotted') child, it could be delivered only by a liberator-saint, a saint who could unite or break through knots and cast off chains.

The bond between mother and child which was established at conception could only be broken by other bonds, symbolic ones this time: Saint Margaret's girdle, or the Virgin's. The theme of the 'body's prisons' thus links with that of magical and religious protection. The 'holy stone' gave freedom from celibacy by giving young girls husbands, and from sterility by allowing the woman to have offspring, while the 'eagle-stone' helped in childbirth. The frequency of vows to Virgins of Deliverance, and the popularity of saints whose name or life had something to do with the breaking of bonds, show how important was the image of the captive body in the minds of people in olden times. Perhaps we should see the Church's pragmatic response to this popular quest as one of the impulses behind the Christianization of rural devotional practices in modern times. In any case, the idea was strong enough to keep hope alive, right up to the last scene of all, the deliverance of bodies at the Last Judgement.

A man in traditional rural society had his own way of understanding time. 'His' time was not 'the Church's time' or 'the merchants' time'; even less was it our time. Through observation, and thanks to his intuition, he had an extensive knowledge of natural rhythms. His behaviour was conditioned by the variable length of day and night, by the unfolding of the seasons. He attributed great importance to the moon's role in the germination and growth of plants, and held her to be in large part responsible for the fertility of women, the development of pregnancy and the accomplishment of the delivery.

Chronobiology has since confirmed some of these empirical discoveries; we now know precisely what seasonal rhythms govern the reproduction of the higher vertebrates. Domestication, in fact, tends to try and stagger the periods favourable to fertilization and birth, which in wild animals are narrowly limited by environmental conditions. Luminous 'synchronizers' can modify fertility, birth and even the length of gestation. And 'the artificial insemination of cattle in a way prefigures the "untimely" birth of the test-tube baby'.

Man has progressively freed himself from seasonal variations in temperature, humidity and length of daylight, and has submitted more and more to 'synchronizers' which are cultural and socioeconomic. Biological rhythms began to be modified very early on: religious taboos became more numerous from the Middle Ages onwards and the scarcity of conceptions during the 'closed seasons' of Lent and Advent in the seventeenth century proves that people did hearken to the Church's decrees. But it is in the last hundred years that change has been most rapid and profound, and we may well ask what remains today of the 'synchronizers' which governed the behaviour of our ancestors. Our rhythms connected with the 'natural environment' fade a little more each day, and our 'internal clocks' strive to take on the new data they are receiving, and to harmonize them as best they can.

The reception of women in labour and of newborn babies is an especially clear token of our growing dependence on the social environment. For the spontaneous births which used to happen 'according to the rhythms of the earth', the medical establishment has substituted a birth closely bound by the techniques and timetables of hospital services. While labour naturally begins at about one o'clock in the morning, with the birth coming most often around three o'clock, nowadays the use of oxcytocics and the increasing number of Caesareans means that children are born between nine o'clock and one in the afternoon, or between four o'clock and nine at night. And everyone knows that it is becoming more and more unusual to give birth over the week-end . . . .

The ancient concept of the cycle of life had its own coherence, but implied submission to the order of nature, of the family line and of God. An individual, once grown up, could not escape his role as a maintainer of tradition; he was the link between past and future; then, when he had 'had his time', he departed in his turn for the world of his ancestors. Disease, epidemics, death in childbirth, were part of the risk of living; and what we call fatalism was no more than acceptance of higher laws against which revolt was unthinkable.

It was only slowly that the idea of belonging to a society which lived in permanent physical contact with the earth began to be questioned. The first signs of a new awareness of life probably goes back to the emergence of towns in the thirteenth century. But it was the cities of the Renaissance which played the decisive part in this alteration: a new 'way of being in the world' appeared there in the fifteenth and sixteenth centuries, just as the horizons of the known world were widening and a new cosmology was being worked out. As we have said, the individual counted for more; above all he was much less dependent on the natural environment which had conferred its coherence on the ancient rural cosmology. In towns there was no place for the Ancestors.

Settling in a place where the regular alternation of the seasons was no longer considered vital, the fact that the family was no longer rooted in a humus which nurtured their life, changes in the intellectual horizon and the collective mentality, probably gave rise to new demographic behaviour: a desire to control natural impulses, to give priority to saving existing life, to spare agonized bodies further suffering. Other places, other times, other visions.

Renaissance optimism is instinct in this powerful desire to live and take care of oneself. And we may ask if the leap forward – demographic, economic and intellectual – of the Western world in modern times was not fundamentally the result of this new will to live, this vital flux which made men revolt against accidents, ill-fortune and death.

In the second half of the eighteenth century, administrators, priests and doctors, 'the new Wise Men' round the baby's cradle, encouraged the emergence of what was to be the contemporary vision of mankind. For a monent the interests of the State, the Church and the medical profession coincided with the desires of the individual. No doubt the model did not gain acceptance everywhere at the same rate; to deny this would be to fail to recognize the weight of different structures and histories, and country districts often held out until the dawn of the present century. But from then on, man was faced with a clear choice about his way of life: a possible choice, and one he accepted.

Notes

Chapter 1   Man, the Earth and the Cosmos

1 J. Duval, *Des Hermaphrodits, Accouchemens des Femmes et Traitement qui est Requis pour les Relever en Santé, et bien Élever leurs Enfants* (Rouen, 1612), p. 6.

2 Ibid., p. 9.

3 C. Viardel, *Observations sur la Pratique des Accouchemens Naturels, Contre-nature et Monstrueux* (Paris, 1674), pp. 29–30.

4 Ibid.

5 Virgil, *Georgics*, Book IV, 11. 282–314.

6 Duval, *Hermaphrodits*, pp. 42, 48.

7 Pr. Bélin-Milleron, 'L'expression bio-sociologique de la plante: les mythes végétaux et la méthode en philosophie des sciences', *VIe Congrès International d'Histoire des Sciences* (Amsterdam, 1950), vol. II, p. 663.

8 V. Perrot et Chipiez, *Histoire de l'Art dans l'Antiquité*, (Paris, 1885), vol. III, p. 715, fig. 526; Houssay, 'Nouvelles recherches sur la faune et la flore des vases peints de l'époque mycénienne et sur la philosophie pré-ionienne', *Revue Archéologique* XXX (1897), pp. 94–6, figs 4–7.

9 Bélin-Milleron, 'L'expression', p. 665.

10 J. Le Goff, *La Civilisation de l'Occident Médiéval* (Paris, 1982 edn), p. 304.

11 E. Cassirer, *The Individual and the Cosmos in Renaissance Philosophy*, tr. M. Domandi (Oxford, 1963), pp. 46–52.

12 Ibid., p. 149.

13 J. Cardano, *De Subtilitate, Libri XXI* (Basel, 1554), vol. V, fol. 152; cited in Cassirer, *The Individual and the Cosmos*, p. 149, n. 24.

14 P. della Mirandola, *Apologia*, fols. 170ff., cited by Cassirer, *The Individual and the Cosmos*, p. 150.

15 A. Chéreau, article on 'Signatures mystiques' in Dechambre, ed., *Dictionnaire Encyclopédique des Sciences Médicales*, pp. 616–17.

16 M. Bakhtin, *Rabelais and His World*, tr. H. Iswolsky (Cambridge, MA & London, 1968), chap. 5–6, pp. 303–436; A. J. Gourevitch, *Les Catégories de la Culture Médiévale* (from the Russian; Paris, 1983), pp. 47–95.

273

17   H. Braibant, *Médecins, Malades et Maladies de la Renaissance* (Brussels, 1966), pp. 153–5.

18   R. Allers, 'Microcosmus from Anaximandros to Paracelsus', *Traditio* (New York, 1944), vol. II, p. 386.

19   Virey, article on 'Nature' in Panckoucke, ed., *Dictionnaire des Sciences Médicales*, (Paris, 1819), vol. XXXV, p. 259.

20   F. Loux, *Le Corps dans la Société Traditionnelle* (Paris, 1979), pp. 47–8.

21   Duval, *Hermaphrodits*, pp. 36–7.

22   M. -C. Pouchelle, *The Body and Surgery in the Middle Ages*, tr. R. Morris (Oxford, Polity, 1990), p. 79.

23   Bakhtin, *Rabelais*, pp. 368–436.

24   'Contrary to modern canons, the grotesque body is not separated from the rest of the world . . .. The stress is laid on those parts of the body that are open to the outside world, that is, the parts through which the world enters the body or emerges from it, or through which the body itself goes out to meet the world . . . on the apertures or the convexities, or on various ramifications and offshoots.' Ibid., p. 26.

25   Ibid.

26   Ibid.; see also Gourevitch, *Les Catégories*, p. 40.

Chapter 2   Daughter, Wife and Mother

1   Duval, *Hermaphrodits*, p. 150.

2   F. -E. Morin, *La Rouge Différence ou les Rythmes de la Femme* (Paris, 1982).

3   Y. Verdier, *Façons de Dire, Façons de Faire* (Paris, 1979), pp. 60–1.

4   Ibid., p. 40.

5   Dr H. Leclerc, 'La médecine des signatures magiques', *Janus* (1918), pp. 21–2.

6   P. Saintyves, *Corpus du Folklore Préhistorique* (Paris, 1934), vol. I, p. 75.

7   'Vieux remèdes du pays nantais', *La France Médicale* (1900), p. 413.

8   J. Dezeimeris, *Les Aphorismes Classés Systématiquement et Précédés d'une Introduction Historique* (Paris, 1836), nos. 453, 457.

9   Henri de Mondeville, *Chirurgie*, cited in Pouchelle, *Body and Surgery*, p. 156.

10   A. S. Morin, *Le Prêtre et le Sorcier* (Paris, 1872), p. 123.

11   Ibid., p. 126.

12   G. Jeanton, *Le Mâconnais Traditionaliste et Populaire* (Mâcon, 1920), vol. I, p. 32.

13   Verdier, *Façons*, p. 70.

14   E. Shorter, 'L'Âge des premières règles en France, 1750–1950', *Annales ESC* (1981/3), pp. 495–11, and *A History of Women's Bodies* (New York, 1982), pp. 17–19.

15   E. Le Roy-Ladurie, 'L'Aménorrhée de famine (XVIIᵉ–XXᵉ siècle)', *Annales ESC* (1969/6), and in *Le Territoire de l'Historien* (Paris, 1973), vol. I, pp. 331–48.

16   L. Heister, *Anatomie* (Paris, 1753), vol. I, p. 457.

17   L. Joubert, *Erreurs Populaires et Propos Vulgaires Touchant la Médecine et le Régime de Santé* (Bordeaux, 1579).

18   Article on 'Erreurs populaires' in Panckoucke, ed., *Dictionnaire des Sciences Médicales* (Paris, 1815), vol. XIII, p. 207.

19   P. -O. Duhaze, 'Étude des prescriptions religieuses et des coutumes concernant la femme pendant la menstruation et les suites de couches', *Thèse de Médecine*, Paris (1922), no. 259, p. 23.

20   E. Deschamps, *Oeuvres*, vol. II, p. 259, cited in P. Sébillot, *Le Folklore de la France* (reprint, Paris, 1968), vol. III, p. 462.

21   Ibid., p. 320.

22   See Verdier, *Façons*, p. 21.

23   Ibid.

24   Duval, *Hermaphrodits*, pp. 152–3.

25   Verdier, *Façons*, pp. 61–73.

26   Joubert, *Erreurs*, p. 108.

27   Ibid., p. 175.

28   J. Durand, *Le Folklore de l'Aube*, vol. I, *Les Âges de la Vie* (Paris, 1961), p. 3.

29   'Im e Rode isch uit ze tröje' cited by J. -G. Barth, 'LÂme alsacienne face au problème de la mort: rites et croyances', Thesis, Faculty of Protestant Theology, University of Strasbourg (1966), p. 100.

30   Ibid., pp. 100–1.

31   Verdier, *Façons*, p. 46–7.

32   In the Charente region, for example: see M. Leproux, *La Vie Populaire; du Berceau à la Tombe; Contribution au Folklore Charentais* (Paris, 1959), vol. II, p. 3. A childless woman was also called 'mule' in Limousin: A. Goursaud, *La Société Rurale Traditionnelle en Limousin* (Paris, 1977), vol. II, p. 290.

33   'A mule's eye makes women barren': Agrippa of Nettesheim (sixteenth century).

34   Cited in H. Polge, 'Un facteur démographique irrationnel: le discrédit attaché à la notion de stérilité', *DH* (1969/11), p. 7.

35   Cited in C. Laborde, *Essai sur les Vieilles Coutumes du Pays Marchois* (Guéret, 1944), p. 3.

36   Polge, 'Un facteur démographique irrationnel', p. 8.

37   P. Chevallier, *Louis XIII* (Paris, 1979), pp. 548–9.

38   D. Jacomme, 'Les saints guérisseurs en gynécologie et obstétrique', *Thèse de Médecine*, Nancy, no. 208, p. 48; J. Sainsaulieu, 'Études sur la vie érémitique en France de la Contre-Réforme à la Restauration', unpublished thesis, University of Paris IV (1973).

39   It was probably not by chance that both brother Fiacre and the superior of the Carmel referred to Saint Margaret: she was habitually petitioned by barren women.

40   'L'art du XVIIᵉ siècle dans les Carmels de France', exhibition catalogue, Musée du Petit Palais, November 1982–February 1983, pp. 130–1.

41   Ibid., p. 104.

42   S. Peigne, 'Les miracles de sainte Anne d'Auray au XVIIᵉ siècle (1634–1647)', MA thesis, University of Paris I (1971–2), p. 100.

43   E. Babel, *Terre de Lorraine* (1917), cited in Jacomme, 'Les saints', p. 39.

44   J. Roland-Gosselin, *Le Carmel de Beaune (1619–1660)* (Rabat, 1969), p. 426.

45   The case of Louis XIII and Anne of Austria is the most striking example, but we should not forget other cases of royal sterility: the French royal dynasty of the seventeenth and eighteenth centuries lived in constant fear that the succession would be interrupted.

46 M. Segalen, *Amours et Mariages dans l'Ancienne France* (Paris, 1981), pp. 173–4.
47 Evidence from a schoolmaster in 1929, reported by Saintyves, *Corpus*, vol. I, pp. 223–4.
48 P. de Thorey, *Usages, Fêtes et Coutumes Existant ou Ayant Existé en Dauphiné* (Grenoble, 1882), pp. 53–4.
49 Saintyves, *Corpus*, vol. III, p. 494.
50 Ibid., p. 74.
51 L. Coutil, *La Chapelle Saint-Éloi de Nassandres* (Évreux, 1918), p. 48.
52 Dr Pommerol, 'Le pèlerinage d'Orcival', *L'Homme* III (1886), p. 630.
53 In Sébillot, *Folklore*, vol. IV, p. 63.
54 *Revue des Traditions Populaires* (hereafter *RTP*), VIII, p. 448.
55 Nose: Saint Guénolé; heel: Saint Christopher, in the church of Avenières at Laval; knees: Saint Nicholas at Nevez (Finistère); neck: Saint Barbara at Guimiliau; etc. Sébillot, *Folklore*, vol. IV, p. 168.
56 *RTP*, X, p. 309. The image of Notre Dame des Ronces, at Nontron in Limousin, was the focus of such a ritual. M. Coissac, *Mon Limousin* (Paris, 1913), p. 172.
57 H. Babou, *Les Païens Innocents* (Paris, 1878), p. 230.
58 Sébillot, *Folklore*, vol. IV, p. 168.
59 Ibid., vol, II, p. 230.
60 J. Lecoeur, *Esquisse du Bocage Normand* (Condé-sur-Noireau, 1887), vol. II, p. 293.
61 Dr E. Bogros, *A Travers le Morvan* (Château-Chinon, 1883), p. 160.
62 C. Thuriet, *Traditions Populaires de la Haute-Saône et du Jura* (Paris, 1892), p. 174. On prenuptial frequentations and their accompanying rites see J. -L. Flandrin, *Les Amours Paysannes (XVIᵉ–XIVᵉ siècle)* (Paris, 1975), pp. 172ff.
63 P. Megnien, *Notre-Dame chez nous* (Joigny, 1958), p. 105.
64 The *aiguillette* was 'a castrating ligature intended to damage the genital region': E. Le Roy-Ladurie, 'L'aiguillette', *Europe* (1974), pp. 134–46; translated as 'The aiguillette: castration by magic' in *The Mind and Method of the Historian* tr. S. and B. Reynolds (Harvester Press, 1981), pp. 84–96. Jean Delumeau notes that 'Between 1500 and 1790, no French ritual omits a condemnation of the *aiguillette* and the prayers intended to conjure it.' *La Peur en Occident (XIVᵉ–XVIIIᵉ siècles)* (Paris, 1978), pp. 54–9. In nineteenth-century Saintonge, 'pegging', also intended to make the husband impotent, was still practised: as the Sanctus was being said during the nuptial mass, the sorcerer would drive a long wooden peg into the church wall while muttering an anathema. J. M. Nogues, *Moeurs d'autrefois en Saintonge* (Saintes, 1891), p. 127.
65 *RTP* XVI, p. 132.
66 D'Eméry, *Nouveau Recueil de Curiositez* (1684), vol. I, p. 73.
67 Abbé Thiers, *Traité des Superstitions*, vol. I, p. 152.
68 F. Daleau, *Notes pour Servir à l'Étude des Traditions, Croyances et Superstitions de la Gironde* (Bordeaux, 1888), p. 45.
69 Bérenger-Féraud, *Superstitions et Survivances* (Paris, 1896), vol. V, p. 45.
70 A. de Gubernatis, *La Mythologie des Plantes, ou les Légendes du Règne Végétal* (Paris, 1882), vol. II, p. 166.
71 A. Duvivier, *Notice sur les Noces de Campagne dans le Morvan* (Nevers, 1840).

72 J. Drouillet, *Folklore du Nivernais et du Morvan,* 2nd edn (Luzy, 1979), vol. I, p. 123.
73 Noted by Dr Pommerol, 'Le pèlerinage d'Orcival'.
74 Segalen, *Amours et Mariages,* p. 147.
75 E. Fleury, *Antiquités et Monuments du Département de l'Aisne* (Paris, 1877), vol. I, p. 105.
76 P. Duffard, *L'Armagnac Noir ou Bas-Armagnac* (Angers and Auch, 1901), p. 90.
77 Bérenger-Féraud, *Superstitions et Survivances,* vol. II, p. 189.
78 L. Martinet, *Le Berry Préhistorique* (Paris, 1878), p. 87.
79 B. Souchet, *Croyances, Présages et Superstitions Diverses* (Niort, 1880), p. 15.
80 A. Van Gennep, *Le Folklore de l'Auvergne et du Velay* (Paris, 1942), p. 225.
81 *RTP* XIX, pp. 288–9.
82 Sébillot, *Folklore,* vol, III, pp. 245–6.
83 Ibid., pp. 515–16.

Chapter 3 What if No Child Appears?

1 Sulphur baths or sea-bathing. A. Limón Delgado, *Costumbres Populares Andaluzas de Nascimiento, Matrimonio y Muerte* (Seville, 1981), p. 24.
2 *Revue Médicale de l'Est* (1893), p. 636; Sébillot, *Folklore,* vol. II, p. 232.
3 F. Sarg, *En Alsace, du Berceau à la Tombe* (Strasbourg, 1977), p. 4.
4 J. Primerose, *Des Erreurs Vulgaires de la Mécedine, avec des Additions de M. de Rostagny* (Lyon, 1689), Book IV, pp. 679–80.
5 Cited by de Gubernatis, *Mythologie,* p. 6.
6 'In the mountains of Pistola, mandragora leaves are thought to be shaped like a human hand, and its roots like a human face,' Ibid., p. 217.
7 Cited by A. du Chesnel, *Dictionnaire des Superstitions Populaires,* 3rd Migne encyclopaedia (1856), col. 610.
8 Brothers Grimm, *Traditions Allemandes* cited by du Chesnel, *Dictionnaire,* col. 610.
9 de Gubernatis, *Mythologie,* p. 214.
10 R. -C. Schule, 'De l'ermite à la cigogne . L'origine des enfants en Valais et en vallée d'Aoste; la religion populaire', *Le Monde Alpin et Rhodanien,* special number (1977/1–4), p. 365.
11 A. Diederich, *Mutter Erde: ein Versuch über Volksreligion,* 2nd edn (Leipzig and Berlin, 1913), pp. 19ff., 126ff.
12 A. Pfleger, 'Roches sacrées: survivance du culte des pierres en Alsace', *Revue d'Alsace* (1954), p. 94.
13 In 1908, a folklorist in Champagne reported on the lumps of granite scattered over the northern flank of the hill of Rheims: 'My grandmother told me that they had come just like that, of their own accord, like mushrooms and truffles.' A. Guillemot, *Essais de Folklore Marnais* (Châlons-sur-Marnes, 1908), vol. I, pp. 40–5.
14 G. Dumézil, *Jupiter Mars Quirinus: Essai sur la Conception Indo-Européenne de la Société et sur les Origines de Rome* (Paris, 1941), pp. 228–9.
15 Saintyves, *Corpus,* pp. 102–3.

Chapter 4   The Cycle of Life

1   In the nineteenth century, parents did not always understand why Christian burial should be denied to their stillborn child; in such a case they would instinctively make their way back to the 'old stone', and bury the little body nearby.

2   *Heel-Konstige Aanmerkkingen Betreffende de Gebreekken der Vrouwen*, 2nd edn (Amsterdam, 1672).

3   Cf. Barth, 'L'Âme alsacienne', pp. 76–7. A. Chanaud, *Ethnologie Française* (1971), vol. I, pp. 59–78; Y. Knibiehler, 'Les Âges de la vie' in *Iconographie et Histoire des Mentalités* (Marseilles, 1979), pp. 168–9.

4   Barth, 'L'Âme alsacienne', p. 76.

5   Pope Gelasius introduced this festival into the Christian calendar at the end of the fifth century.

6   An enquiry conducted in Spain in 1901 by the Ateneo Madrileño proved that candles of the Purification were frequently used in childbirth.

7   Barth, 'L'Âme alsacienne', pp. 57–9.

8   Ibid., p. 17; A. Lambs, *Über den Aberglauben im Elsass* (Strasbourg, 1880), p. 22.

9   See 'Le sermon sur la chasse sauvage' by J. Geiler von Kaysersberg in *Die Emeis. Dies ist das Buch von der Omeissen* (Strasbourg, 1516).

10   M. Eliade, *Myths, Dreams and Mysteries* tr. P. Mairet (London, 1960), p. 166.

11   Even the king of France was granted only a secondary role when the royal line was described. Speaking of the dauphin, it was said: 'The King is the child of the Queen'. Eliade, *Myths*, p. 166.

12   See the comparative study by Crawley, *Mystic Rose*, vol. II, no. 27, pp. 177–8, and the excellent summary study by G. Cohen, 'La couvade', *Psyché* (1949), pp. 27–8.

13   G. J. Witkowski, *Histoire de l'Accouchement chez tous les Peuples* (Paris, n.d.), pp. 532–3.

14   F. Michel, *Le Pays Basque* (Paris, 1857), p. 201.

15   B. Bonnet, 'Étude obstétricale sur le rituel de l'accouchement à propos de quelques sociétés primitives', *Thèse de Médecine*, Paris (1972), p. 57.

16   According to Michel de Zmigrodski, this custom existed in the Tyrol and in Bavaria in 1890: 'La mère et l'enfant: folklore européen comparé', *RTP* V (1980), p. 548. See also Bastian, *Matriarchat und Patriarchat: Verhandlungen der Gesellschaft für Ethnologie und Urgeschichte zu Berlin* (1886), p. 337.

17   *The Savage Mind* tr. anon. (London, 1966), p. 195.

18   B. This, *Le Père, Acte de Naissance* (Paris), pp. 115–17 and 175–205. Cohen writes cautiously about 'an important fact of ethnology from the juridical viewpoint, perhaps not without an unconscious physiological substratum', 'La couvade', pp. 90–1.

19   Primerose, *Erreurs Vulgaires*.

20   G. Bouthoul, *Traité de Sociologie* (Paris, 1946), p. 294.

21   Dr G. Léorat, 'De l'influence de la lune', *Chronique Médicale* (1939), pp. 57–60.

22   Dr Azemar, 'Les phases de la lune et l'agriculture', *Chronique Médicale* (1930), p. 209.

23   J. B. Salgues, *Des Erreurs et des Préjugés Répandus dans la Société* (Paris, 1811), p. 130.

24   Gerlach, *Une Montagne sacrée dans les Vosges, le Donon*, p. 53.

25 S. Reinach, 'Les monuments de pierre brute dans le langage et les croyances populaires', *Cultes, Mythes et Religions* vol, III, pp. 366ff.; L. Rutimeyer, *Urethnographie der Schweiz* (Basel, 1924), p. 374.

26 Barth, 'L'Âme alsacienne', p. 90.

27 J. Séguin, *Comment Naît, Vit et Meurt un Bas-Normand*, 3rd edn (Paris, 1978), p. 21.

28 'Coutumes et superstitions du Loir-et-Cher', *RTP* (1900), p. 370.

29 du Chesnel, *Dictionnaire*, no. 20 (1856), col. 732.

30 N. L. A. Richard, *Traditions Populaires: Croyances Superstitieuses; Usages et Coutumes de l'Ancienne Lorraine*, 2nd edn (Remiremont, 1848), p. 111.

31 Sarg, *En Alsace*, p. 40.

32 Saintyves, *Corpus*, vol. II, p. 327, notes the existence of 'navel stones' and 'stones in the middle of the world'. See also Eliade, *Patterns of Comparative Religion* tr. R. Smeed (London, 1971).

33 R. Christinger, *Mythologie de la Suisse Ancienne* (1947).

Chapter 5   The Body in Pregnancy

1 Viardel, *Observations*, pp. 10–11.

2 L. Bourgeois, *Observations Diverses* (Paris, 1626), p. 51.

3 This was confirmed by a doctor in 1821: 'The public thinks, since it ordinarily happens that if a woman is pregnant the periodic flow ought to be interrupted, that if on the contrary it does not cease, there is no pregnancy.' B. Teulère, 'Quelques erreurs relatives à la grossesse et à l'accouchement', *Thèse de Médecine*, Paris (1821), no. 207, p. 7.

4 Bourgeois, *Observations*, p. 53.

5 J. Guillemeau, *De l'Heureux Accouchement des Femmes* (Paris, 1609), p. 7.

6 Ibid., pp. 6–7.

7 This 'recipe' is to be found in the Hippocratic texts.

8 A. Van Gennep, *Du Berceau à la Tombe* (Paris, 1916), p. 44; R. Devos and C. Joisten, 'Moeurs et coutumes de la Savoie du Nord au XIXe siècle: l'enquête Rendu', *Mémoires et Documents de l'Académie Salésienne* (Annécy, Grenoble, 1978), vol. 87–8, pp. 107–8.

9 C. Coudin, 'Naître autrefois ... en Aunis et Saintonge', *Thèse de Médecine*, University of Bordeaux II (1980), no. 339, pp. 40–1.

10 Goursaud, *Société Rurale*, p. 292.

11 G. Rocal, *Le Vieux Périgord: Folklore* (Paris, 1927), p. 35.

12 H. Meige, 'Les urologues dans l'art', *Aesculape* (1928), pp. 54–67.

13 J. Lévy-Valensi, *La Médecine et les Médecins Français au XVIIe Siècle* (Paris, 1933), p. 506.

14 Duval, *Hermaphrodits*, p. 135.

15 Bourgeois, *Observations*, pp. 9–10.

16 Viardel, *Observations*, p. 15.

17 Cited in *Les Cahiers du Nouveau-né* (Paris, 1980), no. 4, p. 160.

18 Dr Phelippeaux, *Archives de Tocologie* (May 1879), pp. 310–20.

19 *Limoges Illustré* (15 March 1900); Le Goust, 'De la perception des bruits du coeur et de l'enfant contenu dans l'utérus', MS in the library of La Rochelle, no. 8435;

see also H. Stofft, 'Kergaradec à l'écoute du foetus', *Jour. Gyn. Biol. Repr.* 10 (1981), pp. 611–22.

20 Bourgeois, *Observations*, II, pp. 65–7.

21 Duval, *Hermaphrodits*, pp. 146–7.

22 D. Delance, *Au Maroc* (Paris, 1949); most importantly, see G. H. Bousquet and H. Jahier, 'L'enfant endormi: notes juridiques, ethnologiques et obstétricales', *Revue Algérienne* (1941), pp. 17–36.

23 Duval, *Hermaphrodits*, p. 147.

24 Erasmus, *De Matrimonio Christiano.*

25 The greatest wonder of the womb was the Son of God. The theme of *virginis partitura*, 'the Virgin who shall bring forth a son' is very ancient: it persisted up to modern times in many places, such as Chartres, Gildwiller in Alsace, Fontaine in Burgundy . . .. Abbé Grobel, *Notre-Dame de Savoie* (Annécy, 1860), pp. 273–4; Th. de Bussière, *Culte et Pèlerinages de la Très Sainte Vierge en Alsace* (Paris, 1862), pp. 364–6.

26 On the theme of the pregnant Virgin, see pp. 71–3.

27 *Les Légendes Hagiographiques* (Brussels, 1905), p. 110.

28 P. Saintyves, *Les Vierges-mères et les Naissances Miraculeuses* (Paris, 1908), pp. 163–76.

29 P. Saintyves, 'Le thème de l'Annonciation', *En Marge de la Légende Dorée* (Paris, 1930), p. 57.

30 Ibid., p. 160.

31 Ibid., pp. 60–1.

32 A. Maury, *Croyances et Légendes du Moyen Age* (Paris, 1896), pp. 94–5.

33 L. du Broc de Segange, *Les Saints Patrons des Corporations* (Paris, 1888), vol. I, pp. 47–8; R. Lecotte, *Recherches sur les Cultes Populaires du Diocèse de Meaux* (Paris, 1953), pp. 49–50.

34 (Paris, 1749 edn), Book III, p. 92.

35 A. Paré, *Oeuvres* (Paris, 1614), Book XXIV, 'De la génération', p. 935.

36 Voltaire, *Philosophical Dictionary* tr. T. Besterman (Harmondsworth, 1971), article 'Influence'.

37 *Chronique Médicale* (1909), p. 684.

38 Galen, *De Theriaca ad Pisonem* (Venice, 1662), cited by B. Bablot, *Dissertation sur le Pouvoir de l'Imagination des Femmes Enceintes* (Paris, 1788).

39 Montaigne, *Essays*, Book I, chap. XX.

40 Planque, *Observations Rares de Médecine* (Paris, 1758), no. 72.

41 'The power of maternal impression', *Pediatrics* LVIII (1976), p. 901.

42 R. de Westphalen, *Petit Dictionnaire des Traditions Messines* (Metz, 1934), col. 412.

43 Cited in Chambon de Montaux, *Des Maladies de la Grossesse* (Paris, 1785), vol. II, pp. 97–8.

44 Ibid.

45 Comte de Saint-Simon, *Memoirs* tr. B. St John (London, 1964), vol. VI, chap. VI.

46 L. de La Salle, *Croyances et Légendes du Centre de la France* (Paris, 1875), vol. II, p. 2.

47 Guillemeau, *De l'Heureux Accouchement*, pp. 35–6.

48 Cited by Chambon de Montaux, *Des Maladies*, pp. 112–13.

49 Bourgeois, *Observations*, pp. 30–1.

50 Primerose, *Erreurs Vulgaires*, p. 222.

51 Duval, *Hermaphrodits*, p. 107.

52 Ibid., p. 104.

53 Joubert, *Erreurs*, p. 364.

54 Ibid., p. 172.

55 Duval, *Hermaphrodits*, pp. 104–5.

56 Ibid., p. 109.

57 Barth, *L'Âme Alsacienne*, p. 147.

58 Sarg, *En Alsace*, pp. 7–8. Some of these ex-votos are displayed in the Alsatian Museum at Strasbourg.

59 Barth, *L'Âme Alsacienne*, p. 148.

60 Duval, *Hermaphrodits*, p. 105.

61 Ibid., pp. 105–6.

62 du Chesnel, *Dictionnaire*, col. 661.

63 Chambon de Montaux, *Des Maladies*, p. 150.

64 Ibid., p. 151.

65 Joubert, *Erreurs* Book III, chap. II.

66 See J. Roussier, 'La durée normale de la grossesse', *Mélanges Henri Lévy-Bruhl* (Paris, 1959), p. 247.

67 Hippocrates, *Nutriment*, vol. I, tr. W. H. S. Jones, Loeb (London & Cambridge, MA, 1923), p. 356.

68 Chambon de Montaux, *Des Maladies*, pp. 147–8.

69 Darcet, *Journal de Médecine, Chirurgie, Pharmacie* XXV (1766), pp. 53ff.

70 Cited by Fodère, in Panckoucke, ed., *Dictionnaire* (1819), vol. XXXV, pp. 155–7.

71 J. F. Lobstein, *Observations d'Accouchemens* (Paris, 1817), p. 56.

72 F. Max Müller, *Lectures on the Influence of Language* (London, 1891), I, pp. 4–6.

73 Roussier, 'Durée', pp. 250–1.

74 On ways of reckoning time and the change from natural time to 'merchants' time' in the Middle Ages, see J. Le Goff, *Time, Work and Culture in the Middle Ages* tr. A. Goldhammer (Chicago and London, 1980).

75 J. Gélis, 'Enfant pas mûr, enfant pas cuit' in 'Un enfant prématurément', *Les Cahiers du Nouveau-né* VI (Paris, 1983), pp. 105–20.

76 G. Mauquest de La Motte, *Traité des Accouchements*, p. 298, n. f.

77 Bourgeois, *Observations*, p. 221.

78 Hippocrates, 'Du foetus de sept mois' ('On the seven-month foetus') tr. into French in Littré (ed.), *Oeuvres Complètes*, vol. VII, p. 439. (There is no modern English translation of this pseudo-Hippocratic text.)

79 Ibid., pp. 439–40.

80 Paré, *Oeuvres*, cited in *Chronique Médicale* (1892), p. 594.

81 Hippocrates, *Oeuvres*, p. 437.

82 K. Tallmadge, 'On the influence of the stars on human birth', *Bulletin of the History of Medicine* XIII (March 1943), pp. 251–67.

83 Joubert, *Erreurs*, Book III, chap. II.

84 Aristotle, cited in *Chronique Médicale* (1892), p. 595.

Chapter 6   The Experience of Pregnancy

1   At the end of the eighteenth century, the obstetrician Nicolas Saucerotte inveighed against the fashion for wearing corsets among pregnant women in towns.
2   Mme Fouquet, *Remèdes Charitables* (Lyon, 1681), pp. 70–1.
3   Bourgeois, *Observations*, II, p. 2.
4   Benoist, *Recueil de Préceptes sur les Accouchemens* (Auch, 1785), p. 41.
5   Bourgeois, *Observations*, II, p. 96.
6   Duval, *Hermaphrodits*, p. 167.
7   N. Andry, *L'Orthopédie* (Paris, 1741), vol. II, p. 10. Isidore of Seville (seventh century) explains *incicta* as 'Eo quod est sine cinctu'. Young women wore their girdles just over the hips.
8   In the Tiffauges region; *RTP* (1913), p. 86.
9   C. Dubalen, 'Pratiques médicales populaires dans les Landes', *Thèse de Médecine*, Lyon (1906–7), no. 83, cited in *France Médicale* (1907), p. 383.
10 *Chronique Médicale* (1935), pp. 130–2.
11 G. Thuillier, *Pour une Histoire du Quotidien au XIXe Siècle en Nivernais* (Paris, 1977), p. 73.
12 S. Commeau, 'Folklore du canton de Fours', *Mémoires de la Société Académique du Nivernais* (1927), p. 69.
13 A. Van Gennep, *Le Folklore du Dauphiné* (1932), vol. I, p. 33.
14 A. Jacqmart, 'Erreurs, Préjugés, coutumes et légendes du Cambrésis', *Mémoires de la Société d'Émulation de Cambrai*, vol. XXXVI, p. 328.
15 E. Jalby, *Le Folklore du Languedoc (Ariège, Lauragais, Tarn)* (Paris, 1971).
16 Dr Cauvin, 'La médecine populaire en Provence', *Thèse de Médecine*, Lyon (1930–1), no. 16, p. 32.
17 N. Culpepper, *Directory for Midwives* (London, 1737), pp. 99–110.
18 Mauquest de La Motte, *Traité*, p. 587.
19 Abbé Thiers, *Traité des Superstitions*, (Paris, 1704 edn), p. 88.
20 Ibid., pp. 11–12.
21 P. Perdrizet, *La Vierge de miséricorde, Étude d'un Thème Iconographique* (Paris, 1980); M. Vloberg, *La Vierge, Notre Médiatrice* (Grenoble, 1938), chap. V, pp. 109–30.
22 Jacomme, 'Les Saintes', p. 63.
23 Ibid., p. 64.
24 A. Guerreau, 'Les pèlerinages du Mâconnais: une structure d'organisation symbolique de l'espace', *Ethnologie Française* XXI/1 (January–March 1982), pp. 7–30.
25 C. Robet, 'La médecine populaire et les saints protecteurs de la maternité en Bretagne', *Thèse de Médecine*, Lyon (1930–7), no. 10, pp. 58–9.
26 P. Claudel, *Correspondance* (Paris, 1926), p. 231.
27 Cited by Jacomme, 'Les saints', p. 68.
28 *La Légende Dorée* (French translation of the *Golden Legend*, Paris, 1967), vol. I, p. 432. There is no modern English translation.
29 Cited by Robet, 'La médecine', p. 58.
30 *Partus et integritas discordes tempore longo / Virginis in gremio foedera pacis habent.* Noted by Abbé Hamon, *Notre-Dame*, vol. V (1865), p. 507.

31   Didron, *Iconographie chrétienne: Histoire de Dieu*, p. 287, n. 1, cited in J. Sarrète, *Vierges Ouvertes*, pp. 13–14.

32   Exactly the same scenes appear in a painting of the German school of the end of the fifteenth century (Museum of Lyon) and in a sixteenth-century stained-glass window in the church of Saint Nizier in the same city. Sarrète, *Vierges Ouvertes*, pp. 18–20.

33   *Chronique Médicale* (1905), p. 619.

34   P. Bidault, 'Les superstitions médicales du Morvan', *Thèse de Médecine*, Paris (1899), no. 321, p. 71.

35   *Mémoires de la Société Éduenne*, vol. X, p. 514.

36   H. Liegard, 'Les saints protecteurs de la Basse-Bretagne', *Thèse de Médecine*, Paris (1902–3), no. 457, pp. 22–3. See also Robet, 'La médecine', pp. 59–60.

37   H. Labourasse, *Anciens Us, Coutumes, Légendes, Superstitions et Préjugés de la Meuse* (Bar-le-Duc, 1902), cited in Jacomme, 'Les saints', p. 74.

38   Liegard, 'Les saints', p. 19.

39   Dr Fournée, 'A travers la Normandie: les pèlerinages à la Sainte Vierge pour la protection des enfants', *Sanctuaires et Pèlerinages* (1955), p. 37.

40   Jacomme, 'Les saints', pp. 73–4.

41   Cited by A. Molinier, 'Une enquête politique, économique et sociale en Languedoc au milieu du XVIIIe siècle', *Annales de Démographie Historique* (1944), p. 476.

42   'Pregnant women had a particular devotion to this relic, so as to obtain a happy deliverance by its touch; several well-attested cases of deliverances so obtained confirm them in this devotion.' Abbé Hamon, *Notre-Dame*, vol. V, p. 349.

43   Jacomme, 'Les saints', p. 72.

44   Ibid.

45   At Plouer in Brittany, in the last century; see Robet, 'La médecine', p. 59.

46   Ibid., pp. 58–9.

47   J. Goulin, *La Médecine des Dames ou l'Art de les Conserver en Santé* (Paris, 1771), p. 177.

48   Guillemeau, *De l'Heureux Accouchement*, p. 23.

49   Ibid., pp. 32–3.

50   Nicolas, *Le Cri de la Nature en Faveur des Enfants Nouveau-nés* (Paris, 1775), p. 1, n. 1.

51   Letter to her daughter, 27 April 1671; cited in Dr Vignes 'Les sept couches de Mme de Grignan', *Aesculape* (1927), pp. 132–7.

52   Nicolas, *Le Cri de la Nature*, p. 20.

53   Ibid., p. 19.

54   Ibid., p. 20.

55   Chambon de Montaux, *Des Maladies*, p. 210. At the end of the eighteenth century, Nicolas Saucerotte, an obstetrician from Lorraine, emphasized that 'there is still some resistance to bathing': *De la Conservation*, pp. 19–20.

56   Ibid., p. 1, n. 1.

57   *Le Cheval d'Orgueil: Mémoires d'un Breton du Pays Bigouden* (Paris, 1975), p. 419.

58   Nicolas, *Le Cri de la Nature*, p. 22.

59   Bourgeois, *Observations*, p. 62.

60   Guillemeau, *De l'Heureux Accouchement*, p. 49.
61   Ibid., pp. 52–3.
62   Nicolas, *Le Cri de la Nature*, p. 37, n. 1.
63   Ibid.; Saucerotte, *De la Conservation*, p. 20.
64   Goulin, *La Médecine*, p. 186.
65   Nicolas, *Le Cri de la Nature*, p. 24.
66   Saucerotte, *De la Conservation*, p. 15.
67   Guillemeau, *De l'Heureux Accouchement*, pp. 103–4.
68   Ibid., p. 113.
69   Saucerotte, *De la Conservation*, p. 18.
70   Ibid.
71   Guillemeau, *De l'Heureux Accouchement*, pp. 34–5.
72   N. Saucerotte, *Examen de Plusieurs Préjugés et Usages Abusifs Concernant les Femmes Enceintes* (Strasbourg, 1777), p. 15.
73   Duval, *Hermaphrodits*, pp. 162–3.
74   Guillemeau, *De l'Heureux Accouchement*, pp. 34–5.
75   Duval, *Hermaphrodits*, p. 162.
76   Saucerotte, *De la Conservation*, p. 13.
77   Goulin, *La Médecine*, p. 179.
78   Duval, *Hermaphrodits*, p. 163.
79   Nicolas, *De la Conservation*, p. 8.
80   F. A. Deleurye, 'Des passions de l'âme', *Traité des Accouchemens en Faveur des Élèves* (Paris, 1770), p. 93.
81   Guillemeau, *De l'Heureux Accouchement*, p. 39.
82   Nicolas, *De la Conservation*, p. 27.
83   Guillemeau, *De l'Heureux Accouchement*, p. 45.
84   Letter of 4 October 1671, cited in Vignes, 'Les sept couches'.
85   M. Feroger, curé de Mayet, dioc. du Mans, *Instructions de Morale, d'Agriculture et d'Économie* (1769), pp. 220–1.
86   Chambon de Montaux, *Des Maladies*, p. 99.
87   Bourgeois, *Observations*, pp. 71–2.
88   Guillemeau, *De l'Heureux Accouchement*, pp. 10–11.
89   Joubert, *Erreurs*, p. 250.
90   Nicolas, *Le Cri de la Nature*, p. 38.
91   Guillemeau, *De l'Heureux Accouchement*, p. 41.
92   Saucerotte, *De la Conservation*, pp. 11–12.
93   Froger, *Instructions*, p. 221.
94   Dubalen, 'Pratiques Médicales', p. 60.
95   'This cult seems to have been widespread in France.' Jeanton, *Mâconnais*, vol. III, p. 32, n. 1. See also *RTP* IV, p. 745, and *France Médicale* (1909), p. 403.
96   Jacomme, 'Les saints', p. 73; H. Fromage, 'Mythologie de la région de Tournus', *Mythologie Français* CXX (January–March 1981), p. 35.
97   Guerreau, 'Les Pèlerinages', p. 12.
98   A. Ott, *Étude sur les Couleurs en Vieux Français* (Paris, 1899), cited in Guerreau, 'Les Pèlerinages', p. 14.
99   J. G. Bulliot and A. Thiollier, *La Mission et le Culte de Saint Martin* (Autun, 1892), p. 298.

100   T. -J. Schmitt, *L'Organisation Ecclésiastique et la Pratique Religieuse dans l'Archi-diaconé d'Autun de 1650 à 1750* (Autun, 1957), p. 194.
101   Andry, *L'Orthopédie*, p. 10.
102   Sébillot, *Folklore*, vol. II, pp. 120–5.
103   Fromage, 'Mythologie', p. 35.
104   Joubert, *Erreurs*, pp. 196, 203.
105   Sarg, *En Alsace*, p. 15.
106   Mauquest de La Motte, *Traité*.
107   Letter to her daughter, 25 October 1671.
108   Primerose, *Erreurs Vulgaires*, pp. 686–7.
109   Y. Brekilien, *La Vie Quotidienne en Bretagne au XIXᵉ Siècle* (Paris, 1966), p. 143.
110   Dr Ysambert, 'Les superstitions médicales en Touraine', *Gazette Médicale du Centre* (1905), p. 3.
111   Hippocrates, Aphorism 48.
112   Jacqmart, 'Erreurs, préjugés, p. 336; G. Celos, 'Moyen de savoir le sexe de l'enfant à naître', *RTP* (1914), p. 157; P. Cuzacq, *La Naissance, le Mariage et le Décès* (Paris, 1902), p. 21.
113   *France Médicale* (1903), p. 135.
114   Dr Ravon, 'Préjugés populaires dans le Lyonnais', *Correspondent Médical* (1903).
115   Dr Ysambert, 'Les superstitions', p. 41.
116   In the canton of Ligueil: ibid., p. 3.
117   Ibid., p. 4.
118   Brekilien, *Vie Quotidienne*, p. 143.
119   Primerose, *Erreurs Vulgaires*, p. 691.
120   Guillemeau, *De l'Heureux Accouchement*, pp. 12–13.
121   Cited in Boislisle, *Correspondence des Contrôleurs Généraux*, vol. I, article 955, note.
122   Archives nationales 01 3791 (3), House of Queen Marie Antoinette, confinement of the queen.
123   On the way a midwife was chosen and on the intrigues which surrounded this choice, see L. Bourgeois, *Le Récit Véritable de la Naissance de Messeigneurs et Dames les Enfans de France* (Paris, 1624), pp. 111–35.
124   Ibid., p. 140.
125   Ibid., p. 142.
126   Héroard, *Journal*, Bibliothèque Nationale MS f.s. Fonds fs. 10321; cited in G. J. Witkowski, *Les Accouchements à la Cour* (Paris, n.d.), p. 156–7, n. 3.
127   Bourgeois, *Récit*, p. 138.
128   Ibid., pp. 144–5.

Chapter 7   *The Society of Birth*

1   M. Eliade, *The Sacred and the Profane* tr. W. Trask (New York, 1968), pp. 172–9; *Patterns in Comparative Religion*.
2   In his *Traité de la Fièvre Miliaire des Femmes* (Paris, 1778), René G. Gastellier emphasizes the disadvantages of this method, widely used in the countryside throughout the eighteenth century. It was, again, to create heat that the woman was made to drink strong drinks of liqueurs which 'burned'. This springs from the

idea that heat causes ripening, or cooking; just as a drunken man is sometimes said to be 'stewed'.

3   Sarg, *En Alsace*, p. 23.

4   R. Giron, 'Attitudes des parturientes', *Thèse de Médecine* Paris (1906–7), p. 33, n. 1. The story of the birth of St Francis of Assisi is well known: 'Pia, his mother, being unable to bring him to birth, a pilgrim advised taking her to a stable, where she was delivered at once.' Witkowski, *Histoire*, p. 98.

5   P.-J. Helias, *Le Cheval d'Orgueil*, p. 47: 'At about eleven o'clock, Marie-Jeanne Le Goff will leave the washplace where she has been washing a mountain of clothes. She will just have the strength to put the midday meal on to cook before asking a neighbour to call the midwife Marie-Jeanne Le Rest, who will deliver her at about three o'clock.'

6   Dr Munaret, *Le Médecin de Campagne* (Paris, 1837), p. 373, cited in A. Coquin, 'Vécu et pratiques de la grossesse et de l'accouchement en France rurale du XIXe siècle', MA thesis, University of Paris VIII (1980), p. 48.

7   Report from Mlle Audier, schoolmistress at Sainte-Gemme; cited in Coudin, 'Naître autrefois', p. 109.

8   *Les Caquets de l'accouchée*; see the introduction by Leroux de Lincy's edition (Paris, 1855), and M. Jeay, 'De l'autel au berceau: rites et fonctions du mariage dans la culture populaire au Moyen Age' in *La Culture Populaire au Moyen Age: Quatrième Colloque de l'Institut d'Études Médiévales de l'Université de Montréal* (Montreal, 1977), pp. 39–62.

9   La Motte advises 'never letting anyone talk in a low voice, or whisper in the ear of a woman in labour, although it is often nothing but trifles and things of no importance which such people talk about. A woman in this state is only too good at tormenting herself, and always misjudges what is being said about her, and thinks that she is hearing her death sentence.' *Traité*, p. 276.

10   Bourgeois, *Observations*, I, pp. 107–8.

11   La Motte, *Traité*, pp. 278–9.

12   F. Loux, *Le Jeune Enfant et son Corps dans la Médecine Traditionnelle* (Paris, 1978).

13   O. Perrin and A. Bouet, *Breiz Izel ou la Vie des Bretons de l'Armorique* (1835), p. 26.

14   Their knowledge even extended to veterinary gynaecology: they were able to deal with 'meiregea', i.e. prolapse, falls and torsions of the uterus. J. J. Brieude, *Topographie Médicale de la Haute-Auvergne* (1786; new edn 1821), pp. 123–5.

15   A. Raillet and L. Moule, *Histoire de l'École d'Alfort* (Paris, 1908).

16   Archives départementales, Orne, C. 356.

17   Archives départementales, Haute-Garonne, C. 60. At Broye, in the Hesdin region, at the end of the eighteenth century, there was a midwife who came of a line of midwives: 'Her mother, grandmother and great-grandmother all exercised the profession of midwife. A practice which goes as far back as that may be worthy of some consideration.' Archives départementales, Nord, C. 9016.

18   Dr J. F. Caizergues, 'Sur les cours gratuits d'accouchement dans la province de Languedoc de 1781 à 1789', *Bulletin de la Société Française d'Histoire de la Médecine* XVII/5–6 (1933), p. 135.

19   Subdelegation of Bapaume, Archives départementales, Nord, C. 9016.

20   P. Dionis *Traité Général des Accouchements* (Paris, 1718), p. 417.

21   Archives départementales, Gironde, C. 3304.

22 In 1786 the priest of Orthez used the following words to recommend a pupil to the general syndic of the States General: 'Allow me, M. le Syndic, to ask your protection for a young girl, still virgin, who hopes to succour those who are virgin no longer . . .. I promise you the gratitude of all the woman of Orthez and their husbands.' Inquiry into 'Midwives in the Kingdom', archives of the Société Royale de Médecine (hereafter SRM), Box 85.

23 Letter from Mauduit, Mayor of Vire, to the Intendant of Lower Normandy, 3 September 1786; Archives départementales, Calvados, C. 983.

24 The midwife of Mareuil: Archives départementales, Aisne, C. 632.

25 Archives départementales, Doubs, C. 1610. For Guillemeau, who looked to evidence from the ancient authors, especially Plato, a midwife ought not to 'begin to exercise that art until the time when she can no longer bear children; seeing that Diana, the goddess who presides over childbirth, is barren, and the woman who bears children is much incommoded and less fit for work and hard labour': *De l'Heureux Accouchement*, p. 149.

26 J. Gélis, 'Sages-femmes et accoucheurs: l'obstétrique populaire au XVIIe et XVIIIe siècles', *Annales ESC* (1977/5), pp. 934–5.

27 'Her function, which obliged her daily to succour (in particular) poor women who were pregnant, and to bring them to birth, also meant that she most often had to supply them with linen to swaddle the new babies and even to meet the earliest needs of their subsistence.' Report on the midwife of Basly, Lower Normandy, 1786; Archives départementales, Calvados, C. 83.

28 SRM Box 87.

29 Subdelegation of Mirecourt, Box 86.

30 P. Portal, *La Pratique des Accouchemens* (Paris, 1682), pp. 46–8. The phrase 'hunger brings the wolf out of the wood' was proverbial.

31 Subdelegation of Mirecourt and Remiremont, SRM Boxes 86, 87.

32 R. de La Bretonne, *Monsieur Nicolas* (1794), vol. I, p. 90.

33 Archives départementales, Orne, C. 301.

34 SRM Box 87.

35 SRM Box 86.

36 Verdier, *Façons*, pp. 101–8.

Chapter 8   Hastening the Hour of Deliverance

1 M. A. Le Boursier du Coudray, *Abrégé de l'Art des Accouchements*, 6th edn (Paris, 1785), pp. 62–3.

2 F. Bombled, *Catéchisme d'Accouchements à l'Usage des Sage-femmes de Cambrésis* (Cambrai, 1788).

3 'Memoire sur le besoin indispensable de quelques instruments simples et faciles à employer dont les sages-femmes de campagne devraient être pourvues', by J. F. Icart, obstetrician–demonstrator, Municipal Library of Narbonne, CM 2130.

4 La Motte, *Traité*, pp. 574–6.

5 Pointe, *Gazette de Santé* (1780), pp. 89–91.

6 A. Levret, *Essai sur l'Abus des Règles Générales et contre les Préjugés qui s'opposent aux Progrès de l'Art des Accouchemens* (Paris, 1766), p. 51.

7   Matthiolus, *Commentaires sur les Six Livres de Dioscoride*, French translation by A. du Pinet (Paris, 1680).
8   du Chesnel, *Dictionnaire*, p. 902.
9   P. Sébillot, 'Le monde minéral', *RTP* (1901).
10   H. Vaschalde, *Recherche sur les Pierres Précieuses du Vivarais et du Dauphiné* (Paris, 1874), p. 40.
11   H. de Montegut, 'Langues de serpent', *Bulletin de la Société Archéologique et Historique de la Charente* I, series 2 (1910).
12   Pomet, *Traité Général des Drogues*, vol. II, pp. 10–14.
13   Dr Cabanes, *Remèdes d'Autrefois* (Paris, 1905), pp. 208–9.
14   H. Cloquet, *Faune des Médecins*, (Paris, 1828), vol. V, p. 22. The bezoar enjoyed considerable fame throughout Europe, especially among the better-off. Thus, noblewomen in the Grisons used it regularly as a help in the delivery of both child and afterbirth. G. Bauhin, *De Lapidis Bezoar Orientalis et Occidentalis Cervini* (Basel, 1613), p. 69.
15   Matthiolus, *Commentaires*, pp. 402–3.
16   Around Arles, Nîmes and Tarascon, beginning of the twentieth century. *Chronique Médicale* (1936), p. 264.
17   Commune of Saint-Nizier. Van Gennep, *Le Folklore du Dauphiné*, vol. I, p. 34.
18   After a report in the communal archives of Béthune, cited by Dr Cabanes, *Remèdes*, p. 207.
19   J. Varanda, *De Morbis et Affectis Mulierum Libri Tres* (Lyon, 1615), cited by Saintyves, *Corpus*, vol. II, p. 433.
20   P. Peu, *La Pratique des Accouchemens*, pp. 142–3.
21   Ibid., pp. 137–8.
22   Only in exceptional cases is this practice mentioned, for it seemed axiomatic to everyone. 'The pains did not even give time to do the patient's hair': La Motte, *Traité*, pp. 408–9.
23   Drouillet, *Folklore du Nivernais*, 2nd edn, vol. I, p. 246.
24   La Motte, *Traité*, pp. 386–7.
25   F. Mauriceau, *Traité des Maladies des Femmes Grosses et Accouchées* (Paris, 1681), p. 363.
26   Cited by Verdier, *Façons*, p. 93.
27   Bourgeois, *Récit*, p. 157.
28   La Motte, *Traité*, p. 387.
29   R. J. Atwood, 'Positions d'accouchement et comportements s'y rattachant: étude ethnologique', *Les Cahiers du Nouveau-né* IV, 'Corps de mère, corps d'enfant'; J. Gélis, 'L'accouchement au XVIIIe siècle: pratiques traditionnelles et contrôle médical', *Ethnologie Française* VI/3–4 (1976), pp. 325–40.
30   P. Dionis, *Traité Général des Accouchemens* (Paris, 1743), p. 363.
31   M. Odent, *Genèse de l'Homme Écologique, l'Instinct Retrouvé* (Paris, 1979).
32   'Nowadays we have lost the ability to crouch', remarked Marcel Mauss in 1934. See also his pertinent remarks on 'techniques of the body' in *Sociologie et Anthropologie* (Paris, 1950), p. 374.
33   Unpublished memoirs, cited in *Chronique Médicale* (1928), p. 368.
34   Dr C. Bonnemaison, 'Des accouchements rapides et non surveillés et leurs complications', *Thèse de Médecine*, Paris (1898).

35   Giron, 'Attitudes', p. 21. See also G. Thuillier, *Histoire du Quotidien*, p. 72.
36   Description by Dr Merab, reported in Giron, 'Attitudes', p. 52.
37   There are exceptions. Jules Renard notes a case of a woman giving birth alone, in a standing position. 'La mère', *Bucoliques*, in *Oeuvres*, vol. II, p. 226, cited in Thuillier, *Histoire du Quotidien*, p. 84.
38   Dr Morel of Puy-en-Velay, cited by Giron, 'Attitudes', p. 52.
39   Giron, 'Attitudes', p. 53.
40   Collet, 'De l'accouchement spontané rapide et de l'expulsion imprévue du foetus', *Thèse de Médecine*, Paris (1904), cited by Giron, 'Attitudes', p. 52–3.
41   Description by Dr Kerambrun in 1912. According to him, 'nine tenths' of all Breton women gave birth in this way in the countryside. *Chronique Médicale* (1880), cited by Coquin, 'Vécu et pratiques', p. 53.
42   SRM Box 85.
43   Leproux, *La Vie Populaire* vol. II, p. 15.
44   See films made by Dr Wulf Schiefenhovel and his wife in New Guinea. 'These documents perfectly show the need to find a position and the importance of movements, which seem to be carefully concerted, of swaying and rotation of the pelvis.' Odent, *Genèse*, p. 94.
45   SRM Box 87.
46   Dr Legros, 'Lettres obstétricales', *Gazette des Hôpitaux* XXXVII/73 (1864), p. 20.
47   E. Rösslin, *Der Schwangerfrauen und Hebammen Rosengarten* (Strasbourg, 1513).
48   Paré, *Oeuvres*, 10th edn (1641), chap. XVI, pp. 599–600.
49   H. Speert, *Histoire de la Gynécologie et de l'Obstétrique* (Paris, 1976), pp. 265–9. See also L. R. Villerme, article 'Siège' in Panckoucke, ed., *Dictionnaire* (1821), vol. LI, pp. 253–9.
50   Since the sixteenth century the capital of Alsace had been famous for the quality of its midwives and obstetricians. J. -P. Lefftz, 'Aperçu historique de l'obstétrique de Strasbourg pendant la Grande Révolution', *Thèse de Médecine*, Strasbourg (1952).
51   At the beginning of the nineteenth century there was a Dutch carpenter who, because of his great strength, was often called upon to support women in labour; he had the idea of creating a birth chair. Giron, 'Attitudes', p. 33, following *Archives d'Iéna* (1835).
52   Villerme, 'Siège', p. 255.
53   'Among the other curiosities which were to be seen (in the eighteenth century) in the cabinet of the Grand Duke of Florence was one of these chairs, decorated with jewels from top to bottom. *Vanitas vanitatum* . . .' Villerme, 'Siège', p. 254.
54   La Motte mentions that it was used in Caen at the beginning of the eighteenth century. It is known to have been in use in Switzerland, Germany, northern Italy, France, Flanders, the United Provinces and Great Britain.
55   'Country women lie on a little straw, their backs propped on a mattress leaning against upturned chairs, legs and thighs apart, facing the hearth where a good fire is kept up.' Description by Depaul, cited in Giron, 'Attitudes', p. 38.
56   See illustration 4. The Alsatian Museum at Strasbourg has a folding chair once (1837) used by the midwife of Hurtigheim. Sarg, *En Alsace*, p. 29.
57   Odent, *Genèse*, p. 90.
58   Description cited by Giron, 'Attitudes', p. 38.

59   Odent, *Genèse*, p. 94.
60   Observation by Dr Morel, of Puy-en-Velay, cited by Giron, 'Attitudes', p. 52.
61   Bourgeois, *Observations*, pp. 95–6.
62   Ibid., p. 96.
63   Ibid., p. 190.
64   Ibid., p. 187.
65   Didelot, *Instructions pour les Sages-femmes* (Nancy, 1770), p. 7.
66   Joubert, *Erreurs*, pp. 340–1.
67   Cited by Coudin, 'Naître autrefois', p. 92.
68   Pomet, *Traité Général*, II, pp. 50–2 and p. 128.
69   Subdelegation of Saint-Sever: SRM Box 85.
70   M. de Lens, article on 'Ergot' in *Dictionnaire* (Paris, 1831), vol. III, pp. 134–7.
71   J. J. Rigal, 'Mémoire sur la matière des accouchements' (1787), Archives départe-
     mentales, Hérault, D. 179.

Chapter 9   Birth: A Double Liberation

1   M. Laget, *Naissances: l'Accouchement avant l'Âge de la Clinique* (Paris, 1982),
    pp. 119ff.
2   Bourgeois, *Observations*, II, p. 26.
3   Dionis, *Traité Général*, p. 209. He adds that 'These are all good actions which can
    do no harm.'
4   Ovid, *Metamorphoses*, Book IX, ll. 284–324.
5   J. G. Fraser, *The Golden Bough: a Study in Magic and Religion* 3rd edn (London,
    1936), III, pp. 294–9.
6   R. Bayon in *RTP* (1890), p. 220.
7   Pomet, *Traité Général*, vol. II, p. 44.
8   Lucie de V. H., *RTP* (1906), pp. 169–70.
9   M. Leproux, *La Vie Populaire*, I/2, *Les Croyances Populaires* (Paris, 1959), p. 17.
10 G. Vuillier, 'En Limousin' in *Le Tour du Monde* (1893), pp. 65–96; (1899), pp.
    505–40. A scene showing the 'hammering' of a sick child by Chazala, the
    blacksmith, is reproduced in F. Loux, *Pratiques et Savoirs*, p. 143.
11 Similar behaviour was observed among some Siberian tribes at the end of the
    nineteenth century; the Kalmucks 'always have a number of men, with their guns
    in readiness, waiting near the bed of the patient; as soon as the midwife perceives
    the head distending the perineum she signals to the men who fire simultaneously,
    thinking to assist nature by the sudden fright which the noise must cause.' Among
    the Commanches of North America 'a noted warrior mounted on his fleetest
    steed, with all his war paint and equipments on, charged down upon her at full
    speed.' Engelmann, *Labor*, p. 20.
12 Bourgeois, *Observations*, II, p. 78.
13 Duval, *Hermaphrodits*, p. 196.
14 Guillemeau, *De l'Heureux Accouchement*, pp. 25–6.
15 Joubert, *Erreurs*, p. 342.
16 Leproux, *La Vie Populaire*, p. 45.
17 'Journal de F. J. Le Clerc, chevalier seigneur de Bussy (1708–1728)', edited by A.

de Calonne in *Mémoires de la Société des Antiquaires de Picardie*, 4th series, vol. VI (1910), p. 268.

18 du Chesnel, *Dictionnaire*, p. 568.
19 Jacopo da Voragine, *Legende dorée*, (Paris, 1967), vol. II, pp. 268–70.
20 J. Delumeau, *Le Péché et la Peur: la Culpabilisation en Occident, XIIIᵉ–XVIIIᵉ Siècles* (Paris, 1983).
21 Archives départementales, Seine-Maritime, G. 732.
22 Thiers, *Traité des Superstitions*, p. 292.
23 The examples known to us came from the Auvergne and the Cevennes. See A. Aymar, *Le Sachet-accoucheur et ses Mystères* (Toulouse, 1926); 'L'homme et son corps dans la société traditionnelle', catalogue of the ATP exhibition (Paris, 1978), pp. 78–9; 'Religions et traditions populaires', catalogue of the ATP exhibition (Paris, 1979), pp. 89–90.
24 Aymar, *Sachet*, p. 279.
25 Leproux, *La Vie Populaire*, p. 16.
26 See especially Alphonse Dupront's study of pilgrimages and Delumeau's work, especially his inaugural lecture at the Collège de France, 1975; see the dossier edited by Bernard Plongeron, *La Religion Populaire: Approches Historiques* (Paris, 1976).
27 In the southern provinces of France, the use of Saint Margaret's girdle seems to have been less common, but in the south-west there was often recourse to the girdle of Saint Foy at Conques.
28 Abbé J. Corblet, *Hagiographie du Diocèse d'Amiens*, vol. IV, pp. 434–5.
29 Marie de Medici, for every confinement; Marie-Thérèse in 1661; Marie-Anne of Bavaria, wife of the dauphin, in 1662.
30 A. de La Borderie, *La Ceinture de la Vierge Conservée à Quentin* (1890), cited in Dr Lejeune, 'La ceinture de la Vierge de Quintin qui aide aux heureuses délivrances', *Aesculape* (1938), p. 281.
31 Lejeune, 'La ceinture', p. 281.
32 Same substitution at Notre-Dame-de-la-Daurade. On one girdle, dating from 1950, which bears the seal of the sanctuary and is kept in the Musée des Arts et Traditions Populaires in Paris, we read this invocation: 'O Mary, Divine Mother, Pray for me, Protect me. *Basilica Beatae Mariae Deaurate, Tolosae*'.
33 Dr P. Albarel, 'L'oraison de sainte Marguerite pour les femmes en couches', *Chronique Médicale* (1924), p. 233.
34 Some of these images can be seen at the Alsatian Museum in Strasbourg.

Chapter 10 Suffering to Give Life

1 La Motte, *Traité*, p. 208.
2 Ibid., p. 759.
3 Ibid., pp. 453–4.
4 Memoir by the Curé of Merry-Sec in 1683: Archives départementales, Yonne, C. 1660, reported by Alain Demay.
5 Portal, *Les Pratique des Accouchemens*, p. 53.
6 La Motte, *Traité*, p. 800.
7 Joubert, *Erreurs*, p. 398.

8   La Motte, *Traité*, p. 392.

9   J. Ch. Gilles de La Tourette, *L'Art des Accouchemens* (Paris, 1787), p. 111.

10 J. Ruleau, *Traité des Accouchemens Difficiles et Laborieux* (Saintes, 1713), pp. 128–9.

11 Bourgeois, *Observations*, II, p. 115.

12 The formulae for these sponges were familiar to European surgeons in the sixteenth century, having passed from the works of Guy de Chauliac, Nicolas (*Antidotaire*) and Hugo of Lucca into popular textbooks by authors such as Joubert and Falcon. E. Gilbert, *Les Plantes Magiques et la Sorcellerie* (Moulins, 1892); A. Deffarge, 'Les éponges somnifères à base de drogues végétales: histoire critique', *Thèse de Pharmacie*, Toulouse (1927–8), no. 2.

13 To be convinced of the truth of this it is sufficient to read the descriptions of their childhood by Coignet and Jamerai Duval: *Cahiers du Capitaine Coignet* (Paris, 1968); *Mémoires de Jamerai Duval* (Paris, 1981).

14 B. Bonnet, 'Étude obstétricale', pp. 26–8.

15 M. Laulhère, 'Aspects socio-culturels de l'accouchement', *Thèse de Médecine*, Paris (1963), no. 130, pp. 31–8.

16 Dr J. M. Cheynier, 'Douleur, souffrance, violence', *Les Dossiers de l'Obstétrique*, special number, *La Douleur* 73, (April 1981), pp. 15–19.

17 Odent, *Genèse*, p. 131.

18 See evidence collected in western Iran by Wolf Schiefenhovel, presented at the *Congrès d'Ethno-Histoire*, Göttingen, 1978.

19 Engelmann, *Labor*, p. 22.

20 Joubert, *Erreurs*, p. 401.

21 Godeau, *Instructions et Prières Chrétiennes* (1646).

22 La Motte, *Traité*.

23 Portal, *Les Pratique des Accouchemens*, pp. 71–2.

Chapter 11   Stages in the Delivery

1   Guillemeau, *De l'Heureux Accouchement*, pp. 164–5.

2   See the description by Pointe, Doctor of Medicine of Lyon, in *Gazette de Santé* (1780), pp. 89–90.

3   'I had her warmed with linen, because she was shivering violently, as she had been doing even before giving birth; which should cause no astonishment, because it is a sign that the birth will follow shortly.' Portal, *Pratique*, p. 25.

4   Guillemeau, *De l'Heureux Accouchement*, p. 164.

5   Ibid., p. 163.

6   Portal, *Pratique*, p. 136.

7   Ibid., p. 166.

8   Van Gennep, *Folklore du Dauphiné*, vol. I, p. 34.

9   Bourgeois, *Observations*, I, pp. 120–1.

10 Guillemeau, *De l'Heureux Accouchement*, p. 167.

11 Suchard, 'Sur l'expression utérine appliquée au foetus', *Thèse de Médecine*, Paris (1872); G. Keim, 'L'expression du foetus', *Thèse de Médecine*, Paris (1900).

12 Portal, *Pratique*, p. 134.

13 Ibid., p. 84.

14 Mme du Coudray, *Abrégé*, pp. 81–2.

15 Paré, *Oeuvres*, vol. II, p. 677.
16 *Gazette de Santé* (1779). pp. 159–60.
17 In 1786 the Curé of Hinacourt, near Soissons, wrote: 'I have noted that in the said parish there are many children with umbilical hernias, which I attribute to the fact that the cord was not tied at their birth.' Archives départementales, Aisne, C. 631.
18 Joubert, *Erreurs*, p. 353.
19 Dubalen, 'Pratiques médicales'.
20 Joubert, *Erreurs*, pp. 360–1.
21 Portal, *Pratique*, p. 117.
22 Ibid., p. 103.
23 Dubalen, 'Pratiques médicales'.
24 It was called 'blowing on the delivery'. Dr L. Mathe, 'Le folklore médical', *Chronique Médicale* (1925), pp. 42 and 251. See also R. Blancard, 'Réflexions sur l'hygiène de la grossesse, de l'accouchement et du post-partum à la campagne: abus et imprudences des matrones', *Thèse de Médecine*, Paris (1896), no. 120, pp. 19–20.
25 Duval, *Hermaphrodits*, p. 199.
26 Cited by Sue le Jeune, *Essais Historiques* (Paris, 1779), vol. I, p. 582.
27 Duval, *Hermaphrodits*, p. 301.
28 Dubalen, 'Pratiques Médicales', p. 62.

Chapter 12   The Placenta: Double of the Child

1 Their replies show their bewilderment: the women never bothered about the placenta. 'The midwife *must* have taken it away'; 'it *must have been* thrown into the privy, but I'm not really sure'; '*perhaps* it was buried in a corner of the garden . . . I'll have to ask my husband'.
2 Odent, *Genèse*, p. 111.
3 Bonnet, 'Étude obstétricale'.
4 'The females all more or less share this propensity to eat the afterbirth, herbivores as much as carnivores.' Dr Rainard, *Traité Complet de la Parturition* (1845), vol. I, p. 327.
5 Mauriceau, *Traité des Maladies*, vol. I, p. 227.
6 Saint-Cyr and Violet, *Traité d'Obstétrique Vétérinaire*, p. 346.
7 Cornevin, *Traité de Zootechnie Générale* (Paris, 1891), p. 825.
8 Dr L. Bouchacourt, 'De l'utilisation naturelle de la partie extra-embryonnaire de l'oeuf', *L'Obstétrique* (1902), p. 112.
9 Buffon, *Oeuvres Complètes, Variétés sur l'Espèce Humaine*, vol. II, p. 200.
10 Galliot, 'Sur l'avortement criminel', *Thèse de Médecine*, Lyon (1884), p. 14. The Tasmanians and the Chavante of Uruguay are convinced that the soul of the child is then reabsorbed into the bodies of its parents, and that, especially for the mother, this is the best way to regain the strength and vigour which she lost during her pregnancy. See C. Letourneur, *La Sociologie* (1892).
11 We now know that the placenta performs the essential function of synthesizing proteins and hormones; at the end of gestation, it also supplies the foetus with the maternal antibodies. P. Beaconsfield, G. Birdwood and R. Beaconsfield, 'Le placenta', *Pour la Science* (October 1980), pp. 29–37.

12   It is so designated in all the romance languages. The Latin *placenta* also originally meant 'cake'. *Tr.*

13   F. Loux, *Le Jeune Enfant* (Paris, 1978). See in particular 'Les soins à l'enfant après la naissance' and 'Le placenta et le cordon ombilical'.

14   N. Belmont, *Les Signes de la Naissance* (Paris, 1971), p. 76.

15   Dubalen, 'Pratiques médicales', p. 62.

16   Fraser, *Golden Bough*, vol. I, pp. 186ff.

17   E. Hoffmann-Krayer, *Handwörterbuch der deutschen Aberglauben* (1927–42), article 'Nachgeburt', vol. II, p. 327.

18   Loux, *Le Jeune Enfant.*

19   In the province of Tras Os Montes. Verbal communication.

20   In Belmont, *Signes*, p. 75.

21   But in Würzberg in 1555 there was a 'Regulations for midwives' which recommended sinking placentas in water: to put them out of reach of sorcerers? Or to prevent trade in them?

22   Peu, *Pratique*, p. 489.

23   Jacobs, *École Pratique des Accouchemens* (1785), p. 13, notes that in Belgium 'there are people who bury the placenta in hot ashes'.

24   Leméry, *Dictionnaire des Drogues* (Paris, 1697), p. 803.

25   Dubalen, 'Pratiques médicales', p. 62.

26   Eighteenth and nineteenth-century doctors noted cases in which women, girls or grandmothers had succeeded in suckling a child by simply giving it the breast in order to stop it crying.

27   Report by Ortali in *Gazetta degli Ospedali* (1904/55).

28   Nineteenth-century veterinarians and doctors noted the aphrodisiac powers of the afterbirth in rabbits and guinea-pigs. Bouchacourt, 'De l'utilisation', p. 120.

29   A. van Andel, 'L'hippomanes, un remède anti-épileptique', *Bulletin de la Société d'Histoire de la Médecine* XV (1921), pp. 369–72.

30   J. de Léry, *Relation de Voyage au Brésil* (Paris, 1558), chap. VI. According to Engelmann, *Labor among Primitive Peoples*, the custom still existed at the end of the nineteenth century: Brazilians, 'if it can be done secretly, eat the organ which has been recently expelled in a solitary labor' (p. 173).

31   *Voyages de Gemelli Carreri* (Paris, 1719).

32   My italics.

33   In the Comminges, where the ceremony of churching was observed less and less as the French Revolution approached, 'the offering of the rolls of bread', was still kept up. See *Les Paroisses de Comminges en 1786*, documents edited by A. Sarramon (Paris, 1968), p. 21.

34   J. M. Tiffaud, 'L'exercice illégal de la médecine dans le Bas-Poitou: les toucheurs et les guérisseurs', *Thèse de Médecine*, Paris (1898), no. 274.

35   L. -F. Sauve, *Le Folklore des Hautes-Vosges* (Paris, 1889).

Chapter 13   The Governance of Mother and Child

1   Duval, *Hermaphrodits*, p. 256.

2   L. de la Salle, *Croyances et Légendes*, vol. I, p. 7.

3   Bourgeois, *Observations*, I, p. 153.

4 Guillemeau, *De l'Heureux Accouchement*, p. 179.

5 On licking of newborn babies in certain Eskimo tribes see Ashley Montagu, *La Peau et le Toucher: un Premier Langage* (Paris, 1979).

6 Dubalen, 'Pratiques médicales'.

7 Gardien, article on the 'Nouveau-né' in Panckoucke, ed., *Dictionnaire*, p. 389.

8 Carrère, *Manuel pour le Service des Malades* (Paris, 1786), pp. 64–70.

9 Paré, *Oeuvres*: 'De la génération', chap. XVII.

10 La Motte, *Traité*, p. 470.

11 SRM Box 87.

12 Cited by A. Franklin, *La Vie Privée d'Autrefois*, vol. XVII, *L'enfant* (Paris, 1895), pp. 72–3.

13 Subdelegations of Gordes and Grasse, 1786; SRM Box 87.

14 du Coudray, *Manuel*, p. 74.

15 Paré, *Oeuvres*, vol. II, chap. XXXVIII. On the similarity between the methods of obstetricians and midwives up to the eighteenth century, see J. Gélis, 'L'accouchement au XVIIIᵉ siècle', pp. 325–40.

16 Subdelegation of Grasse, 1786.

17 J. J. Bruhier d'Ablaincourt, *Dissertation sur l'Incertitude des Signes de la Mort* (Paris, 1749), vol. II, p. 286.

18 du Coudray, *Manuel*, p. 6.

19 Guillemeau, *De l'Heureux Accouchement*, p. 183.

20 Bourgeois, *Observations*, I, pp. 127–9.

21 Duval, *Hermaphrodits*, p. 261.

22 Portal, *Pratique*, p. 35.

23 Bourgeois, *Observations*, I, p. 150.

24 Guillemeau, *De l'Heureux Accouchement*, pp. 175–6.

25 Duval, *Hermaphrodits*, p. 240.

26 Portal, *Pratique*, p. 25.

27 Bourgeois, *Observations*, p. 150.

28 Duval, *Hermaphrodits*, p. 243.

29 Portal, *Pratique*, p. 44.

30 Duval, *Hermaphrodits*, p. 236.

31 Bourgeois, *Observations*, I, p. 130.

32 Portal, *Pratique*, p. 163.

33 E. Badinter, *The Myth of Motherhood: an Historical View of the Maternal Instinct* (London, 1981). On the debate initiated by that work, see the papers from the colloquium *Mères et nourrissons (XVIIᵉ–XIXᵉ siècle)* by the Société de Démographie Historique, 28 November 1981, published in *Annales de Démographie Historique* (1983).

34 Duval, *Hermaphrodits*, pp. 260–2.

Chapter 14   Welcoming the New Baby

1 Goubelly, *Connaissances Nécessaires sur la Grossesse* (Paris, 1785), vol. II, pp. 129–30.

2 A. Durant-Tullou, 'Un milieu de civilisation traditionnel: Le Causse de Blandas', *Thèse-lettres*, Montpellier (1959).

3   A. Goursaud, *Société Rurale*, vol. II, p. 297.
4   Sarg, *En Alsace*, p. 44.
5   N. L. A. Richard, *Traditions Populaires*, p. 225.
6   Courval-Sonnet, *Les Toilettes de Nuict et les Coiffes de Couche* (Paris, 1622). Cited by Dr Le Maguet, 'Le monde médical parisien sous le Grand-Roi', *Thèse de Médecine*, Paris (1899), pp. 309–10.
7   See the description by L. S. Mercier, *Tableau de Paris*, vol. VI, p. 46, cited by Franklin, *L'enfant*, p. 55.
8   Some of these 'new mothers' cups' or 'plates' are on show in the museum of the Petit Palais (Dutuit collection) and in the municipal museum of Rouen.
9   Leproux, *La Vie Populaire*, p. 22.
10   Dr P. Noury, 'L'alimentation des accouchées dans l'art', *Chronique Médicale*, XVI, pp. 369–77; 652–3; 682–5.
11   C. Seignolle, *Le Folklore de la Provence*, new edn (Paris, 1967), p. 36.
12   Goursaud, *Société Rurale*, p. 297.
13   Goursaud tells of an absent-minded visitor at Cussac who forgot to leave her offering, whereupon the mother's breasts ran dry. Someone went to the visitor's home to ask for the gift; when the coin was returned, the milk came back that same evening. *Société Rurale*, pp. 297–8.
14   Ibid.
15   There is evidence of this custom in the twelfth century; perhaps these 'three loving fairies' represent a memory of the Three Mothers of Antiquity, who decided the destiny of men as they entered into life. *Journal des Sages-femmes* (1878), p. 191.
16   Goursaud, *Société Rurale*, p. 297.
17   Bibliothèque de l'Arsenal, MS 6087, p. 299.
18   Cited in *RTP* XV, p. 232.
19   Bourgeois, *Récit*, p. 165.
20   Ibid., p. 163.
21   Franklin, *L'enfant*, p. 78.
22   Ibid., p. 82.
23   Bourgeois, *Récit*, p 165.
24   Rouanet de La Vigne private collection, Rennes; communicatin by J. -P. Goubert.
25   In November 1602, Marie de Medici bore a second child, a daughter, Madame Elisabeth. 'She was taken aback,' reports Louise Bourgeois, 'because she thought that the King would be angry; but he showed no sign of it: on the contrary, he consoled the Queen and said that God knew well what was best for them, that it was necessary to make alliances with Spain and England.' *Récit*, pp. 177–8.
26   Laborde, *Essai*, p. 7.
27   Linguet's diary for 15 May 1776, cited in *RTP* XV, p. 233.
28   A. Hugo, *La France Pittoresque* (Paris, 1835), vol. III, p. 174.
29   J. Michelet, *Origine du Droit français et Étranger*, cited by Laisnel de La Salle, *Croyances et Légendes* (Paris, 1875), vol. II, p. 6.
30   'As soon as a man has a son, people tell him, "You're renewed". It is an important way to congratulate someone.' J. M. Rouge, *Le Folklore de la Touraine* (Tours, 1935), p. 2.
31   Barth, 'L'Âme alsacienne', p. 97.

32 J. L. M. Nogues, *Moeurs d'autrefois en Saintonge*, p. 21.

33 M. Higelin, *Die Sagen des Kreizes Altkirch* (Altkirch, 1909), p. 14.

34 Witkowski, *Histoire*, p. 161. Nogues, *Moeurs d'autrefois en Saintonge*, p. 21.

35 Barth, 'L'Âme alsacienne', p. 98.

36 Dr C. Vidal, 'De quelques superstitions populaire concernant la médecine dans le Castrais', *France Médicale* (1909), p. 197.

37 A. Pfleger, 'Das Stündlein bringt's Kindlein', *Elsassland Lothringer Heimat* (1938), p. 80.

38 Leproux, *La Vie Populaire*, I/2, p. 22; Seignolle, *Le Folklore de la Provence*, p. 35.

39 Communication from R. Samson of Coudray-Saint-Germer.

40 J. Roy, *Us et Coutumes de l'Ancien Pays de Montbéliard et en Particular de ses Communes Rurales* (Montbéliard, 1886), no. 1, p. 11.

41 In Brittany Alain Croix found some 'astrological predictions written in the margin of certificates of baptism': *La Bretagne au XVIe et au XVIIe Siècle: la Vie, la Mort, la Foi*, (Paris, 1980), vol. II, p. 1061, n. 123.

42 Lyon edn, p. 39. Cited in J. -C. Nardin and J. Labaste, 'L'enfant au XVIIe siècle, à travers les collections de la bibliothèque Mazarine', exhibition catalogue (March–June 1980), p. 5.

43 *Astrologia Gallica* (The Hague, 1661), pp. 544–55, cited by Nardin and Labaste, 'L'enfant', p. 5.

44 On the state of research see M. Stupfel, 'Chronobiologie, environnement et néonatologie', *Cahiers du Nouveau-né* VI (1983), pp. 123–39.

45 A. Niquet, 'L'influence de la pression atmosphérique et des phases lunaires sur le nombre quotidien des naissances', *Thèse de Médecine*, Paris. Cochin-Port-Royal (1979), no. 125, pp. 48–9.

46 M. Bramou-Spyropoulos, 'Influence des variations du potentiel de la lune et du soleil sur le travail obstétrical', *Thèse de Médecine*, Geneva (1963), no. 16.

47 Cited by Abbé J. Durand, *Le Folklore de l'Aube*, vol. I, pp. 2–3.

48 Goursaud, *Société Rurale*, vol. II, p. 300; A. Taverne, *Coutumes et Superstitions Foréziennes*, vol. IV, *Les Étapes de la Vie* (Ambierle, 1972), p. 6.

49 Sauve, *Le Folklore des Hautes-Vosges*, p. 21.

50 C. Rumeau-Rouquette, *Naître en France. Enquêtes Nationales sur la Grossesse et l'Accouchement (1972–1976)*, INSERM (Paris, 1979). G. Breard and C. Rumeau-Rouquette, 'Rythmes spontanés et rythmes induits par le déclenchement et le déroulement du travail et de l'accouchement', *Journal of Interdisciplinary Cyclical Research* (1979/10), pp. 195–205 (specimen of 4,330 births studied in France in 1979).

51 Sarg, *En Alsace*, p. 35.

52 Canon E. Sol, *Le Vieux Quercy* (Paris, 1929), p. 10.

53 Dr A. Fournier, *Vieilles Coutumes, Usages et Traditions Populaires des Vosges* (Saint-Dié, 1891), p. 59.

54 Sarg, *En Alsace*, p. 36.

55 Limousin proverb quoted by Goursaud, *Société Rurale*, p. 300.

56 Leproux, *La Vie Populaire*, p. 18.

57 Ibid.

58 Barth, 'L'Âme alsacienne', p. 100.

59 Ibid.

60 Sol, *Le Vieux Quercy*, p. 10. Daniel Fabre is currently researching into the *armier*, and hopes to publish shortly.

61 *Niau* comes from the late *nidasius*, whence also *niquedaille*, *niquedouille* 'stupid'. In the Beauce, *niau* can also mean a plaster or stone model put in nests to encourage hens to lay, i.e. the egg that stays in the nest. *RTP* vol. XIV, p. 511. See also A. Van Gennep, *Manuel de Folklore Contemporain*, vol. I, p. 124, n. 2.

62 M. Bloch, *The Royal Touch* tr. J. E. Anderson (London, 1973), pp. 168–71.

63 C. Ginzburg, *The Night Battles* tr. J. and A. Tedeschi (London, 1983), pp. 61–2.

64 Cited by Mousson-Lanauze in *Paris-Médical*, 24 March 1924.

65 Cited by M. Gille, 'Les enfants nés coiffés', *Revue Pratique de Biologie Appliquée* (1929), pp. 363–8.

66 On children born with cauls, and on the great variety of denotations for the caul in European culture, see Belmont, *Signes*, Part I, pp. 29–38.

67 In Ginzburg, *The Night Battles*, p. 15.

68 On 25 December 1647, two women of Udine were brought before the Holy Office for having placed 'a little caul' under the altar of a church: they wanted to have masses said over it, so as to send it to a young man who was at the war and make him invulnerable. Ibid., n. 6.

69 Joubert, *Erreurs*, IV, chap. VI, pp. 367–8. The allusion to people being born 'fully clad' is a play on the word *coiffé*, meaning both '[born] with a caul' and 'wearing a hat'.

70 Ginzburg, *The Night Battles*, p. 61.

71 Ibid., p. 57.

72 La Motte, *Traité*, p. 260.

73 Bourgeois, *Récit*, pp. 187–8.

74 Pliny, *Natural History*, Book VII, chap. VI, p. 8.

75 Ibid.

76 Belmont, *Signes*, p. 136.

77 Ibid., p. 134.

78 Ibid., pp. 144–5.

79 H. Coulon, *Erreurs et Superstitions Médicales du Cambrésis* (Cambrai, 1911), pp. 13–14.

80 P. Saintyves, *La Guérison des Verrues: de la Magie Médicale à la Psychotherapie* (Paris, 1913).

81 Sarg, *En Alsace*, p.37.

82 Sébillot, *Folklore*, vol. I, p. 405.

83 Guillemeau, *De l'Heureux Accouchement*, p. 34.

84 Richard, *Traditions Populaires*, p. 227.

85 Barth, 'L'Âme alsacienne', pp. 94–6.

86 Sébillot, *Folklore*, vol. III, pp. 432–3.

87 La Fontenelle de Vaudore, 'Recherches sur les vigueries et les origines de la féodalité en Poitou', *Mémoires des Antiquaires de l'Ouest* (1838), p. 404.

88 Laget, *Naissances*, p. 94; Leproux, *La Vie Populaire*, p. 22.

89 Laborde, *Essai*, p. 7.

90 Peu, *Pratique*, pp. 199–200.

Chapter 15   Socializing the Child: Giving a Name

1   C. Lévi-Strauss, *The Savage Mind*, chap. VII, 'The individual as a species'.

2   F. Zonabend, 'Prénom et identité' in *Le Prénom, Mode et Histoire*, ed. J. Dupâquier et al. (EHESS, Paris, 1980), pp. 23–8.

3   See *Le Prénom*, and the special number of *L'Homme*, XX/4 (October–December 1980).

4   A. Burguière, 'L'attribution du prénom en France: approche historique', *Le Prénom*, p. 32.

5   C. Klapisch-Zuber, 'Constitution et variations temporelles des stock de prénoms', *Le Prénom*, p. 39.

6   On the dwindling of the 'feudal names' and the changes which occurred in the 'courts of heaven', see J. Chiffoleau, *La Comptabilité de l'au-delà: les Hommes, la Mort et la Religion dans la Région d'Avignon à la Fin du Moyen Age*, École Française de Rome (1980), pp. 375ff.

7   A. Collomp, 'Un stock de prénoms dans deux groupes de villages de Haute-Provence de 1730 à 1770', *Le Prénom*, pp. 169–76.

8   J. Dupâquier, 'Prénoms, parrains, parenté', *Mémoires de la Société Historique et Archéologique de Pontoise, du Val d'Oise et du Vexin* (1980).

9   M. Vovelle notes 'a passion, around 1760, for Saint Joseph as patron of the good death', *Piété Baroque et Déchristianisation en Provence au XVIIIe Siècle* (Paris, 1973), p. 441.

10   F. Lebrun, 'Les prénoms dans une paroisse rurale de l'Anjou entre 1751 et 1797: note sur l'exploitation d'un fichier de famille', *Le Prénom*, pp. 241–6.

11   M. Gresset, 'Les prénoms dans le monde judiciaire comtois aux XVIIe et XVIIIe siècles', *Le Prénom*, p. 214.

12   Trent catechism, cited by J. Dupâquier, 'La fréquence des prénoms dans le Vexin français', *Le Prénom*, pp. 357–68.

13   Ibid.

14   S. Hoyez and A. Ruffelard, 'Prénoms protestants au XVIIe siècle en Brie et en Provence', *Le Prénom*, pp. 223–9.

15   Ibid., p. 229.

16   Goursaud, *Société Rurale*, vol. II, p. 302; G. Rocal, *Le Vieux Périgord*, p. 50.

17   A. Fine-Souriac, 'Transmission des prénoms et parenté en pays de Sault', *Le Prénom*, pp. 109–26.

18   M.-N. Dénis, 'Usage des prénoms dans l'Alsace rurale aux XVIIIe et XIXe siècles', *Le Prénom*, p. 318.

19   Durand, *Le Folklore de l'Aube*, p. 7.

20   J. Boutier and L. Pérouas, 'L'évolution des prénoms en Limousin, du XIe au XXe siècle', *Le Prénom*, p. 69.

21   F. Zonabend, 'Le nom de personne', *L'Homme*, XX/4, pp. 7–23; 'Jeux de noms: les noms de personne à Minot', *Études Rurales* LXXIV (April–June 1979), pp. 51–85.

22   Chiffoleau, *Comptabilité*, pp. 378, 381; J. Hajnal, 'European marriage patterns in perspective', *Populations in History* (London, 1965), pp. 101–43.

23   Chiffoleau, *Comptabilité*, pp. 381–7.

24   *Les Caquets de l'Accouchée*, pp. 12–13.
25   Thiers, *Traité des Superstitions*, vol. II, chap. VII; cited by Burguière, 'L'attribution', p. 15.
26   Gresset, 'Les prénoms', pp. 212–13.
27   D. Schnapper, 'Essai de lecture sociologique', *Le Prénom*, especially pp. 13–27.
28   Gresset, 'Les prénoms'.

Chapter 16   The Falling of the Flower

1   E. Brissaud, *Histoire des Expressions Populaires Relatives à l'Anatomie, à la Physiologie et à la Médecine* (Paris, 1892), p. 322.
2   In 1622, Anne of Austria, six weeks pregnant, miscarried as a result of a foolish accident. 'The affair was kept from the King for as long as possible, so long as he was in Paris': *Mémoires de Basompierre*, cited by Witkowski, *Les Accouchements à la Cour*, p. 171, n. 1.
3   Portal, *Pratique*.
4   Didelot, *Instructions pour les Sages-femmes*, pp. 45–6.
5   Peu, *Pratique*, pp. 87–110.
6   La Motte, *Traité*, pp. 404–5.
7   Manuscript catalogue, Carnegie library of Rheims. J. Gélis, 'Un accoucheur rémois au XVIIIe siècle: le chirurgien Pierre Robin (1726–1804)', *Travaux de l'Académie Nationale de Reims* vol. CLXII (1983), pp. 121–36.
8   Archives départementales, Marne, C. 2881.
9   J. Gélis, 'La pratique obstétricale dans la France moderne: les carnets du chirurgien–accoucheur Pierre Robin (1770–97)', *Annales de Bretagne et des Pays de l'Ouest* (1979/2), p. 195.
10   Laget, *Naissances*, p. 51.
11   Gélis, 'La pratique', p. 195.
12   La Motte, *Traité*, p. 700.
13   Tissot, 3rd edn (Paris, 1767), pp. 387–9.
14   Bourgeois, *Observations*, pp. 39–40.

Chapter 17   The Unripe Fruit

1   Cf. J. Gélis, 'Enfant pas mûr, enfant pas cuit', *Les Cahiers du Nouveau-né* (1983) Special no. 6, pp. 105–19.
2   Perrault, *Contes*, ed. G. Rouger (Paris, 1967), p. 187. For an English version of the story, which emphasizes Tom's wit and 'nimbleness', see I. and P. Opie, *The Classic Fairy Tales* (Oxford, 1974), pp. 32–46.
3   La Motte, *Traité*, p. 204, n. g.
4   Ibid.
5   Mauriceau, *Traité des Maladies*, p. 131.
6   N. Venette, *Traité de l'Amour Considéré dans l'État de Mariage* (Paris, 1686), vol. I, p. 180, art. 4.
7   La Motte, *Traité*, pp. 312–13.
8   Mauriceau, *Traité des Maladies*, pp. 172–6.
9   At Rheims, 15 per cent of Robin's interventions concerned premature babies between seven and nine months. In modern France, there has been a most

spectacular decline in the number of premature births: 8.2 per cent in 1972, 6.8 per cent in 1975–6. Rumeau-Rouquette, *Naître en France*.

10 La Motte, *Traité*, pp. 304–5.
11 Planque, article 'Accouchement' in *Bibliothèque Choisie de Médecine* (Paris, 1748), vol. I, pp. 304–5.
12 'Prématurité et créativité', *Les Cahiers du Nouveau-né* (1982/6), pp. 177–80.

Chapter 18   Unnatural Delivery

1 La Motte, *Traité*, pp. 406–7.
2 Bourgeois, *Observations*, II, pp. 7–11.
3 Portal, *Pratique*, Observation XII, p. 40.
4 La Motte, *Traité*, pp. 239–41.
5 Ibid., p. 1009.
6 Report of Nédey, surgeon–obstetrician, Archives départementales, Doubs, C. 91.
7 Portal, *Pratique*, p 83.
8 Nédey's report to the Royal Academy of Surgery on 22 June 1778: Paris, Académie de Médecine, Box 27.
9 Portal, *Pratique*, pp. 48–9.
10 Peu, *Pratique*, pp. 153–4.
11 La Motte, *Traité*, pp. 259–60.
12 Anne-Amable Augier du Fot, memoir to the Intendant of Soissons, 1 July 1773, Archives départementales, Aisne, C. 360.
13 Portal, *Pratique*, pp. 68–9.
14 See *Gazette de Santé*, 6 July 1783, pp. 106ff.
15 *Journal des Sçavans* (1749), p. 34–5.
16 M. J. A. Chaptal, 'Observations de médecine pratique', no. 32. MS, Bibliothèque de l'Académie de Médecine, SRM Box 198, text quoted and analysed by J. -P. Peter, 'L'Histoire par les oreilles' in *Le Temps de la Réflexion* (Paris, 1980), pp. 286–7.
17 *Histoires Anatomiques*, cent. 2, p. 304.
18 J. -J. Bruhier d'Ablaincourt, *Dissertation sur l'Incertitude des Signes de la Mort* (Paris, 1749), vol. II, pp. 266–7.
19 Obstetrical textbooks give numerous examples of the family's refusal to allow this operation.
20 Cited by Witkowski, *Accouchements*, pp. 148–9.
21 On the cult of San Ramón in Spain at the dawn of the twentieth century, see A. Limón Delgado, *Costumbres Populares*, pp. 44–7.

Chapter 19   Death, the Greatest Aberration

1 La Motte, *Traité*, pp. 245–7.
2 Portal, *Pratique*, p. 108–9.
3 'Mémoire sur la nécessité de faire instruire les sages-femmes de la campagne', by Desfarges, a surgeon of Meymac (1786); Acádemie de Médecine, SRM Box 85.
4 La Motte, *Traité*, pp. 815–18.
5 Ibid., pp. 1041–3.

6   Paré, *Oeuvres*. See also P. Darmon, *Le Mythe de la Procréation à l'Âge Baroque* (Paris, 1977), chap. XII.

7   'Observation sur un enfant pétrifié dans le sein de sa mère et dont les os sont sortis par le nombril, à la suite d'un dépôt', by M. Génil, surgeon of the town of Montbrison-en-Forez, *Journal de Médecine* LX, pp. 334–7.

8   A. Planchon, *Traité Complet de l'Opération Césarienne* (Paris, 1801), pp. 89–103.

9   La Motte, *Traité*, p. 1127–9.

10 Observations by Moussard, doctor of Aubagne, to the Société Royale de Médecine, 1788. SRM Box 196 *bis*, dossier 28. See A. Farge, 'Accouchement et naissance au XVIIIe siècle', *Revue de Médecine Psychosomatique et de Psychologie Médicale* I (1976), p. 23.

11 'Observations sur la fièvre puerpérale', by M. Archier, doctor of medicine in the Faculty of Montpellier, *Journal de Médecine* LXI (1784), pp. 372–3.

12 A. Gordon, *A Treatise on the Epidemic Puerperal Fever of Aberdeen* (London, 1795), p. 74.

13 J. -J. Brieude, *Topographie Médicale de la Haute-Auvergne* (1786), new edn (1821), p. 125.

14 J. and E. de Goncourt, *Germinie Lacerteux* tr. anon. (London, 1955), pp. 75–6; cited by D. Tucat, 'Les sages-femmes à Paris (1871–1914)', *Thèse 3e cycle*, University of Paris VII (1983), pp. 96–7.

15 A. Planchon, 'Sur la fièvre miliaire des femmes en couches et sur leur traitement', *Journal de Médecine* LIII (1780), pp. 340–3.

16 Statistics by Tenon; see H. Carrier, *Les Origines de la Maternité de Paris, ses Maîtresses Sages-femmes et l'Office des Accouchées de l'Ancien Hôtel-Dieu (1378–1796)* (Paris, 1888), pp. 192–203.

17 N. Stockman, 'La gynécologie et l'obstétrique dans la vie française du XVIIIe siècle', Thesis, EHESS, Paris (1974), pp. 237–41. On the mortality amongst women, see M. Laget, 'Les fièvres puerpérales en Languedoc au XVIIe siècle' in 'La qualité de la vie au XVIIe siècle', *Marseille* review, no. 109, pp. 63–8.

18 *Journal de Médecine* LVIII (1782), pp. 454–5.

19 D. Delaroche, *Recherches sur la Nature et le Traitement de la Fièvre Puerpérale* (Paris, 1783).

20 'This fever seemed to be brought on by cold, or errors in diet, but much oftener by anxiety of mind', *Practical Observations on the Child-bed Fever* (London, 1772), p. 41.

21 R. G. Gastellier, *Traité de la Fièvre Miliaire*, pp. 108ff.

22 Report by the doctors of the Hôtel-Dieu in Paris, 1778, cited by Carrier, *Les Origines*, p. 193.

23 A. Doublet, 'Remarques sur la fièvre puerpérale', *Journal de Médecine* LXI (1784), p. 4.

24 Gordon, *Treatise*, p. 63.

25 'I was myself the means of carrying the infection to a great number of women', Ibid., p. 64.

26 As late as 1879, Dr Fichot, a practitioner in the Nevers region, reported that in the countryside 'the malady is usually transmitted by a midwife. It is not sufficient to isolate the new mother . . .': in Thuillier, *Histoire du Quotidien*, p. 90, n. 77.

27 'The infection was carried by practitioners of midwifery from Aberdeen to

Gilcomston and the Hardgate, villages in the suburbs of the city': Gordon, *Treatise*, pp. 65–6.

28 'Mémoire sur la maladie qui a attaqué, en différents temps, les femmes en couches à l'Hôtel-Dieu de Paris', *Journal de Médecine* LVIII (1982), p. 456.

29 Ibid., pp. 456–9.

30 'In 1787, the government had the "American elixir" purchased for pregnant women, and sent quantities of it into the provinces with instructions for its use': A. Babeau, *La Province sous l'Ancien Régime* (Paris, 1894), vol. II, p. 299.

31 'The patient's apparel and the bed-clothes ought to be burnt, or thoroughly purified; and the nurses and physicians, who have attended patients affected with the puerperal fever, ought carefully to wash themselves, and to get their apparel properly fumigated, before it be put on again.' Gordon, *Treatise*, pp. 98–9.

32 See Loux, *Le Jeune Enfant*, and Gélis et al., *Entrer dans la Vie: Naissances et Enfances dans la France Traditionnelle* (Paris, 1978), p. 120.

33 Bourgeois, *Observations*, pp. 166–7.

34 Ibid., pp. 170–1.

35 In 1787, the obstetrician Rigal de Gaillac reported on the case of a woman who could not bring her child to birth: 'She had said very firmly that she did not want me to touch her: that it was natural for her to die for her child and not to sacrifice it to a parricidal hand.' 'Mémoire sur la matière des accouchemens', Archives départementales, Hérault, D. 179.

36 Bourgeois, *Observations*, pp. 197–204.

37 J. d'Arras, *Le Roman de Mélusine ou l'Histoire des Lusignan*, ed. M. Perret (Paris, 1979), p. 261.

38 A. Stoeber, *Die Sagen des Elsasses* (Saint-Gall, 1852), p. 130); cited by Barth, 'L'Âme alsacienne', p. 150.

39 J. Adam, 'Abergläublische Sitten und Gebräuche in den Strassburger Landegemeinden', *Elsass-Lothringischer Familienkalender* (Strasbourg, 1894), cited in Barth.

Chapter 20   Where Does the Beast End and Man Begin?

1 At the end of the eighteenth century the surgeon Tenon noted that in the 'wine country', where female workers were needed, 'sucklings remain unattended in the cradle, hungry, wallowing in filthy nappies, uttering screams which often bring on a prolapse.' Cited in A. Chamoux, 'L'enfance abandonnée à Reims, à la fin du XVIIIᵉ siècle', *Annales de Démographie Historique* (1973), p. 285.

2 Bourgeois, *Observations*, p. 169–70.

3 Morin, *Le Prêtre et le Sorcier*, p. 283.

4 Thiers, *Traité des Superstitions*, vol. I, p. 383.

5 *Bulletin de la Société d'Anthropologie* (1890), p. 896; cited by Sébillot, *Folklore*, vol. III, p. 417–18.

6 Morin, *Le Prêtre et le Sorcier*, pp. 264, 271, 273, 276, 277. Saint Corneille's power is owing to his name, which means 'crow'.

7 Saintyves, *La Guérison des Verrues* (Paris, 1913).

8 Chaussier and Adelon, article 'Monstruosité' in Panckoucke, ed., *Dictionnaire*, vol. XXXIV, pp. 191–2.

9   *Journal de Physique*, November 1774.
10 Maupertuis, *Oeuvres*, vol. II, Letter XIV.
11 Percy and Laurent, article 'Multimamme' in Panckoucke, *Dictionnaire*, vol. XXXIV, p. 525.
12 Ibid., p. 528.
13 Ibid., p. 526.
14 Deleurye, *Traité des Accouchemens*, p. 390.
15 Murat, article 'Môle' in Panckoucke, ed., *Dictionnaire*, vol. XXXIV, p. 5.
16 Ibid., pp. 6–7.
17 Buffon's classification.
18 *A Parisian Journal* (end of the Hundred Years' War), tr. J. Shirley (Oxford, 1968;, pp. 235–6.
19 Description of a monstrous child by M. Gacon, doctor of Bagé-en-Bresse, *Journal de Médecine* XXXIX (1773), pp. 42–5.
20 P. Camper, 'Réponse à une question posée en 1783 par la société batave de Rotterdam', *Oeuvres*, vol. II, year XI, pp. 334ff.
21 Saint-André, 'A short Narrative of an extraordinary Delivery of Rabbits perform'd by Mr John Howard', included in R. Manningham, *An exact Diary of what was observed during a close attendance upon Mary Toft, the pretended Rabbet-breeder . . .*, 2nd edn (London, 1926), pp. 9–10.
22 Ibid., pp. 25–6.
23 Ibid., pp. 63–4.
24 J. Céard, *La Nature et les Prodiges: l'Insolite au XVIe Siècle en France* (Paris, 1977), p. viii; see also Darmon, *Procréation* (Paris, 1977).
25 J. Wauquelin, *Traité des Merveilles de l'Inde Découvertes par Alexandre*, cited in Dr Cabanes, *Les Curiosités de la Médecine* (Paris, 1925), p. 123.
26 M. Delcourt, *Stérilités Mystérieuses et Naissances Maléfiques dans l'Antiquité Classique* (Liège and Paris, 1938), p. 39.
27 Aeschinus, *Against Ctesiphon*, cited in Delcourt, *Stérilités*, p. 12.
28 J. Obsequens, *Prodigiorum Liber*, chap. LXV, cited in Delcourt, *Stérilités*.
29 Livy XXVI.37, cited in Delcourt, *Stérilités*.
30 Delcourt, *Stérilités*, pp. 34, 65.
31 Ibid., p. 66.
32 See Céard, *La Nature*, chap. II.
33 Saint Augustine, *City of God*, XXII.19, cited in Céard, *La Nature*, p. 28.
34 J. -L. Flandrin, 'L'attitude à l'égard du petit enfant et les conduites sexuelles dans la civilisation occidentale', *Annales de Démographie Historique* (1973), p. 154.
35 J. -L. Flandrin, *Un Temps pour Embrasser: aux Origines de la Morale Occidentale, VIe–XIe Siècles* (Paris, 1963).
36 Cited in Flandrin, *Un Temps*, p. 119, and 'L'attitude', p. 155.
37 Cited by Céard, *La Nature*, p. 81–2.
38 Ibid.
39 *Miracle Arrivé dans la Ville de Genève en Ceste Année 1609*, cited in *Chronique Médicale* (1907), pp. 396–7.
40 Chambon de Montaux, *Des Maladies*, vol. II, pp. 85–7.
41 Ibid., p. 91.

42 A passage in Gregory of Tours reveals that in the early Middle Ages, mothers customarily killed the monsters they brought forth: quoted in Flandrin, *Un Temps*, p. 119.

43 J. Telinge, *Cours d'Accouchements en Forme de Catéchisme, par Demandes et Réponses* (Paris, 1776).

44 M. Beaussier, 'On two children joined together', *Journal de Médecine* XXXIV (1770), pp. 90–1.

45 Céard, *La Nature*, p. 438.

46 Ibid., pp. 440–1.

47 Salgues, *Des Erreurs*, vol. III, pp. 122–3.

48 Ibid., pp. 118–19.

49 J. Deshayes, *La Civilisation de l'Orient Ancien* (Paris, 1969), p. 247.

50 J. Libis, *Le Mythe de l'Androgyne* (Paris, 1980), p. 42.

51 M. Delcourt, *Hermaphrodite* (Paris, 1958), chap. V.

52 G. Lapouge, review of Libis, *Androgyne* in *Le Monde*, 2 January 1981.

Further Reading

Background and Approach

Ariès, P., *Le Temps de l'Histoire*, new edn. (Paris, 1986)
—— *Histoire des Populations Françaises et de Leurs Attitudes Devant la Vie Depuis le XVIIIᵉ Siècle* (Paris, 1948)
Braudel, F., *The Structures of Everyday Life*, tr. M. Kochan, rev. edn (London, 1987)
Cassirer, E., *The Individual and the Cosmos in the Renaissance*, tr. M. Domandi (Oxford, 1973)
Certeau, M. de, *L'Écriture de l'Histoire* (Paris, 1975)
—— *L'Absent de l'Histoire* (Paris, 1973)
Chaunu, P., *L'Histoire, Science Sociale: la Durée, l'Espace et l'Homme à l'Époque Moderne* (Paris, 1974)
Davis, N. Z., *Society and Culture in Early Modern France* (Stanford, 1965)
Delumeau, J., *Le Christianisme de Luther à Voltaire* (Paris, 1971)
Dupront, A., 'Problèmes et méthodes d'une histoire de la psychologie collective', *Annales ESC* (January–February 1961)
Eliade, M., *La Nostalgie des origines. Méthodologie et Histoire des Religions* (Paris, 1974)
Febvre, L., *Le Problème de l'Incroyance au XVIᵉ Siècle. La Religion de Rabelais*, new edn (Paris, 1968)
Foucault, M., *The History of Sexuality*, vol. I: *An Introduction*, tr. R. Herley (London, 1979)
Ginzburg, C., *The Night Battles*, tr. J. and A. Tedeschi (London, 1983)
Gourevitch, A. J., *Les Catégories de la Culture Médiévale* (from the Russian) (Paris, 1983)
Laslett, P., *The World We Have Lost* (London, 1965)
Le Goff, J., *Time, Work and Culture in the Middle Ages*, tr. A. Goldhammer (Chicago and London, 1980)
—— and Nora, P., *Constructing the Past: Essay in Historical Methodology* (Cambridge, 1985)
Le Roy Ladurie, E., *Le Territoire de l'Historien* (Paris, 1979); partial translation by S. and B. Reynolds, *The Mind and Method of the Historian* (Harvester Press, 1981)
Lévi-Strauss, C., *Structural Anthropology*, tr. C. Jacobson and B. G. Schoepf (New York, 1964)
—— *The Savage Mind*, tr. anon (London, 1966)

Muchembled, R., *Culture Populaire et Culture des Élites dans la France Moderne des XVe– XVIIIe Siècles* (Paris, 1979)

Pouchelle, M. C., *The Body and Surgery in the Middle Ages*, tr. R. Morris (Oxford, Polity, 1990)

Family, Mother, Child

Ariès, P., *Centuries of Childhood*, tr. R. Baldick (London, 1982)

Badinter, E., *The Myth of Motherhood: an Historical View of the Maternal Instinct* (London, 1981)

'Enfant et société', *Annales de Démographie Historique*, special number (1973)

'Famille et société', *Annales ESC*, special number (1972)

Fouquet, C. and Knibiehler, Y., *L'Histoire des Mères, du Moyen Age à Nos Jours* (Paris, 1980)

—— *La Femme et les Médecins, Analyse Historique* (Paris, 1983)

Flandrin, J. -L., *Les Amours paysannes* (Paris, 1975)

—— *Familles, Parenté, Maison, Sexualité dans l'Ancienne Société*, new edn (Paris, 1984)

Gélis, J., Laget, M., Morel, M. -F., *Entrer dans la Vie: Naissances et Enfances dans la France Traditionnelle* (Paris, 1978)

Laget, M., *Naissances: l'Accouchement avant l'Âge de le Clinique* (Paris, 1982)

Lebrun, F., *La Vie conjugale sous l'Ancien Régime* (Paris, 1975)

Mause, Ll. de et al., *The History of Childhood* (New York, 1974)

Segalen, M. *Mari et Femme dans la Société Paysanne* (Paris, 1981)

Shorter, E., *The Making of the Modern Family* (New York, 1975)

Stone, L., *The Family, Sex and Marriage in England (1500–1800)* (New York, 1977)

Birth and the Life Sciences

Darmon, P., *Le Mythe de la procréation à l'âge baroque*, new edn (Paris, 1976)

Delaunay, P., *La Vie Médicale aux XVIe, XVIIe et XVIIIe Siècles* (Paris, 1935)

Devraigne, L., *L'Obstétrique à travers les Âges* (Paris, 1939)

Dumont, M. and Morel, P., *Histoire de l'Obstétrique et de la Gynécologie* (Lyon, 1968)

Engelmann, G. J., *Labor among Primitive People*, 2nd edn (St Louis, 1883)

Guyenot, É., *Les Sciences de la Vie aux XVIIe et XVIIIe Siècles: l'Idée d'Évolution* (Paris, 1957)

Laignel-Lavastine, M., *Histoire Générale de la Médecine, de la Pharmacie, de l'Art Dentaire et de l'Art Vétérinaire*, 3 vols. (Paris, 1936–49)

Lenoble, R., *Histoire de l'Idée de Nature* (Paris, 1969)

Pecker, A., *Hygiène et Maladies des Femmes au cours des Siècles* (Paris, 1972)

Roger, J., *Les Sciences de la Vie dans la Pensée Française au XVIIIe Siècle* (Paris, 1963)

Rostand, J., *Maternité et Biologie* (Paris, 1966)

Siebold, E. J. K., *Versuch einer Geschichte der Geburtshülfe*, 2 vols. (Berlin, 1839–45)

Speert, H., *Iconographia Gyniatrica: a Pictorial History of Gynecology and Obstetrics* (Philadelphia, 1973)

Taton, R., ed., *Enseignement et Diffusion des Sciences en France au XVIIIe Siècle*, new edn (Paris, 1986)

Thomas, K., *Man and the Natural World: changing attitudes in England (1500–1800)* (Harmondsworth, 1983)

Witkowski, G. -J., *Histoire des Accouchements chez tous les Peuples* (Paris, 1890)

Childbirth: Myth, Practice and Culture

Baltrusaitis, J., *Le Moyen Age Fantastique: Antiquités et Exotismes dans l'Art Gothique*, new edn (Paris, 1981)

Belmont, N., *Les Signes de la Naissance. Étude des Représentations Symboliques Associées aux Naissances Singulières* (Paris, 1971)

Bouteiller, M., *Médecine Populaire d'Hier et d'Aujourd'hui* (Paris, 1966)

Caillois, R., *Le Mythe et l'Homme* (Paris, 1972)

Dontenville, H., *La France Mythologique* (Paris, 1966)

Eliade, M., *The Forge and the Crucible*, tr. S. Corrin (London, 1962)

—— *Aspects du mythe* (Paris, 1963)

—— *Myths, Dreams and Mysteries*, tr. P. Mairet (London, 1960)

—— *Patterns of Comparative Religion*, tr. R. Sheed (London, 1971)

Franklin, A., *La Vie Privée d'autrefois*, vol. 17, *L'enfant, la Naissance, le Baptême* (Paris, 1895)

Imhof, A., ed., *Der Mensch und sein Körper, von der Antike bis heute* (Munich, 1983)

Jordan, B., *Birth in Four Cultures* (Montreal, 1978)

Loux, F., *Le Jeune Enfant et son Corps dans la Médecine Traditionnelle* (Paris, 1978)

—— *L'Homme et son Corps dans la Société Traditionnelle*, Catalogue of an exhibition at the Musée des Arts et Traditions Populaires (Paris, 1979)

—— *Le Corps dans la Société Traditionnelle* (Paris, 1979)

Mandrou, R., *De la culture populaire aux XVIIᵉ et XVIIIᵉ Siècles* (Paris, 1965)

Ploss, H., *Das Kind in Brauch und Sitte der Völker* (Leipzig, 1884)

Rieves, H. and Monchicourt, M. -O., *L'Homme et le Cosmos* (Paris, 1984)

Saintyves, P., *Les Saints Successeurs des Dieux. Essai de Mythologie Chrétienne* (Paris, 1930)

Sarg, F., *En Alsace, du Berceau à la Tombe* (Strasbourg, 1977)

Sébillot, P., *Le Paganisme Contemporain, chez les Peuples Celto-latins* (Paris, 1908)

—— *Le Folklore de France*, 4 vols, new edn (Paris, 1968)

Servier, J., *L'Homme et l'Invisible* (Paris, 1980)

Thomas, K., *Religion and the Decline of Magic. Studies in Popular Beliefs in Sixteenth and Seventeenth-Century England* (New York, 1971)

Van Gennep, A., *Les Rites de Passage* (Paris, 1909; reprinted 1969, 1981).

—— *Manuel de Folklore Contemporain*, vol. I/1–2, *Du Berceau à la Tombe*, new edn (Paris, 1979)

Verdier, Y., *Façons de Dire, Façons de Faire* (Paris, 1979)

Warsage, R. de, *Le Folklore de la Vie Humaine* (Liège, 1937)

Zonabend, F., *La Mémoire Longue: Temps et Histoire au Village* (Paris, 1980)

Birth, Death and the Sacred

Ariès, P., *The Hour of Our Death*, tr. H. Weaver (London, 1981)

Auge, M., *Pouvoirs de Vie, Pouvoirs de Mort* (Paris, 1977)

Caillois, R., *L'Homme et le Sacré* (Paris, 1939)

Chiffoleau, J., *La Comptabilité de l'Au-delà: les Hommes, la Mort et la Religion dans la Région d'Avignon à la Fin du Moyen Age* (Rome, 1980)
Delumeau, J., *La Peur en Occident, XIVᵉ–XVIIIᵉ siècles* (Paris, 1978)
—— *Le Péché et la Peur: la Culpabilisation en Occident, XIIIᵉ–XVIIIᵉ Siècles* (Paris, 1983)
Dupront, A., 'Pèlerinages et lieux sacrés', *Encyclopaedia Universalis*, vol. XII (Paris, 1972)
—— 'Anthropologie du sacré et cultes populaires. Histoire et vie du pèlerinage en Occident', *Miscellanea Historiae Ecclesiasticae* (Leuven, 1974), vol. V
L'Espace et le Sacré, special number of *Annales de Bretagne et des Pays de l'Ouest*, XC (1983), no. 2.
Eliade, M., *The Sacred and the Profane*, tr. W. Trask (New York, 1968)
Isambert, F. -A., *Rite et Efficacité Symbolique* (Paris, 1979)
Jung, C. -G., *Man and his Symbols* (London, 1964)
Thomas, L. -V., *Anthropologie de la Mort* (Paris, 1980)
Religions et traditions populaires, exhibition catalogue, Musée des Arts et Traditions Populaires (Paris, 1979)
Vovelle, M., *Mourir Autrefois* (Paris, 1974)
—— *La Mort et l'Occident de 1300 à Nos Jours* (Paris, 1983)

History of Midwifery

Aveling, H., *English Midwives: Their History and Prospects* (1872, reprint London, 1967)
Donnisson, J., *Midwives and Medical Men. A History of Interprofessional Rivalries and Women's Rights* (London, 1977)
Forbes, T. Y., *The Midwife and the Witch* (New Haven and London, 1966)
Gélis, J., *Accoucheur de Campagne sous le Roi-Soleil: le Traité de l'Accouchement de G. Mauquest de la Motte* (Toulouse, 1979)
Hallema, A., 'Vroedvrouwen in staden dorp in het essten van Noord-Brabant. Hoe stadsen dorpsbesturen zorgden voor verloskundige hulp gedurende de 16° tot den 18° eeuw.' *Ned. Te Geneesk*, XCIX (1955), pp. 2660–7
Laforce, H., *Histoire de la Sage-femme dans la Région de Québec* (Quebec, 1985)
Pancino, C., *Il Bambino e l'Acqua Sporca. Storia dell'Assistenza al parto, dalle Mammane alle Ostetriche (secoli XVI–XIX)* (Milan, 1984)
Ringoir, D. J. B., *Plattelands chirurgie in de 17° en 18° eeuw. De rekeningboeken van de 18°-eeuwse Durgerdamse chirurgijn Anthony Egberts* (Amsterdam, 1973)
Shorter, E., *A History of Women's Bodies* (New York, 1982)
Schrader's, C. G., *Memoryboeck van de Vrouwens. Het Notitieboek van en Friese Vroedvrouw (1693–1745)*, with introduction and notes by M. J. van Lieburg and G. J. Kloosterman (Amsterdam, 1984)
Van Reeuwijk, A. J., 'Vroedkunde en vroedvrouwen in de Nederlanden in de 17° en 18° eeuw', Thesis, Universiteit Amsterdam (1941)
Witkowski, G. J., *Accoucheurs et Sages-femmes célèbres* (Paris, 1902)

Birth in Figures

Armengaud, A., *La Famille et l'Enfant en France et en Angleterre, du XVIᵉ au XVIIIᵉ Siècle: Aspects Démographiques* (Paris, 1975)
Bardet, J. -P., *Rouen aux XIVᵉ et XVIIᵉ Siècles. Les Mutations d'un Espace Social*, 2 vols, (Paris, 1983)

310   *Further Reading*

Bergues, H. et al. *La Prévention des Naissances dans la Famille* (Paris, 1960)
Croix, A., *La Bretagne aux XVIᵉ et XVIIᵉ Siècles: la Vie, la Mort, la Foi*, 2 vols, (Paris, 1981)
Drake, M., *Population in Industrialization* (London, 1969)
Dupaquier, J., *La Population Rurale du Bassin Parisien à l'Époque de Louis XIV* (Paris, 1977)
—— *La Population Française aux XVIIᵉ et XVIIIᵉ Siècles* (Paris, 1979)
Garden, M., *Lyon et le Lyonnais au XVIIIᵉ Siècle* (Paris, 1970)
Imhof, A. E., *Die Gewonnenen Jahre* (Munich, 1981)
—— (ed.) *Mensch und Gesundheit in der Geschichte* (Husum, 1980)

Modern Childbirth

Cohen, A., *Les Mains de la Vie* (Paris, 1981)
'Corps de mère, corps d'enfant', *Cahiers du Nouveau-né*, no. 4
Damstra-Wijmenga, S. M. I., *A Comparative Study of the Outcome of Deliveries at Home and in Hospital* (Groningen, 1983)
Jeanson, C., *L'Accouchement sans Douleur* (Paris, 1964)
Leboyer, F., *Birth Without Violence* (London, 1979)
Merger, Dr R., *La Naissance* (Paris, 1970)
Minkowski, A., *Pour un Nouveau-né sans Risques* (Paris, 1973)
Montagu, Ashley, *Touching: the Human Significance of the Skin* (Columbia, UP, 1971)
'Naître ... et ensuite', *Cahiers du Nouveau-né*, no. 1–2
Oakley, A., *Women Confined: Towards a Sociology of Childbirth* (Oxford, 1980)
—— *Becoming a Mother* (Oxford, 1980)
Odent, M., *Entering the World* (New York and London, 1984)
—— *Genèse de l'Homme Écologique: l'Instinct Retrouvé* (Paris, 1979)
Roberts, H. et al. *Women, Health and Reproduction* (London, 1981)
Sureau, Claude, *Le Danger de Naître* (Paris, 1978)
Smulders, B. and Limburg, A., 'Medicalizzazione e parto in casa in Olanda: ina contraddizione?' in *Le Culture del Parto* (Milan, 1985)
This, B., *Naître* (Paris, 1980)
—— *Le Père, Acte de Naissance* (Paris, 1980)
'Un Enfant Prématurément', *Cahiers du Nouveau-né*, no. 6

Index